P9-DUX-260

The Rabbinic Mind

The Rabbinic Mind

MAX KADUSHIN

THIRD EDITION

With an Appendix by Simon Greenberg

BLOCH PUBLISHING COMPANY
New York

Third Edition, 1972
Library of Congress Catalog Card Number: 75-189016
First Edition, 1952; Second Edition, 1965
SBN: 0-8197-0007-X
Printed in the United States of America

TO
E. G. K.

Foreword to the Third Edition

Religion and morality have something in common, it has long been felt; but though that feeling is sound, the various philosophical attempts to identify that "something" have been more or less unsuccessful. A modern school of thought has, however, made the problem stand out in bold relief. Insisting that the proper function of language is to deal with matters of sense, these thinkers describe the assertions of religion and morality as referring to non-sense. At best, therefore, what we do have here is a negative description. Religion and morality can be classified together on the ground that neither refers to matters of sense. But is there no positive relation between them?

A fundamental factor in all languages is almost ignored by this modern theory of language. In that theory the contention is made that language reflects the logical processes of the human mind. Granted that this contention is correct, language must nevertheless also reflect another, and different, process of the human mind. We speak of language in general but the truth is that there are only particular languages, not language in general. To be sure, the particular languages possess characteristics in common, one of these being that they reflect the logical processes of the mind. However, the sine qua non is the presence of particular languages. It is this basic factor, with all its implications that the modern theory tends to obscure by dwelling on "the essence of language."

A particular language implies a particular people that used

or still uses that language. Now a people existing for generations is usually unified, kept a people, not by a factual language alone but by certain concepts, generalizing ideas, possessed by all the members of the people. Those concepts must be expressed as simply as possible for they are generalizing ideas common to *all* the individuals, intellectual or otherwise, clever or simple. A concept expressed as simply as possible is one which is conveyed by a single word or a single term. However small the basic vocabulary of a people may be, it must also contain the words expressing the unifying concepts.

But these words do not stand for any aspect of sensory experience and hence do not reflect logical processes. They reflect an entirely different process of the human mind. At the same time, they are not insulated from the rest of the vocabulary. An integral element of the basic vocabulary, they are used in concert with the rest of the vocabulary. What is probably the best illustration of all these matters is to be found in the rabbinic mind.

The rabbinic vocabulary contains certain words that, with respect to the rest of the vocabulary, constitute a type all their own. Such words are Torah, *Miẓwot* (commandments), *Zedaḳah* (charity), *Teshubah* (repentance), *Tefillah* (prayer), *Derek 'Ereẓ* (ethics), *'Adam* (man), and many others. They constitute a type of their own because they do not designate objects, relationships or qualities in sensory experience, do not stand for "matters of sense." They do, however, represent generalizing ideas and therefore must be conceptual terms of some kind.

Not referring to "matters of sense," these terms do not reflect the logical processes of the mind. To be involved with or connected to logical processes, a word must possess a more or less fixed, stable meaning. That is not the case with these rabbinic terms. As we shall now see, the concept for which a rabbinic term stands is not static. Employed in various contexts, it grows in meaning and expands in content. The abstract conceptual terms themselves cannot thus be otherwise than merely connotative, suggestive.

Rabbinic concepts of this type take on idea content only when they are combined in a statement or situation. For example, in an act of charity not only are objects involved, such as a coin or perhaps clothing, but also the concepts of charity itself and man. Indeed, had these concepts not been embodied in the act, it could hardly have taken place at all. But the concept of charity does not combine solely with the concept of man. Rabbinic statements tell of God's charity in judgment and such statements reveal how the concept of charity is combined with those of God's love, forgiveness and sin. An early chapter of this book similarly describes how the concept of *Malkut Shamayim* (God's Kingship) combines with God's love, His justice, the Nations of the World, Israel and *Miẓwot,* and shows that in the process there emerges one idea after another about the concept of *Malkut Shamayim*. The content of any given rabbinic concept of this type is, therefore, a function of that entire group of concepts as a whole. If every rabbinic concept depends for its meaning on all the rest, then all the concepts of this type constitute an organismic whole. This is also to say that the rabbinic concepts reflect organismic thought.

Organismic thought or organic thinking is not an independent mode of thought. The abstract rabbinic concepts themselves, though crystallized in words, are no more than indicants of organismic thought, for these words are merely connotative. Only when several rabbinic concepts in combination are embodied in a concrete statement or act has organismic thought actually come into play. But concretizing the rabbinic concepts in this manner also reflects logical thought. In a sentence the context consists of words reflecting logical processes, but most often this context is implicit. Motivated or interpreted by unspoken rabbinic concepts, an act or a situation is a complete experience in itself, an experience which includes sensory data that precondition logical processes. Furthermore, in the derivation of laws and in juristic discussions the Rabbis employ logical, inferential processes directly. The laws usually represent ways of applying the rabbinic concepts in daily life, and their derivation and elucidation are marked by acute logical reasoning.

The conclusion is inescapable that, if Rabbinic Judaism is a criterion, religion and morality have a common, positive character. They have a positive character because they are crystallized in concepts so essential that without them there would be no particular peoples, and consequently no particular languages, which is to say, no words reflecting logical processes. They have a common character because all the concepts are dynamically related to each other as elements of a single organismic complex. This organismic relationship enables any concept to be combined with any other concept, whether we regard either as belonging to religion or morality. We need only recall the instance of how the concept of charity combined with that of God's love and other concepts of religious experience. Proof of the positive, common character of religion and morality thus does not rest on any philosophical theory but on the demonstration of the positive, common character of the concepts which they employ.

In this Foreword to the study of the rabbinic mind, we have used the term "rabbinic concepts" as a designation for the rabbinic organismic concepts. Though this designation has served our purpose here, it is too inclusive, since certain legal and even logical concepts are also rabbinic concepts. For that reason we shall, in this study, designate the organismic concepts as "value concepts." Whatever shortcomings that term may have, it does convey the idea that there are concepts which endow acts or situations or things with value, with significance. By using this general term, moreover, we indicate that our study of the rabbinic mind may be relevant to the study of any social tradition.

Preface to the Second Edition

ON THE ONE HAND the rabbinic mind is expressed in Halakah: law and juristic discussions and interpretations; and on the other it is expressed in Haggadah: nonjuristic interpretations and statements. Since both Halakah and Haggadah are aspects of the rabbinic mind there must be a large factor common to both, a factor that ought to be identified at the very beginning of our inquiry. It cannot possibly consist of statements, however inclusive, nor of laws, no matter how fundamental, for it must inform all the laws in Halakah and all the statements in Haggadah. What is common to both Halakah and Haggadah are rabbinic concepts embodied in the particular laws and statements.

Rabbinic concepts common to both Halakah and Haggadah are represented by single words or terms such as *Ẓedaḳah* (charity), *Middat Raḥamim* (God's love), *Teshubah* (repentance), *Ḳedushah* (holiness), *Malkut Shamayim* (the Kingship of God), *Gemilut Ḥasadim* (deeds of loving-kindness), *'Adam* (man), to mention but a few. These terms are connotative or suggestive. This is to say that they are not definable and, furthermore, that they cannot be made parts of a nicely articulated logical system or arranged in a hierarchical order. Nevertheless, despite being simply connotative, these rabbinic terms are genuine concepts, general ideas, although neither scientific nor philosophic concepts, nor yet concepts referring to objects or relations in sensory experience. They deal exclusively with the sphere of value, performing there the functions of classifying and abstracting. They are, in fine, value-concepts. Concepts that not only interpret situations but also create them, these value-concepts evoke unique, not actually repeatable events. Can concepts so indeterminate exhibit coherence, a relatedness of some kind? They do possess coherence, but not of a static order. Instead of being connected in diagrammatic fashion, they are all elements of an integrated whole, an organismic, dynamic complex in which all the concepts constantly interweave with each other.

I must confess that I could glean little that was helpful from the modern literature on the problem of value and on the value act. Apparently the outlook of the writers prevents them from realizing that a value act embodies value-concepts, and that such concepts have a distinctive character of their own, different from other types of concepts. Some thinkers, indeed, attempt to obliterate the distinction between a value act and other acts, selecting such examples of "valuation" as can be made to illustrate "experimental logic."

Integrated in an organismic complex, the value-concepts were not produced by logic and are not united in any logical scheme. At the same time logic plays an enormous rôle, especially in Halakah. Rabbinic laws indicate how value-concepts, in themselves abstract, are to be concretized in daily life, and logical, inferential thinking marks both the derivation and the elucidation of the laws. The Mishnah reflects another logical procedure, that of classification of the laws. Even in Haggadah there is effortful, if not exactly inferential, thought. Haggadah employs various forms for combining what are primarily discrete statements; devising and utilizing those forms of composition called for effortful thought, although of a type characteristic of art rather than of analytic reason.

The rabbinic mind, then, reveals how an organismic process and logical processes are not antagonistic but complementary. Still, the dominant process is the organismic. Without inferential reasoning and other logical processes the value-concepts could not have functioned, but the problems thereby solved are set, directly or indirectly, by the value-concepts.

If the value-concepts are dominant in rabbinic literature, it is because they were dominant in life, and not in the lives of the Rabbis alone. The Rabbis were at once representative of the folk and its intellectual leaders, bringing to the people at large the fruits of their work and insights. So far as the valuational life is concerned, the rabbinic mind was also the mind, at its best, of the common man.

Although the pagination of the original edition has been retained, this new edition is the result of a careful revision. Corrections have been made in the text wherever necessary, and new material has been added to the notes. Also new is the Appendix by my friend and colleague, Professor Simon Greenberg, to whom I hereby express my warm thanks. It consists of guiding questions bound to stimulate further thought as well as to make the ideas in the book more salient.

Preface to the First Edition

BY THE TITLE *The Rabbinic Mind* I wish to call attention to two of the book's features. Rabbinic literature is viewed here as an expression of the concepts of the Rabbis, creative concepts that canalized their thinking. But I hope that the term may suggest something more – the great realm of awareness, the realm of ideas that endow life with significance.

My earlier works are devoted primarily to the problem of the nature of the rabbinic concepts. Not united in any logical scheme, must not these apparently disparate concepts be integrated in some other manner? They are found to be the elements of a dynamic organismic complex; by the same token, the rabbinic concept is seen to be dynamic, fluid, experiential. The analysis of a large number of rabbinic concepts is involved in the demonstration of these and cognate matters.

The present book is concerned chiefly with the wider aspects of the rabbinic mind. It discusses such problems as the transmission of social values, the integration of the self, the relation of the self to society. It treats of such topics as the category of significance, indeterminacy of belief, normal mysticism, the commonplace and the holy, rabbinic dogma, the relation of rabbinic thought to philosophy. The sources on which these discussions are based are drawn from both the Haggadah and the Halakah.

There is no sharp line of demarcation, however, between the method here and that of my earlier works. Embodying the results of those earlier studies and building upon them, the present volume further enlarges on the nature of the rabbinic concept; moreover, the discussions here often demand that a concept be analyzed, as in the discussion concerning the rabbinic concepts of "natural order" and the concept of *Nes* ("miracle"). On the other hand, *Organic Thinking*, an earlier book, deals with the category of the ethical and with kindred topics, and hence the subject of rabbinic ethics is not given separate treatment in the present volume.

These studies of the rabbinic mind have implications for the study of religion in general. For example, the tendency of late has been to place religious tradition in an unfavorable contrast with religious mysticism – a contrast in which routine and formalism are associated with religious tradition and fresh experience with religious mysticism. But the very assumption that such a dichotomy exists is wrong, if we are to judge from the normal mysticism of the Rabbis. Not consisting of visions or locutions, but stimulated by normal, everyday life and everyday activities, it was mystical experience to which the common man as well was sensitized. As a matter of fact, rabbinic tradition sensitized the folk to the entire realm of values; it made the many-toned experience of significance the usual means for the expression of the self. How can the deep and latent forces of historic tradition be so rashly ignored in favor of an easy dichotomy?

No attempt at completeness has been made in these studies, either as to range of concepts and topics or as to full details of such as have been taken up. I trust, nevertheless, that an insight has been given into the nature of the rabbinic mind, and perhaps also into that of historic tradition in general.

Professor Max Arzt and Professor Simon Greenberg have read the entire manuscript. Their encouragement and interest have meant more to me than I can tell. I also wish to extend my warm thanks to the colleagues and organizations that have made possible the publication of this book; and to Dr. Maurice Jacobs and his able staff for their helpfulness and courtesy.

MAX KADUSHIN

New York, June, 1952.

Contents

CHAPTER I. Introductory

I. *Value, Self and Society:* The problem of the relation of self to society • The problem of the identification of the values of an historical tradition • Value-concepts of Rabbinic Judaism • They consist of single terms and are undefined concepts • Can thus express the *differentia* of human personalities • At same time are common to all members of the group • Value-concepts are not "value-judgments" • They are usually imbedded in action or statement • Why the term "value-concept" is not entirely satisfactory • Value-concepts are dynamic whereas philosophic concepts are not • The rôle of logic in a value-complex • Theories of religion are wont to overemphasize either society or the individual • Society and self are not two distinct entities. 1

II. *Modern Interpretation:* Our descriptive vocabulary not to be confused with rabbinic terms • A modern presentation of rabbinic thought is also an interpretation • Why our presentation here is "justified". 8

III. *A Psychology of Religion:* The new psychological approach called for by the phenomena of Rabbinic Judaism • Psychological study alone can cope with a number of problems in rabbinic literature • The problem of the relation between Halakah and Haggadah • The problem of *peshaṭ* and *derash* • Psychological approach stresses indigenous elements in the rabbinic mind • "The problem of anthropomorphism" obscures an indigenous problem • Value-complex not the same as a *Weltanschauung* • Realm of the subconscious and realm of awareness. 10

CHAPTER II. The Organism of Rabbinic Value-Concepts

I. *Organismic Coherence:* The problem of the coherence of rabbinic thought • The four fundamental concepts • The subconcepts are concepts in their own right • The conceptual phases • The process of integration as exemplified by passages on *Malkut Shamayim* (the Kingship of God) • Fundamental concepts interweave with each other and with every other concept • The conceptual term only *suggestive,* and the idea-content of a value-concept is a function of the complex as a whole • Unpredictability • Process of integration is also process of individuation • Rabbinic value-complex is a mental organism. 14

II. *Supplementary Forms of Coherence:* These are supplementary to, but do not take the place of, organismic integration • Concepts that are obverses of each other • Subconcepts not of one but of two separate concepts • Concepts that overlap. 26

III. *Experiential Concepts:* Value-concepts are inherent in situations • They are inseparable from normal, everyday experience • Coherence more complex and more flexible than in hierarchical thought • Use of abstract value-concepts found only in developed religious forms. 30

CHAPTER III. The Conceptual Term and Its Implications

I. *The Value-Term:* A genuine rabbinic value-concept must possess a noun form • The concept of *Bereshit* • Noun form enables value-concept to abstract and to classify • Abstract value-terms reflect genuine abstract thought • Habit of abstract valuational thinking practiced by the people at large • Each rabbinic value-term has its own connotation • Examples: *Ẓaddiḳ* and *Ḥasid*; *Goy, Nokri,* and *'Ummot Ha-'Olam*; *'Emunah* and *Biṭṭaḥon*; the apparent exceptions • Through entire rabbinic period no new valuational term. 35

II. *Definition:* Value-terms are never defined • The value-terms are connotative only • Function of a definition in philosophy and science • Value-concept not a conclusion reached by speculation or observation. 45

III. *The Cognitive Concept:* What is perceived through the senses is usually conceptualized • How these cognitive concepts differ from the value-concepts. 50

IV. *Auxiliary Ideas:* They are not represented by conceptual terms • Ideas of God's omniscience, freedom of the will and the like • The idea of the election of Israel • All such ideas act in the service, so to speak, of genuine value-concepts • A true rabbinic value-concept must possess a conceptual term in rabbinic literature. 52

CHAPTER IV. Haggadah, Halakah and the Self

I. *Haggadah as Valuational Expression:* The value-concepts are integrating agents • This is reflected in Haggadah, each haggadic statement being an integrated whole, a unitary entity • Exemplified in all haggadic contexts, whether in exegetical Haggadah or in haggadic compositions • Haggadic statements are unitary entities even in rabbinic sermons • Example from the Yelammedenu • The function of the various forms of haggadic composition is to unify statements in themselves independent • Independent haggadic statements reflect the way value-concepts function in everyday life • Value-concepts fuse all the elements in a situation, whereas cognitive concepts "break down" a total situation • Because each haggadic statement is a unitary entity, there can be variety of opinion • A biblical verse may receive a variety of interpretations • The same is true of events • Examples • Conflicts of opinion. 59

II. *The Self and the "Social Mind":* There is no collective mind • What endows the historic group with a special character are its value-concepts • Cognitive concepts are readily translatable but not value-concepts • Character of the historic group remains constant because value-concepts are stable • Value-concepts possess a drive toward concretization • The dynamic value-concepts play an enormous rôle in the process of the integration of the self • The integrative process of the self to be seen in the integrative process of the value-concepts • The same concepts that give a group its special character make for the uniqueness of the individual self • A value-complex with a larger number of concepts allows greater opportunity for the expression of the self. 76

III. *The Rabbis and the Folk:* Haggadah is a necessary supplement to the speech of ordinary social intercourse • The three requirements the Rabbis had to meet in order to produce this form of literature • No gap between the authors or teachers and the folk • Occasions for training the folk. 84

IV. *Halakah and its Nexus:* Halakah prescribes way for concretization of the value-concepts • Instead of consisting of independent units like Haggadah, Halakah possesses an internal nexus among the laws • The nexus is implicit, and is made explicit only by the work of individual teachers and by their discussions • Except for the classification of subject matter, emergence of nexus incidental to elucidation of laws • Hermeneutic rules • Nexus becomes more explicit in talmudic period • Halakah reflects in its own way the qualities of the value-concepts: Divergent opinions and divergence in actual practice. 89

CHAPTER V. The Category of Significance

I. *Rabbinic Interpretation and Philosophic Interpretation:* Haggadic interpretations of biblical texts embody *rabbinic* concepts • The problem of *peshaṭ* (simple meaning) and *derash* (rabbinic interpretation) • Haggadah is not figurative interpretation • Maimonides' rationale for figurative, philosophic interpretation • Rabbinic interpretation presents a point for point contrast to philosophic interpretation of Bible • There is no such thing as "the logic of revealed religion". 98

II. *Category of Significance–Haggadah:* A reconsideration of the types of concepts • In contrast to the other types, value-concepts do not stand for something objective • How value-concepts use defined concepts and cognitive concepts • Value-concepts fuse the elements in a situation into a unitary entity, and give the situation significance • Value-concepts in a situation are the projection of a personality • A work of art is also a complete entity and bears the imprint of a personality • The differences and the kinship between valuational significance and aesthetic significance • The rôle of a stimulus in poetry and how that rôle differs in the case of haggadic statements • The use of biblical texts as stimulus for haggadic interpretation • The "sequence of thought" between the stimulus and the resultant interpretation must always be given in Haggadah • The same biblical text can serve as stimulus for any number of haggadic interpretations, that is, for multiple interpretations. 107

III. *Category of Significance—Halakah:* The mishnah form and the midrash form • A demarcation between *peshaṭ* and *derash* not possible in Halakah • No basic difference in method between *'asmakta* and other halakic derivations • Some halakic interpretations do exhibit characteristics of haggadic interpretations, usually in a form greatly modified • Some halakot are influenced by haggadot • Multiple interpretation in Halakah and how it differs from multiple interpretation in Haggadah • Halakah reflects organismic character of value-concepts when applied in action, and in the liturgy. 121

IV. *Indeterminacy of Belief:* Category of significance has to do with the element of indeterminacy in thought and action • The value-concepts are indeterminate, and cease to be indeterminate only when concretized • The biblical texts are a non-determining stimulus to haggadic interpretations • Element of indeterminacy also affects attitude toward Haggadah • Indeterminacy of belief which, on occasion, can harden and become determinate • Examples • Can become determinate not only in affirmation but also in negation • Rabbinic legends subject to indeterminacy of belief • Makes for vividness in concretization of value-concepts. 131

V. *Concepts of "Natural Order":* Category of significance goes hand in hand with grasp of objective character of physical world • Value-concepts and cognitive concepts exist as a generally consistent dichotomy • This dichotomy not present in primitive societies • Lévy-Bruhl's theory of "preformed" connections • "Preconnections" are admixture of the valuational and the cognitive • The rabbinic concepts of *sidre Bereshit* and *sidre 'Olam* indicate people as a whole possessed an idea of the regularity and order of the physical world • They are quasi-scientific concepts. 143

VI. *The Concept of Nes ("Miracle"):* One aspect of concept of *Nes* is defined, though not formally • *Nes* characterized as a change in *sidre Bereshit* • Corresponds to philosophic idea of a miracle • A rationalistic tendency in rabbinic literature limiting *Nissim* • Examples indicating that this tendency is not a dominant one • Another aspect of the concept of *Nes*, one in which the question of conformity to *sidre Bereshit* does not enter • Everyday *Nissim* • Striking events as *Nissim* • The "defined" aspect or phase of the concept of *Nes* a phenomenon unparalleled in rabbinic value-complex, being an admixture of a value-concept and an abstract, quasi-scientific concept • The functioning of this abstract phase of *Nes* is restricted by the Rabbis, both in Haggadah and Halakah. 152

VII. *The Commonplace and the Holy:* Halakah makes of certain objects and phenomena occasions for recurrent or fixed concretizations of value-concepts • Eating of food, the *Berakot* involved, and the value-concepts concretized • The commonplace becomes the significant • Ritualistic objects, those employed in rites which evoke a consciousness of holiness • *Ḳedushah* as related to personal conduct • *Miẓwot* as a source of holiness • objects employed in rites are governed by Halakah but are not holy • A rite is a representative part of the *Miẓwot* as a whole • Why consciousness of holiness could not accompany performance of any and every *Miẓwah* • How a rabbinic rite differs from other acts that require a *Berakah* • Rabbinic rite as epitome of category of significance • The several objects that are holy in themselves • Not physical or theurgic efficacy is involved here but reverence • Holy days, too, are fixed concretizations of concept of *Ḳedushah* • How Halakah reifies the holy days • No efficacy inherent in them either • The association of angels with the concept of *Ḳedushah* • Angel is cognitive concept, and so is *shed* • Angelology as background for value-concepts. 167

VIII. *Summary:* The main features of the category of significance. 189

CHAPTER VI. Normal Mysticism

I. *Conceptual Terms for God:* The terms *'Eloah* and *'El* may refer to pagan deities as well as to God • The term *'Elohim* • These terms are not genuine generic terms, and are not really classificatory • The generic terms are also used as proper nouns, that is, as names • Concept of God is *sui generis.* 194

II. *The Experience of God:* Rabbinic experience of God is mystical, but not altogether ineffable • Ways of experiencing God crystallized in concepts like *Middat Ha-Din, Middat Raḥamim, Nes,* prayer, repentance and in a number of other concepts • Ordinary, everyday things and occurrences constitute occasions for experience of God • Again, every member of the group, since he possesses the value-concepts, has some experience of God • This kind of experience can only be characterized as normal mysticism • The various epithets or appellations for God as reflecting normal mysticism • The use of the conceptual terms for God accounted for • The awareness of God as illustrated in prayer • The rôle of the Halakah in this experience of God • Mystical practice in reciting the *Shema'* • Study of Torah as a means of experiencing God • Any concept in the value-complex may be integrated with a concept symbolizing mystical experience; hence, once more, mystical experience of God was an aspect of the normal valuational life of the individual • Concepts of God's love and His justice render this mystical experience expressible • *Middat Ha-Din* and *Middat Raḥamim* are genuine concepts • Rabbinic thought dominated by idea of God's love rather than by the idea of His justice • Ideas of God's omnipotence, God's omniscience and the like are not experiential concepts but auxiliary ideas • The fallacy of treating auxiliary ideas as though they were rabbinic concepts. 201

III. *Revelation of Shekinah (God): Shekinah* is a name for God, although medieval philosophers hold a different opinion • *Shekinah* is used as a name for God when the Rabbis speak of God's nearness to man • Consistent with idea of God's nearness is the use of the word in the term, *Gilluy* (revelation of) *Shekinah,* a concept standing for occasions when God manifested Himself to man's sight or to some other human sense • *Gilluy Shekinah* is a value-concept, but unlike the usual value-concepts, it involves man's senses • Being an admixture of the valuational and the cognitive, the concept does not function as readily as the other concepts • In most of the passages involved, *Gilluy Shekinah* is, with respect to rabbinic period, depicted as being either in the past or in the future • Examples from the Haggadah • Further, the term itself occurs but a single time • Concretization of *Gilluy Shekinah* also restricted in the Halakah • Halakic instances • *Gilluy Shekinah* as associated with prophecy refers to prerabbinic times • In general, then, the Rabbis' experience of God, and that of the folk as well, was *unaccompanied* by psychic phenomena such as visions and locutions • There is no implication of the "immanence of God" in the contexts of *Gilluy Shekinah,* nor in the use of the word *Shekinah* • It is not likely that the Rabbis had *Merkabah* mysticism in mind when they spoke of *Gilluy Shekinah.* 222

IV. *Bat Ḳol:* The several kinds of *Bat Ḳol* had no association with experience of God • Rejection of *Bat Ḳol* in Halakah • *Bat Ḳol* is not a pure value-concept. 261

V. *The Relationship to God:* The steady consciousness of a relationship to God in normal mysticism can be suggested but not depicted • A sense of intimacy is present but so is another and an opposite feeling • How the *Berakah* expresses both feelings by shifting from the second to the third person • Mystical consciousness of relationship to God also expressed in terms of *various* human relationships, and by use of the appellatives. 263

CHAPTER VII. This Side of Philosophy

I. *The Question of Anthropomorphism:* The Rabbis apparently object to biblical statements about God that seem to limit Him • Has this apprehension anything to do with the philosophers' objection to anthropomorphism? • The many anthropomorphisms that are unqualified • The various solutions offered all have philosophical implications • Vantage point of the Rabbis lost whenever a stand is taken on anthropomorphism • How postrabbinic Jewish thought confirms this contention • Problem of anthropomorphism foreign to indigenous Judaism • Medieval Jewish philosophy does not represent a development in the Jewish idea of God • Kaufmann's theory. 273

II. *Organismic Development:* Rabbinic thought is a development out of the Bible • Rabbinic value-concepts are all rooted in the Bible, but have greater applicability and range • Rabbinic concepts with conceptual terms not found in the Bible • Rabbinic concepts with biblical conceptual terms, but now having a wider, more universal connotation • The bond between the Rabbis and the prophets • Rabbinic concepts having conceptual terms found in the Bible but which are now used in a different sense • Emphatic trends in rabbinic thought • A living bond unites both Haggadah and Halakah with the Bible • Rabbinic emphasis on the experience of God, an emphatic trend, has its roots in the Bible • Some aspects of normal mysticism as emphasized by the Rabbis represent an enlargement of a particular idea, and hence are, to a degree, a departure from the Bible. 288

III. *The Otherness of God:* Every experience of God brought the recognition that God is like none other • Rabbinic conceptual terms for God are, in a sense, terms for God's otherness • The need for cultivating the recognition of God's otherness • Rabbinic passages with which this chapter began are not strictures on anthropomorphisms but means of cultivating idea of God's otherness • It is a biblical idea but accented still more strongly by the Rabbis • Certain haggadic stereotypes teach the idea but stress God's love and His justice • How the Rabbis teach the idea of God's otherness, not incidentally, but as an idea in its own right • Phrases in Scripture that are only intended "to soothe the ear" • What the Rabbis regard as prophetic license • How the Rabbis emphasize the idea of God's otherness when they discuss Temple sacrifices and ritual • How the Rabbis teach the idea by interpreting away biblical verses that seem to contradict the idea • The data in these passages indicate that it is not an aversion to anthropomorphism that the Rabbis express here • Neither, however, did they accept anthropomorphism as a principle • The idea of God's otherness represents an emphatic trend, and like the other rabbinic emphatic trends is a development out of the Bible • Idea of God's otherness, nevertheless, is a very indefinite idea and has no real power of generalization; hence rabbinic literature teems with "anthropomorphisms" • Indefinite character of the idea is in accord with the entire midrashic approach. 303

IV. *Anthropomorphism and Targum Onkelos:* According to Maimonides and other medieval philosophers, the paraphrases in Onkelos' translation of the Pentateuch represent the true meaning, and have the purpose of opposing the belief in God's corporeality • Naḥmanides refutes Maimonides on this • Fallacy of Arama's theory • Luzzatto also not free from the philosophic approach • Our view is that Targum Onkelos, in its deviations from literal translation, teaches the idea of the otherness of God • How the terms *Memra'*, *Yeḳara'* and *Shekinta'* teach that idea • Deviations out of reverence for God also teach the idea of His otherness • Why the inconsistencies in Targum Onkelos are to be expected. 325

V. *Summary.* 336

VI. *Rabbinic Dogma:* The words "acknowledge" and "deny" as associated with rabbinic dogmas • Acknowledgment of God, however, involves experience of God, and denial of God is willful rejection of Him despite that experience • Examples in rabbinic literature and in the liturgy • A dogma is a matter of belief, not a matter of daily personal experience, and a belief to which all must subscribe • *Mattan* (the giving of) *Torah* as a dogma • Terms indicative of belief here are applied not only to Decalogue but also to Pentateuch, and the dogma is also associated with Prophets and *Ketubim* • How *Mattan Torah* was regarded as reënforcing the experience of the individual • Concept of Torah itself as a modification of the dogma • Rabbis were cognizant of their creative rôle in the emergence of the oral Torah • Rabbis felt empowered to make *taḳḳanot* (ordinances) and *gezerot* (prohibitory decrees) on their own authority, and this considerable body of legislation is also Torah • Dynamic value-concept of Torah tends to modify the quasi-determinate concept, the dogma, of *Mattan*

Torah • Belief that God brought Israel out of Egypt is another dogma • Attempt is made to render this dogma, too, a matter of personal experience • The dogma of the resurrection of the dead • The room here for differences of opinion, however • The other hereafter concepts • Why all the hereafter concepts are not real value-concepts • Why they also are not pure dogma • Rabbinic dogmas are not marshaled into a creed, nor are they otherwise presented as the basic principles of Judaism. 340

NOTES 369

APPENDIX 373

INDEX 379

The Rabbinic Mind

CHAPTER I

Introductory

I. VALUE, SELF AND SOCIETY

What is the relation of the individual to society? What kind of ideas make both for the stabilization of society and for the expression of the self? At least partial answers can be given when we discover the nature of values.

How can the values contained in any great historical tradition be identified? The general assumption seems to be that a tradition does not formulate or crystallize its values. When modern scholars and thinkers, therefore, wish to describe the values in a tradition, they attempt to make their own formulation of them based on their own individual insights. This is the invariable method for depicting such values, whether in philosophies of history, or in sociological studies, or in general articles. The formulation of values is exactly, however, what in our present study of rabbinic values we have no need for doing. In Rabbinic Judaism, values are crystallized in specific terms, every value having its own name or symbol. If Rabbinic Judaism is a criterion, this must be true of values of all civilized societies.

The values of Rabbinic Judaism consist of ideas. Rabbinic Judaism, in the course of the many centuries of its creative period (roughly the second B.C.E. to the seventh C.E.), produced a vast literature, and its religious values are embodied in every branch of that literature. One branch, the Haggadah, is of such character as to make it especially amenable to our analysis. The Haggadah is a unique literature, unique in that it reflects quite faithfully, as we shall come to recognize, the way the rabbinic values functioned in everyday life. Now ideas which constantly affect the ever changing situations of daily life and moment-to-moment conduct must be ideas that are grasped and manipulated in a flash. Can any idea be communicated more quickly, grasped more quickly, acted on more quickly, than that contained in a single word or term commonly understood? We can now see why any attempt to formulate rabbinic values does violence to them. The only authentic way to express abstractly a rabbinic value is by means of the term for it found in rabbinic literature. Even to define that term is to distort the value. A definition would have to present the value as a complete idea, a proposition; it would thereby change the character of the value. We may say, therefore, that the rabbinic value-terms stand for ideas, but not for complete, fully formulated ideas. The rabbinic value-terms can thus be characterized as undefined concepts. Again, if rabbinic value-terms are a criterion, value-concepts in general are apparently not defined.

The absence of a definition, instead of being a defect, is what enables the rabbinic value-concept to function easily and effectively. We shall find that the value-concepts are not only undefined but nondefinable, and that this accords with the dual nature of the task which is accomplished by them. Being nondefinable, the value-concepts are extremely flexible, and they can, therefore, respond to and express the *differentia* of human personalities. At the same time the value-term does convey an abstract, generalized idea of the concept it represents, and this generalized idea is common to all the members of the group. The complex of value-concepts as a whole is hence meaningful enough and colorful enough to make of the individuals who employ it a unified group, a society with a clearly recognizable character.

Value-concepts are, then, decisive factors both in the development of the self and in the stabilization of society — are crucial factors in the relation of the self to society. That the value-concepts played these rôles in the lives of the Rabbis and their followers will, we believe, become apparent in this work. But it is hardly possible, bearing in mind the basic function of the value-concepts, that the entire phenomenon can be characteristic of that society alone. Value-concepts are most likely decisive factors in every civilized society, each society owing its stability and character to such value-concepts, or at least to such aspects of value-concepts, as are peculiarly its own. If this is the case, then it is hard to understand why value-concepts were not identified and described long ago. So far as we know, however, even the term "value-concepts" has not been used before; people spoke of "values," by which they meant all manner of subjective attitudes toward sundry matters and objects, and they spoke of "value-judgments," by which they meant statements revealing a bias of some kind. But they have not employed the term "value-concepts" as a designation for a distinct type of concept possessing certain characteristics and *differing*, because of those characteristics, from other types of concepts. This has perhaps been due, among other causes, to the fact that the value-concepts are frequently "invisible." Value-concepts are symbolized, as we have said, by words or terms, but these terms stand for the concepts only when the latter are referred to abstractly. In all other instances, the value-concepts present are not mentioned by name but are, as it were, imbedded in an action or a statement. Thus, the very first rabbinic passage we shall have occasion to quote in the next chapter contains the concept of *Malkut Shamayim*, the Kingship of God, yet the term itself, though found elsewhere often enough, is not mentioned there. Instead, the concept is imbedded in the statement, "My dominion is everywhere." Very likely, to repeat, it is this property of being imbedded rather than named that has helped keep value-concepts from being noticed. Not having been actually noticed, the value-concepts in any tradition could not have been recognized, of course, as examples of a distinct conceptual type.

The term "value-concepts" is not an entirely satisfactory one. This compound term has the great advantage of pointing, through its two components, to two important things. The component "concepts" tells that the values referred to are communicable ideas, that is, ideas that may be shared by the group as a whole; whilst the component "value" tells that these ideas are nevertheless also, in a degree, personal and subjective, and that they are ideas held warmly. At the same time, the term has its disadvantages as well. It does not make evident that the concepts are not only communicable, but that they are common ideas, folk-ideas. And it has other disadvantages, those associated with the component "value". This word can be taken to mean that the concepts evaluate, appraise, or estimate. It is true that some of the rabbinic value-concepts have such a connotation, as in the case of *Ẓaddiḳ* (righteous man) and in that of *Rasha'* (wicked man). But many value-concepts do not appraise. The Kingship of God is not an appraising concept, nor is God's loving-kindness — nor, to mention a modern value-concept, is "freedom of speech." On the other hand, the word "value" does apply to "freedom of speech" if we use "value" in the sense of esteem, of holding in high regard. So used, the word could apply to all goals or ends. Concepts like God's love and God's Kingship, however, are obviously not goals or ends of man; neither can they be properly associated with man's esteem. As we shall go on to analyze the character of value-concepts, we shall find that they endow actions or situations or events with "significance" – not with significance in general, but with significance in terms of the particular concepts embodied in the situation or event.

The value-concepts are dynamic. They cannot be organized into a static system, one neat proposition following upon another, because the concepts are single words or terms, not propositions. It is only when the value-concepts are employed in speech or action, when they are active or dynamic, that the coherence of the concepts, their interrelationship, can be demonstrated. The coherence of the concepts is an organismic coherence, as we shall endeavor to prove in the next chapter, and it has many and far-reaching consequences. One of them is the atomistic effect of the value-concepts, each statement and each deed embodying value-concepts being a complete and independent entity in itself. This is reflected in the Haggadah, where certain literary forms bring together statements that are essentially single units in themselves. Statements of that kind, whether in Haggadah or in ordinary speech, are vehicles for the expression of the individual's personality. Not articulated in a hard-and-fast system, they can convey an individual's moods, his reactions under varying circumstances, his own peculiarities of temperament, as well as his deep seated convictions. All this would be impossible were the value-concepts congealed in a static, hierarchical system of thought. Were that the case, instead of leaving room for the *differentia* of personalities, the value-concepts would impose a uniform set of ideas upon everybody, a rigid structure of dogmas. This does not mean that rabbinic thought admits of no dogmas at all. But the dogmatic elements are few, and these few are of a sort that does not impede the operation of the value-complex as a whole.

Particularly since the Middle Ages, thinkers have worked

to achieve an integrated philosophy, a system of ideas compelling assent by the force of its logic. Many thinkers today have a similar ideal, and they would doubtless stigmatize value-concepts answering to our description as nothing but naïve, unsophisticated ideas. It is not a question, however, as to whether value-concepts are "naïve" as compared to philosophical concepts, but rather as to which type can actually function in the ever shifting situations of life. To meet these situations, there is need for dynamic concepts, and the value-concepts are dynamic whereas the philosophic concepts are not. The fact of the matter is that our basic attitudes, our value-concepts, are not logically ordered because they are not the outcome, not the product, of cold logic. We had a concept of human equality, for example, long before it was proved "correct" during recent decades by the various studies on racial traits; nor would unfavorable conclusions in those studies have disturbed our value-concept. But though logic does not build up the value-concepts, it has nonetheless an extremely important function in the valuational life. Logical analysis enables us to find ways of applying the value-concepts, both by means of laws and in situations not covered by law. Acute logic marks that branch of rabbinic literature which has to do with law, the Halakah.

If the value-concepts seem simple, it is only because they are common, familiar. Actually, the value-concepts involve one subtle experience after another. Theirs is the domain of the interior life as well as that of social relationships. Because of them, there is a completely objective grasp of things at the very time these things are the occasions for subjective experiences. They play a major part in the creation of new ethical events, and they also make possible a type of literary creativity. At times they can allow for shadings in belief, for an attitude which is neither complete assent nor complete dissent. They are the means of rendering the experience of God a normal element in the life of every man.

Theories of religion are wont to overemphasize either society or the individual. According to the social theories of religion, sacred rites and activities are always symbols of society: those who engage in them express thereby their consciousness of community, of belonging to one another in a common life. But is this really what is in the minds of those performing the rites? May not a value-concept be embodied in the rite, namely, the value-concept of holiness, and may not this consciousness of holiness be uppermost when the rite is performed? That is certainly what happened, we shall see, in Rabbinic Judaism: many of the rites are performed not in assembly but by the individual; of the two ideas current — the concept of holiness and the idea of community — the concept of holiness is distinctly the one emphasized, and is the one that gives the rite its significance. The result is that the performance of the rite becomes a personal experience, an experience with overtones and commitments that concern personal conduct. Here as always, a value-concept affords a means for the expression of the self.

On the other side, some theories overstress the individual. According to these theories, religious feelings are purely personal intuitions, religious ideas the apprehensions of a few great souls. These notions are negated by what we know about value-concepts. Value-concepts are not intuitions. They are, it is true, charged with feeling and on occasions with intense feeling, but they have a conceptual, an ideational core. As to the part played by great religious personalities, that is a matter we shall discuss in some detail later on. Now we need only point out that great religious personalities could have played no part at all had they not communicated their ideas; and communication was possible because the concepts they used — the value-concepts — were represented by common terms in the general vocabulary. Society at large was the repository of the value-concepts, that is to say, every member of society.

What is the relation of the individual to society? Society and the individual cannot be set up one against the other, for the reason that they are not two distinct and different entities. Every individual expresses his personality by means of the value-concepts. He can do so only because all the other individuals in his society have the same means for expressing and developing their personalities. As Whitehead puts it, "The individual is formative of the society, the society is formative of the individual."

II. MODERN INTERPRETATION

In our endeavor to depict the rabbinic mind, we are obliged to use a fairly large number of descriptive terms. Any attempt at scientific analysis is bound to bring into play a descriptive vocabulary of some kind; that vocabulary is justified if it calls attention to phenomena and properly describes them. Our own descriptive vocabulary is justified if it calls attention to, and correctly depicts, the character and the qualities of rabbinic thought. But we must caution against regarding our vocabulary as anything other than descriptive; our descriptive terms must not be confused with the rabbinic terms; only rabbinic terms can be rabbinic value-concepts. Our own descriptive terms are pointers merely, calling attention to the value-concepts and to other phenomena characteristic of rabbinic thought.

Every modern presentation of rabbinic thought is also an interpretation. Scientific procedure demands that we refrain from imposing on the material an outlook that is foreign to it, but this does not mean that interpretation is necessarily ruled out. As a matter of fact, interpretation cannot be entirely ruled out. Even if we do no more than classify rabbinic statements in a manner not classified by the Rabbis themselves, we are interpreting those statements. The classifying rubric calls attention to an aspect of rabbinic thought that might otherwise not have been noticed, and in doing so, the rubric has put an interpretation on the passage thus classified.

Exceedingly cautious as the modern authorities are, therefore, they cannot avoid interpretation. No one is more suspicious of interpretation than Schechter. "I considered it advisable," he says, "not to intrude too much interpretation or paraphrase upon the Rabbis. I let them have their own say in their own words, and even their own phraseology, so far as the English idiom allowed."[1] Among his chapter-headings, however, are such rubrics as "The Kingdom of God (Invisible)," "The Visible Kingdom (Universal)," "The Kingdom of God (National)" – and "invisible," "visible," "universal," "national," are not terms used in these connections by the Rabbis themselves. They are terms that Schechter employs in order to call attention to various aspects of the Kingdom or Kingship of God; they are interpretative terms.

Our own descriptive vocabulary, of course, also constitutes an interpretation. It goes without saying that we have tried to render accurately the rabbinic passages employed here, whether in translation or in paraphrase. But that is not the only consideration, we feel, if our presentation is to be faithful to rabbinic thought. Once the rabbinic materials are subjected to analysis, an injustice is done if we reckon merely with this or that specific statement; such specific statements then stand unrelated to rabbinic thought as a whole. How can this difficulty be overcome,

[1] S. Schechter, Some Aspects of Rabbinic Theology (New York: The Macmillan Co., 1910), p. viii.

at least in some degree? By so treating the rabbinic statements we employ as to point up the value-concepts which they embody, the value-concepts being common to rabbinic thought as a whole. Our present study ought to meet that requirement. The earlier chapters, dealing with the organization of the rabbinic value-concepts and with the ways of identifying them, are devoted exclusively to the rabbinic value-concepts. Furthermore, as we go on to discuss other topics – the category of significance, normal mysticism, the emphatic trends, to mention several – our very approach compels us to take account of the value-concepts embodied in the rabbinic statements under discussion.

We have just mentioned several of our descriptive terms. They are justified, it seems to us, on two counts. First, they epitomize genuine aspects or qualities of rabbinic thought. Second, they represent an analysis that attempts to relate the specific rabbinic statements to rabbinic thought as a whole. Our descriptive vocabulary constitutes an interpretation, but a justified interpretation.

III. A PSYCHOLOGY OF RELIGION

Our work may well be characterized as a psychological study of Rabbinic Judaism. Such a study, however, cannot be based on the studies already made in the field of religious psychology. The phenomena of Rabbinic Judaism call for an entirely different approach. We shall see, for example, that the rabbinic consciousness of holiness is not at all dependent on the presence of things mysterious and awesome; and further that this consciousness has a decided bearing on personal behavior. Similarly, there is little in the modern analysis of mysticism that is relevant to the rabbinic experience of God. That experience is indeed a form of mysticism, but it is a form that can only be described as "normal mysticism." To the modern students of mysticism, the term "normal mysticism" will doubtless appear to be self-contradictory. The same thing can be said of our term, "indeterminacy of belief"; yet that attitude of mind issues from the very character of Rabbinic Judaism as an organismic complex of thought. The factor of indeterminacy is a feature of all organisms.

The psychological study of Rabbinic Judaism alone can cope with a number of problems in rabbinic literature. A basic problem there is the relation between Halakah and Haggadah. It is not enough merely to recognize the obvious fact of a close relationship, nor even that the ideas in both are similar. Can we depict that relationship explicitly? Can we point to the common ideas, not just here and there, but to an entire, discernible pattern of common ideas accounting for that relationship? Despite the common ideas, the Halakah is often stricter than the Haggadah, less bending, certainly far more precise. What kind of ideas are they that can have one character in the Halakah and another in the Haggadah? As soon as we have to describe a *kind* of idea, a *type* of concept, we are in the field of psychology. The common ideas, according to our study, are the value-concepts, concepts that, because of their special characteristics, can serve the purposes of both Halakah and Haggadah. Haggadah and Halakah are so closely related because both are concretizations of the value-concepts – Haggadah in speech, Halakah in law and action.

More specific literary problems also belong to the field of psychology. The Rabbis designate the plain meaning of the biblical texts as *peshaṭ,* and their own haggadic interpretations as *derash.* The Rabbis are thus aware of the simple meaning of the texts. How is it, then, that they can also engage extensively in textual interpretation that departs so radically from the simple meaning? The allegorical interpretation of Scripture which is the product of the Jewish philosophers cannot be taken as a parallel; we shall find that the two methods of scriptural interpretation — the philosophical and the rabbinic — are essentially different, and that the rationale given by the philosophers for their allegorical interpretation cannot apply to rabbinic interpretation. Neither can we say that the Rabbis merely utilized the biblical texts so as to make their own statements more authoritative; to say this would be to do the Rabbis a monstrous injustice. The fact of the matter is that any explanation is bound to be wrong which deals with the problem externally, that is, only in terms of the method of interpretation. Haggadic interpretation is characteristic of an entire aspect of the rabbinic mind. It cannot be explained without recourse to our "category of significance."

The psychological approach has the virtue of stressing the indigenous elements in the rabbinic mind. This is sound scientific practice, not apologetics. In post-rabbinic times, problems in rabbinic thought have often been treated as though they were philosophic problems, with the result that their indigenous character has been obscured. It has become a tradition, for example, to speak of the problem of anthropomorphism in rabbinic literature. But the negation of anthropomorphism is a metaphysical principle, a principle arrived at in the course of discursive, philosophical ratiocination. Can we, like many medieval philosophers, see in the paraphrases of Targum Onkelos the endeavor to conform to this metaphysical principle? Modern authorities only go so far as to attribute to the Rabbis the attempt to "mitigate" anthropomorphic expressions. Notwithstanding these apparent "mitigations," however, rabbinic literature simply teems with anthropomorphisms. What has been regarded as a problem of anthropomorphism in rabbinic literature is indeed a problem, but not of anthropomorphism. It is a problem that arises, as we shall notice, out of the rabbinic experience of God, a problem that demands a psychological, and not a philosophic, approach.

A value-pattern or a value-complex is not the same as a *Weltanschauung*. It is not achieved by an individual as the result of taking thought, or after years of experience; it is not something added, so to speak, to a personality. The rabbinic value-complex, by supplying the means for experiencing significance in everyday life, also supplied the means for the expression of personality, and this from earliest childhood. Growth in personality meant greater sensitivity to situations that yield significance, that is also to say, an ever-deepening awareness of the value-concepts.

A healthy corrective is to be found here for our present-day views of personality. We have been wont for some time to think of personality chiefly in terms of the subconscious or the unconscious; no one can now deny the importance of this realm. Our study, however, demonstrates that of even greater importance is the realm of *awareness*. The active, dynamic concepts of civilized man, the concepts which mold a man from earliest childhood, are concepts of which he is aware. The more a person is aware of the value-concepts, the more sensitive he is to them, the greater will be the significance he will experience in everyday life, and the richer his personality.

* * *

We shall try to keep purely technical discussion, whether on textual matters or on conceptual theory, down to a minimum. At times, however, the nature of a particular topic is such that a technical analysis is unavoidable, and this is true of the first major topic we shall consider, the organism of the rabbinic value-concepts.

CHAPTER II

The Organism of Rabbinic Value-Concepts

I. ORGANISMIC COHERENCE

It was Schechter who recognized that the lack of logical system in rabbinic thought was a virtue, not a defect. The absence of dogmatic formulation allowed the Rabbis, as he shows, to dwell upon one doctrine, when there was need, rather than upon another; to enunciate religious ideas without spinning them out into creedal principles; to present aspects of a subject which may well be modified or qualified by other aspects of that subject.[1] These observations are extremely important for the insight they give us into rabbinic thought. Yet they leave the essential problem unsolved. If rabbinic thought does not present a logical system, does it have no integrating principle at all?

But rabbinic thought must have coherence, must have a cohesiveness of some sort. Rabbinic midrashic literature seeks to impart ideas: it is a literature which deals with concepts, its statements having to do with such concepts as charity, Torah, *Malkut Shamayim*, *Derek Ereẓ* and scores of other value-concepts. Now ideas, to be coherent, must be in a system of some kind; an idea can be conveyed only when it is related in some manner to other ideas, when it can be placed in context with other ideas, in other words, when it is part of a larger whole. The literature of Rabbinic Judaism conveys ideas, and the ideas are, therefore, undoubtedly

[1] Solomon Schechter, op. cit., pp. 11–17.

coherent with each other. The question is, however: what is the nature of that coherence? Can we discern in the great array of ideas or concepts any form of organization or, at least, any organizing principle? This is, we believe, the central problem in the study of Rabbinic Judaism.

The coherence or organization of the rabbinic value-concepts was the subject of our earlier works on rabbinic thought.[2] We make use in this section of some of the essential conclusions found there, conclusions reached after tracing every rabbinic concept through every passage in two representative Midrashic Tractates and confirmed by corroborative selections from rabbinic literature generally.

There are four concepts which have a special character — God's justice (*Middat Ha-Din*), God's love (or mercy) (*Middat Raḥamim*), Torah, and Israel. Each of these four possesses its own subconcepts: God's justice the subconcepts of chastisements, merit of the fathers, merit of the children, and "measure for measure"; God's love the subconcepts of prayer, repentance, and atonement, the latter having its own subconcept in vicarious atonement; Torah the subconcepts of the study of Torah, *Miẓwot,* good deeds, and ethical *Derek Ereẓ,* the latter also having its own subconcepts in charity and deeds of loving-kindness and in such ethical matters as humility, honesty, reverence and the like; and Israel the subconcepts of the righteous and the wicked, the learned and the ignorant, the patriarchs, and the pious.[3] This list of subconcepts is not exhaustive. We wished merely to indicate that it is characteristic of these four concepts to have fairly numerous subconcepts. Of the subconcepts not given here, only a few belong to

[2] The Theology of Seder Eliahu (New York: Bloch Publishing Co., 1932), hereafter referred to as TE; Organic Thinking (New York: The Jewish Theological Seminary of America, 1938), hereafter referred to as OT; and Aspects of the Rabbinic Concept of Israel in the Mekilta, Hebrew Union College Annual, Vol. XIX (Cincinnati, 1945–46), pp. 57–96.

[3] On these topics see the references in the General Index of OT. On *Middat Ha-Din* and *Middat Raḥamim* see below, p. 215 f.

other than the four concepts, and we ought, therefore, to regard such instances as exceptional.

The subconcepts are not designated as such by the Rabbis, and are not in any sense inferred from or subsidiary to the main concepts. They are, in fact, treated in rabbinic literature in exactly the same way as are the main concepts. Only after some scrutiny do they stand revealed as "belonging" to their respective main concepts, and this because they appear to share in the ground provided by the latter. "Measure for measure", for example, is an independent manifestation of the concept of God's justice, sharing in the general ground provided by that concept for all forms of God's justice, and is in no manner inferred or derived. In stressing thus the independent character of the subconcepts, however, we do not mean to imply that by classifying them as subconcepts, we did violence to their nature. A real kinship exists among a general concept and all its subconcepts, so that they tend to be employed as a unit. It is not accidental, for example, that in a compilation like Pirḳe 'Abot wherein Torah is the central concept, the subconcepts *Miẓwot, Derek Ereẓ*, and good deeds are the other concepts most often involved in the rabbinic dicta. The relation of a general concept to its subconcepts, in the case of the four concepts, is one form of integration to be found then in the complex of the rabbinic value-concepts.[4]

[4] The concept of man and its various subconcepts can serve as illustrations of the fact that subconcepts which are values are treated completely as general concepts and never as derived from a main concept. The concepts of the nations of the world and Israel are, apparently, subconcepts of the concept of man. Chronologically, Israel is a branching out of man, and so are the nations of the world, in the rabbinic view of history; man would thus precede both in time; Israel and the nations would thus be derived from man. But the Rabbis speak of Israel as among the things preceding creation although realized later (Bereshit R. I. 4, ed. Theodor, p. 6). And there are other rabbinic ideas regarding Israel and the nations equally at variance with the notion of these concepts as being derived from man. Since Israel and the nations are value-concepts, they are always treated as concepts in their own right, not derived.

The four concepts — God's justice, His love, Torah, and Israel — are distinguished in another regard. Besides subconcepts, they may also possess conceptual phases, our designation for what appear to be subconcepts which are without the benefit of conceptual terms. The concept of God's justice has two such conceptual phases. There is the phase of the justice due the individual, the idea that whatever befalls anyone, for good or evil, comes as recompense for his own acts, and there is also the phase of corporate or collective justice, a phase of the general concept of God's justice which permits the Rabbis to regard reward or punishment for the deeds of an individual as visited by God not only upon him alone but upon others in some way associated with him, as well. These two conceptual phases act very much, so far as we can see, as do the genuine subcepts. The phase of corporate justice even possesses, like some of the genuine subconcepts, subconcepts of its own in merit of the fathers and merit of the children, and the latter do not exhaust but only share in the ground provided by the phase of corporate justice, once more exactly as is the case with genuine general concepts and subconcepts. The concept of Torah, too, possesses a conceptual phase, the efficacy of Torah, which is the idea that knowledge of Torah has an immediate, though not an inevitable, effect upon conduct.[5] Conceptual phases seem, therefore, to be subconcepts which the Rabbis left unnamed. But this very fact — the omission of the names or terms — should make us unwilling to place the conceptual phases in the same category with the genuine subconcepts. Not characterized by rabbinic terms, the conceptual phases, despite their definite characteristics, have not crystallized out into genuine subconcepts, perhaps because of some amorphous qualities which further study may yet reveal.

[5] See the references under the topics God's justice, corporate justice, and efficacy of Torah in the General Index of OT.

Ramified into subconcepts and conceptual phases, the four concepts, we can plainly see, play a large rôle in integrating the entire complex of concepts. "Ramified," however, is the wrong word to use. It gives the impression of static or diagrammatic organization; moreover, it takes no account of the peculiar relation of general concept to subconcept whereby the latter acts in all ways like the general concept itself. These erroneous impressions are corrected only as we perceive not the large but the dominating rôle of the four concepts in the integration of the complex as a whole, not their relation to their own subconcepts and conceptual phases but to all the concepts in the complex.

To illustrate the process of integration, let us take passages dealing with the concept of *Malkut Shamayim*, the Kingship of God (lit., of Heaven).[6] We shall preface each passage or group of passages with a sentence summarizing the idea concerning *Malkut Shamayim* the passage contains.

(a) God's dominion is everywhere. According to Exod. 12:15, God will punish him who eats leavened bread during the seven days of Passover — "For whosoever eateth leavened bread from the first day until the seventh day, that soul shall be cut off from Israel." The Rabbis, in a comment on the words "from Israel," add: "I might understand it to mean: that soul shall be cut off from Israel, but go to live among another people. But it says, 'From before Me; I am the Lord' (Lev. 22:3). My dominion is everywhere."[7]

[6] The term *Malkut Shamayim* is found in two of the passages about to be cited — Mekilta, ed. Lauterbach, II (Philadelphia: Jewish Publication Society of America, 1933), 227; also ibid., 230, according to the printed editions which is the reading rightly preferred by Horovitz-Rabin in their edition of the Mechilta (Frankfort am Main: Kauffmann Verlag, 1928–31), p. 219. The phrase לקבל מלכות שמים בשמחה is identical in the two passages and is a cliché, and hence the variant in Lauterbach II, 230 is very likely incorrect. Quotations from the Mekilta throughout this book refer to Lauterbach's edition, except when otherwise indicated.

[7] Mekilta I, 67; ibid., 79. The relevant phrase in Lev. 22:3 reads in full: "that soul shall be cut off from before Me; I am the Lord."

In (a) above, the concept of *Malkut Shamayim* is interwoven with the concept of God's justice.

(b) God will ultimately be *recognized* as King by the whole world. This will come to pass, one passage says, when God will punish those who destroyed His Temple which He will then build again. This passage makes its point by means of a parable which tells of a king who sat in judgment over the robbers who had destroyed his palace and which concludes with "And thereafter his kingship was recognized in the world."[8] In another passage R. Eleazar says, "When will the name of these people [Amalek and, apparently, the other enemies of Israel] be blotted out? At the time when idolatry will be uprooted together with its worshipers, and God alone will be (recognized as God) in the world, and His Kingship will be established forever and for all eternity. For at that time, 'shall the Lord go forth and fight' etc. (Zech. 14:3), 'And the Lord shall be King over all the earth; in that day shall the Lord be One, and His name one.' (*ibid.* v. 9)."[9]

The combination of concepts in (b) above consists of *Malkut Shamayim*, God's justice, the nations (enemies), and idolatry.

(c) The Kingship of God negates, basically, the dominion of the nations of the world over Israel. They rule over Israel, the Rabbis state, only because Israel said, "The Lord will reign (i. e. in the future) for ever and ever" (Exod. 15:18). "Had Israel said at the sea, 'The Lord is King for ever and ever,' no nation or kingdom would ever have ruled over them. But they said: 'The Lord will reign for ever and ever' – *le'atid labo*."[10]

Again, in (c) above, God's justice and *Malkut Shamayim* are interwoven.

[8] Mekilta II, 79–80.

[9] Ibid., 158–9.

[10] Mekilta II, 80. The passage immediately following is corrupt but a better text is in Horovitz-Rabin, p. 150.

All the four concepts, not God's justice alone, interweave with the concept of *Malkut Shamayim*. In the following the latter is combined with God's love or mercy:

> (a) God's Kingship is accepted by Israel after they have experienced His loving-kindness in His many deeds on their behalf. Following a parable in which a king is accepted by a people only after he had benefited them by his deeds, the midrash says: "Likewise, God. He brought Israel out of Egypt, divided the sea for them, sent down the manna for them, brought up the well for them, brought the quail for them, fought for them the battle with Amalek. Then He said to them: I am to be your King (in the First Commandment – 'I am the Lord thy God'). And they said to Him: Yes, yes!"[11]

> (b) God's Kingship negates the rule of all others over Israel – an idea met with above, but given here more general form: "I shall not appoint nor delegate any one else, so to speak, to rule over you, but I Myself will rule over you. And thus it says, 'Behold, He that keepeth Israel doth neither slumber nor sleep' (Ps. 121:4)."[12]

Torah interweaves with the concept of *Malkut Shamayim*:

> (a) The practical implication of the acceptance of God's Kingship is the observance of the *Miẓwot* of the Torah, God's commandments; although thus implied in each other, there can be no observance of the *Miẓwot* before there is acceptance of His Kingship. In one passage, the Rabbis start with a parable concerning a king of flesh and blood who, upon entering a province, was advised by his attendants to issue decrees to the people, but who refused to do so until the people should accept his kingship. "For if they will not accept my kingship they will not carry out my decrees. Likewise, God said to Israel: 'I am the Lord thy God, who brought thee out of the land of Egypt . . . Thou shalt have no other

[11] Ibid., 229–30. The term for God here is *Ha-Maḳom*.

[12] Ibid., 204.

> gods (Exod. 20:2–3) – I am He whose Kingship you have taken upon yourselves in Egypt.' And when they said to Him, 'Yes, yes!' He continued: 'Now, just as you accepted My Kingship, you must also accept My decrees – Thou shalt have no other gods before Me (*ibid.*)."[13] The first statement in the Ten Commandments – "I am the Lord thy God" – is taken here by the Rabbis to state that Israel accepted God's Kingship when He took them out of Egypt; the Commandments or decrees proper would begin, then, with the second statement – "Thou shalt have no other gods before Me." There seems to be a difference of opinion, however, as to when Israel did accept the Kingship of God, for the passage immediately goes on to give R. Simeon b. Yoḥai's view that Israel accepted it at Sinai, although he, too, indicates that "I am the Lord thy God" is a prefatory declaration referring to God's Kingship.[14] Elsewhere, also, Israel's acceptance of God's Kingship is said to have taken place at Sinai when the Torah was given. "Rabbi (R. Judah the Prince) says: This proclaims the excellence of Israel. For when they all stood before Mt. Sinai to receive the Torah, they all made up their mind alike to accept the Kingship of God with joy."[15] And according to another passage, at Sinai, before the Ten Commandments were given, Moses said to Israel: "Be ready to accept the Kingship of God with joy."[16]

We hardly need to point out that the concept of Israel is combined with the concept of *Malkut Shamayim* in most of the passages cited above, though not in all. It may also have been remarked that some passages involve other concepts besides the four and *Malkut Shamayim.*

[13] Ibid., 237–8. (I followed the reading of Horovitz-Rabin, p. 222.)

[14] Ibid., 238.

[15] Ibid., 230. The reference is to the singular form "*thy* God" in the statement "I am the Lord thy God" — again taken to be a declaration of God's Kingship — and this suggests that each one individually accepted God's Kingship. On the reading here see above, note 6.

[16] Ibid., 227.

Our analysis of the way in which the four concepts combine with that of *Malkut Shamayim* is an illustration of the manner in which they combine or interweave with *every* value-concept of the rabbinic complex of concepts. In like manner the four concepts also interweave with each other and with all their subconcepts and conceptual phases, as we have demonstrated at length in our earlier studies. Apparent now is an all-embracing principle of coherence, making by and large for the organization of the rabbinic value-complex, for, since the four concepts combine with one another and with all the rest of the concepts, every concept can interweave with every other concept in the complex. That is why even among the few passages just cited other concepts could be involved besides the four and *Malkut Shamayim*. In this organization of the complex, the four concepts thus play the dominant rôle, whether we view them as integrating factors or whether they are, as seems much more likely, simply the concepts by means of which we can trace the organization of the complex which acts as one integrated whole.

The latter view is the correct one, moreover, if only because it saves us from a fatal error. When we regard the four concepts as simply tracer concepts, we are not apt to place them above the others, to see in them concepts of major importance and hence to relegate the others to secondary rank. There are concepts of major and concepts of minor importance only in an hierarchical system, that is, in a system wherein the minor concept is something which is in a degree derived from the major concept so that the structure of the concepts assumes a geometrical aspect. But the rabbinic complex of values is not a ramified, hierarchical structure. *Malkut Shamayim*, *Ḳiddush Ha-Shem*, *Derek Ereẓ* and the other concepts are not derived from the four concepts; they merely interweave with the four concepts and with each other. If this is borne in mind, we can, without harm, designate the four concepts as fundamental concepts in order to stress their rôle in the integration or organization of the complex.

The process of integration has enormous bearing on the meaning of the individual concepts. The conceptual term is only *suggestive* of the meaning of the value-concept. The idea-content of any particular rabbinic value-concept is a function of the entire complex of concepts as a whole, more specifically, of the process of the integration of the particular concept with the rest of the concepts of the complex. Depending on how we view the process, we can say, therefore, either that a value-concept takes on idea-content, or that its idea-content becomes explicit, only as it interweaves with other concepts of the complex. Thus, in the example above, *Malkut Shamayim*, in itself merely the conceptual term, became explicit and took on content as it combined with the four fundamental concepts and with other concepts like the nations of the world and idolatry. As it combined with other concepts, we learned that *Malkut Shamayim* signifies that God's dominion is everywhere, that God will ultimately be recognized as King by the whole world, that it negates basically the dominion of the nations of the world over Israel, that it is acknowledged after experiencing God's love or mercy, that it immediately implies the observance of the *Miẓwot*. Had we found it necessary to cite more passages, we should have drawn forth more ideas implicit in the concept of *Malkut Shamayim*.

But the meaning of a value-concept, it must be noticed, is not made explicit by fixed combinations with the other value-concepts after the manner of a mechanism. There is no way to predict, on the basis of the particular concepts involved, precisely what idea any given combination of concepts may be made to express. The idea above, for example, that God's Kingship negates the rule of all others over Israel is an idea that was expressed once in a combination of the concepts of Israel and God's justice and again in a combination of the concepts of Israel and God's love. In the natural sciences, say in chemistry, knowledge of the order to which the elements conform enables us to repeat experiments and to predict results. Here, however, knowledge of the form of conceptual coherence, of the organization of the concepts, still leaves decided room for unpredictability.

What is the principle of coherence or order which governs the concepts? We have to do here not with a fixed, static form of unity but with a dynamic process. It is a process of *integration*, on the one hand, in which the four fundamental concepts combine with each other and with the rest of the concepts so that each individual concept is always free to combine with any other concept of the complex; and it is also a process of *individuation*, on the other hand, in which any particular concept takes on meaning or character in the very process whereby it combines with the other concepts of the complex. What we have just described is an organismic process. In Coghill's discussion of behavior as the function of the organism as a whole we find a parallel identification between "the processes of integration and individuation of parts."[17] The rabbinic complex of value-concepts is an organism. It conforms to the definition of an organism given by Ritter and Bailey, namely, that "wholes are so related to their parts that not only does the existence of the whole depend on the orderly coöperation and interdependence of its parts, but the whole exercises a measure of determinative control over its parts."[18] We need not wonder now that the rabbinic value-complex gives room for novelty or unpredictability, for that is one of the chief characteristics of an organism.

[17] E. G. Coghill, The Neuro-Embryologic Study of Behavior, in Science, Vol. 78, pp. 131–8.

[18] Ritter and Bailey, The Organismal Conception (Berkeley, California: U. of California Press, 1928), p. 307.

The rabbinic value-complex, since it is composed of concepts and ideas, is a mental organism. If we are to judge from the rabbinic complex of value-concepts, a mental organism, *qua* organism, differs in a very suggestive respect from a physical organism. In a physical organism, though all the parts are interdependent, certain parts are vital to the life of the organism and others are not. As W. Kohler puts it, "Certain parts are more strictly indispensable for the existence of others than the latter are for the existence of the former," and he goes on to characterize this kind of interdependence by saying that it thus exhibits "an hierarchical order."[19] Now at first blush, a close analogy in the rabbinic complex to the vital organs of a physical organism appear to be the four fundamental concepts, the tracer concepts, by means of which, from one point of view, the rabbinic value-concepts are integrated into one unified whole. But, unlike the vital organs of a physical organism, the fundamental concepts are not more indispensable than are any of the other concepts. All the concepts are equally indispensable. The four fundamental concepts depend for their meaning and character no less on the other concepts than the latter depend on the fundamental concepts, all the value-concepts being thus, so to speak, "vital organs." This being so, we are forced to conclude that the rabbinic value-complex, a mental organism, actually conforms more closely to our definition of an organism, a definition which emphasizes the organismal quality to the exclusion of any other factor, than does a physical organism. Only if all the parts are indispensable, if all parts are vital parts, "are wholes so related to their parts that . . . the existence of the whole depends on the orderly cooperation and interdependence of its parts." The physical organism definitely retains something of "an hierarchical order," the type of

[19] W. Kohler, The Place of Value in a World of Facts (New York: Liveright, 1938), p. 17. The discussion on "statements" in that chapter is interesting but not clear.

structure characteristic of the geometric and the spatial, whereas the mental organism of the rabbinic complex does not unless, indeed, the rôle of the fundamental, tracer, concepts admits of a faint comparison with hierarchical order. The physical organism is still physical, and hence *must* possess something of an hierarchical order; only the mental organism is pure organism.

II. SUPPLEMENTARY FORMS OF COHERENCE

The organismic principle of integration is an all-embracing principle, taking in all the value-concepts in the complex and relating every concept to every other concept in an identical manner. Within this general, all-inclusive type of integration or relationship, however, there is room also for additional forms of integration having to do not with the complex as a whole but with numerous specific concepts. There are at least five such additional forms of relationship, one of which we noticed above when we described the relation of a fundamental concept to its subconcepts. As we pointed out in that instance, concepts related in an additional fashion, being "closer" to one another, are quite often associated together in midrashic statements. But this is by no means a general rule. The dominant relationship remains organismic and this enables *any* concept, whether in a special group or no, to unite with *any other* concept. In fact, the organismic relationship is so all-powerful that it prevents complete exclusiveness on the part of the special groups by allowing, in many cases, a concept to belong to several special groups at once. The additional forms of integration are supplementary to, but do not take the place of, organismic integration.

Some concepts are related by being obverses of each other. Examples are (examples here throughout are illustrative, not exhaustive): the righteous and the wicked,[1] the learned and the ignorant,[2] *Ḳiddush Ha-Shem* (sanctification of the Name) and *Ḥillul Ha-Shem* (profanation of the Name),[3] *Malkut Shamayim* and idol worship,[4] *Miẓwah* (commandment) and *'Aberah* (transgression).[5] Like the other forms of relationship which we are about to mention, this is not a general characteristic of rabbinic value-concepts, for any number of rabbinic concepts have no obverses. Prayer, repentance, Torah, *Derek Ereẓ*, the Holy Spirit, to take only some instances, have no obverses.

There are rabbinic concepts which are subconcepts not of one but of two separate concepts, and what we now know about obverses helps us to bring into relief an example of extraordinary ethical significance. Among the nations of the world, certain individuals could not be designated by the Rabbis as other than "wicked", and thus they speak of "Pharaoh the wicked,"[6] "Balaam the wicked,"[7] "Hadrian the wicked."[8] Israel also, however, had its wicked men, and the Rabbis have much to say concerning רשעי ישראל, "the wicked of Israel."[9] The concept of the wicked is, then, a subconcept of the nations of the world on the one hand, and of Israel on the other – a subconcept of each of the latter independently. But the concept of the wicked has an obverse in the concept of the righteous. If our analysis is correct, we should expect the obverse also to be a subconcept of the same two concepts, and the concept of the righteous, to be, therefore, not only a

[1] Bereshit Rabba I. 6, ed. Theodor, p. 3; ibid., X. 6, ed. Theodor, p. 86; and elsewhere.

[2] Seder Eliahu, ed. Friedmann, p. 69; 'Abot III. 8–10; and elsewhere.

[3] Giṭṭin 57b; Bereshit R. XXXVIII. 13, ed. Theodor, p. 361; and elsewhere.

[4] Mekilta II, 158–9; Berakot 57b; and elsewhere.

[5] 'Abot IV. 2; Kohelet R. III. 12; and elsewhere.

[6] Mekilta, I, p. 199.

[7] 'Abot V. 19.

[8] Yerushalmi Pe'ah VII. 1, 20a.

[9] Tos. Sanhedrin XIII. 2; Sanhedrin 110b; and elsewhere.

subconcept of Israel but of the nations of the world. And this is indeed the case. According to the Rabbis there are צדיקי אומות העולם, "the righteous of the nations of the world,"[10] among whom were to be found Jethro and Rahab, even before their conversion,[11] and contemporary Gentiles like "Antoninus (Pius) and his comrades."[12] We are not here concerned so much with the statements on Gentiles by individual Rabbis, reflecting views however broad or limited,[13] as with the fact that the very structure of the rabbinic value-concepts necessitates the concept of "the righteous of the nations of the world." This necessary character of the concept, even more than some of the sublime statements to which it gave rise, is evidence of the breadth of ethical outlook in Judaism.

Incidentally, we need not be surprised to find a necessary element in rabbinic thought, even though the rabbinic value-complex is a mental organism which, by its very nature, allows so much of the novel and the unpredictable. The necessary element consists of a concept, צדיקי אומות העולם; and have we not indicated that every rabbinic concept in the complex is vital and indispensable?

The righeous and the wicked are subconcepts *either* of Israel *or* of the nations of the world, depending on the occasion. The subconcept has in this instance *either* of two grounds. Another type of subconcept shares in two grounds simultaneously, and a prime example of that type is the concept of the learned, subconcept of the study of Torah and Israel at once. In conformity with the parallelism

[10] Ḥullin 92 a; Yalḳuṭ Shime'oni on Isaiah 26:2, par. 429; also the term צדיקים באומות העולם — Tos. Sanhedrin XIII. 2; Yerushalmi Berakot II, 5c (cf. L. Ginzberg, A Commentary on the Palestinian Talmud, New York: The Jewish Theological Society of America, 1941, I, p. 391), and see Tanḥuma, ed. Buber, I (Wilna: Verlag Romm, 1885), 54b; and elsewhere.

[11] Ibid.

[12] Yalḳuṭ, l. c.

[13] For rabbinic statements on Gentiles, both broad and limited, see Moore, Judaism I (Cambridge, Mass.: Harvard University Press, 1927), p. 279 and II, pp. 385–6 and the references there. Cf. also ibid., III, p. 87 and p. 205.

demanded of obverses, the concept of the ignorant, which is the obverse of the concept of the learned, also shares simultaneously in the same two grounds.

Finally, concepts may be related in such a way as to overlap. For example, the concept of the righteous, emphasizing good conduct, and the concept of the learned, emphasizing the study of Torah, are two distinct concepts, each having a character of its own. But there is, we may remember, a conceptual phase, the efficacy of Torah, which implies that knowledge of Torah has an immediate, though not an inevitable, effect upon conduct. The learned, therefore, are likely also to be the righteous; the two concepts overlap. This overlapping allows the two concepts to be used interchangeably, on occasion, as in the following passage: "Blessed be God, blessed be He who chose *the learned* and their pupils and their pupils' pupils. He observes toward them the rule of 'measure for measure.' Just as they sit in the synagogues and in the houses of study and, on every day free to them, study the Bible for the sake of Heaven and study the Mishnah for the sake of Heaven with fear (of God) in their hearts . . . so the Holy One blessed be He gives them, *the righteous*, joy (even) against their will (i. e., even whilst they mourn over the exile)."[14] Concepts which overlap are characterized by the fact that they are used, when circumstances warrant, interchangeably for each other; and all together they constitute quite a large group. Elsewhere we described the overlapping of the concepts of charity and deeds of loving-kindness,[15] and we shall have occasion to discuss more such concepts in our present study.[16]

[14] Seder Eliahu, ed. Friedmann, pp. 96–7. See Friedmann, ibid., note 50. The term for God here is *Maḳom*.

[15] OT, pp. 138–9.

[16] See below, p. 150 f. — *Bereshit,* man, the world; pp. 250–251 — *Gilluy Shekinah, Dibbur, Ruaḥ Ha-Ḳodesh*; p. 318, note 57 — *Zekut 'Abot* and *Kapparah.*

The following statement by Pierce indicates that "overlapping" is a general type of relationship: "It may be quite impossible to draw a sharp line of demar-

III. EXPERIENTIAL CONCEPTS

The organization of the rabbinic value-concepts is, then, a highly complicated affair, complex enough because of the constant interweaving of all the concepts in their organismal relationship and made still more complex because of further, supplementary types of relationship permitted by the organismic integration. But this complexity of organization does not mean that there is great mental strain or effort in the use of the value-concepts. On the contrary, the rabbinic value-complex functions easily, simply, often almost casually, and is similar in that respect to organismic biologic forms which are likewise so complex in organization yet so integrated, direct and effortless in action. The rabbinic value-concept is not a meaning added or applied to objective facts or situations but *inherent* in the situations, and as easily apprehended. "See how (great) is the power of charity," the Rabbis say, "because of a small coin which one may give to a poor man he merits and receives the presence of *Shekinah* (God)."[1] The concept of charity and the literal situation of one man giving a coin to another are not divisible: the concept is concretized in the action; the action is both motivated and interpreted by the concept. The same is true of all the other rabbinic concepts. When a man is engaged in prayer or in the study of Torah, for example, again the concepts are concretized in the actions,

cation between two classes, although they are real and natural classes in strictest truth. Namely, this will happen when the form about which individuals of one class cluster is not so unlike the form about which individuals of another class cluster but that variations from each middling form may precisely agree. In such a case, we may know in regard to any intermediate form what proportion of the objects of that form had one purpose and what proportion the other; but unless we have some supplementary information we cannot tell which ones had one purpose and which the other" — C. S. S. Peirce, Collected Papers, ed. by Hartshorne and Weiss (Cambridge: Harvard Univ. Press, 1931–35), Vol. I, pp. 87–88.

[1] Midrash Tehillim XVII.14, ed. Buber (Wilna: Verlag Romm, 1891), 67b.

and again the actions are both motivated and interpreted by the concepts.

Rabbinic value-concepts are inseparable from normal, everyday, moment-to-moment experience. They are mental habits that are become second nature, more correctly, in view of their organismic character, part of nature.

It is precisely the naturalness, the everyday quality of the rabbinic midrashim that led the modern authorities in this field, accustomed to philosophic and ethical systems in which deliberate, careful, effortful demonstration is the rule, to despair of finding any principle of organization in rabbinic thought. They looked, apparently, for an organizing principle which would systematize the many and varied rabbinic *statements,* and they soon found that these statements would not fit into any logical scheme. We went behind the statements to the *concepts* which the statements embodied, to the concepts which the Rabbis themselves had crystallized into single words or terms. We found that the concepts, not the statements, are elements of a great organismic complex, and that rabbinic thought, far from being chaotic, is completely coherent. The simple, natural quality of the rabbinic statements reflects the character of that organismic complex. We have to do here not with a system of thought *projected* by a mind but with the rabbinic mind itself, with the elements of that mind as they grasp the facts of normal, everyday experience.

The contrast between the philosophic or ethical systems and the type of mental organism represented by the rabbinic value-concepts ought to be more fully appreciated. In any philosophic or ethical system, indeed, in any system of thought devised by an individual, the ideas must be marshaled in a logical, hierarchical order, with the validity of the system regarded as dependent, in large part, on the tightness of its logic. Such systems, requiring tremendous mental effort and concentration, never were, and never could be, guides in daily conduct for most men, not even for philosophers in their off-moments. Have not the philosophic and ethical systems, however, the virtues of order and clarity as against the hodge-podge of naïve notions entertained by the people at large? If the rabbinic concepts are a criterion, nonphilosophic, nonhierarchical value-concepts are not a hodge-podge. On the contrary, they exhibit an order infinitely more complex than can be devised by an individual, an order infinitely more flexible and thus more suitable to everyday needs. The organismic order which they exhibit is something which is native to man, completely in keeping with the rest of his organismic nature, part and parcel of that nature. Contrasted with the religious values typified by the rabbinic concepts, philosophic systems are seen to be stiff, brittle and artificial.

In an attempt to focus on the kind of religious thought and behavior which is native to man, students of religion have emphasized the study of primitive religions. Primitive religions, they say, represent the elementary religious forms which the religions of civilization have only elaborated. They conclude, therefore, that in penetrating to the fundamental traits of primitive religion we discover the basic, fundamental traits of all religions. Even if we grant the very doubtful assumption, sometimes expressed and often implied, that primitive religions are less complicated than the religions of civilization and hence more amenable to research, this entire approach is fallacious on two counts. Supposing the primitive religions to be indeed the earlier forms out of which the religions of civilization developed, how can we study the early undeveloped forms without first having a firm knowledge of the developed forms? Would an anatomist recognize all the traits and features of an embryo without a knowledge of the developed form? There is a second, even graver, fallacy. We commit the gravest scientific error possible when we wash away facts.

Yet here we are bidden to disregard the new elements in the developed religious form, to leave them out of consideration, and to be satisfied with an analysis of such phenomena as existed before the new facts came into being, before, indeed, the new form characterized by the new phenomena came into being. The methods of abstraction and generalization used by the primitive mind, as Lévy-Bruhl has demonstrated, do not result in the development of a variety of abstract concepts, and this is particularly true in regard to religious matters.[2] The use of abstract value-concepts in a religion is thus a new phenomenon found only in the religions of civilization. To ignore it is to ignore one of the chief traits common to man in a civilized state.

Neither philosophies of religion nor the science of anthropology are, then, very helpful in the study of the rabbinic religious mind. They are not helpful because philosophy deals with artificial systems and anthropology with the primitive, not the civilized, mind. By the same token, the study of the rabbinic religious mind may well inaugurate a new approach to the study of religion and of the valuational life in general. The rabbinic value-concepts constitute a mental organism, a form of conceptual organization in complete consonance with the rest of man's organismic nature. To study that mental organism is to penetrate to the very core of matters vital to civilized man, to gain new insight into such fundamental relationships as that of self to society, of mind to language, of folklore to religion, of beliefs to values. And the conceptual character of rabbinic thought makes the analysis of these and similar problems altogether feasible. It enables us to break up a passage into its elements, namely, into the concepts of which it is composed, as we did in order to demonstrate their organismic

[2] Lucien Lévy-Bruhl, How Natives Think, trans. Clare (New York: Knopf, 1925), esp. pp. 116–136. The entire matter is elaborated on below, pp. 144 ff.

interrelation. Indeed, there is hardly any aspect of the investigation of our subject that is not aided by the fact that rabbinic thought is both conceptual and organismic, that it possesses its own natural elements and its own natural organization.

Rabbinic thought will probably always remain the domain largely of Jewish scholars who alone, because of their interest, will be attracted to it and because of their knowledge, qualified to study it. Their conclusions will be of direct benefit to Jewish life and thought today. It is quite possible, however, that their method of approach, and some of their conclusions as well, will have important implications for the study of religion in general.

CHAPTER III

The Conceptual Term and its Implications

I. THE VALUE-TERM

Although only suggestive of the meaning of the value-concept, the conceptual term is indispensable. We can, as we shall soon see, use the term as a test for establishing the presence of a genuine rabbinic value-concept. Moreover, by studying the characteristics of the conceptual terms we learn much concerning the character and function of the value-concept, and are enabled to distinguish value-concepts more readily from other types of concepts.

All the conceptual terms are substantives, noun-forms. The terms Torah, *Miẓwah, Malkut Shamayim, Derek Ereẓ, Middat Ha-Din, Ẓedaḳah, Ḳiddush Ha-Shem,* to take only a few instances at random out of the large number of the rabbinic conceptual terms, are noun-forms, and so are all the rest. The one apparent exception only confirms the rule since it is a word which the Rabbis nounized. We refer to the word *Bereshit,* the first word in Scripture. *Bereshit* is used as a conceptual term in rabbinic literature, where it stands, according to Professor Ginzberg, "for anything created during the six days of Creation."[1] Grammatically an adverb, *Bereshit* is used as a noun by the Rabbis in phrases like "the waters of *Bereshit*"[2] and in prayers and benedictions like "Blessed be He who maketh

[1] L. Ginzberg, op. cit., I, p. 187.

[2] Bereshit R. XV.7, ed. Theodor, p. 138; Tos. Ta'anit I.8, ed. Zuckermandel-Lieberman, Second Edition (Jerusalem: Bamberger and Wahrmann, 1937), p. 215.

Bereshit."[3] Nor was this use of the word confined to the Rabbis alone. In common with all the other conceptual terms, *Bereshit*, too, was employed as a conceptual noun by the people in general, as we can judge from those places where it occurs in Targum Jonathan on the Prophets, an Aramaic version intended for the Aramaic-speaking masses. Not only does *Bereshit*, on three separate occasions, occur there as a substantive, but it was left untranslated, proof positive that such use of the term in the original was habitual with the people in general.[4] It is, then, a rule that the conceptual terms indicative of rabbinic value-concepts are, without exception, always substantives.

Being a noun-form, the conceptual term is really the *name*-form of the concept. And it is only by virtue of having a name that the value-concept is able to perform the dual function of abstraction and classification. The Rabbis, for example, designate as *Derek Ereẓ* the prohibition against building houses with wood of fruit-bearing trees[5]; but they also designate as *Derek Ereẓ* the behavior of the stranger, who, instead of eating of the sustenance which he has brought with him into the strange land, puts that food aside and buys from the local storekeeper to the latter's profit.[6] In these instances, the Rabbis have obviously abstracted from two otherwise totally different matters a

[3] Berakot 54a, 59a. That עושה בראשית is the correct reading throughout is to be seen from Rabbinovicz, Diḳduḳe Soferim I, 168a; see also Ginzberg, l. c.

On the same use of the word in the Prayer Book see the references in S. Baer, סדר עבודת ישראל, Schocken ed., p. 58.

[4] Targum Jonathan on Isaiah 28:29; ibid. on Isaiah 66:9 and Jeremiah 23:23; and ibid. on Habakkuk 3:4. Quoted in Baer, l. c., who calls attention, on the basis of these passages, to the popular character of the term. The term מעשה בראשית designates the *section* in Genesis (first chapter) which tells the story of creation, as can be seen from the use of this term in Ḥagigah II.1 and Ḥullin 83a ("It is said in מעשה בראשית"), and from the similar use of מעשה מרכבה in Ḥagigah 13a and elsewhere to designate the section in Ezekiel (first chapter) which tells of the "Chariot."

[5] Shemot Rabba XXXV.2.

[6] Bemidbar Rabba XIX.7.

common quality named "*Derek Ereẓ*," and it was the name "*Derek Ereẓ*" that made that abstraction possible. At the same time, of course, the name "*Derek Ereẓ*" has been the classifying agency, the means whereby the two disparate matters were put into the same category or classification. The conceptual term accomplishes this dual function because it is the concept in generalized, abstract form, not tied, that is, to any particular manifestation but the symbol for all the manifestations of the concept or for any one of them. We should remember, moreover, that these abstract conceptual terms are not abstractions of, or generalizing terms for, objects or other such concrete data of sensory experience. They are abstractions of value-content, in other words, symbols for concepts with idea-content, as we saw above. The presence in rabbinic literature of conceptual terms standing for value-concepts reflects, therefore, the phenomenon of genuine abstract thought, albeit of a definite type. Other types are represented by philosophy and by scientific theory; but the notion that abstract thought is confined to philosophy and science becomes absurd as soon as we begin to analyze the nature of value-concepts.

The conceptual terms were known to the masses and were, in fact, words in current use, as was exemplified even in the case of the nounized conceptual term of *Bereshit*. This means that the habit of abstract valuational thought was practiced not by the Rabbis alone but by the entire people, that it was a common mental habit. Everyone was able to abstract and to generalize insofar as the valuational life was concerned. Part of the common vocabulary, terms like *Miẓwot*, *Ẓedaḳah* (charity), *Tefillah* (prayer), Torah and so on bespeak numerous occasions when the ordinary man was called upon at least to recognize situations involving these concepts, and so to abstract and to classify. Every normal person in the community knew and used those concepts and hence such use involved a common mental habit.

We do not wish to imply, however, that the habit of abstraction and generalization in valuational matters was a single, unrestricted habit. It was definitely conditioned by the conceptual terms, and some conceptual terms differed in their generalizing powers. The concept of *Derek Ereẓ*, for example, refers to a quality in any number of acts or situations[7] whereas the concept of *'Abot* (patriarchs) refers usually to only three individuals, namely, Abraham, Isaac and Jacob, although it may sometimes include others as well.[8] Since the range of generalization is not the same for all the rabbinic concepts, each conceptual term would seem to represent a distinct habit of generalization by itself. But this is only a likely conjecture. While the concepts of *Derek Ereẓ* and *'Abot* — to use the examples we just cited — obviously differ in their generalizing powers, the range of both is quite indeterminate. If the range of many rabbinic concepts is indeterminate, then we can only roughly compare but not actually gauge the generalizing powers of the rabbinic value-concepts.

Be that as it may, the conceptual term certainly does point to the individual character of the concept for which it stands. We saw above that the organismic complex represents a process both of integration and of individuation of concepts, and that the process of integration is responsible for the idea-content of each individual concept. But

[7] OT (see above p. 15, n. 2), pp. 124–5.

[8] The Rabbis speak also of seven patriarchs — Adam, Noah, Shem, Job, Abraham, Isaac, and Jacob — though, to be sure, they say these are "patriarchs of the world" (see L. Ginzberg, Legends of the Jews, IV, p. 158 and VI, p. 296, note 69, end.) They also designate, however, the sons of Jacob as patriarchs (see Ginzberg, ibid., V, p. 378, note 2); and speak of Moses as the seventh and most beloved of the patriarchs (see Ginzberg, ibid., III, p. 226 and VI, p. 81, note 430). David, too, is spoken of as the "head of the three," that is, of the patriarchs (see Ginzberg, ibid., VI, p. 265, note 94.) See also Ginzberg's discussion of the term "patriarchs" in his Eine unbekannte jüdische Sekte (New York: The Jewish Theological Seminary of America, 1922), pp. 295–7.

how is any particular concept known and what draws our attention to it? We are aware of it because of the distinctive verbal symbol which connotes it. The entire function of this verbal symbol or conceptual term is, therefore, connotation. Connotation is to the abstract valuational term what denotation is to other terms. This means, for one thing, that each rabbinic conceptual term has its own connotation and, for another, that it represents a rabbinic concept which differs in some respects from any other rabbinic concept. However closely related certain concepts may be, the very fact that they are represented by different conceptual terms is an indication that they are to be distinguished from one another. Let us demonstrate with the following examples of kindred concepts deliberately selected from various areas of experience.

The same individual may be regarded both as a *Ẓaddiḳ*, a righteous man, and as a *Ḥasid*, a pious man. The *Ẓaddiḳim* of the former generations, say the Rabbis, were *Ḥasidim*.[9] From this statement we infer that a *Ḥasid* is higher in the scale of virtue than a *Ẓaddiḳ*, since the Rabbis extol the righteous of former generations by calling them *Ḥasidim*, and, by implication, withhold such praise from others in their own day who may have been *Ẓaddiḳim*. Elsewhere the Rabbis speak of *Ḥasid*, *Ẓaddiḳ*, and *Rasha*' (a wicked man) in this descending order,[10] a gradation which Rashi justifies in his commentary with the explanation that "a *Ḥasid* is superior to a *Ẓaddiḳ*."[11] For our present

[9] 'Abot de R. Nathan VIII, ed. Schechter, p. 38.

[10] Niddah 17a.

[11] Ibid., a. 1. The references in this and the two preceding notes are cited by S. Lieberman, Greek in Jewish Palestine (New York: The Jewish Theological Seminary of America, 1942), p. 71, note 27.

Lieberman also concludes that גירי הארץ and גירי אומות העולם, terms that occur only rarely, "are special names for the different categories of semi-proselytes" — ibid., p. 84. Even terms used only rarely, then, bespeak distinct and separate concepts. The concepts identified here by Lieberman are related by being sub-concepts of גרים.

purpose, it is not necessary to enter into a discussion as to how the *Ḥasid* is superior to the *Ẓaddiḳ*. It is sufficient to notice that the Rabbis carefully discriminate in their use of these two terms. So closely related in idea as to be descriptive, on occasion, of the general conduct of the same individual, the words *Ḥasid* and *Ẓaddiḳ*, nevertheless, represent two distinct concepts.[12]

The Rabbis use the terms *Goy, Nokri, and 'Ummot Ha-'Olam* when speaking of non-Jews. All three terms reflect the same social fact of demarcation between Jew and non-Jew, yet each term has a connotation of its own. In the case of the word *Goy* we must not attempt to deduce its rabbinic meaning from its biblical usage; the two are radically different. In the Bible, the word *Goy* means "nation," and is applied both to Israel[13] and to other nations.[14] As used by the Rabbis, however, *Goy* refers to the individual non-Jew, and it retains that meaning for the Rabbis often even when it occurs in the biblical passages they interpret. This new meaning necessitates new grammatical forms of the word. Since, in rabbinic usage, the word is no longer a collective noun but refers to the individual, it now possesses not only a masculine form,[15] as in the Bible, but also a feminine form,[16] and plurals of these respective forms which again apply not to collective groups but to disparate

[12] *Ḥasid* and *Ẓaddiḳ* are related by being subconcepts of Israel. The close kinship in idea, however, reflects still another relationship. Both concepts have the same obverse, *Rasha'*, as can be seen from the passage in Niddah 17a, and also from 'Abot V.10, where the *Rasha'* has characteristics which are the opposite of those ascribed there to the *Ḥasid*. It would seem, therefore, that there is a sixth form of supplementary relationship in addition to the five mentioned in the previous section, the sixth form being instances where two concepts have the same obverse. SEE NOTES, P. 369.

[13] Exod. 19:6; ibid., 32:10; Deut. 4:6; and elsewhere.

[14] Gen. 15:13–14; Hab. 1:6; and elsewhere. Compare, however, I. Heinemann, Darke Ha-Agadah (Jerusalem: Hebrew University, 1949), p. 113.

[15] Bemidbar R. XX.12; Tos. Pe'ah II.9, ed. Zuckermandel-Lieberman, p. 19; and elsewhere. The context demonstrates that the word refers to the individual.

[16] גויה — Yer. Yebamot II, 4a; ibid., 'Abodah Zarah I, 40a.

individuals.[17] But though referring to non-Jews as individuals, *Goy* does not stand for all non-Jews. It does not apply to a Samaritan.[18] Finally, despite the fact that it ordinarily refers to a pagan, it does not necessarily have that connotation. "All *Goyim* who forget God" (Ps. 9:18) implies, according to R. Joshua, that there are also *Goyim* who do not forget God and are righteous.[19] We have dwelt at some length on this term because it has so often figured in controversy and particularly because it affords a good illustration, as evidenced by the new grammatical forms, of the refinement of conceptual terminology in rabbinic usage.[20]

The other terms for the non-Jew, too, have their own connotations. *Nokri* means "stranger" and, whilst usually referring to the non-Jew,[21] may also refer to a Jew who is a stranger in the sense that he is not a member of a particular family.[22] *Goy* and *Nokri* appear to be subconcepts of the more inclusive concept of *'Ummot Ha-'Olam,* the nations of the world, with which we are already acquainted, and which regards the entire non-Jewish world as a single entity.[23] The demarcation here, unlike that connoted by *Goy* and *Nokri,* is not with respect to the individual non-Jew but with respect to the whole Gentile world conceived as having a collective personality. Each of these several terms, then, has its own special connotation; each represents a distinct and different concept.[24]

[17] גויים — Yer. Giṭṭin I, 43b; גויות — Yer. Yebamot IV, 6b.

[18] See, for example, Tos. 'Abodah Zarah III.5, ed. Zuck.-Lieb., p. 463, where *Goy* is in contradistinction to *Kuti,* Samaritan; cf. also Giṭṭin I.5.

[19] Tos. Sanhedrin XIII.2, ed. Zuck.-Lieb., p. 434; Sanhedrin 105a. We have here an example of the Rabbis taking the word *Goyim* in a biblical verse where it means "nations" to refer to *disparate individuals.*

[20] For an abstract term involving the same concept, see below, p. 295.

[21] Shabbat XVI.8; 'Erubin VIII.5; and elsewhere.

[22] Cf. Yebamot III.7.

[23] See above, p. 19.

[24] We have not dealt here at all with the term *'Akkum* because, though found

Equally distinctive in connotation are different terms which, at first glance, may seem to describe the same inward attitude. Both *'Emunah* and *Biṭṭaḥon* are words for faith or trust in God, yet the connotations of each are different. Neither word, incidentally, is used by the Rabbis in the sense of belief in the existence of God, a meaning which *'Emunah* has for the medieval Jewish philosophers. The Rabbis used that word in quite the same way as it is used in the Bible. "And they believed in the Lord and in His servant Moses" (Exod. 14:31) – if they believed (האמינו) in Moses, the Rabbis say in order to give the basis for a later homily, they believed in God *à fortiori*.[25] Belief, *'Emunah,* obviously means here trust or faith, since there was no question of belief in the existence of Moses, either in the biblical account or in the Rabbis' view of that account. As Moore remarks, "The words for faith in the literature and thought of this age are not used in the concrete sense of creed, beliefs entertained – or to be entertained – about God."[26]

'Emunah has the connotation of general trust in God, general in the sense that it does not necessarily imply reliance on God for security or personal welfare. The Rabbis extol Israel, applying to them the text "The Lord preserveth the faithful (*'Emunim*)" (Ps. 31:24). For they (i. e. the people of Israel) say, Blessed be the Lord who quickens the dead, though the resurrection of the dead has not yet come; and they say, (Blessed be the Lord) who redeems Israel, though Israel is not yet redeemed; and they say, Blessed (be the Lord) who rebuilds Jerusalem, though Jeru-

in our editions, it is not a rabbinic term but a substitution imposed by the censorship. It does differ from the rest, of course, by having unequivocally the connotation of "pagan." See H. L. Strack, Introduction to the Talmud and Midrash (Eng. trans.) (Philadelphia: Jewish Publication Society of America, 1931), p. 262, note 66, and the reference to Hoffmann there.

[25] Mekilta, I, p. 252.

[26] Moore, op. cit., Vol. I, p. 238.

salem is not yet rebuilt. The Holy One blessed be He says, Israel was redeemed for only a little while and then went back into servitude, and (yet) they have faith (*ma'aminim*) in Me that I shall redeem them in a time to come![27] In this passage trust in God's promise to Israel, in His ultimate redemption of the people as a whole, is characterized as *'Emunah.* It is otherwise when *Biṭṭaḥon* is used. Then the note is one of reliance on God for security or safe-keeping, and usually for personal security, as can be seen from the following typical statement: "Everyone that puts his trust (בטחונו) in the Holy One blessed be He has a Refuge in this world and in the world to come."[28] We must conclude once more, therefore, that different conceptual terms indicate different and distinct concepts, even though, as here, the different terms appear at first to represent the same inward attitude.

There are, apparently, two exceptions to our rule, two instances where, in addition to a concept's original symbol, an alternative term has also come to represent that concept. What makes this seem to be a total violation of our rule is the fact that in each instance the alternative term, too, is an old, original term and stands for another concept in its own right. Both *Ḥakam* and *Talmid Ḥakam* refer to "one of the learned," and both are old terms, as Ginzberg points out. He demonstrates[29] that *Ḥakam* was the designation for the ordained scholar fully empowered to decide on all questions of law whereas *Talmid Ḥakam* (as the word *talmid* implies) referred to the student who was permitted only to answer questions on the sections he had been taught, and that the latter term came also to be used in the wide sense of "the learned" in general and thus as equivalent

[27] Midrash Tehillim, ed. Buber, p. 120b. Cf. the references there. The benedictions are from the Eighteen Benedictions of the daily prayers.

[28] Menaḥot 29b. See also Seder Eliahu, ed. Friedmann, pp. 90, 91.

[29] L. Ginzberg, Commentary, I, pp. 405–8.

to *Ḥakam.*[30] *Ḳiddush Ha-Shem* and *Ḳedushat Ha-Shem* present a completely analogous instance. Originally employed only as a designation for the Third *Berakah* of the *'Amidah,*[31] which includes the *Kedushah* – "Holy, holy, holy," etc. (Isa. 6:3 and Ezek. 3:12) – the sanctification of the Name by declaration,[32] *Ḳedushat Ha-Shem* came to stand for the sanctification of the Name in general[33] and hence as an equivalent for *Ḳiddush Ha-Shem.*[34] In both cases, however, terms are only expanded, as we can see, and employed in a "borrowed" sense. Nevertheless, had there been many such instances, the individual character of the various concepts would soon have been obliterated.

Every conceptual term is a stable term, and the terminology as a whole is a fixed terminology. Throughout the entire rabbinic period no valuational term is either altered or displaced by another. This is true of all the conceptual terms in the rabbinic value-complex, whether like Torah and *Miẓwah* they are terms carried over from the Bible; or whether like the word *Goy* they are biblical terms given a new turn; or whether like *Malkut Shamayim, 'Abodah Zarah* (idol-worship) and so many other rabbinic value-terms they are terms purely characteristic of this period. And the terminology is not only stable but fixed: no new valuational term arises during this entire period. The only two terms which arise to serve as alternatives, *Talmid Ḥakam* and *Ḳedushat Ha-Shem,* are themselves old, original terms. This static aspect of the organismic complex, we shall now endeavor to show, is not fortuitous but inherent in its very nature.

[30] *Talmid Ḥakam* is used in this wide sense already in the Mishnah itself — Nedarim X.4 and Nega'im XII. 5 (references quoted from Ginzberg, l. c.) Professor Ginzberg, in conversation with me, remarked that it is only in the earlier parts of the Mishnah that *Ḥakam* and *Talmid Ḥakam* are two distinct terms.

[31] See Rosh Ha-Shanah IV.5.

[32] See Seder Eliahu, ed. Friedmann, pp. 163, 193; cf. also ibid., pp. 84, 156.

[33] See Song of Songs Rabba II.18; Berakot 20a (Ta'anit 24a; Sanhedrin 106b); Sanhedrin 74b.

[34] Cf. the references above, p. 27, note 3.

II. DEFINITION

The valuational concepts are never defined. They are abstract concepts, as we saw above, representing a form of abstract thought. Now the abstract concepts of science and philosophy are defined by the scientists and philosophers; the meanings of the concepts are agreed upon in some formal manner, so that each concept is given its own precise meaning distinct from those of other concepts employed in the same field. But the abstract valuational concepts were employed by the plain people, not by the Rabbis alone. They did not represent philosophic or scientific generalizations. They were concepts which expressed human experience, both in its ordinary manifestations and its rarer moments. The academically-minded, from the days of Socrates down to our own, have attempted to define terms of this type, but the common folk have paid no heed. In fact, the plain people have probably never seen or heard of these attempts at definition. The Rabbis were at one with the plain people in this as in so many respects, and made no attempt to define the valuational concepts.[1]

What is not defined usually cannot be defined. A definition delimits the meaning of a concept and puts precise boundaries to it; and to do this with a valuational concept is to destroy its meaning. A value-concept, we have learned, takes on meaning as it interweaves with the other value-concepts, grows in meaning, expands in idea-content

[1] We must not assume that attempts at explaining the conceptual terms are attempts at definitions. Rashi, for example, gives an explanation of *Ḥillul Ha-Shem* in his comment on that term in Shabbat 33a. But his explanation ought not to be taken as an attempt at definition, for he limits *Ḥillul Ha-Shem* to its interplay with the concepts of Torah and *Miẓwot*. The concept of *Ḥillul Ha-Shem* interweaves, however, with other concepts. Notice its combination with Israel and with God's justice as depicted in TE (see above, p. 15, n. 2), pp. 67–69 ("robbing a Gentile") and ibid., p. 71.

in accordance with its use in combination with other concepts. That is why the term which represents it can only be suggestive, connotative. We can, of course, describe a concept by setting down its idea-content as gleaned from passages or statements, which we did above in the case of *Malkut Shamayim* or when we tried to convey what certain terms connoted. Such descriptions of rabbinic concepts cannot, however, be regarded as definitions, for no matter how detailed, the descriptions will always remain partial, incomplete. Were a person even to succeed in utilizing all the rabbinic material extant on a concept, his task would remain undone. What cannot be collected and classified are the actual situations in everyday life in which the concept played a part. Presenting all the data on a valuational concept is quite like presenting all the data contained in the daily "stream of consciousness" of which, indeed, it was an element.

When a concept is defined, it is really the definition that performs the functions of abstraction and classification, and hence the conceptual term is of only secondary importance. It may be discarded for another symbol considered more adequate, it may be redefined and so change its meaning as happens not infrequently in the science of psychology, and it may even be an ephemeral term for which there are many alternatives as often happens in philosophy. The permanent aspect of the concept, then, is the definition; the lifespan of the concept, so to speak, depends on that rather than on the conceptual term. But the valuational concept must rely solely on its verbal symbol for abstraction and classification. Here it is the verbal symbol, the conceptual term, that must be permanent if the concept is to continue functioning. Nor can any new conceptual term be introduced. The individual character of the valuational concept depends, again not on a definition, but on the play of all the concepts in an *integrated* complex of concepts. That integration would be broken by the injection of a new, and thus foreign, concept. Below we show that changes in terminology do occur and new concepts are introduced, but only when there is an organismic development, that is, a general development of the complex as a whole.[2]

There is a noteworthy implication in the distinction just drawn between philosophic or scientific concepts and value-concepts. Why must a philosophic concept consist of a definition — a statement — and not of a single term? Because a philosophic or scientific statement is always a conclusion of some sort, a complete idea which is the final result of speculation or observation, an inference derived from given data. If put precisely, an inference is always a statement; and since a definition aims at preciseness, a defined concept will always be a statement. Philosophic and scientific concepts are inferred concepts.

Not so value-concepts. A value-concept cannot be delimited by a definition or statement. It is not a complete idea in itself. But an idea which is the result of speculation or observation is always a complete idea, an inference that can be summarized in a statement. A value-concept, therefore, is not an idea which is inferred, and can never be the result of speculation or observation. This is not to say that value-concepts have no "history"; the latter is a complicated problem which we hope we may discuss on another occasion. But to ascribe the *origin* of religious ideas, ideas that are valuational in nature, to speculation or observation is to commit an error of the first magnitude, and it is this error which mars the work of the earlier anthropologists and of many modern writers on religion. Tylor and his

[2] See below, pp. 288 ff.

school regarded the idea of the soul among primitive people as an inference from dreams.[3] George Adam Smith finds in the irregularity of Palestine's climate a contributory cause to the rise of the belief in Providence. "To such a climate, then, is partly due Israel's doctrine of Providence."[4] Other modern writers attribute the origin of religious ideas to reflection on definite political events in Israel's history, some going as far as to ascribe the origin of the idea of a universal God to an assumed deduction or inference. The prophets of Israel, they say, foresaw in the might of Assyria and Egypt the impending doom of Israel. Was, then, the God of Israel powerless to save His people? Were the gods of Assyria and Egypt more powerful? Here, say our modern writers, the prophets made their crucial inference which spelled the change from henotheism to monotheism: There is only one God, the God of Israel, and He uses the great empires as a rod with which to punish Israel for her sins.[5] All such theories would make religious ideas out to be of the same stuff as philosophic and scientific ideas, inferences from facts or events. If so, these theories, consciously or otherwise, are not free from a certain condescension toward religion. The element of ratiocination which these theories attribute to religion is certainly far stronger in philosophy than it is in religion, and religious thought is thus relegated to a lower rank, conceived, indeed, to be a kind of pre-philosophy.

According to our analysis, religious concepts are in a

[3] Cited by Durkheim, The Elementary Forms of The Religious Life, trans. Swain (New York: Macmillan), pp. 49 ff. See below, p. 49, note 7.

[4] George Adam Smith, Historical Geography of the Holy Land, 4th ed. (Richard R. Smith, New York) pp. 73–4.

[5] This is, in general, the position of the Wellhausen school. But even a more cautious scholar like O. C. Whitehouse has this to say: "If Assyria finally overthrew Israel and carried off Yahweh's shrine, Assur, the tutelary deity of Assyria, was mightier than Yahweh . . . This problem of religion was solved by Amos and the prophets . . ." — Encyc. Brit., 13th ed., Vol. 13, pp. 182–3.

totally different category. They do not originate in reflections aroused by this or that event, and they are not inferences or deductions after the manner of philosophy or science. Is there not evident, in fact, a certain superficiality in all such explanation of origins, no matter how detailed and circumstantial? Can we pin down a basic religious idea, obviously the fruit of long historical processes, to a definite origin, the mechanism of which it is given us quite plainly to see? More, examination of the various inferences offered as the "origins" of religious ideas shows that they are only *assumptions* made by our modern authors; they are never actually stated in the religious texts analyzed by these authors. Thus, the prophet Isaiah does indeed speak of Assyria as "the rod of Mine (i. e., God's) anger"[6]; but where, in all the chapters of the Prophets, is there a single, even remote, reference to the inference of which this statement is supposed to be the outcome? Unless we recognize that religious valuational concepts are simply not of the same nature as inferred concepts, that they belong in a different category, we shall lack a sound, realistic approach to the entire subject.[7]

[6] Isaiah 10:5

[7] Durkheim, in his book cited above, does not attribute the origin of religious ideas to any sort of inference on the part of the primitive man. That is one of the chief virtues inherent in a theory which posits a social origin for religious concepts. Yet this important implication of his theory escapes Durkheim, as it escapes so many social theorists. When Durkheim deals with Tylor's notion, for example, he demonstrates that the inference assumed by Tylor is not a necessary one, and that the primitives might just as well have made other, more plausible, inferences from their dreams. He does not seem to have recognized that Tylor's very approach is wrong.

This is not the place to make an extensive criticism of Durkheim's theory from our point of view. Since we have touched on the matter of "origins," it may be remarked, however, that his theory, too, advances an "origin" for religious concepts. It is a complicated theory and is much less mechanistic than those we have touched upon; nevertheless, like those theories it, too, is a construct.

III. THE COGNITIVE CONCEPT

There is another class of concepts which are not dependent on definitions. This consists of the terms we use in order to describe whatever we perceive through the senses, the terms which constitute the bulk of every man's everyday vocabulary. But these terms do not merely *describe* the world of human perception. In an excellent study on speech published some years ago,[1] Prof. G. A. de Laguna develops the thesis that human perception itself is, to a very great extent, conceptualized, that it is not raw perception. "The lenses we acquire with language are not merely colored, but blocked out in more or less regular designs, so that the world we see through them is *patternized* to our earliest view. The ability to speak, then, to attach names to things and to make statements about them, does not leave unaltered the world which we see and hear. Perception remains primarily a preparation for direct primary response to things, but there is superadded the capacity for a more detached and disinterested scrutiny . . . Human perception is, then, *conceptualized* to an indefinite degree."[2] What is accomplished by conception when it is superadded to perception? "The capacity for a more detached and disinterested sort of scrutiny" is the capacity to perceive the objective relation of things or of persons *to each other*[3] and to respond, as well, to the elements of the objective world without regard to the particular setting in which they may be at any given time.[4] Conceptualization, in other words, not only brings the features of the physical world we perceive into bold relief but, by naming them, gives them a certain fixity and independence. If the world we perceive

[1] Speech: Its Function and Development (New Haven: Yale University, 1927).

[2] Ibid., p. 290.

[3] Ibid., pp. 293, 298.

[4] Ibid., p. 249.

as the result of conceptualization is already "*patternized* to our earliest view," the concepts involved are, obviously, not dependent on formal definitions.

De Laguna has rather little to say concerning valuation; indeed, she apparently fails to realize that valuation also is conceptualized,[5] a very common error. What she describes as conception in general is, in our opinion, applicable to only one class of concepts, even though that class is so broad and inclusive as to cover the entire range of man's perceptual experience. But man also has valuational experience, and this, too, is expressed in conceptual terms, distinctly different in type from those described by de Laguna. The latter, as de Laguna herself points out, are cognitive in nature[6] — and hence we may call them "cognitive concepts" — while the value-concepts are largely affective in character. The cognitive concepts refer to objective matters, such as "table," "chair," "tall," "round," and are therefore denotative whereas the value-concepts, as we saw, are never denotative but only connotative. "Denotative" and "connotative" here point to a broad, basic difference in character, and we shall expand upon that in a later chapter. This basic difference in character makes for certain differences in the way the two types of concepts are employed.

Thus, cognitive concepts differ from value-concepts in regard to the use of the conceptual terms. When we speak of a table or chair, we usually must employ the words "table," "chair"; only when we indulge in artificial circumlocutions do we refrain from calling a spade a spade

[5] She speaks of valuation as though it were distinct from conception; conception to her seems to be associated only with objective sense-experience: "Valuation and conception are mutually determining psychological phenomena. A value represents an objectification of affective quality, parallel to the objectification which we find in a conceptualized property of a perceived thing. Valuation, like conception, is also a fruit of cooperation. The objectivity of values is constituted in large part by their social character" — de Laguna, ibid., p. 354, note.

[6] Ibid., pp. 191 f., 207–212.

and speak of an "agricultural implement" instead. When we use concepts referring to perceived things we do so by uttering the conceptual terms which stand for those perceived things. This is frequently not the case when we employ value-concepts. A statement may be an excellent expression of a particular value-concept without containing the conceptual term; the concept is, as it were, imbedded in the statement. The following statement, for example, speaks of a manifestation of *Middat Raḥamim*, God's love, without mentioning the term itself: It is God "from whom go forth brightness and light to the world; and who causes rain to fall and grass to grow."[7] And the following is a vigorous and lofty rabbinic passage concerning God's justice, yet it does not contain the term itself: "I call heaven and earth to testify for me: whether Gentile or Israelite, whether man or woman, whether male-slave or female-slave — according to the deed done thus does the Holy Spirit rest upon him!"[8] The value-concept is often imbedded in its concretizations, whether in speech or action, and there is no need then for the conceptual term to serve as label.

IV. AUXILIARY IDEAS

This supposes, however, that the rabbinic statement in question contains a genuine rabbinic value-concept, a concept with a conceptual term found somewhere in rabbinic literature. Without a conceptual term there can be no abstraction and classification, no possibility for the value-concept to function. And we can be fairly certain that no matter how often a genuine value-concept is only imbedded or implied in various passages, the conceptual term itself does occur somewhere in rabbinic literature. Vast in scope

[7] Seder Eliahu, p. 8.

[8] Ibid., p. 48. Cf. ibid., p. 65.

and in extent, that literature will hardly fail to mention a valuational term current among the people. On the contrary, it is very likely that the Rabbis, in the homilies and sermons embodying the value-concepts, had more occasion to use the abstract conceptual terms than the people at large. We can safely count, then, on finding a conceptual term in rabbinic literature for every genuine rabbinic value-concept.

The rather few rabbinic ideas not represented by conceptual terms do not offer exceptions to the rule just laid down. Unlike the genuine value-concepts, these ideas are constant and static and do not expand when used in combination with other concepts. This becomes evident as soon as we compare a general formulation of an idea of this kind with its use in any particular situation.

The Mishnah declares: "All is foreseen (by God), and freedom (of action) is given (to man)."[1] Here we have in general terms an affirmation of what have come to be known as God's omniscience and the freedom of the will. The idea of God's omniscience is also to be found in passages of a more specific nature, as in the midrash which attributes the death of Adam not to his own sin but to that of some of his descendants. Adam had not deserved to taste death, says this midrash. Why, then, was death decreed for him? Because the Holy One blessed be He foresaw that Nebuchadnezzer and Hiram, king of Tyre, would pronounce themselves gods.[2] This is an inversion of the more familiar rabbinic notion that all descendants of Adam are doomed to die because of Adam's sin, although both are applications of the idea of corporate justice.[3] Our midrash also contains the implication that man's mortal character testifies to the

[1] 'Abot III.15.

[2] Bereshit Rabba IX.5, ed. Theodor, p. 70.

[3] See above p. 17. On the different rabbinic explanations of the presence of death in the world, see OT, p. 209 and the references there.

falseness of the worship of human beings. The value-concepts of God's justice and *'Abodah Zarah* (idolatry) are thus imbedded in this midrash, and, in addition, the passage tells us that God knew beforehand events which were to occur in later generations. Does this instance of God's omniscience add anything, however, to the general statement "All is foreseen by God?" Indeed all rabbinic instances of the idea of God's omniscience are only exemplifications of the general idea, specific illustrations and no more. Between such an idea and a value-concept there is a marked difference. We need only recall how the concept of *Malkut Shamayim* expanded in meaning in passage after passage, in one midrash signifying that God's dominion is everywhere, in another that He will ultimately be recognized as King of the whole world, and in a third that it immediately implies the observance of the *Miẓwot*.

A rabbinic idea for which there is no conceptual term is an *auxiliary* idea. It is usually in the service, so to speak, of a true concept, broadening the range of the latter's manifestations or else placing the concept into bolder relief. In our midrash, for example, the idea of God's omniscience serves the concept of God's justice, one of the fundamental concepts, and expands it to include an application of corporate justice, a conceptual phase, we may remember, of God's justice. The positive concept of God's justice and the negative concept of *'Abodah Zarah* are the values emphasized in this midrash, with the idea of God's omniscience merely an auxiliary idea.

Similarly, the idea of the freedom of the will serves as an auxiliary idea in rabbinic thought. What, for example, is the point of emphasis in the statement, "Everything is in the hands of Heaven (i. e., God) except the fear of Heaven?"[4] Freedom of the will? Hardly. The Rabbis tell

[4] Berakot 33b (and parallels).

us here that fear of Heaven, *Yir'at Shamayim,* is not forced upon man but rests with him alone, and can be acquired by every man. They stress a value-concept, and the idea of the freedom of the will is present only as an auxiliary idea. This is borne out by the ensuing discussion which is on *Yir'at Shamayim* and in which free-will is not even mentioned.[5] Kindred ideas, such as God's omnipotence and eternity and the like, also are not represented by conceptual terms in rabbinic literature and, like the ideas of God's omniscience and the freedom of the will, are only auxiliary ideas.[6]

Tested by the rule that every rabbinic value-concept must have a conceptual term, the idea of the chosen people or the election of Israel, too, appears to be an auxiliary idea. In all of rabbinic literature, so far as we have been able to discover, there is no conceptual term, no valuational noun form equivalent to the terms "the chosen people" or "election of Israel." However the idea functioned, therefore, it does not seem to have crystallized into a value-concept.

The word "Israel" by itself is, of course, a genuine concept. It is a name-form, a collective noun referring, in rabbinic literature as in the Bible, to the people as a collective entity,[7] but which the Rabbis, unlike the Bible, also employ, without any change in grammatical form, in order to designate the members of that people individually as well.[8] And it is a valuational term: it is one of the four

[5] Ibid.

[6] See "Independent Attributes," TE, pp. 34–38. A far better name is "auxiliary ideas," for "attributes" is a philosophic term, and "independent" is a misnomer.

[7] E. g., Berakot IX.1; Sheḳalim II.4; Yoma VIII.9.

[8] E. g., Shabbat XVI.8; Pesaḥim II.3; Baba Ḳamma IV.3.

In the Bible, as we said, the word "Israel" always refers to the people in the collective sense. But the Rabbis will sometimes interpret the word even when it occurs in the Bible to refer to an individual member of the people. " 'Israel hath sinned' (Josh. 7:11) — Said R. 'Abba b. Zabda: An Israelite, even though he has

fundamental concepts and has value-concepts such as the righteous and the wicked, the pious, and *Gerim* (proselytes) for its subconcepts. Incidentally, collective nouns may be conceptual terms but not proper nouns; since a proper noun designates but a single specific individual entity it is not a generalization and therefore not a concept.

The warrant offered for the use of the phrase "the election of Israel" usually consists of passages from the liturgy. There is no gainsaying the fact that the liturgy often expresses the idea that God has chosen Israel from all the peoples. Thus, it is declared in the benediction on the Torah that God chose Israel and gave them the Torah,[9] and in the *Ḳiddush* for the Sabbath that God chose Israel and gave them the Sabbath.[10] In these instances, however, and in all the rest to be found in the liturgy, the idea of election is always only a part of a more extensive idea involving several rabbinic concepts; the emphasis seems to be on those concepts, not on the idea of election. Moreover, the verb *baḥor*, "to choose," as used in the liturgy, does not necessarily imply the idea of selection. The benediction introductory to the reading of the lesson from the Prophets concludes with, "Blessed art Thou, O Lord, who hast chosen (literally, who chooses) the Torah, and Moses Thy servant, and Israel Thy people, and prophets of truth and righteousness."[11] If this benediction contains the idea that God chose the Torah from among other possible Torot, that He *selected* the Torah and rejected other Torot, then we have here an idea without a parallel in all of rabbinic literature.[12]

sinned, remains an Israelite," that is, great though his sin may be, he does not lose his status as an Israelite — Sanhedrin 44a. SEE NOTES, P. 369.

[9] Daily Prayer Book, ed. Baer, p. 225.

[10] Ibid., p. 198.

[11] Ibid., p. 226. The shift here from second to third person cannot be translated; see below, p. 267 f.

[12] The rabbinic notion that God tested and tried the words of the Torah (see OT, p. 31) has nothing in common with this.

It is more likely that the benediction intends, rather, to emphasize the authenticity of the Torah and to declare God's own love for it. Similarly, Moses and Israel and the prophets are declared here to be "chosen" or loved by God without any implication that they were selected from among others and that the others were rejected. This interpretation renders the second half of the benediction entirely consistent with the first half which says that God "has chosen good prophets and has found pleasure in their words which were spoken in truth." Here, too, there are an emphasis on the authenticity of the words of the prophets and a suggestion of God's love for the prophets themselves, but no necessary implication that others were rejected in their favor.[13]

It is not our purpose to engage now upon an analysis of the religious concepts used by modern Jewish writers. That demands separate treatment. But our study here points to one criterion, at least, that obviously ought to be employed. Are these concepts, set forth as representing Jewish tradition, rabbinic concepts? Are the conceptual terms used, rabbinic terms? If not, the concept may be anything from an auxiliary idea to a concept borrowed from another religion and totally unsuited to any Jewish context. We hear, for example, Jews speaking of "communion with God" as though it were a concept rooted in Jewish tradition. But there is no rabbinic term for "communion"; prayer (*Tefillah*) is not communion; communion is not even an auxiliary idea. Even the term "revelation," which has become hallowed in certain Jewish quarters, is not rabbinic, if that term is intended as a designation for the giving of the Ten Commandments on Sinai. The rabbinic term is *Mattan Torah* (the giving of Torah) and it is not confined to the

[13] For a more extensive treatment of the idea of the chosen people or the election of Israel see Beḥirat Yisra'el Bedibere ḤaZaL, Proceedings of The Rabbinical Assembly of America, Vol. VIII, 1941–44, pp. 20 ff.

occasion at Sinai.[14] If by revelation is meant revelation of *Shekinah, Gilluy Shekinah*, that too cannot be limited to Sinai, for according to the Rabbis there were many other occasions when the *Shekinah* was revealed.[15] Both *Mattan Torah* and *Gilluy Shekinah* are concepts, generalizations, and hence neither is limited to a single concretization or instance. The criteria laid down here ought, then, to be helpful in determining whether a modern religious concept is or is not rooted in Jewish tradition.

The Rabbis possessed their own abstract valuational terminology. Each and every rabbinic value-concept is represented by a conceptual term, always a substantive, connotative of, and peculiar to, that particular value-concept. The conceptual term does not act as a label; it is not necessarily present whenever the concept is embodied in a rabbinic statement, but it is bound to occur in some passages. Rabbinic ideas not represented by conceptual terms serve only as auxiliary ideas, different in character from the dynamic value-concepts. The conceptual term itself is stable and fixed because the value-concept is never defined and depends on the term alone to perform the functions of abstraction and classification. These considerations point to the conceptual terms as the only authentic generalizations of the rabbinic value-concepts; we must not make the error of taking our own generalizations, however helpful in analysis, to represent genuine rabbinic concepts.

[14] According to the Rabbis, certain laws were given Israel at Marah, before they came to Sinai. Interpreting the words "statute" and "ordinance" in Exod. 15:25, Rabbi Joshua says the law concerning the Sabbath and the law to honor father and mother were given them then, while R. Eleazar says the laws against incestuous practices and the laws concerning robberies, fines and injuries were given at that time — Mekilta II, p. 94. The laws given at Marah are referred to as "the words of the Torah which had been given (*shenittenu* — from the same root as *Mattan*) them at Marah" — ibid., II, p. 98.

[15] See below, pp. 228 ff.

CHAPTER IV

Haggadah, Halakah and the Self

Rabbinic literature consists of Haggadah and Halakah. Both are necessary vehicles for the value-concepts, although Halakah is of even greater importance in that respect than Haggadah. It is from Haggadah, however, that we can learn most regarding the nature of the value-concepts. Haggadah is an almost perfect reflection of the way in which the value-concepts function in day-to-day living, in speech and action. It mirrors the relation of the self to the group. Its very manner of expression is determined by the nature of the value-concept, and that fact enables us further to differentiate value-concepts from cognitive concepts.

I. HAGGADAH AS VALUATIONAL EXPRESSION

The value-concepts are integrated not in a fixed, static manner but by virtue of being elements in a dynamic, organismic process. Each value-concept is a factor in the organism, is itself an integrative agent. The value-concepts do not just organize the data of experience or of history. They integrate that data. Every haggadic statement is an integrated whole, a unit.

We have found that the value-concepts are usually imbedded in a midrash, inseparable from the data which they interpret.[1] Why? Because in the process of interpreting the data, the value-concepts, instead of merely organizing

[1] See above, p. 51 f.

the data, *fuse* everything in the midrash — including the data — into an integrated unit. We noticed above, for example, that both God's justice and *'Abodah Zarah* (idolatry) are imbedded in the midrash which says that Adam had not deserved to taste death, but that death was decreed upon him because the Holy One blessed be He foresaw that Nebuchadnezzer and Hiram, descendants of Adam, would pronounce themselves gods.[2] Obviously, both value-concepts — God's justice and idolatry — are essential elements in this statement, just as much so as Adam's death and Adam's descendants, the data which they interpret and explain. In fact, we cannot distinguish between data and interpretation. The statement is an integrated whole, a unit, and the value-concepts have been the integrating agents. When data and concepts are fused, the thought expressed, or the situation described, is an integrated whole, complete in itself.

The characteristic mode of haggadic expression is precisely that kind of statement. Haggadic statements are independent entities, containing ideas or describing situations that are complete in themselves. This does not preclude a later author or editor taking an earlier midrash and adding to it an idea of his own[3]; the earlier midrash, the original statement, is still, of course, a complete entity in itself. On the other hand, when an editor or a copyist has left with us only a fragment of a midrash, that fragment, though it may make sense, seldom conveys the point of the midrash. Only when research has restored the whole passage, the complete entity, does the midrash yield its real meaning.[4]

[2] Above, p. 53.

[3] For example, to the midrash in Bereshit Rabba XIX.4 (ed. Theodor-Albeck, pp. 172–3) on the slandering of God by the serpent, there is added in Tanḥuma, Bereshit, par. 8, the idea that this caused the death of Adam. See Ginzberg, Genizah Studies I (New York: Jewish Theological Seminary of America, 1928), p. 454.

[4] For example, see Lieberman's brilliant collation of passages which, taken

The independent character of the haggadic statement can be discerned no matter in what context the statement is found, in a homiletic composition no less than in an exegetical context.

In an exegetical context, the haggadic statements are usually altogether discrete. So unconnected are they, in fact, that we may have several consecutive interpretations of the same biblical verse, each of them an independent entity.[5] But even when passages are connected in exegetical Haggadah, they are connected by a device, used also in midrashic works of other types, which assures the practical independence of such passages. A statement interpreting a biblical text may be followed by other statements, each joined to the one preceding by an association of ideas, whilst none but the first is an interpretation of the biblical verse which is the homiletic origin for the entire passage. For instance, in the verse "And the Lord spoke unto Moses and Aaron in the land of Egypt, saying" (Exod. 12:1), the Rabbis interpret the words "in the *land* of Egypt" to imply that God spoke to Moses not in the city but outside of it – "in the land" – because the city "was full of abominations and idols." The passage then continues: "Before the land of Israel had been chosen, all lands were suitable for divine communications (*Dibberot*); after the land of Israel had been chosen, all other lands were eliminated. Before Jerusalem had been chosen, the entire land of Israel had been suitable for altars; after Jerusalem had been chosen, all the rest of the land of Israel was eliminated . . . Before Aaron had been chosen, all Israel were qualified for the priesthood . . . Before David had been chosen, all Israel were eligible for the kingship . . ." When the passage does close, it is with a statement that the patriarchs and prophets offered their

together, convey the point of R. Me'ir's interpretation of Gen. 24:1 — S. Lieberman, in קבץ מדעי לזכר משה שור (New York, 1945), pp. 186–188.

[5] See below, p. 71.

lives in behalf of Israel.[6] Now the statements in the passage are connected, but the connection is from statement to statement only, so that the last statement has no connection whatever with the first, nor indeed, with any but the one immediately preceding it. In other words, there is no concluding statement based on all that has been said before because there is no single chain of thought. Each statement is an independent fusion of concepts and data. This is a far cry from the carefully articulated systems of philosophy and, in fact, from the chain-like, analytic reasoning exhibited by a section of Halakah in the Talmud.

The various forms of haggadic composition also testify to the independence of the haggadic statements they contain. A loose form of composition is the proem, found in Bereshit Rabba and also in other midrashic works. As exemplified in Bereshit Rabba, the proem form consists of different interpretations of the same verse, usually one taken from the Hagiographa, so given that the last interpretation leads directly to a verse in the lection from the Pentateuch.[7] In this haggadic form, each statement is practically discrete, a distinct entity in itself. Except for the proem form there is, in fact, no difference between this type of composition and the plain, discrete, exegetical Haggadah. Indeed, as Albeck has shown, a number of these proem passages were originally not proems at all but statements found elsewhere which the compiler made into proems by introducing them with the simple proem formula.[8]

Most pertinent to our inquiry is the demonstration of the independence of the haggadic statements in the rabbinic sermons. Midrash Haggadah arose primarily as a mode of

[6] Mekilta, I, pp. 3–11. Actually, there is a tacking back to the original theme with the question regarding the prophets (p. 5), but to have taken this into account would have needlessly complicated our discussion.

[7] See for example the first passage in Bereshit Rabba, ed. Theodor-Albeck, pp. 1–2.

[8] See ibid., Introduction (by Albeck) (Berlin: Akademie-Verlag, 1931), pp. 15–17.

public instruction, and constituted the sermons preached by the Rabbis.[9] The sermons contained midrashim as the latter were actually employed in the course of public instruction; the sermon itself had necessarily some form of coherence or unity; if, nevertheless, the various midrashim in the sermon can still be recognized as independent entities, we must conclude that even unified haggadic compositions consist essentially of independent statements. Unfortunately, almost none of the great midrashic works has come down to us in its original form. There has been recension after recension, and compilers added or deleted as they saw fit. The present fragments are, however, in many instances, large enough for our purpose, as we can gather from Mann's recent work.[10] Mann has endeavored to prove that the structure of the rabbinic sermon was largely determined by the *Hafṭarah* — the lection from the Prophets — read on the occasion when the sermon was preached, and when the reading from the Prophets as well as from the Pentateuch was in accordance with the Palestinian triennial cycle.[11] Although Mann drives his theory too hard,[12] it has cast new light on many midrashim, especially of the Yelammedenu type, and has made us realize that a large number of the latter are not mere fragments but entire sections of sermons. We can, therefore, use a Yelammedenu passage for the purpose of our inquiry — the first one found in "the printed Tanḥuma."[13]

[9] Krochmal, מורה נבוכי הזמן (ed. Rawidowicz, Berlin, 1924), p. 248. "The great majority of the older haggdot were those which were preached in sermons to the people" — ibid., p. 242. See also below, p. 86 f.

[10] Jacob Mann, The Bible as Read and Preached in the Old Synagogue, Vol. I (Cincinnati: Ajanoth, 1940).

[11] See ibid., pp. 3–19. In Palestine, the reading of the Pentateuch was completed, as the result of public reading on the Sabbaths, once every three years.

[12] See the appraisal by S. Lieberman, op. cit., p. 186. Note his use of Mann's theory.

[13] Tanḥuma, Bereshit, par. 4. "The printed Tanḥuma" as distinguished from the Tanḥuma, ed. Buber.

It begins with the Yelammedenu formula, "Let our master teach us." The master is asked to tell them the benediction to be made when one has built a new home. The answer starts off the sermon. The benediction to be made, begins the master, quoting a halakah,[14] is שהחיינו. A few words are apparently missing here, but this does not affect the point made, which is clear from the sequence. The point is that when man thus blesses God, God in turn blesses him.[15] This is illustrated by the Festivals given Israel, (on which the benediction שהחיינו – "who has kept us in life . . . and enabled us to reach this season" – is recited). From Exod. 13:10, and alternatively from Num. 29:39, the idea is derived that God utters the wish that the individuals who enjoyed the Festivals this year enjoy them also the coming year. As we can see, the illustration serves as proof that when the blessing שהחיינו is recited by men, God, in accordance with this benediction acknowledging gratitude for life, in turn blesses them with life. The preacher supports this idea by calling attention to scriptural verses telling of blessings by God. Scripture states that when God created His world, He blessed the Sabbath (Gen. 2:3), and that when He created the beasts and the fowl, He blessed them (*ibid.*, 1:22), and so, also, He blessed man (*ibid.*, 5:2) when He created him, and so, also, the creeping things (*ibid.*, 1:20–22). "And so, too," adds the preacher, "in regard to the matter we discussed," meaning, God also blesses man when man recites שהחיינו.[16] The passage closes with three examples of God's unlimited power in contrast to man's. The last example contrasts the way of man, who must build the lower part first and then the upper, with the way of God who created the upper parts first, and then the lower,

[14] Berakot IX.3.

[15] הוי אומר שכשם שהאדם מברך להקב״ה כך הוא מברכו.

[16] We have taken the reading וכן לענין דאמרינן in ed. Venice, 1545 — see Mann, op. cit., p. 25, note 7. וכן לענין מזון does not carry out the point of this section.

"as it says 'In the beginning God created the heaven' (Gen. 1:1) and then after that 'and the earth' (*ibid.*)." By referring to the idea of building, the closing part is linked with the beginning of the sermon, and by its leading up to Gen. 1:1, the first verse of the *Sidrah* of the day, that verse becomes "the occasion" of the sermon.

Though there are no doubt deletions, this passage exhibits a certain unity. Nevertheless, several statements in it are seen at a glance to be independent in character, despite the skillful way in which they have been woven into the sermon. What is said about the Festivals, even if used here as illustration and proof, is manifestly a complete idea in itself. As we might suspect, it is also found elsewhere[17] as a discrete statement. The three closing examples of God's power are explicitly quotations from three different authorities, and so are indubitably independent statements. One of them is also a discrete statement elsewhere.[18] In Mann's summary of the sermon, the independent character of the statements is lost for the simple reason that he inserts connective ideas not contained in the sermon itself.[19]

Sometimes a haggadah serves as the basis for a new haggadic statement. In those instances, however, the new statement is a complete entity in itself, despite its point of departure in the older haggadah. This is illustrated by

[17] See L. Ginzberg, Genizah Studies I, p. 454, no. 1. The concepts imbedded in the statements are God's love, *Berakah* (blessing), and Israel.

Ginzberg regards the Yelammedenu fragment he edited in that volume, pp. 37–50, as part of the original Yelammedenu. See ibid., pp. 23–36, and pp. 449–454. But we might also have indicated the presence of independent statements in these sermons also. Ginzberg notes a number of instances where statements given in these sermons are also found elsewhere — see, for example, ibid., p. 39, notes 25 and 26; p. 40, note 29; p. 41, note 8; p. 42, note 19; etc.

[18] Ibid., p. 454, no. 1. The concepts imbedded are that of *Bereshit* and that of man. On *Bereshit* as a concept, see above, p. 35 f., and on the concept of man ibid., p. 16, note 4.

[19] Note how he introduces the idea of the imitation of God and other ideas in order to make transitions — op. cit., p. 25.

many midrashim in Seder Eliahu, a literary composition which Ginzberg has shown to consist of a Mishnah-like text and of a later Talmud-like commentary.[20] The midrashim in the commentary, though using the earlier text as a point of departure, are complete and independent ideas in themselves. An earlier passage, for example, tells of how God divides the day into three equal parts – one in which He studies Torah, another in which He judges the world, and a third in which He dispenses charity and feeds and sustains the world. "And He laughs [lit., there is laughter before Him] only a single brief while."[21] The commentary takes up this last sentence by asking, "When does He laugh?" and it answers: when wicked nations of the world arrogantly challenge Him to come upon them and destroy them.[22] In this "comment", we have a new and complete idea, namely, the implication that the arrogant nations who challenge God will ultimately be destroyed. The new idea is so far from being a necessary corollary of the older haggadah that another version elsewhere has it that God's sport is with Leviathan, a symbol for Satan.[23] Similarly, the Seder also has two different "comments", two different haggadot, based on one and the same statement from an older haggadah.[24]

In the foregoing analysis, we had occasion to notice that the same haggadic statements also occurred elsewhere than in the passages under discussion. These parallels are a feature of midrashic literature in general. Practically every midrashic work which has come down to us has utilized previously collected midrashim, and this holds true of the

[20] See TE, pp. 13–16; OT, pp. 263–4. (See above, p. 15, n. 2.)

[21] Seder Eliahu, ed. Friedmann, pp. 61–2.

[22] Ibid. As to this part being commentary, see Ginzberg's remarks in OT, p. 297, note 101. The proof-text of the "comment" is appropriately Ps. 2:1–4.

[23] See OT, ibid., and the reference there to 'Abodah Zarah 3b.

[24] Seder Eliahu, ed. Friedmann, p. 123—on the statement: "And the Israelites in Egypt would circumcise their sons." See also OT, p. 294, note 50.

early[25] as well as the later[26] midrashic texts. Again, this was possible because the haggadic statements contain complete ideas and are therefore not dependent on a particular context.

It has not been our intention to imply that the various forms of haggadic composition can be disregarded. True, due to the integrative nature of the value-concepts, every haggadic statement is an independent entity. This is the primary mode of haggadic expression, whether the statement is discrete, as in an exegetical passage, or whether it is combined with other statements in a haggadic composition. But the recognition of this fact only makes the character of haggadic composition more evident. The unity of the haggadic composition is inherent in its form rather than in a logical order of the statements. This is obvious in the case of the comparatively simple form of the proem; the connection between the statements is the proem form itself. It is also true, however, of the more complicated forms. The statements in the first part of the Yelammedenu sermon, we may recall, are associated with a halakah, the typical beginning for that sermonic form, whilst the statements in the latter part are associated with the final statement which, in turn, both leads directly to the verse which is the "occasion" for the sermon and also refers to the idea in the halakah.[27] Here a larger structure has been built up of smaller units complete in themselves, and this larger unity was achieved by the Yelammedenu form. Every haggadic composition owes its unity to a particular form

[25] E. g., the relation between the Pesiḳta and Bereshit R.; Wayyiḳra R. and Midrash 'Ekah — see H. Strack, Introduction to the Talmud and Midrash (Eng. trans.) (Philadelphia: The Jewish Publication Society of America, 1931), pp. 211–12.

[26] E. g. Midrash Ḳohelet — see Strack, op. cit., pp. 220–21.

[27] On the basis of fragments from the Genizah (see above, p. 65, note 17), Ginzberg describes the original form of the Yelammedenu — "its special form of composition" — in a note communicated by him to G. F. Moore, and found in Moore, Judaism, III, p. 49.

whereby smaller independent entities have been combined so as to achieve a larger unified structure.

The forms of haggadic composition had a definite function. They overcame the difficulty posed by the fact that every haggadic statement was an independent entity. The purpose of Haggadah was the instruction and edification of the masses. But any extended discourse was made difficult by the very mode of haggadic expression: discrete, independent statements in a spoken discourse do not make for sustained and steady interest on the part of an audience. It was this difficulty that gave rise to the haggadic forms, each with its own manner of unifying otherwise independent statements. We may perhaps generalize and add that some such relationship always exists between the forms developed by an art and the materials which those forms shape. An aesthetic form apparently overcomes the difficulties engendered by the materials with which the artist chooses, or with which he is obliged, to work.

Having studied how the value-concept functions, we can now further differentiate between value-concepts and cognitive concepts. Conceptualization, as de Laguna has said, enables us to perceive the objective relation of things or of persons to *each other,* and to respond to the elements of the objective world without regard to the particular setting in which they may be at any given time.[28] But this applies, we have already pointed out, only to what we have called cognitive concepts. A cognitive concept like "table," for instance, allows us to recognize and to use — "to respond to" — any number of different entities symbolized by this concept, though we may find them in as many different settings. By the same token, cognitive concepts have the tendency to "break down" total situations, enabling us to perceive the objective relation of things and persons to each other; and it is this perception of objective relationships that has

[28] See above p. 50.

played so great a rôle in the development and use of tools. Cognitive concepts, then, have the function of rendering objects, and qualities too, *separable* elements in a total situation. But value-concepts, we have seen, do just the opposite. Like all concepts, they abstract and classify, but they also do more than that. They *fuse* all the elements in a situation — including cognitive data — into a single entity, into a unique whole, into "a particular setting." Cognitive concepts are disintegrating mental agents; value-concepts, on the contrary, are integrating mental agents.

Value-concepts are not simply general ideas having to do with the valuational life. In the preceding chapter we distinguished between value-concepts and inferred concepts. We have now observed that there is also a basic difference between value-concepts and cognitive concepts. Value-concepts constitute a class of concepts in their own right, with characteristics different from those of other classes of concepts.

It may be that language, including the cognitive concepts, is some kind of organic whole. "Language grows up as an organic whole. This does not mean simply that the various linguistic *forms* reciprocally imply each other, although this is a significant fact. But beyond this, the organic nature of a language means that any particular sentence, phrase, or word has determinate, albeit complex, connections with other particular sentences, phrases, and words. The essential constitutive relations of the things we cognize in the world, and the acts we perform to, or with, or on them, are reflected in the structure of language. But while the basic structure of language is ultimately determined by the interrelations of things and human acts, it develops an organic structure peculiarly its own, relatively independent and autonomous."[29]

We are not prepared to say what is the relation between

[29] De Laguna, op. cit., pp. 305–6.

the organic structure of a language as a whole and the organismic complex of value-concepts which it contains. That a relationship exists there can be no doubt. On the other hand, the character of the organismic complex of value-concepts is certainly not the same as that of the organic structure of the language as a whole. Valuational terms remain constant in the vocabulary, whereas new cognitive terms are continuously added to the language as the result of new political, social and economic conditions. Moreover, valuational terms, as we have just learned, differ in function from the cognitive terms. Valuational concepts, being usually imbedded in a particular setting, are integrating mental agents; cognitive concepts, being separable elements in a total situation, are in themselves disintegrative, analytic agents. And valuational concepts also differ, we have learned, from the inferred concepts.

We have demonstrated that the value-concepts constitute an organismic complex in themselves. We have also seen that the value-concepts possess characteristics different from those of the other types of concepts. If the other types of concepts also constitute an organic whole, the latter would seem to be a different, though related, organismic complex.

Let us return to the consideration of the independence, the wholeness, of the haggadic statement. We have recognized the truth of the oft-repeated observation that rabbinic thought cannot be coordinated into a system. But we have gone beyond that and observed two things more: First, that rabbinic thought as a whole does possess coherence, an organismic, conceptual coherence which can be traced and demonstrated. Second, that because of this kind of conceptual coherence each statement is an integrated, independent entity. The independent character of the haggadic statement is not an indication that rabbinic thought is chaotic or haphazard, which is often what is meant by the word "unsystematic." On the contrary, it is the result of a conceptual organization far more subtle than is to be found in any "system," one that is inherent in value-concepts and in them alone.

Because each haggadic statement is an independent unit, the midrashic texts exhibit remarkable variety in opinion. With each opinion or statement an independent entity, none is more authoritative than the others; all deemed worthwhile are given. Often placed side by side are many different interpretations of the same verse or the same event, and even, occasionally, opinions directly contradicting each other. This is amply illustrated by almost any midrashic text we happen to choose. We happen to have chosen the Mekilta, from which most of the following illustrations have been taken, and these illustrations are really only a few out of a possible multitude. We may recall, incidentally, that we had found novelty or variety of opinion to be the hallmark of an organismic mental complex.[30] Variety of opinion is made possible by the independence of each haggadic statement. The independence of each haggadic statement is thus once more seen to be inherent in the very nature of the rabbinic organismic complex.

A biblical verse, a phrase from a verse, may receive various interpretations, no one of them more authoritative than the others. The phrase "and how I bore you on eagles' wings" (Exod. 19:4) is given three different and consecutive interpretations in a single brief passage. The first two take "eagles' wings" to indicate miraculous swiftness, R. Eliezer saying that it refers to "the day of Rameses" when "they were all gathered and brought to Rameses within a little while," and R. 'Aḳiba saying that it refers to a *Nes* (miracle) at Mt. Sinai. The third interpretation, prefaced by the term *dabar 'aḥer*, "another interpretation," gives a totally different turn to the metaphor. "How is the eagle distinguished from all other birds? All the other birds carry

[30] Above, pp. 23–24.

their young between their feet, being afraid of the birds flying higher above them. The eagle, however, is afraid only of men who might shoot at him and he prefers that the arrows lodge in him rather than in his children." The passage concludes with the parable of a man walking on the road with his son whom he shields with his own body against all harm.[31] If the same verse can be the subject of diverse interpretations, each interpretation must be considered as independent and none as more authoritative than the others. In fact, our texts themselves seem to say this very thing in so many words when they preface a statement by the term, "another interpretation," as is the case here with our third interpretation. "Another interpretation" can only mean that the preceding interpretations as well as that about to be given are each of them independent of the others and that all are of the same rank. And this prefatory term is employed profusely[32] throughout all of midrashic literature.

Since each haggadic interpretation is an independent entity, there can be no demand for consistency in the interpretation of Scripture. The same individual may offer more than one interpretation of a verse. We have an instance, in another midrashic work, of an authority, R. Ḥama bar Ḥanina, who presents six consecutive interpretations of Gen. 29:2–3 which are introduced, so as to emphasize their single authorship, by the statement "R. Ḥama bar Ḥanina interpreted it (i. e., the verse) in six

[31] Mekilta, II, p. 202–3.

[32] Occasionally the term *dabar 'aḥer* also prefaces a halakic interpretation, as in Mekilta, I, p. 48 (Horovitz-Rabin, p. 20 and the note there); ibid., I, p. 50; Sanhedrin 63a; ibid., 63b. Such occasional instances are possible because Halakah, too, reflects in its own way the organismic qualities of the value-concepts. See below, p. 129 and p. 93 f. But in contrast to the use of the prefatory term in haggadic interpretation, the term is certainly not "employed profusely" in halakic interpretation. Notice, moreover, how in Sanhedrin 63a the different interpretations of Lev. 19:26 are united by means of the principle of לאו שבכללות and are thus not completely independent.

(different) ways."[33] If such multiplicity of interpretation on the part of a single individual is taken as a matter of course, it is primarily because each interpretation is independent of all the others.

What makes it possible for the same verse to be variously interpreted also makes variation in the interpretation of the same event possible. Each interpretation is independent of any other. The exodus from Egypt, for example, is accounted for in various ways, each one involving another value-concept. R. Nathan says that Israel was redeemed because of the conduct of the pious women among them, and thus employs the phase of corporate justice; R. Eleazer ben Azariah says that the event took place "because of the merit of our father Abraham," and thus employs the concept of the merit of the fathers; and R. Simeon ben Yoḥai says that it was their reward for having observed the rite of circumcision, and thus employs the concept of God's justice and that of *Mizwot*. And these different views are given, be it noted, consecutively in the same section.[34] Similarly, in a later section, there are numerous consecutive opinions accounting for the crossing of the Red Sea. Following is a partial list of these opinions and their authors: Because of Jerusalem – R. Ishmael; God only fulfilled the promise He had made their fathers (the patriarchs) – anonymous; because of the *Mizwah* performed by Abraham ("he cleaved the wood" – Gen. 22:3, and so "the waters were cleft" – Exod. 14:21) – R. Banaah; because they observed the rite of circumcision – Simeon of Teman; be-

[33] Bereshit R. LXX.8, ed. Theodor-Albeck, pp. 805 ff.

A. Gulack's opinion (יסודי המשפט העברי, Vol. IV [Berlin: Dwir, 1922], p. 12) that the מופלא שבבית דין was resented and that proof for this can be adduced from R. Ḥama's reference to him is not sound. Comp. Theodor-Albeck's notes p. 808 and L. Ginzberg, Commentary, III, pp. 212–219. See now also S. Lieberman, Hellenism in Jewish Palestine (New York: Jewish Theological Seminary of America, 1950), p. 66, note 153.

[34] Mekilta, I, pp. 140–1. Of course all the views are also supported by biblical verses.

cause God was reconciled to His sons (Israel) — R. Absalom the elder; God did it for the sake of His name — the *Ḥakamim*; because they (Israel) "trusted in Me" — Rabbi (Judah the Prince); "because of the merit of their father Abraham" — R. Eleazar ben Azariah; "because of the merit of the tribes (the sons of Jacob)" — R. Eleazer ben Judah; because their father Abraham "trusted in Me" — Shema'yah; because they (Israel) "trusted in Me" — Abṭalyon; because "I (God) am a Brother to Israel when they are in trouble" — R. Ḥananyah ben Ḥalnisi; because of Moses and his prayer — R. 'Aḥa.[35] Here, too, the various opinions mostly involve different value-concepts, although there are also repetitions of ideas and near repetitions. All such things are possible because each opinion is independent of all the others.

We have thus far cited whole passages in which divergent interpretations or opinions are in juxtaposition, not so much contradicting one another as simply different from each other, independent of each other. To so large a degree, however, are haggadic statements independent of each other that even contradictory statements lie peaceably side by side. One opinion has it that God ("the Holy One blessed be He") bent the heavens down to Mt. Sinai, and in this wise God ("the Glory") descended. Immediately following is a contradictory statement by R. Jose. For, basing himself on Ps. 115:16 — "The heavens are the heavens of the Lord, but the earth hath He given to the children of men" — R. Jose declares that "neither Moses nor Elijah went up to heaven, nor did the Glory come down to earth," and he adds that God merely told Moses that He would call him from the top of the mountain whereupon Moses should ascend the mountain.[36] Sometimes an authority contradicts

[35] Ibid., pp. 216–222.

[36] Ibid., II, p. 224; the parallel in Sukkah 5a has *Shekinah* in place of the Glory (*Ha-Kabod*), and says that "*Shekinah never* came down below (i. e., to earth)."

a colleague by raising a seemingly valid objection to the latter's interpretation of a verse. Thus, Rabbi (Judah the Prince) rejects a colleague's interpretation on the ground that it would appear to make God go back on His word, and presents another interpretation of the same verse instead. But our text does present the colleague's view also; the objection has apparently not invalidated it.[37]

Views most widely held and emphatically stated, not just the opinions of individuals, are not exempt from contradiction. In one place, "Because he has despised the word of the Lord" (Num. 15:30) is applied to him who says "the Torah is not from heaven" (i. e., God did not give the Torah), and is specifically applied as well even to him who says that the entire Torah is from heaven except for a single verse uttered "by Moses himself", not by the Holy One blessed be He.[38] Yet this view on Torah, though conforming to a mishnah, is flatly contradicted by another passage which declares that the comminations in the Book of Deuteronomy were uttered "by Moses himself."[39] Nor should the similarity in style, involving a Hebrew idiom, be overlooked![40]

The Rabbis seem, then, to be altogether indifferent to conflict in haggadic views. But we must not suppose that they are indifferent to contradictions or inconsistencies in general; on the contrary, in the halakic, or legal, sections of post-mishnaic rabbinic literature, the elucidation of the law demands the most rigorous examination of all possible conflicts of opinion, an examination that often results in the refutation of what is deemed logically untenable. In fact, this halakic, logical approach is occasionally carried

[37] Ibid., pp. 207–8.

[38] Sanhedrin 99a.

[39] Megillah 31b — the authority is 'Abaye, an 'Amora! S. D. Luzzatto calls attention to this contradiction in a comment on Deut. 28:23 in his commentary to the Pentateuch, and sees in it proof that research or investigation was not trammelled by the Rabbis.

[40] משה מפי עצמו (אמרן) — in both passages.

over into the sphere of the non-legal, or the haggadic type of dicta we have just been discussing. Thus, R. 'Ammi's dictum that death and suffering are always the result of sin is taken up, challenged by contradicting instances from the Haggadah, and the refutation announced in a formula usually reserved for halakic refutations.[41] If, therefore, on the whole the Rabbis take conflicts in haggadic view completely for granted we must look for the cause in the nature of the Haggadah itself. We have found the cause to consist in the organismic organization of the value-concepts which renders each statement embodying the concepts an independent entity.

II. THE SELF AND THE "SOCIAL MIND"

A literary mode has, in this instance, psychological bearings. The independence of each particular statement encourages and reflects diversity of opinion, the *differentia* of individual minds. But the organismic integration of the value-concepts as a whole also has important psychological bearings. All the characteristic features of Haggadah superbly reflect the relation between "the social mind" and the individual mind, and the manner in which the personality of the individual is integrated and enriched. We can probably learn more about these things from Haggadah, for reasons given below, than from any other literature of western civilization.

The existence of a social mind is denied by most writers today, and with good reason. How can a mind exist apart from individuals who think and feel? Social phenomena are explained as due to the interaction of individuals, and not the result of what a recent writer caustically dubbed

[41] Shabbat 55a–b. The argument closes with ותיובתא דרב אמי תיובתא. Instances of attempts at harmonization of haggadic dicta are in Yoma 85b and 86a.

"the communal ghost." Granted, however, that there can be no mind distinct and apart from individual minds. Granted, too, that there are no social phenomena without the interaction of individuals. But having granted all this, basic questions still remain unanswered. What is it which gives any historic group its special character, a character different from that of any other group? How does it happen that a group character goes hand in hand with full development of *differentia* in the individual? And since the group character persists generation after generation, is there not something fixed and stable within the very flux and change of the individuals' interaction?

It is in the attempt to answer such questions that social mind theories have been invented. Our answer, however, posits the existence of no actual collective mind. Data on the rabbinic value-concepts, part of which we have already noticed, in a measure explain the phenomena associated with "the social mind" so far as the Rabbis and their people are concerned. It is highly probable that our explanation, by and large, holds good in analogous fashion for historic groups in general.

What primarily endows the historic group with a special character are its value-concepts. We have been at pains to indicate that value-concepts function differently from other types of concepts, that they are different *in kind*. Their unique quality is such, indeed, that unlike other concepts they are, largely, almost untranslatable. Hebrew words for "table," "chair," "tree" and the like have, as can be seen, their corresponding English words: cognitive concepts are readily translatable. Scientific concepts are by convention international. A term like "Torah", however, is practically untranslatable and, as we have demonstrated, also undefinable, and that is why conscientious writers today refrain from translating it as "law." They let it simply stand for itself. Translations of rabbinic valuational terms are poor makeshifts as a rule, and this is no less true, we must say, of the few translations attempted here. "Commandment" is not a full equivalent for *Miẓwah* by any means, nor "sanctification of the Name" for *Ḳiddush Ha-Shem.* In fact, the rabbinic valuational terms are really even less translatable than idioms. While not literally translatable, the latter usually have meanings that can be completely conveyed in another language, but that is not the case with the valuational terms. The valuational terms, in fine, represent concepts that are the group's very own, and that distinguish it from all other historic groups.

The maintenance of the special character of the group is thus, to an extent, a matter of the transmission of the valuational terms. The rabbinic valuational terms formed part of the vocabulary of the people as a whole, of every individual member of the people, high or low, scholarly or non-scholarly. And being part of the vocabulary, they were transmitted from generation to generation as an integral element of the language, by interaction from infancy. Yet despite dynamic interaction within the group and with members of other groups, and despite changes in times and circumstances, all of which had their effect on the rest of the language, the valuational terms, as we know, remained fixed and stable throughout the entire rabbinic period. Since the terms which spelled the special character of the people were fixed and stable, that character remained constant generation after generation.

Had the valuational terms been left abstract, they could not have had so powerful an effect. Here, again, Haggadah reflects the manner in which the concepts functioned in daily life. We found that the abstract conceptual term is not used often, and that the concept is usually imbedded in a concrete haggadic statement. We saw, too, that this is due to the way in which the value-concepts functioned, not to mere literary artifice.

The way in which the value-concept functioned in haggadic literature is a true parallel to the way it functioned in daily life. The value-concepts were not just terms in the vocabulary. They could not be left abstract. *Every rabbinic value-concept had a drive toward actualization or concretization*; and many of them, such as charity, *Teshubah* (repentance), the study of Torah, and numerous others, directly impelled the individual to appropriate overt actions. But impulse alone would have made such drives only sporadic at best; it could hardly have ensured steady concretization. Being mental factors, however, the concepts were subject to conscious direction. They could not only be embodied in Haggadah but also in Halakah, in commonly observed laws or rules for concretization. These laws, fashioned by the Rabbis, who usually based themselves, as in Haggadah, on the Bible, ensured steady concretization. The concretization of the concept of charity, to give several examples, was made certain by the various agricultural regulations, including the tithes for the poor, *pe'ah* ("corner of the field"), *leḳeṭ* ("gleaning") and *shikḥah* ("forgotten sheaves"), and by the institutions of *tamḥuy* (community plate) and *ḳuppah* (community chest), and by the laws concerning personal charity[1]; that of repentance by the practices during the ten days of repentance[2]; and that of the study of Torah by the public reading of the Torah on Monday and Thursday and on the Sabbath and the Festivals, as well as by the institution of the *bet ha-midrash* and by the sermons and lectures of the Rabbis.[3] Even so highly subjective a matter as the acceptance upon oneself of *Malkut Shamayim* (the

[1] See the entire tractate Pe'ah. Cf. S. Schechter, Studies in Judaism, Vol. III (Philadelphia: Jewish Publication Society of America, 1924), pp. 238 ff.; E. Frisch, An Historical Survey of Jewish Philanthropy (New York: Macmillan, 1924); OT, pp. 131–140; and י. ברגמן, הצדקה בישראל (ירושלים, תש"ד).

[2] See S. Schechter, Some Aspects of Rabbinic Theology (New York: Macmillan, 1910), p. 342 and note 5 there.

[3] See G. F. Moore, op. cit., I, Chaps. IV–V.

Kingship of God) is not left solely to an individual's mood, but is given a place in the prescribed prayers, and hence is expressed by every individual daily in a declaration, an overt gesture.[4]

These and all the other concretizations of the value-concepts in law – Halakah – are not "legalism." They did not crowd out the possibilities for spontaneous concretizations; for proof, we need only point to such a rabbinic concept as deeds of loving-kindness which has reference also to deeds of love done beyond what is required by law.[5] Moreover, Halakah itself is a product of the value-concepts' drive toward concretization, and without doubt the most important product. Lacking Halakah, the value-concepts, with their need for steady concretization in actual life, might not have functioned at all.

It is easy enough to recognize the outward manifestations of the value-concepts, the concretizations. But unless we also realize that they *are* concretizations of warmly felt value-concepts, we shall completely fail to apprehend such outward actions. For here we are dealing with the springs of human actions, in other words, with the self, wherein inner experience and outward action are hardly separable. The rabbinic concepts are only *symbolized* in words. They are, in fact, often drives to action and hence bound up with the self. This is as true of matters of law as of more "spontaneous" concretizations. Can there be any more crucial expression of the self than martyrdom? Yet the following rabbinic tribute to contemporary martyrs reveals martyrdom for matters of law. " 'Them that love Me and keep My commandments' (Exod. 20:6)," says R. Nathan, "refers to those who dwell in the land of Israel and give their lives for the sake of the *Mizwot* (commandments). 'Why are you being led out to be decapitated?' 'Because I

[4] See TE, p. 60.
[5] See OT, pp. 137–8.

circumcised my son (that he be) an Israelite.' 'Why are you being led out to be burned?' 'Because I read the Torah.' 'Why are you being led out to be crucified?' 'Because I ate unleavened bread (i. e., observed Passover).' "[6] The practice of the laws was certainly as whole-souled an expression of the self as other concretizations of the concepts.

The self is less an entity than a continuous process making for an entity. Every individual is a more or less successful integrative process in constant function. In this process of integration, the value-concepts seem to play an enormous, perhaps a decisive, rôle; and this can be said even after reckoning with other influences upon man's personality – those revealed by research into man's chemistry and by the clinical studies of the various psychological schools. For in describing the individual as an integrative process in constant function, we have been describing the complex of value-concepts as well. And when we spoke of outward action as being hardly separable from the inner experience of the self, we were speaking of the drive toward concretization as being inherent in the value-concept. The integrative process of the individual self and the integrative process of the value-complex are thus certainly not two distinct processes. And it is the latter – the integrative process of the value-complex – that persists generation after generation. Is not this process, then, an important integrative factor in every individual's development? Further, being integrated not rigidly but organismically, the value-complex gives play to the individual's temperament and to his circumstances. The value-concepts thus allow – better, supply the means of – expression to each different personality, whether that expression consists of opinion, as in Haggadah, or of an actual concretization in life.

We can understand now how it happens that a group

[6] Mekilta II, p. 247, and the parallels there.

character goes hand in hand with full development of *differentia* in the individual. The very concepts that make for the special character of a group also make for the distinctiveness and uniqueness of the individual self, for the integrative process which *is* the self. There is no actual group mind. There are only individual minds, each of which employs the common heritage of value-concepts in an original and distinctive manner. But though there is no group *mind*, there can be no gainsaying that the group does possess a kind of personality. The commonly held value-concepts give the group a special character but so, too, do the laws, practiced by all and embodying these concepts. That interaction of the individuals without which there could be neither group nor individuals is always conditioned by these concepts and laws, and is therefore different in every group. Just as we cannot deny that the group, despite the fact that it is composed of disparate individuals, is an entity, so we cannot deny that it is always a peculiar, singular entity. It seems to possess a corporate personality or character, shared by all the individuals who belong to it. The corporate personality itself is grasped by a value-concept, in our case, the concept of Israel.

The sheer number of the concepts in the value-complex has a decided effect on the individual's personality. Since the value-concepts supply the means of expression to each personality and since each value-concept has a character of its own,[7] the more value-concepts there are the greater the range of expression. It is a common error to say, as Mead does, that "the difference between primitive human society and civilized human society is that in primitive human society the individual self is much more completely determined, with regard to his thinking and behavior, by the general pattern of the organized social activity carried on by the particular social group to which he belongs, than he

[7] See above, pp. 38–44.

is in civilized society."[8] Unless we see in license an expression of the self, the individual self in civilized society depends quite as much on the value-concepts peculiar to the group as it does in primitive society. The underlying difference consists in the number, the variety, of the value-concepts. In primitive society, the value-concepts allowing for the expression of the self are either comparatively few or, as we have reason to think, not crystallized into distinct and separate concepts,[9] and so individuals express themselves along very similar lines. On the other hand, the rabbinic value-complex, with its rich and large variety of concepts, encouraged the development of rich and differentiated personalities. The multitude of concepts gave both scope to temperament and the capacity to respond to the slightest change in circumstances; and temperament and circumstances differ, of course, with every individual. Every individual was thus given ample opportunity, nay, stimulus, for rich and varied self-expression.

Our entire discussion here, incidentally, confirms the remarks made above concerning attempts at defining value-concepts. If the value-concepts make for the uniqueness and distinctiveness of the individual self, it is folly, perhaps worse than that, to attempt to define them. It is folly because a defined concept is the same for all, negating the flexibility which allows for the play of every individual's *differentia*. It is worse than folly when such definitions are taken seriously and the attempt is made to cast the minds of all individuals into the same mold.[10]

[8] G. H. Mead, Mind, Self and Society (Chicago: University of Chicago, 1934), p. 221. SEE NOTES, P. 369.

[9] See below, pp. 144–147.

[10] Hankering after definitions, many of our American thinkers have failed in their true function. They have sought to define democracy, trying in this way, no doubt, to give it firmness. Fortunately, these academic definitions have no chance of success. Had the effort been successful, value-concepts would have become rules uniform for all men. We should be having totalitarianism, not democracy.

The true function of our American thinkers is quite otherwise. Can we actu-

III. THE RABBIS AND THE FOLK

It is only partly true that the value-concepts, being represented by terms, were transmitted from generation to generation in the same way as the other words of the language. Ordinary social interaction suffices for the maintenance and transmission of the terms constituting the bulk of the usual vocabulary. These terms are cognitive concepts. They refer to things, qualities, relationships, and are rooted in everyday objective, perceptual experience. But value-concepts are not rooted in perceptual experience. For the maintenance and transmission of value-concepts, concepts which do not refer to objective things and qualities, ordinary social interaction is not enough. There must be a supplementary form of communication that will help make the value-concepts as vivid as the objective cognitive concepts, and their use as frequent. That supplement to the speech of ordinary social interaction was the Haggadah. Arising primarily as sermons to the masses, it approximated the actual manner in which the value-concepts were imbedded in daily situations and in ordinary conversation. Haggadah

ally identify democratic concepts by their noun-forms? Has such an attempt to identify them been made? Had we crystallized our democratic concepts, — had our thinkers helped to crystallize them, — these concepts would be far more potent drives than they are now. They could be, far more than at present, means for individual self-expression. (See also below, p. 89, note 17.)

A news item appeared in The New York Times (March 16, 1946) telling of an attempt on the part of a group of educators, acting as an advisory board to a company making classroom movies, to formulate a definition of democracy. An official of the company reported that they debated the question for eighteen months in perhaps seventy-five conferences, and he recalled that at the first meeting, "at 10 A. M., everybody agreed, but by 4 P. M. there was no agreement on what democracy was." Finally, they settled on the proposition that "the signs of democracy are shared power and shared respect and the conditions of democracy are economic balance and enlightenment."

We have here what amounts to an experiment in formulating a definition for a value-concept. But how helpful are such vague terms as "shared respect" and "economic balance?"

was, therefore, a kind of extension of the use of value-concepts in ordinary social intercourse, and that accounts for its effectiveness as a means of instruction.

In order to produce this literature, the Rabbis had, apparently, to meet three requirements. Obviously, to teach they had first to learn, and the Rabbis remained students throughout their lives. The great academies not only handed down the learning of the past, they promoted interchange of views and opinions among the mature scholars; and these creative discussions served to train the younger disciples, who were allowed to put questions and even to venture opinions.[1] And yet, despite the fact that the Rabbis "spent more time in the *Bet ha-Midrash* (the academy) than beyond its walls,"[2] they were not a cloistered group and not a professional class. Thus they met the second requirement, namely, that there be no gap between the authors or teachers and the folk. They taught the adult members of their communities but received therefor neither salaries nor gifts.[3] Instead of forming a separate professional class, the Rabbis were bound up with the life of the people as a whole, and members of every economic group were to be found among them. Ginzberg has noticed that "more than one hundred scholars mentioned in the Talmud were artisans, a considerable number were tradesmen, and others were physicians or followed various professions."[4] Some of the greatest of the Rabbis made their living with their hands — Hillel was a carpenter, Joshua b. Ḥananiah a smith, Joḥanan a shoemaker.[5] Such men

[1] L. Ginzberg, Students, Scholars and Saints (Philadelphia: Jewish Publication Society of America, 1928) pp. 48–50. The Rabbis recognized and emphasized the creative function of the *bet ha-midrash* — see OT, p. 38, bottom, and the references there.

[2] L. Ginzberg, Students, etc., p. 51.

[3] See OT, p. 283, note 291 and references; and Ginzberg, Students etc., p. 55.

[4] L. Ginzberg, Students etc., p. 40.

[5] Solomon Goldman, The Jew and the Universe (New York: Harper and Bros., 1936), p. 191, note 50 and the references there.

were representative of the folk, albeit of the folk at its best. By the same token, the value-concepts embodied in their teachings were the value-concepts of the folk. That is why Haggadah was an extension of the use of the value-concepts in ordinary social intercourse. Finally, for their teaching to be effective, they had themselves to embody the ideals which they preached. "It was not the learning of the *Talmid Ḥakam*," says Ginzberg, "that gave him his position but his ideal life."[6] The high regard for the *Ḥakam* or the *Talmid Ḥakam*[7] was not something fleeting or fluctuating but has permanently affected the character of the concept itself. We may recall that *Ḥakam* and *Ẓaddiḳ* are overlapping concepts, that *the learned* is a term used interchangeably, on occasion, with *the righteous*.[8] And if the Rabbi was effective as an example, it was, again, because the circumstances of his life were the same as those of the folk in general. The people could not help but feel that, under the very circumstances in which they lived their lives, the teachings of the Rabbis could be carried out into practice.

The Rabbis took every possible opportunity to instruct and to train the folk. They spoke at betrothals and weddings; they delivered eulogies at funerals, and on returning gave talks of comfort to the mourners; they combined the amenities of social life with instruction or edification, as when they were guests anywhere, or at leave-taking[9] Their main occasions for instruction were, however, on the Sabbath and the Festivals, when they interpreted the day's lection from the Pentateuch or the Prophets to the members of

[6] L. Ginzberg, Students etc., pp. 40–41. See also his fine characterization, illustrated by incidents, ibid., pp. 52–57.

[7] On the relation between the two concepts see above, p. 43.

[8] See above, p. 29.

[9] See L. Zunz, Die gottesdienstlichen Vorträge der Juden (Berlin, 1832), pp. 334–336.

the community at large, both men and women.[10] It is the content of these sermons, which included things of such popular appeal as parables, folk-tales, fables and the like,[11] that has come down to us in the great compilations forming the bulk of Haggadah.

Characteristic of the Rabbis' relation to the folk, of the identity of their interests with those of the folk, is the Rabbis' own attitude toward Haggadah. They did not view it as something fit only for the masses, but to which they themselves were superior; on the contrary, they felt themselves deeply in need of Haggadah, regarding it as one of the great divisions of Torah, and the study of which was incumbent upon them. "Thou shalt not say, 'I have studied Halakot – that is sufficient for me,'" warns a statement in a tannaitic Midrash, and it goes on to interpret "for by everything that proceedeth out of the mouth of the Lord doth man live" (Deut. 8:3) as referring both to Halakot *and* Haggadot.[12] Younger scholars were stimulated toward becoming skillful in Haggadah as well as in Halakah.[13] True, as Lieberman points out, the Rabbis were mindful of their audience, suiting the style and content of their message in accordance with the background of their hearers.[14] In contrast, for example, to one interpretation of Koh. 12:2 R. Levi had given the scholars, he gave an-

[10] Ibid., pp. 336–340. These homilies sometimes included instruction in law — the Yelammedenu and She'eltot types, (ibid., p. 354 f.) ; cf. above, p. 64.

[11] N. Krochmal, op. cit., pp. 242–245.

[12] Sifre on Deut. 11:22. See also end of that paragraph — By studying Haggadah you know the Holy One blessed be He and cleave to His ways.

When the Rabbis object to Haggadah, they have in mind, as Krochmal has shown, not genuine but spurious haggadot. See his treatment of the subject, op. cit., pp. 246–248, 250–255. See also OT, pp. 217–18, where the point is made that these spurious haggadot do not embody value-concepts.

[13] Bacher, אגדות התנאים (Jerusalem: Dvir, 1932) , trans. Rabinowitz, p. 26 (R. Johanan b. Zakkai) , p. 68, (R. Gamaliel of Yabne) .

[14] S. Lieberman, Greek in Jewish Palestine, pp. 161–2.

other for the masses which was more "earthy."[15] But such differences in approach do not vitiate the factors which all types of Haggadah have in common. Whether any particular midrashic statement was intended for the scholars or for the masses, it contained value-concepts that were common to all, scholars and masses alike.

Seldom do we find the gap between the scholars and the folk, as here, all but closed, and still more seldom over so extended a period. In fact, the tendency in the western world has been the other way. The medieval scholars and thinkers spun out abstract doctrines, far beyond the ken of the common folk, and insisted that these are the truths of religion and morality. Nor are we closing the gap today. A philosopher like Bergson, much in vogue among the intellectuals, divides the world into "society," on the one hand, and mystics and saints, on the other. Society only develops obligations, and it exacts obedience to these obligations through pressure; new moral and religious ideas, which are also warm, all-pervasive emotions, are achieved by the mystics through intuition; these new ideas do not compel, but attract and inspire.[16] Bergson merely substitutes in persuasive and glowing terms his mystic for the medievalist's philosopher, but society is stigmatized in either case. Now if Bergson does not realize that the all-pervasive, warm emotions are, in truth, social value-concepts, it is perhaps not his fault. The literary works of western civilization are not, on the whole, produced under the conditions or by the type of men that produced the Haggadah. The Haggadah is a unique literature. Con-

[15] Ibid.

[16] H. Bergson, The Two Sources of Morality and Religion (Eng. trans.) (New York: Henry Holt and Co., 1935), Chap. I.

One of the "new" religious emotions, according to Bergson, is "the emotion introduced by Christianity under the name of charity" (ibid., p. 40). But the term is already found in the Book of Ben Sira and in the Book of Tobit — see OT, p. 303, note 194.

taining the value-concepts of the people as a whole, including the scholars and thinkers, it is a reflection of how these concepts functioned in daily life.[17]

IV. HALAKAH AND ITS NEXUS

Haggadah made the value-concepts vivid, and by means of sermons nurtured and cultivated them. The other product of the Rabbis, Halakah, had an altogether different function. It prescribed ways for the concretization of the concepts in day-by-day living. Does Halakah also reflect the qualities of the value-concepts, and if so, how?

In contrast to Haggadah, Halakah does not consist of independent units or entities. Definite forms of haggadic composition — literary, aesthetic forms — enabled the Rabbis, as we saw, to build up larger structures out of the independent haggadic statements. The literary forms overcome the barrier which the independence of the haggadic statements places in the way of any organization of haggadic

[17] Modern democratic values would be far more vivid were there a genuine interaction between the intellectuals and the people at large. We have not yet produced a supplement to the speech of ordinary social interaction embodying democratic value-concepts. Educators attempt to offset this lack by encouraging democratic procedures and conditions in schools and clubs. These worthwhile enterprises must remain, however, quite limited in scope; it is hardly possible to duplicate on this small scale the varied opportunities for the expression of democratic values in everyday life. More promising is the attempt to develop neighborhood organizations in which the adults of the community will find a much wider scope for democratic action. Such a movement, if it gathers momentum, may in time call forth a supplementary form of communication that will evoke the democratic concepts and make them more vivid.

A development of this kind will be arrested if its proponents are influenced either by the definition seekers (see above, p. 83, note 10) or by the educators who abhor "indoctrination." The latter have gone to the opposite extreme of the definition seekers. There is a denial here of all that we have found to be true of the value-concepts, of their rôle in the popular vocabulary, and of the need for their deliberate maintenance.

material. But the halakic material — the laws —presents no such barrier. There is an internal nexus between the laws themselves which, in the first instance, allows them to be classified and organized in accordance with their content. In other words, the various subjects with which the laws deal — tithes, the Sabbath, divorce, damages, and so on — constitute natural classifications and can be used for that purpose and for the more detailed organization of the laws. By and large, this is the principle of classification and organization employed by the Mishnah as we have it, with its six major divisions and sixty-three tractates.[1] It was on the basis of this principle that the Rabbis of the Talmud, the 'Amoraim, would account for the presence of an identical law in two different tractates of the Mishnah. That particular law primarily belongs in the one tractate, they would say, because of its subject matter, and is repeated elsewhere only incidentally.[2]

The nexus between the laws, unless brought to light, is always merely implicit. It becomes increasingly explicit only as the result of the work of individual Rabbis and, especially in the Talmud, of discussions among the Rabbis. Thus, though the organization of the laws was implicit in the natural classifications of the subject matter, it remained for a great mind to bring these classifications to light. This, it appears, was achieved by R. 'Aḳiba, whose work was continued by his pupil, R. Me'ir, and was utilized by Rabbi

[1] Strack, op. cit., pp. 26–64, gives a summary of each tractate.

By and large, the principle of classification and organization we have described holds for the Mishnah. But there are occasionally departures from it. On departures in the sequence of the tractates, see ibid., pp. 27–28 and the references; on departures within a tractate, see ibid., 24–5 and the references. Add to the references on the order in the Mishnah, L. Ginzberg, Tamid the Oldest Treatise of the Mishna, Journal of Jewish Lore and Philosophy, I, pp. 33–44, 197–209, 265–295.

[2] Shebu'ot 40b — הא עיקר ההיא אגב גררא נסבה; see also Rashi, a. l. Cf. Baba Meẓi'a 4b. So also in regard to a law apparently given in two different chapters of the same tractate — Zebaḥim 11b. For another type of repetition, see Ketubbot 72a.

Judah the Prince in his authoritative edition of our Mishnah made at about the end of the second century.[3]

Apart from the classification of the laws according to subject matter, the task of establishing the nexus between the laws was not undertaken by the Rabbis for its own sake. It was a concomitant of their efforts to formulate and elucidate the laws, although not a necessary concomitant. In the mishnaic period, the laws were often formulated with the aid of hermeneutic rules, methods for deriving laws from the Bible[4]; and it is in the course of the application of these rules that the nexus between specific laws may be brought to light. The application of a certain hermeneutic rule, for example, results in the formulation of a general law based on four distinct classes of damages.[5] But that general law also reveals the nexus between these four classes: it describes the characteristics common to them all (הצד השוה). The famous rabbinic interpretation of *lex talionis* — "an eye for an eye" (Exod. 21:24) — offers an instance of another type. Here the use of hermeneutic rules by R. Ishmael and by R. Isaac apparently but confirms what was already accepted as law — namely, not *lex talionis* but monetary compensation. The use of hermeneutic rules elicits in this instance too, however, a relation between this law and other laws.[6]

Nevertheless, the nexus between the laws is not made fully explicit in the mishnaic period. It was not always brought to light when the hermeneutic rules were employed. The very passage just cited contains a third interpretation of "an eye for an eye" which also applies a hermeneutic

[3] See Z. Frankel, דרכי המשנה, second ed., (Warsaw, 1923), pp. 220–228.

[4] For a description of the hermeneutic rules, see M. Mielziner, Introduction to the Talmud, third ed., (New York: Bloch, 1925), pp. 130–176; Strack op. cit., pp. 93–95.

[5] Baba Ḳamma I.1. This is an application of *binyan 'ab*; cf. Mielziner, op. cit., pp. 161–162.

[6] Mekilta, III, 67–68.

rule, but one that does not involve relations between laws.[7] Moreover there were laws, representing an older tradition, unsupported by any hermeneutic rule at all.[8] The classification of the laws, it is true, marks an advance in the direction of establishing the nexus between the laws. But it is an advance limited by its own objective. It relates the laws within any classification but not across classifications. We may say, therefore, that though the nexus between the laws becomes evident in the mishnaic period, it is still somewhat implicit.

It becomes more and more explicit in the talmudic period. As Krochmal has pointed out, there is a distinction, so far as the Babylonian Talmud is concerned, between the kind of discussion engaged in by the earlier generations of 'Amoraim and that engaged in by the later. The earlier discussions, initiated by Rab and Samuel and hence associated with their names,[9] were directed toward the clarification of the Mishnah, and this involved comparing the manner in which a law is stated in our Mishnah with the manner in which it is stated in extra-mishnaic collections, tracing a dispute back to its earliest protagonists, and similar matters.[10] The later discussions, initiated by 'Abaye and Raba and hence associated with their names,[11] were often based on the earlier discussions but exceeded them in the minute analysis of the law. They deal with the discrepancies between the mishnaic and the extra-mishnaic statements of the laws, with the reasons that may be attributed to a law, with the assumptions or principles

[7] Ibid., pp. 68–9. This interpretation by R. Eliezer, as many have said, does not mean that he does not accept the rabbinic law, but only that he insists that the biblical meaning was otherwise.

[8] Such laws were designated הלכה למשה מסיני, or else were introduced by באמת אמרו or by אמרו — see Frankel, op. cit., pp. 20, 304–305, and Krochmal, op. cit., pp. 213–214.

[9] הוויות דרב ושמואל.

[10] Krochmal, op. cit., p. 234.

[11] הוויות דאביי ורבא.

apparently underlying conflicting views or disputes among the older authorities.[12] It is in the course of these discussions that a nexus may be established between laws in different classifications. Thus, it is elicited in a discussion that an identical principle underlies both a law concerning the building of the booth for the Festival of Tabernacles and a law in a totally different classification, that of tithes.[13] When relations are established among laws in different classifications, the nexus between the laws is being made fully explicit.

We have depicted Halakah as the most important product of the value-concepts' drive toward concretization.[14] And now we shall see that, like Haggadah, Halakah also reflects the qualities of the value-concepts, although in its own way. Haggadah is characterized by diversity of opinion. But Halakah differs from Haggadah in not being composed of discrete, independent entities which encourage diversity of opinion. There is a nexus between the laws, an implicit nexus that becomes more and more explicit. Does Halakah, nexus and all, nevertheless have room at any time for wide divergence in law? It does, and so reflects in its own way the organismic, nonrigid nature of the value-complex.

During the mishnaic period, there was achieved the classification of the laws. To this degree only had the nexus been made explicit for the laws in general. Classification according to subject matter, however, is one thing and the elimination of controversial opinion quite another. The "code" may simply be a collection of divergent opinions organized according to subject matter, and this is indeed what the Mishnah, until its final redaction, tended to be.

[12] Krochmal describes these later discussions as characterized by: הקושיא והתירוץ התשובה והפירוק בכלל, הפלפול ועיון הסברא בכל הנמצא מכבר — op. cit., p. 234.

[13] Sukkah 23a–24b; see a. l. the commentary of R. Ḥananel, beg.: ושנינון איפוך. See notes, p. 369.

[14] Above, p. 80.

There are only six complete chapters in the Mishnah which are "anonymous," that is, chapters in which no controversies are recorded.[15]

But divergence in law is not only a matter of diversity of opinion; it means that and much more. The differences of opinion which the Mishnah exhibits pertain not to theoretical questions alone. They often represent actual divergence in practice, Ginzberg has shown, even when it is the view of one authority as against that of the majority of his colleagues. Providing the law was not fixed, the individual authority had the right — the duty — to render a decision in accordance with his own view, although knowing that the majority disagreed with him.[16] Thus, for a long time the School of Shammai differed from the School of Hillel in respect to hundreds of halakot, and both decided cases in accordance with their own views, though the School of Shammai recognized that it was in the minority.[17] That this was true of individual opinions also, we can see from the instances of R. Eliezer and R. Jose.[18] Naturally, there were certain limitations on divergence in practice. When a case came before a group of Rabbis, the decision was by a majority vote, and dissenting opinions in that case had no validity.[19] A further limitation consisted of the ordinances and verdicts of The Great Court (בית דין הגדול). An ordinary court was obliged to decide a case as it saw the law, notwithstanding the fact that another court may have decided a similar case differently[20]; but the ordinances and verdicts of The Great Court were binding on all other courts and on all individuals.[21] Since, however, the decisions of

[15] See L. Ginzberg, A Commentary on the Palestinian Talmud, I, p. 83, where these chapters are listed. See notes, p. 369.

[16] Ibid., I, pp. 81–2, 90.

[17] Ibid., p. 82.

[18] Ibid., pp. 81–2.

[19] Ibid., p. 81 and p. 91, note.

[20] Ibid., p. 82.

[21] Ibid.

The Great Court were comparatively few, and usually made only in times of extreme national danger, ample room was left for decisions by the individual authority in accordance with his own views.[22] As Ginzberg sums it up: "Hence we need not wonder at the many conflicts of opinion among the Rabbis from the days of Shammai and Hillel to the close of the Mishnah. Not only could each of the Rabbis differ from the majority when dealing with theoretical questions, but the individual authority could decide according to his own opinion without regard to the opinion of the majority in any specific case that came before him, outside of those matters already decided by The Great Court."[23] In the course of time conflicts of opinion among the Rabbis became so numerous that there was hardly a law which was not indefinite. The rule was then made that, if an individual authority could not decide a specific case either on the basis of a tradition he had received or on that of legal reasoning, he must decide the case in accordance with the view of the majority of the Rabbis.[24]

Halakah reflects the organismic character of the value-concepts in other ways as well. But we shall not pursue them here. Some of them will become apparent in subsequent discussions.

The value-concepts are concretized in Haggadah and Halakah. Because of the intimate relation of the Rabbis to the folk, rare among creators of written literature, the sermons of the Rabbis as preserved in the Haggadah constitute a unique literature. Informed by the value-concepts common to the whole people, these sermons reflect the manner in which the value-concepts functioned in everyday speech and action. In speech, the value-concepts are

[22] Ibid., pp. 82–3.

[23] Ibid., p. 83.

[24] Ibid. — a later and enlarged application of יחיד ורבים הלכה כרבים. See notes, p. 369.

inseparable from the data which they interpret, and render every valuational statement a fused, independent entity. Only by means of literary forms were the Rabbis able to overcome the atomistic nature of the haggadic statements and to organize these statements into sermons. The value-concepts affect not speech alone, however, but the whole personality. If the independence of the valuational statement encourages diversity of opinion, reflects the *differentia* of individual minds, it is because the entire value-complex encourages and makes possible the development of distinctive personalities. The common character of the group and the differentiated personality of every individual member of it go hand in hand, and both derive from the value-concepts.

The value-concepts have a drive toward concretization, and Halakah is the most important product of that drive. It ensures the steady concretization of the concepts. In contrast to Haggadah, Halakah does not consist of independent entities. There is an implicit nexus between the laws, a nexus that becomes fully explicit only in the talmudic period. Yet so long as the nexus remains more or less implicit, there is room for wide divergence in law, and this is actually the case in the mishnaic period. Halakah, too, thus reflects in a measure the nature of the value-concepts. It is because Halakah is a manifestation of the value-concepts that the practice of the laws can be so whole-souled an expression of the self.

CHAPTER V

The Category of Significance

Value-concepts, as we concluded in the last chapter, make for the distinctiveness and uniqueness of the self. They supply the means of expression to each individual personality. This is to say that every action or situation fraught with value-concepts is unique and original, holding however briefly the distinctive essence, as it were, of a personality. A true work of art is likewise unique and original — in fact, valuational expression and artistic expression are but different modes of one great category. In the present chapter we are attempting a description of that category, largely in connection with valuational expression but touching also on aesthetic expression.

Concepts supplying the means of expression to each individual personality are bound to be, in some degree, subjective. How could they be otherwise and still respond to the unique quality of each individual personality? But these value-concepts express personality only when they are embodied in a concrete situation or action. The subjective value-concepts act not by themselves but always in concert with objective, concrete, cognitive concepts, and even with defined concepts. As we noticed above, value-concepts are fused with cognitive concepts in any concrete situation. Does this "acting in concert" make for a kind of coalescence of conceptual types, blur the demarcations between them? We expect to show that the contrary is true. A value-concept functions easily only when it is free from admixture with a concept of a different type. Subjective valuational experience goes together with a firm grasp of the impersonal, objective nature of things that contribute to that experience. When concepts of various types can act steadily in concert, it is because they do so as a category of thought, speech and action in which each conceptual type remains pure. This category, which we call "the category of significance," is a hallmark of civilized societies; valuational expression in primitive societies, we shall see, manages without it.

Situations fraught with value-concepts have their literary parallel in the discrete haggadic statements. This means that the problems raised by the consideration of these discrete statements are not primarily literary but valuational. For example, is not belief involved in the acceptance of haggadic statements? What kind of belief was it that could also be inspired by legend? This is a problem in religious psychology, and its solution will throw light on the nature of the category to which the rabbinic statements and legends belong. Even what is a genuine literary device — the peculiar manner in which haggadic statements are attached to the Bible — is also much more than that. To account for it we shall have to describe a major aspect of "the category of significance," a description comprehensive enough to include the reasons for that name. With this "literary" problem we shall therefore begin.

I. RABBINIC INTERPRETATION AND PHILOSOPHIC INTERPRETATION

Haggadic statements are, for the most part, interpretations of biblical texts. Yet these interpretations are often not concerned with the literal meaning of the texts to which they are attached. On the contrary, they depart from the literal meaning, frequently in a radical fashion. When a haggadic interpretation departs from the plain text of the Bible, the idea conveyed is generally a concretization of a rabbinic concept.

Even when a haggadic comment reckons with the context of a biblical verse, it usually presents a new, a rabbinic, idea. A few examples will suffice to illustrate. "And Abram took Sarai his wife, and Lot his brother's son, and all their substance that they had gathered, and the souls — *ha-nefesh* — that they had gotten — *'asu* — in Haran" (Gen. 12:5). By taking *'asu* in its literal sense of "made" and by utilizing the higher connotation of *nefesh*, the Rabbis deduce that Abram and Sarai went about making converts (*Gerim*) in Haran. He that makes a convert, they add in explanation of *'asu*, is considered "as though he created him."[1] But the Rabbis' poetic idea is not contained in the verse itself: the very concept of *Ger* as convert is a rabbinic and not a biblical concept.[2] Similarly, a rabbinic comment on Gen. 18:25 injects the rabbinic concept of God's mercy, *Middat Raḥamim*. "Shall not the Judge of all the earth do justly?" is a plea for justice, as given in the Bible. By a slight vowel-change, R. Levi reads it as a declarative sentence: The Judge of the whole world must not act with justice — else there will be no world.[3] Abraham's plea for justice is in this wise turned into a plea for mercy.

Haggadic interpretations of Scripture, then, represent departures from the literal, simple meanings of the texts. What is more, the Rabbis themselves were quite aware of that fact.

The terms פשט and דרש, כמשמעו and ודאי testify that the Rabbis differentiated between midrashic interpretation and

[1] Gen. R. XXXIX.14, ed. Theodor, pp. 378–9. See Theodor's note there for the parallels.

[2] See below, p. 290 f.

[3] Gen. R. XXXIX.6, ed. Theodor, pp. 368–9, and Theodor's notes there. In R. Levi's interpretation, the ה of השופט is vowelized as the definite article.

simple meaning. פשט and דרש are designations, respectively, for the simple meaning and for rabbinic interpretations.[4] Employed by the 'Amoraim, the Rabbis of the Talmud, these two terms of classification were taken over by the medieval exegetes and are used to this day by biblical scholars. In the mishnaic period there was yet no term for דרש, but two terms were used which are the equivalents of פשט – כמשמעו and ודאי.[5] Either of the two tannaitic terms served to designate the simple meaning, and so to set it off from midrashic interpretation. For the purpose of bare classification this was sufficient. If there is a designation for the simple meaning, the other classification is obviously also recognized. Among those asked to return to his home and not to go into battle, for example, was "the man that is fearful and faint-hearted" (Deut. 20:8). "R. 'Aḳiba says: 'that is fearful and faint-hearted' — כמשמעו: he that cannot endure to participate in battle and to see a drawn sword. R. Jose the Galilean says: 'that is fearful and faint-hearted' — this refers to him who is fearful because of the transgressions he committed (lit., in his hand)."[6] In contrast to the simple, literal meaning which R. 'Aḳiba upholds in this passage, and which he designates as כמשמעו, R. Jose offers a midrashic interpretation embodying the concepts of *'Aberah* — transgression, and *Middat Ha-Din* — God's justice.[7] Supported by a proof-text, these rabbinic concepts are made to stand out more prominently in a

[4] See Bacher, Terminologie, Hebrew trans. ערכי מדרש (Tel Aviv, 1923) p. 269, s. v. פשט, p. 174, s. v. דרש. As Bacher points out in a note on p. 269, most of the examples he cites which the Rabbis refer to as *peshaṭ* we should regard as *derash*; we shall account for that presently. On the other hand, two of the examples he cites — 'Erubin 23b (on Exod. 27:18) and Ḳiddushin 80b (on Deut. 13:7) — are definitely in the class of *peshaṭ*.

[5] See Bacher, ibid.; p. 129, s. v. משמע and p. 34, s. v. ודאי.

[6] Soṭah VIII.5; Sifre Deut. to Deut. 20:8 (with a slight variation).

[7] The *derash* is on the words ורך הלבב. Mr. Chaim Sachs suggests that לבב = יצר (comp. Ber. IX.5) — he who is weak in control of his יצר.

variant, where, incidentally, the interchangeable ודאי occurs in place of כמשמעו.[8]

Not only did the Rabbis differentiate between the midrashic interpretations of a verse and its simple meaning, but they also taught the simple meaning. They have a fine sense for the niceties of the Hebrew language and a workable approach of their own to its grammar and syntax, and so produced much that is sound biblical exegesis.[9] Schechter points out that a great portion of Midrash literature is simple commentary and, after giving several illustrative instances, adds: "Such instances of mere פשט (simple meaning) could be cited by hundreds, and it is not impossible that many more were omitted by the scribes, who considered such renderings of words and definitions of terms as universally known through the medium of the various versions, and hence not sufficiently important to be copied."[10] Among these versions, the so-called Targum Onkelos is the standard rabbinic translation of the Pentateuch into Aramaic, and was used for the purpose of instruction in the synagogues where it accompanied the reading of the lection of the day. This translation for the most part renders פשט, the simple meaning.[11]

How is it that the Rabbis could indulge in haggadic interpretations when they knew that these were departures from the simple meaning of the texts? As Schechter has emphasized, a considerable portion of Midrash literature is simple commentary; yet the fact remains that so much of that literature consists of haggadic interpretations. How could the Rabbis' concern with simple meaning have been

[8] Tosefta Soṭah VII.22, ed. Zuck.-Lieb., p. 309; cited by Bacher, op. cit., p. 34.

[9] See Samuel Rosenblatt, The Interpretation of the Bible in the Mishnah (Baltimore: Johns Hopkins Press, 1935), pp. 10–20.

[10] S. Schechter, Studies in Judaism, Third Series, p. 214. See S. Lieberman, Hellenism in Jewish Palestine, pp. 49–52.

[11] See Moore, op. cit., I, pp. 101–2, 174–5, 302–5, and the references.

compatible with the creation of a vast haggadic literature, with a veritable flow of interpretations completely at variance with the simple meaning? We cannot dismiss the problem by saying that haggadic interpretation is just another example of "figurative interpretation." This is precisely what haggadic interpretation is *not*. Haggadic interpretation presents a striking contrast to figurative interpretation.

The clearest rationale of figurative interpretation is the famous one given by Maimonides, although the method itself is old and was employed by the Hellenistic philosophers centuries before it was taken up again by medieval philosophy.[12] In the Books of the Prophets, according to Maimonides, there are obscure figures that are not characterized as figures and that greatly perplex the well-informed person who takes them literally (על פשוטיהם).[13] What need is there for such figures? They are inherent in the purpose of Scripture. Desiring to bring us (the educated) to perfection and to improve the state of our masses, God gave His practical regulations.[14] But these laws can properly be practiced only after the acquisition of rational ideas or truths – meaning, first of all, a conception of God according to our capacities.[15] This becomes possible only through the study of metaphysics which, in turn, presupposes the study of physics.[16] That is why God commenced His Writ (ספרו) with *Ma'aseh Bereshit*, that is, with physical science.[17] (*Ma'aseh Bereshit*, the account of creation, consists of physical science, and *Ma'aseh Merkabah*, the descrip-

[12] See M. Guttmann, משמעות הכתוב ודרכי המדרש, Hazofeh, 5th year, no. 1 (Budapest, 1921), pp. 19–27.

[13] Maimonides, Moreh Nebukim, Part I, Introduction; ed. Ibn Samuel (J. Kaufman), I (Tel Aviv, 1935), p. 12— משלים סתומים מאד שבאו בספרי הנביאים ולא . . . פרש שהם משל . . . וכשיתבונן בהם היודע באמת ויקחם על פשוטיהם תתחדש לו . . . מבוכה גדולה.

[14] Ibid., ed. Ibn Samuel, p. 19. See his notes there.

[15] Ibid. — אשר לא יתכן זה אלא אחר דעות שכליות, תחלתם השגתו ית׳ כפי יכלתנו.

[16] Ibid.

[17] Ibid.

tion of the Chariot, of metaphysics).[18] God communicated these profound matters to us in allegories and figurative language so that the masses might comprehend them in one sense, according to the measure of their intelligence and feebleness of apprehension, whilst the educated might take them in another sense.[19] Indeed, so elusive and difficult are these matters that they can be communicated only by means of figures: he who dispenses with such figures in his teaching must use language even more obscure.[20] There are biblical verses, then, that have a double sense – a plain meaning and a hidden one[21]: the hidden meaning must be superior to the plain one, and the plain meaning must direct the discerning reader to the purport of the hidden meaning.[22] Maimonides also declares that many midrashic interpretations must be taken figuratively.[23]

The manner in which figures are employed varies. The hidden meaning may be contained in only part of a figure; various parts of a figure may each refer to a different idea; a single hidden meaning may be scattered over separate figures; a single figure may, at times, refer to two closely related ideas.[24]

Three characteristics of figurative interpretation emerge from Maimonides' rationale for it. First, the literal meaning and the hidden meaning of a verse are actually not separate things, separate meanings. The literal meaning is only the

[18] Ibid., p. 13.

[19] Ibid., pp. 19–20 — see the notes there.

[20] Ibid., pp. 17–18.

[21] Ibid., p. 25 — שהדבר שהוא בעל שני פנים רצונו לומר שיש לו נגלה ונסתר.

[22] Ibid. — וצריך שיהיה תוכו טוב מנגלהו . . . וצריך שיהיה בגלויו מה שיורה המתבונן על מה שבתוכו. According to Maimonides, these ideas are contained in Prov. 25:11 which he takes to say: "A word fitly spoken is like golden apples in a *network* of silver." For a vivid view of Maimonides' method, see I. Friedlaender, Maimonides as an Exegete, in Past and Present (Cincinnati: Ark Pub. Co., 1919), pp. 193–216. SEE NOTES, P. 370.

[23] Moreh Neb., ed. Ibn Samuel, p. 20. See the references and the summary given by Ibn Samuel in his Introduction, ibid., p. XXXI.

[24] Ibid., p. 18.

pointer, as it were, directing "the discerning reader" to the hidden meaning. Second, the hidden meaning, being the real meaning of a verse, is superior to the plain meaning. The plain meaning is altogether secondary. Third, a biblical verse or part of it can convey only one hidden idea, at the very most two such ideas closely related to each other. In any case, for any one interpreter a verse cannot possess two *alternative* interpretations, let alone a number of such alternative hidden meanings. The manner in which different verses employ their figures may vary. But the hidden meaning represented by any particular verse cannot vary.

To these characteristics of figurative interpretation, rabbinic interpretation presents a contrast point for point. In the Rabbis' view, the literal meaning and their own interpretations are two separate things. We need but recall how R. 'Akiba's rendering of a verse, a rendering designated by him as the literal meaning, is set off against R. Jose's midrashic interpretation of the same verse. The Rabbis, in fact, lay stress on the simple meaning of a verse as being an entity in itself, something quite apart from its rabbinic interpretation. It is a rabbinic principle that "a biblical verse never loses its literal meaning,"[25] however the verse may be employed in rabbinic interpretation. The idea here that it is the literal meaning which is stable, and that rabbinic interpretations are added matters, is a far cry from the idea that the literal meaning is secondary or inferior.

In clear contrast to figurative interpretation is also another rabbinic principle. "One biblical verse or expression," say the Rabbis, "is susceptible of many (different) interpretations."[26] We have met with illustrations of this principle in the preceding chapter.[27] Among them is the

[25] Shabbat 63a; Yebamot 11b; (ibid., 24a) — אין מקרא יוצא מדי פשוטו.
[26] Sanhedrin 34a — מקרא אחד יוצא לכמה טעמים.
[27] Above, p. 71 f.

instance in which one authority, R. Ḥama bar Ḥanina, gives six interpretations of Gen. 29:2–3, consecutive interpretations that are introduced by the Midrash, so as to emphasize their single authorship, by the statement "R. Ḥama bar Ḥanina interpreted it (i. e., the verse) in six (different) ways."[28] All this is at the opposite remove of the notion inherent in figurative interpretation, namely, that there cannot be alternative interpretations to a verse, and certainly not for any one interpreter. Even when the Rabbis themselves take a biblical theme to be a figure essentially, their principle of multiple interpretation still holds. They regard the Song of Songs as an allegory which depicts God's love for Israel and Israel's love for God; but their comments on that Book, too, abound in multiple interpretations of verses.[29] And among the latter is another instance wherein different interpretations of the same biblical phrase are given by one author, and these consecutive interpretations are also prefaced by the formula emphasizing their single authorship.[30]

The Rabbis find warrant in biblical texts for this principle of multiple interpretation. The School of R. Ishmael, for example, reads the principle in Jer. 23:29 – "Is not My word like as fire? saith the Lord; and like a hammer that breaketh the rock in (many) pieces?"[31] To put the rabbinic idea prosaically: a word of God's, unlike that of a human being, can express at once many different things.[32] Modern writers in the field have seized upon this idea and have made it the foundation on which they reared their represen-

[28] Ibid., p. 72.

[29] See Canticles Rabba, on any verse.

[30] Canticles Rabba on 1:5 — R. Levi bar Ḥayta.

On the attitude of the Rabbis in general to the Song of Songs, see I. Heinemann, Darke Ha-Agadah (Jerusalem, 1949), p. 156 f.

[31] Sanhedrin 34a. See Tosafot a. l.; but I have taken Rashi's view as given in his comment on the version in Shabbat 88b.

[32] See also the scriptural warrant found by 'Abaye in Ps. 62:12 (Sanhedrin 34a).

tations of Rabbinic Judaism. They see in it a theory of interpretation which made possible the growth both of new laws and new doctrines, a premise on which was based the whole structure of rabbinic thought, — a premise, therefore, to be characterized as nothing else than "the logic of revealed religion." This approach, however, is but another illustration of how conditioned we are today to seek for logic everywhere in the realm of ideas. Actually, the idea that God can say many things at the same time is not a premise involving a whole theory of interpretation. It does not take into account, for instance, the distinction between the literal meaning and rabbinic interpretations, a distinction which, as we know, the Rabbis do emphasize elsewhere. The idea is an important one, to be sure, but is only one of the concretizations of the concept of Torah.

There is no such thing as "the logic of revealed religion." From the idea that God revealed or gave the Torah, it does not necessarily follow that the words of the Torah are susceptible of many interpretations. No one has insisted more firmly than Maimonides that the Torah was given by God; he made of that idea an Article of Faith, the Eighth of his famous Thirteen Articles of Faith.[33] And it is none other than Maimonides, a master of logic, who also insists that a biblical phrase usually has but one true, although hidden, meaning. The fact of the matter is that, when it comes to interpretation, everything depends on the *type* of the concepts that the interpretation is made to convey. Maimonides tried to find in the Bible — as do all who engage in figurative interpretation of the Bible — a system of philosophic or scientific concepts. Were the same biblical phrase to represent any number of different ideas, the latter could not be reduced to a system. Accordingly, Maimonides limits the number to a minimum. The same

[33] See his statement היסוד השמיני in his Commentary to the Mishnah, Sanhedrin, Introd. to Chap. X.

biblical phrase may refer to only two hidden ideas, and at that only occasionally, and then only if the two ideas are closely related.

The rabbinic interpretation of the Bible is in a completely different universe of discourse. When the Rabbis depart from the literal meaning and offer their own interpretations, what do these interpretations contain? They contain rabbinic value-concepts, concepts shared by the learned and ignorant alike, concepts common to all the people. It is because rabbinic concepts differ so radically from philosophic concepts that rabbinic interpretation is so radically different from figurative interpretation. The Rabbis employ multiple interpretation. The Rabbis are aware of departing from the simple meaning of the text and yet feel quite free to do so. We shall comprehend these phenomena if we take into account all we have learned concerning the nature of the value-concept.

II. CATEGORY OF SIGNIFICANCE — HAGGADAH

A summary of the traits of the value-concept, however, will amount to more than a mere recapitulation of them. The various traits of the value-concept all contribute to its general character, and it is this general character that we are now able to see more clearly. Moreover, in establishing the general character of the value-concept, we shall also penetrate to the core of the difference between value-concepts and other types of concepts. We shall see, finally, how this distinctive character of the value-concepts enables the Rabbis to utilize the biblical texts as they do.

Cognitive concepts and defined concepts are similar in one respect. A cognitive concept — a word like "chair" or "brown" or "near" — stands for something *definite* in our sensory experience. That is why cognitive concepts can be translated; the same definite sensory fact or object possesses a different symbol in another language. Variability of the symbol thus emphasizes the definiteness, the objectivity, of the thing to which the different symbols refer. Defined or inferred concepts are, of course, much more abstract than cognitive concepts. Instead of referring directly to concrete things or sensory qualities, a defined concept stands for a statement, a definition. Yet the defined concept has, if anything, an even more definite character than the cognitive concept, since every defined concept is strictly limited by its definition. The variability of the symbol is, again, greater in the case of the defined concept. The lifespan of the defined concept, so to speak, depends on the definition rather than on the conceptual term or symbol. The same definition or statement can be represented by different symbols.[1] Both cognitive and defined concepts, then, refer, in different ways, to matters that are definite, objective.

But the value-concept does not refer to definite things in sensory experience, and it is not defined. Unlike both cognitive and defined concepts, it does not stand for something merely objective. Every value-concept is an element in the integrative process which constitutes the self, is an aspect of the self.[2] That is why all the value-concepts together form an organismic complex: the self is just such an organism. That is why, too, a value-concept "grows in meaning": the self grows, the individual grows, in experience. And that is also why the value-concept is only suggestive, connotative. A concept that does not have a definite and constant meaning at all times cannot be anything else. On the other hand, to say that both cognitive and defined concepts always refer to something definite is to say that both types are primarily denotative.

What is the relation of the value-concept to the other

[1] See above, p. 46.

[2] The background for this paragraph is on pp. 81–82, above.

types of concepts? In order to ensure steady concretization of the value-concepts, laws are necessary, and laws involve definitions. To ensure, for example, the concretization of the concept of charity there are the laws of *pe'ah* ("corner of the field"), *leḳeṭ* ("gleaning") and *shikḥah* ("forgotten sheaves"), as we have already pointed out.[3] Each of these terms is carefully defined,[4] and so, necessarily, is the state of poverty entitling a man to take these forms of charity.[5] These definitions not only help to ensure the concretization of the concept of charity but, as statements embodying that concept, are themselves concretizations. All such halakic, legal definitions are concretizations of value-concepts, and are in that regard like haggadic statements. The difference lies in the fact that between halakic definitions there is always an explicit or else an implicit nexus.[6] The haggadic statement, however, reflects rather the nature of the value-concept itself. Between the various rabbinic value-concepts there is no implicit nexus which becomes more and more explicit; the rabbinic value-concepts are not defined; the rabbinic value-concepts are not inferred. Only halakic concretizations of value-concepts are subject to these logical procedures, not the value-concepts themselves.

Value-concepts make use only of such defined concepts as are necessary for the elucidation and application of the laws. On the other hand, any and every cognitive concept may have relations with the value-concepts, since nothing in man's sensory experience is excluded from his valuational experience.[7] Valuational experience has to do with particular situations, and sensory data are always elements of particular situations. It is this fact which determines the relation

[3] Ibid., p. 79.

[4] *Pe'ah* — Tractate Pe'ah I.2 ff.; *leḳeṭ* — ibid., IV.10 ff.; *shikḥah* — ibid., V.7 ff.

[5] Ibid., VIII. 8 f.

[6] See above, pp. 89 ff.

[7] Cf. OT (see above, p. 15, n. 2), pp. 179–80.

of value-concepts to cognitive concepts. The value-concepts have to do with particular situations, that is, with situations as particular entities, as distinct wholes. An act of charity, to keep to our example above, may consist of the giving of money or food or clothing or other necessities of life.[8] But we can name every single cognitive concept such an act may involve and yet omit — what? The significance of the act as a whole. The significance of the act as a whole is summed up in the concept of charity, a concept which has the connotation of love.[9] Cognitive concepts refer to definite elements of a situation, to factors which, because they are definite, objective, are also discrete. But these discrete cognitive elements do not yield significance. It is only as an entity, as a complete whole, that a situation or act possesses significance — a significance conveyed by the value-concepts involved in the situation. That is why a haggadic statement is always a complete entity in itself, intrinsically not connected with other haggadic statements. A haggadic statement is a concretization in speech of the value-concepts; it is a reflection of the way the value-concepts are concretized in a situation; it must therefore always be, as in a situation involving value-concepts, a complete entity in itself.

To judge by the haggadic statement, where the value-concepts "fuse" everything in the statement, the value-concepts in a situation give that situation its unitary character. That does not mean that the value-concepts act merely as unifying agents, and are external to the situation. They are as inextricable from a situation as are the cognitive elements in it. What happens, then, if a situation involves several value-concepts at once, as is usually the case? If they func-

[8] See ibid., p. 131.

[9] On love as the connotation of charity in rabbinic literature, see OT, pp. 132–33, and 303, notes 193 and 194; also The Rabbinic Concept of Israel, Hebrew Union College Annual, Vol. XIX, p. 89, note 163 and p. 95, note 190.

tion as separate concepts, how can the situation possibly have a unitary character? How can a situation be a single unit if it contains different unifying concepts? The answer is that the value-concepts in a situation, no matter how many they may be, do *not* function as separate concepts. Because of their organismic character, they not only integrate all the elements of a situation but are themselves integrated in any concrete situation. This is reflected in the haggadic statement: the value-concepts there are usually not mentioned by name but "imbedded", and are thus not to be distinguished as separate elements. The significance inherent in a situation may be many-toned but the situation does not thereby lose its unitary character.

A valuational situation is not only an embodiment, a concretization, of value-concepts. In a literal sense, there is no real demarcation between the valuational situation and the individual who experiences it. Just as the value-concepts integrate the self so they integrate the situation. The value-concepts concretized in a situation represent the projection of the personality, the fullest projection possible under any given set of circumstances. Each valuational situation bears the full stamp of the individual who is experiencing the significance of that situation — the full imprint of his personality. But the self, in its very nature, is projective, dynamic. Being a dominant aspect of the self, the value-concepts are therefore likewise projective and dynamic. That is why every value-concept has a drive toward concretization.

Different from, yet also related to, valuational significance is aesthetic significance. A work of art, like a valuational situation, is a complete entity in itself and bears the imprint of the personality which achieved it. To yield aesthetic satisfaction, any work of art — a painting, a piece of sculpture, a symphony, a lyric poem — must be a harmonious whole; and if it be such it will be charged with the personality of the artist who created it. But the unity achieved in a work of art is the result of balance, rhythm, form. It is not the result of unifying concepts as in a valuational situation or in a midrashic statement. Even in a lyric poem, where the mood or experience is conveyed in words, can we sum up that mood or experience in a concept? The idea conveyed in a lyric poem is an *ungeneralized* idea, inseparable from the figures clothing it, and inseparable, too, from the rhythm and structure of the poem. To be sure, aesthetic form and valuational content are not mutually exclusive. The Rabbis themselves employed aesthetic forms in order to overcome the particularistic, atomic character of the midrashic statements, as we saw above.[10] In that case, however, what gave the sermon its unity was the aesthetic form, not the valuational content. The same is true, in different ways, of the unity achieved in dramas, narratives, and epic poems. In these, too, structure and form are responsible for unity, not sheer valuational content.

A haggadic statement, therefore, is not art, is not poetry. Its unitary character is due not to form and rhythm but to the value-concepts it embodies. Nor is this difference between Haggadah and poetry of little moment; it spells the difference between two different kinds of experience – between the experience of valuational significance and that of aesthetic significance. A person sensitive to the one type of significance may be almost insensitive to the other. Valuational experience, however, possesses the advantage of being far more communicable than aesthetic experience.[11] Only the select few can apprehend the ungeneralized idea

[10] See above, p. 67 f.

[11] My friend, Prof. W. R. Agard, does not agree. He comments as follows: "Aesthetic communication is primarily through a response to color, sound, line, rhythm, mass. Does not such communication make more direct and clear contact than the complex intellectualization, with its many possibilities of varied connotation, of value-concepts?"

conveyed in a lyric poem. But valuational experience is expressed in concepts, and in concepts common to all members of society, learned and unlearned alike. A literature which expressed and reflected such valuational experience would be a literature which represented, and in turn could affect, the folk. If ever a literature conformed to this description, it was the Haggadah.

Despite these differences, there is a certain kinship between Haggadah and poetry. Haggadah communicates valuational significance, poetry aesthetic significance. They express or reflect different modes of one great category, the category of significance — the category of unitary experiences bearing the imprint of personality, whether these experiences be valuational situations or aesthetic insights.

Haggadah and poetry, therefore, do have one important feature in common. Neither a haggadic statement nor a poem is an integral part of a system of thought, an idea logically inferred from other ideas. On the contrary a poem, as well as a haggadic statement, is a discrete and individual entity. Not being the product of other ideas, both a poem and a haggadic statement need something to touch them off, a point of departure, a stimulus of some sort. In poetry, the stimulus is often also the subject of the poem. Stephen Spender, for example, depicts how a view "of the sea stretched under a cliff" served as both the inspiration and the subject of one of his poems. "The idea of this poem," he says, "is a vision of the sea. The faith of the poet is that if this vision is clearly stated it will be significant."[12] In this case, the poem is the vision or inspiration itself "clearly stated." But it happens, too, that an experience will only be a hint and nothing more, that the stimulus will be something quite distinct from the significant statement which does finally emerge. Spender tells us of

[12] Stephen Spender, The Making of a Poem (Partisan Review, Vol. XIII, No. 3 [1946]), p. 298.

how he was moved to write the line "A language of flesh and roses" after seeing a landscape of pits and slag-heaps. He is obliged to give us his "sequence of thought" in order to show the connection between the line and its remote stimulus.[13]

In Haggadah, the stimulus is *always* something distinct from the idea which is touched off. The stimulus to haggadic ideas or statements is usually the plain meaning of biblical texts. In the several implications of that relationship we find the answers to the questions with which we began this discussion.

A haggadic statement is not, as some have supposed, merely attached to a biblical text. Rather, it is precisely what it claims to be — an interpretation of a biblical text. The concepts imbedded in a haggadic statement are, true enough, rabbinic. But the idea developed, the particular thought expressed in a statement, was certainly in some degree stimulated by the biblical text to which the statement refers. We have pointed out above, for example, that the concept of *Ger*, proselyte, imbedded in the haggadic interpretation of Gen. 12:5, is rabbinic and not biblical.[14] But that haggadic statement begins with the query: "Were all the nations to come together in order to create a single flea, they could not inject into it a soul — and you say 'the souls, *ha-nefesh*, which they made, '*asu*?' " The entire rabbinic idea thereupon developed, the idea that one who makes a convert in a sense creates a soul, hinges on these renderings of *ha-nefesh* and '*asu*. The rabbinic idea is an interpretation of the biblical text; the biblical text has acted as stimulus to the rabbinic idea. In the haggadic statement next cited, the rôle of the biblical text is even larger. That text — Gen. 18:25 — is made to convey a rabbinic idea merely by a single, slight vowel change.[15] The

[13] Ibid., pp. 300–1.

[14] See above, p. 99.

[15] See above, ibid.

biblical texts, then, were not employed simply as pegs for rabbinic ideas that had already been thought out. The texts played a rôle in the development of the rabbinic ideas; the ideas are midrashim, interpretations of the texts.[16]

The use of the Bible as stimulus has a double implication. Obviously it implies the midrashic method, דרש. But it also implies a knowledge of, and an appreciation for, the simple meaning, פשט. In order to develop haggadic ideas, unitary ideas, a stimulus is necessary. The midrashic method of interpretation enabled the Rabbis to employ the Bible as that stimulus. Now the Bible proved an effective and steady point of departure, far more steady than the chance stimulus of a poem. It was counted on. But no stimulus of that kind can function with the inevitability of a mechanism. The knowledge of the Bible did not inevitably produce haggadic interpretations. By and large, therefore, the Rabbis could not help but be aware of the simple meaning of the text. They distinguished between פשט, the plain meaning and דרש, midrashic interpretation[17]; they set off the former against the latter[18]; they went so far as to formulate the principle that "a biblical verse never loses its literal meaning."[19] This principle says in so many words that when a text is given a haggadic interpretation, the interpreter must bear in mind, too, the literal meaning of the verse.[20] At the same time, they also looked for,

[16] A careful study of the rabbinic use of biblical texts has recently been made by Prof. I. Heinemann in his Darke Ha-Agadah. He depicts how the Rabbis interpret letters, words, sentences, and chapters or sections of the Bible (ibid., Chaps. 11, 12, 13 and 14). He, too, accounts for the characteristics of the rabbinic method by a theory of "organic thinking," though that theory differs from ours in many basic respects. But his entire treatment is very suggestive, and we shall have occasion later to refer to various aspects of it. For a summary and review of the book, see Jewish Social Studies, Vol. XIII, No. 2 (April 1951), pp. 181–4.

[17] See above, p. 99 f.

[18] Ibid.

[19] Ibid., p. 104.

[20] In a discussion given in Shabbat 63a, R. Kahana declares that he "had not

expected, haggadic interpretations. A passage of the Talmud exhibits this dual attitude with exceptional clarity. In reply to a question, R. 'Ashi tells R. Huna bar Nathan that Josh. 15:22, a verse consisting of the words "And Kinah and Dimonah and Adadah," simply lists several cities of the land of Israel. Said R. Huna: "Do I not know that it lists cities of the land of Israel? R. Gebiha of Argiza, however, has given the verse an interpretation (טעמא)." After hearing the haggadic interpretation, R. 'Ashi asks if Josh. 15:31, a verse consisting of the words "And Ziklag and Madmannah and Sansannah," can also be haggadically interpreted. "Indeed," replies R. Huna, "were R. Gebiha of Argiza here, he would have given it an interpretation." The passage does close with a haggadic interpretation of the verse, though by another authority.[21] The literal meanings are not erased for R. Huna when the verses are interpreted haggadically. But he is not only aware of the literal meanings. He expects them to serve as points of departure for haggadic interpretations.

It is because the Bible is used as a stimulus that we have the dual phenomenon of פשט and דרש. That stimulus is counted on but is not mechanical. When it does not function, the Rabbis are aware of the plain פשט. When it does function, the knowledge of the פשט is not erased. Again, when the stimulus does function the product is דרש.

Haggadic statements, midrashim, are thus interpretations of the Bible but not exegesis. Stimulated, touched off, by the Bible, these midrashim constitute a body of literature in their own right, religious teachings and lore distinct from, though connected with, the Bible. That is why they

known that a biblical verse never loses its literal meaning until just now," despite his having learned all the orders of the Mishnah by the time he was eighteen. But this very statement indicates that R. Kahana did differentiate between פשט and דרש; he knew that a verse has its literal meaning. From the discussion it would appear that he had not given preference to the literal meaning.

[21] Giṭṭin 7a.

are designated by the Rabbis as Haggadah and are a division of Torah in themselves, whilst *Miḳra*, Bible, is another division.[22] An authority apparently need only classify a statement as Haggadah, indicate that it is a דרש, to remove the objection that it contradicts a biblical account.[23]

Nevertheless, the Rabbis do not always distinguish between the simple meaning and haggadic interpretation.[24] That is altogether understandable. The truth is that the connection of biblical texts with haggadic statements is only a surface indication of the deeper relation of Haggadah to the Bible. There is an intrinsic kinship between Bible and Haggadah; how else could the biblical texts have been so steady a stimulus to haggadic interpretations? The intrinsic kinship is a conceptual one, as we shall endeavor to demonstrate at some length in a later chapter (p. 288 f.). Although in any particular instance, therefore, the biblical text acts only as a stimulus, Haggadah as a whole is conceptually akin to the Bible. Because of this general conceptual kinship, it is natural for the Rabbis occasionally to assume that a midrash represents a text's simple meaning.[25] Moreover, a biblical text may contain a word or term often

[22] See OT, p. 39 f.

[23] See R. Isaac's answer, quoting R. Joḥanan, — מקרא אני דורש — to the objection raised by R. Naḥman — Ta'anit 5b. Notice that in Malter's critical edition (editio major, New York: The American Academy for Jewish Research, 1930), p. 14 (editio minor, Philadelphia: Jewish Publication Society of America, 1928, p. 30), there is the full phrase מלתא דאגדתא, thus characterizing the statement as haggadic. R. Naḥman's objection refers to the biblical verses: Gen. 50:2 and 10.

[24] This matter has also been treated by I. Heinemann, op. cit., pp. 129 f., 153 ff. His conclusions are, on the whole, similar to ours, although his approach is different.

[25] A good example is to be found in Sifre on Deut. 1:2. R. Jose objects to a number of R. Judah's interpretations, exclaiming in each case against R. Judah's "twisting of the verses" (למה אתה מעוות עלינו את הכתובים). R. Jose offers instead what are obviously intended as simple renderings of the texts in question. With one exception, we should so classify them today. We should regard as דרש his association of Zech. 9:1 — "And in Damascus shall be His resting place" with Ps. 132:14 — "This is My resting place forever." The two verses spell for him the idea that in the glorious future Jerusalem's boundaries will reach to Damascus. But if this is a midrash rather than simple rendering, it is also in consonance

regarded by the Rabbis as a symbol. "Water", for example, is frequently a symbol for Torah,[26] and so is "bread",[27] whilst "battle" or similar terms are sometimes taken to refer to discussions of Torah.[28] For some Rabbis, especially later ones, the symbolic meaning of a word completely displaced the literal meaning in certain verses, and what was originally a haggadic interpretation becomes for them the simple meaning.[29]

We are always given the "sequence of thought" between the plain biblical text acting as stimulus and a resultant haggadic idea. This is required by the midrashic method. The peculiar rendering of a particular word or of several words of a text must have an evident, even if faint, connection with the plain meaning. Sometimes that connection consists of hardly more than a play on words. " 'And thou shalt have a paddle among thy weapons – *'azeneka* (Deut. 23:14): read not *'azeneka* but *'ozneka* (thy ears) – if a man hear a thing that is not proper, let him put his finger in his ears."[30] This verbal connection was quite sufficient, however; it was necessary only that there be a recognizable sequence. If only sequence mattered, considerations of style were certainly not uppermost, as Maimonides would have it. Inveighing equally against those who insist that haggadic homilies are explanations of the biblical texts and

with the entire content of the verse in Psalms. For R. Jose's midrash is a concretization of the concept of *Gilluy Shekinah*, and contains the thought that *Shekinah* will "rest" ("resting place") in an enlarged Jerusalem.

[26] Ta'anit 7a; ed. Malter (New York), p. 19, and the references there in note 24. (Editio minor, p. 41, and the references there in note 4).

[27] Bereshit R. XLIII.7, ed. Theodor, p. 421; Shemot R. XLVII.8; and elsewhere.

[28] Megillah 15b; Sanhedrin 42a; and elsewhere.

[29] In Ḥullin 6a, R. Ḥiyya's interpretation of Prov. 23:1–2 is taken by the Talmud to be פשטיה דקרא. The word ללחום (ibid., v. 1) was probably symbolic of Torah in a double sense, both "bread" and "battle." Notice that there is no indication that R. Ḥiyya himself regarded his interpretation as simple meaning.

[30] Ketubbot 5a–b. The lack of vowel signs in the scroll of the Pentateuch made it possible for the Rabbis to say in this and in numerous other instances, "Read not ... but ..."

against those who ridicule such homilies because they are not explanations of the texts, Maimonides asserts that the Rabbis often employ דרש as a means of poetic expression (*meliẓat ha-shir*).[31] As an example he gives the midrash just quoted, declaring that it was not intended as an explanation of the verse but that it is "a very beautiful poetic expression."[32] Has Maimonides' reference here to poetry anything in common with our own use of poetry as an analogy? Emphatically, no. We likened the biblical texts to the stimulus which touches off a poem, but there the analogy ended. When there is an evident sequence between the biblical texts and the midrashim, the stimulus has been demonstrated, and nothing more is required. Maimonides introduces a new and a gratuitous criterion when he would have that sequence judged by standards of style, of beauty, of form — of *meliẓah*. Some of the finest midrashim cannot meet this criterion. Were the midrashic method prompted by stylistic considerations, ought not conformity to ordinary grammar be a primary requisite? Yet the appealing midrash on Gen. 18:25, cited above, (and which emphasized God's mercy toward the world), is a midrash by virtue of what is an obvious grammatical fault.[33] But by the same token, grammatical fault and all, there is a sequence between text and haggadic idea.

A recently discovered work enumerates thirty-two or thirty-three rules for haggadic interpretation of Scripture.[34] They stem, very likely, from the tannaitic period and so, it

[31] Moreh Nebukim, Part III, Chap. 43.

[32] Ibid. — אבל היא מליצת שיר נאה מאד.

[33] See above, p. 99 and note 3 there. The definite article is always omitted when a noun is in the construct state; the דרש here which takes the ה of השופט as the definite article commits, therefore, a grammatical fault.

[34] See Mishnat R. Eliezer, ed. Enelow (New York: Bloch, 1933), pp. 10–11 (the rules); pp. 11–41 (the examples). The book was known and quoted in the Middle Ages, and perhaps earlier — see ibid., pp. 21 ff., and Bacher, op. cit., p. 70, notes 1–5.

would seem, do many of the examples illustrating them.[35] But the author or editor who incorporated this earlier material in his book immediately adds still another method of interpretation. "After the rules for the Agadic interpretation of the Scriptures are disposed of," as Enelow says, "our author deliberately proceeds to state that in addition to the Agadic construction of Scriptures provided by some of those rules, there is the Midrashic method."[36] Our author obviously recognized that the midrashic method is not confined by, or limited to, the thirty-two rules of interpretation. Apparently those rules, many of which are either borrowed from halakic methodology or else have to do with the elucidation of simple meaning,[37] were at most but helpful guides to haggadic interpretation. Not confined by rules, the midrashic method required only that there be a sequence between the biblical text and a haggadic idea.[38]

We can now fully account for multiple interpretation in Haggadah. Far from being sanctioned by any peculiar logic, multiple interpretations arise for a reason precisely

[35] See Mishnat R. Eliezer, English Introd., pp. 17–18.

[36] Ibid., p. 19. The reference is to p. 45 of the text.

[37] Fourteen are borrowed from halakic methodology, and five have to do with the elucidation of simple meaning — see Bacher, אגדות התנאים (Hebr. trans. by Rabinowitz), Vol. II, part 2, pp. 15–16.

Lieberman has demonstrated that a number of the rules for haggadic interpretation "were current in the literary world at that time," and that their nomenclature and formulation were largely Greek. Their origin, however, he relates back to "hoary antiquity," for thy were used by both Jews and non-Jews in the interpretation of dreams, and by non-Jews in the interpretation of oracles as well. See his Hellenism in Jewish Palestine, pp. 68 f. Such rules or devices, we can thus add, were familiar to the folk at large, and hence made the sequence of thought between biblical text and haggadic idea all the more recognizable.

[38] The text does state, it is true, that the midrashic method consists of forty-nine aspects (p. 45). But the number "forty-nine" in this connection is also found elsewhere, (see the note ibid.), and wherever it occurs the intention seems to be merely to indicate a large, indefinite number, and to emphasize the variety and multiplicity of interpretations. No attempt is made anywhere to indicate explicitly what these forty-nine aspects (טעמים or פנים) are.

the opposite. Every haggadic idea is an entity in itself, logically unconnected with other haggadic ideas. When we account for multiple interpretations in this way, as we did above,[39] we tell only half the story, however. The category of significance requires that the individual thought-entities be touched off by a stimulus of some sort. In Haggadah, biblical texts usually serve as that stimulus; hence the connection of haggadic ideas with biblical texts is something conditioned by the category to which this type of composition belongs, and is not just a matter of style or literary ornament. But this connection or sequence is the only thing required by the category, so far as the stimulus — the biblical text — is concerned. There is nothing to prevent the same text from acting as stimulus to any number of haggadic ideas; all that is required is to indicate the sequence between text and idea in each particular case. When such different sequences are presented, whether by various individuals or by a single authority, we have multiple interpretation.

III. CATEGORY OF SIGNIFICANCE — HALAKAH

Does Halakah, too, belong to the category of significance? It would be easier to answer this question had a complete and thorough study been made of the relation of the Halakic Midrashim to the Mishnah and Tosefta. The halakic literature of the mishnaic period has come down to us in two forms. There is the midrash form, wherein the halakot, laws, are given as interpretations of biblical texts, and there is the mishnah form, wherein the halakot stand by themselves and are not interpretations of biblical texts. Halakot in the midrash form are contained in the Halakic Mid-

[39] Above, p. 71 f.

rashim — the Mekilta, Sifra and Sifre; halakot in the mishnah form are the rule in the Mishnah, although the latter contains also some halakot in midrash form.[1] Now a great many halakot of the Mishnah have parallels in the Halakic Midrashim, and these parallels are thus in midrash form.[2] The question is: which form is the earlier — mishnah or midrash? If the midrash form is the earlier, then the biblical texts were in some sense the points of departure for the halakot. Opinion among modern scholars is divided, some holding the midrash form and others the mishnah form to be the earlier.[3] There can be no solution to this complicated problem, as Ginzberg has said, until a detailed comparison has been made of the Mishnah and the Halakic Midrashim.[4]

A comparison of the haggadic with the halakic approach to the biblical texts need not wait on this study, however. It can be seen that the methods of halakic interpretation of texts differ widely from those employed in haggadic interpretation. Not only do the methods of interpretation differ, but the basic approach to the texts differs as well.

In Haggadah, it is sufficient if a sequence is established between the biblical text and a haggadic idea, any kind of sequence. We must be made aware of how the text suggests the haggadic idea, and that is all that is required. If rules of interpretation were in any wise employed, it was only as helpful guides. But in Halakah, the rules of interpretation were much more than that, and were introduced at a very

[1] On the Mishnah and Tosefta, see Strack, op. cit., Chaps. III, IV, and VII; on the Halakic Midrashim, ibid., Chap. XVI.

[2] See the parallels from the first five chapters of the Mekilta — L. Ginzberg, על היחס שבין המשנה והמכילתא in קבץ מדעי לזכר משה שור (New York, 1945) , pp. 57–95; also the parallels in C. Tchernowitz, תולדות ההלכה, I (New York, 1934) , pp. 51–53, 56–58.

[3] See the summary of these opinions in Tchernowitz, op. cit., pp. 37–49.

[4] Ginzberg, op. cit., p. 57. In this article, he begins the publication of such a detailed comparison.

early period. A large number of halakot were derived from the Bible by the application of the Thirteen *Middot* of R. Ishmael, rules of interpretation based on those formulated by Hillel, but probably going back beyond him. From very early times, therefore, inference, analogy and literary considerations were factors in the derivation of halakot. Even the methods of R. 'Aḳiba, with far less emphasis on logical procedure than those of R. Ishmael, require more than mere sequence.[5]

The entire approach to the biblical text is different in Halakah from what it is in Haggadah. In Haggadah, דרש is set off against פשט, and this demarcation is kept to, by and large. Such a demarcation is not possible in Halakah. Biblical texts may contain implications that have to do not only with the law in question but that are in the nature of general principles. Yet these principles can only be drawn forth by means of inference or analogy; they are not explicitly given in the biblical text itself. The biblical law regarding the paschal lamb, for example, states that "they shall take to themselves every man a lamb, according to their fathers' houses, a lamb for a household" (Exod. 12:3). This law, enjoining that "every man" take a lamb, is modified in the same verse by "according to their fathers' houses, a lamb for a household," since a household contains a number of other persons besides the one who does the taking or the buying. The injunction is upon "every man," yet it is not necessary for each to take or buy a lamb for himself; hence the Rabbis deduce the principle that a man's agent is like a man himself.[6] This far-reaching principle of agency, of prime importance to the urban, commercial centers of rab-

[5] On the references to the hermeneutic rules, see above, p. 91, note 4. On the norms of interpretation associated with Hillel and with R. Ishmael, see now S. Lieberman, op. cit., pp. 53 ff. Lieberman here shows that there is a decided kinship between these norms and the methods of the rhetors in Alexandria, and even in the terminology.

[6] Mekilta, I, p. 25; comp. ibid., p. 40. SEE NOTES, P. 370.

binic times, is certainly not explicitly given in literal terms in the biblical law. Yet can we say that it is altogether דרש?

We have no parallel in Halakah to the dichotomy of פשט and דרש. It is true that the Rabbis differentiate among halakic interpretations. Some halakot they describe as ordained by the Rabbis, and they designate a verse used in "deriving" such a non-biblical law as *'asmakta,* "support."[7] (This is the term employed in the Babylonian Talmud; the same idea is conveyed in tannaitic literature by a Hebraic term — זכר לדבר.[8]) So far as the sheer approach to the biblical texts is concerned, however, there is no marked difference between those halakic interpretations designated *'asmakta* and those not so designated. This becomes evident as soon as we attempt to classify halakic interpretations on the basis of their approach to biblical texts. A study of this kind has been made by Michael Guttmann, and his three major classifications — *derashot* explanatory of the text, *derashot* eliciting halakic principles, and "symbolic" *derashot* — hold, in his analysis, for the one group as for the other.[9] No doubt other ways of classification are also possible, and here and there objection may be raised in regard to details;[10] nevertheless, his study as a whole, broad in scope and bold in method, is highly indicative. There is no basic difference in method between interpretations labeled *'asmakta* and other halakic interpretations.

[7] Yoma 74a; Ḥagigah 4a; and elsewhere. Verses supporting הלכה למשה מסיני are also designated as *'asmakta* — see Sukkah 6a. (The parallel in Berakot 41b has an incorrect reading — see Rabbinovicz, Diḳduḳe Soferim a. l.)

[8] See Bacher, Terminologie, Hebr. trans. ערכי מדרש, p. 152, s. v. אסמכתא and p. 38, note 11, end.

[9] Michael Guttmann, מפתח התלמוד, Vol. III, Part I (Breslau, 1924), supplement, אסמכתא, pp. 1–48.

[10] See, for example, Tchernowitz's objection (op. cit., p. 66, note) to Guttmann's taking . . . סמכו to refer to an *'asmakta.* We have here, by the way, another instance in rabbinic terminology of how careful we must be before assuming that verb-forms of a root have the same sense as the nominative. Compare the remarks on "the chosen people", above, pp. 55–57.

We reach a similar conclusion when we consider halakic interpretations designated as implications "from the Torah." In several such instances, there are Rabbis to whom the particular interpretations are not acceptable, and who regard them as invalid. These interpretations are, therefore, no different in kind from other disputed halakic interpretations. For example, a biblical law prohibits the use of the new products of the field before the Omer-offering, and the law concludes with the statement: "It is a statute for ever throughout your generations in all your dwelling-places" (Lev. 23:14). The Mishnah takes this law to apply "everywhere," that is, not only to the land of Israel, and designates the wide application of the law as being "from the Torah."[11] The Mishnah here sides with R. Eliezer,[12] who alone gives this wide interpretation to the phrase "in all your dwelling-places."[13] His colleagues disagree with him[14]; for them, his interpretation does not represent an implication of the Torah. Another example is the interpretation of Deut. 6:7 — "And thou shalt talk of them . . . when thou liest down and when thou risest up." From the Mishnah onward, that verse was taken as the warrant for the recital of the *Shema'*,[15] and the recital to be thus enjoined by the Bible.[16] A view in the Talmud, however, has it that the recital was ordained by the Rabbis, and that "And thou shalt talk of them . . ." refers to "words of the Torah," that is, to general Study of Torah.[17]

It would seem, therefore, that the textual methods and approach are quite the same, whether the halakic inter-

[11] 'Orlah III.9.

[12] Ḳiddushin I.9. See Bertinoro a. l.

[13] Yer. 'Orlah III.8 (9), 63b.

[14] Ibid.; cf. Ḳiddushin 37a.

[15] The *Shema'* consists of Deut. 6:4–9; ibid., 11:13–21; and Num. 15:37–41 — see Berakot II.2.

[16] See the discussion in Tosafot to Soṭah 32b, s. v. ורבי.

[17] Berakot 21a.

pretation be designated *'asmakta* or as an implication "from the Torah". This is again reflected in the discussions pertaining to this matter in the Middle Ages. Maimonides states that laws not found in the Bible but derived by the Rabbis by means of any of the Thirteen *Middot* are to be regarded as biblical only if the Rabbis themselves explicitly declare or explain them to be so.[18] Naḥmanides takes issue with this view of Maimonides. He brings proof to the contrary, namely, that all matters derived by means of the Thirteen *Middot* are to be regarded as biblical unless the Rabbis explicitly declare a "derivation" to be an *'asmakta.*[19] These great authorities could differ so radically only because there is no way to distinguish, so far as interpretation of text goes, between an implication "from the Torah" and an *'asmakta.*

Halakic interpretation is, then, altogether different from haggadic interpretation. In haggadic interpretation the biblical texts serve as a spring-board merely, as a stimulus, whereas halakic interpretation of Scripture employs logical procedures expressed in hermeneutic rules. The very dichotomy of פשט and דרש, so basic in Haggadah, does not hold for Halakah. A general principle may be inherent in a specific biblical law, even if it is not explicitly stated there but only drawn forth by inference or analogy. Nor is there a halakic parallel to פשט and דרש in the fact that some laws are designated as "from the Torah" and others as *'asmakta.* The same methods of textual interpretation are employed in order to "support" laws labeled *'asmakta* as to "derive" laws described as "from the Torah."

Yet there are halakic interpretations that do exhibit the characteristics of haggadic interpretation. Thus there are some halakic interpretations that are related to biblical texts by nothing more than bare sequence, and hence that

[18] Maimonides, ספר המצוות, שורש שני.

[19] Naḥmanides' comments, ibid.

are quite analogous to haggadic דרש. It is on that very ground, in fact, that objection to such interpretations is voiced at times. At R. Eliezer's interpretation of Lev. 13:47, his colleague R. Ishmael exclaimed: "Thou sayest to the verse, 'Keep silent until I shall interpret (thee)!'" And the root of the verb "I shall interpret," be it noted, is דרש.[20] When, in a passage cited above, R. 'Aḳiba's rendering of Deut. 20:8 is designated כמשמעו, we must infer that R. Jose's interpretation of that verse is regarded as not כמשמעו.[21]

But ordinarily halakic interpretations that exhibit the characteristics of haggadic interpretation do so in a form greatly modified. Sometimes a law in its general aspect, as Guttmann points out, is implied in a text of the Bible, but not the details of that law. These details, such as the number and order of *teru'ot and teḳi'ot* on Rosh Ha-Shanah, or the four benedictions in the grace after meals, are connected with the texts by no more than the barest sequence.[22] Many derivations of this type are, however, only midrashic support for laws previously established. When the Rabbis ask as to why there should be exactly eighteen benedictions in the daily '*Amidah*, different reasons are given, all of them warrants from Scripture and all of them characterized by mere sequence.[23] Obviously, the eighteen benedictions had long ago been established; the Rabbis are here but seeking biblical support for that number.[24]

[20] Sifra to Lev. 13:47 — עד שאדרוש. Malbim's explanatory comment a. l. is: "Thou sayest to the verse that it keep silent until thou shalt interpret according to thy wish."

[21] See above, p. 100.

[22] See Guttmann, op. cit., supplement, pp. 25–6, and the references there. Several such derivations are to be found in Sanhedrin 3b–4b.

[23] Yer. Berakot IV.3, 7d. The same query is raised in regard to the number of benedictions on other occasions, and the same type of answer is given — ibid.

[24] Ginzberg remarks that the Rabbis deliberately searched in Scripture until they found support of one kind or another for the number and order of the benedictions — Commentary, III, p. 248.

We meet also with halakot that are influenced by haggadot. For example, a certain rite prescribed for fast-days during a drought is regarded by the Rabbis as a symbol. Two authorities disagree as to the specific meaning of the symbol; and the difference in these haggadic ideas spells also a difference in the halakah concerning the rite.[25] The haggadic ideas, we may add, are connected with a biblical text by mere sequence. But, again, very often halakot that are associated with haggadot have not actually been influenced by the latter. The haggadot may be only either interpretations of, or else support for, the halakot. Why is a *shofar* made of a cow's horn not a proper *shofar*? A sound halakic reason is given in the Mishnah.[26] But the Midrash supplies another reason, a haggadic interpretation of the law as manifestly already known and practiced.[27] R. Joshua B. Levi's statement which associates the patriarchs with the morning, afternoon and evening prayers[28] is an instance of a haggadic support for a halakah. The wording of this statement in the original source, to which Ginzberg has called attention, indicates that R. Joshua b. Levi himself regarded the haggadah here as only a support for the halakah. In the original source — the Yerushalmi — the words מאבות למדום imply that those who ordained the prayers "learned" to do so from the examples provided by the patriarchs, and not that the patriarchs themselves ordained the prayers.[29] The examples provided by the patriarchs are adduced, as in Haggadah generally, by mere sequence.

It is thus in a modified form that Halakah employs the type of interpretation characteristic of Haggadah. However tenuous the sequence between a biblical text and a hag-

[25] Yer. Ta'anit II.1, 65a, cited by Guttmann, op. cit., p. 28.

[26] Rosh Ha-Shanah III.2.

[27] Leviticus R. XXVII.3.

[28] Yer. Berakot IV.1, 7a. The parallels are given by Theodor, op. cit., p. 778.

[29] Ginzberg, op. cit., III, pp. 24–7. R. Joshua b. Levi's statement is, moreover, later than the one which attributes the prayers to Daniel and also found in Yer. Berakot IV.1, 7a — Ginzberg, op. cit., III, p. 25.

gadic idea, the text actually serves as a stimulus to the idea. This is rather seldom true when Halakah employs that method of interpretation, whether directly or through the medium of a haggadah. In most cases, a tenuous connection between a biblical text and a halakah is a fairly good indication that the halakah in question existed before it was connected with the biblical text in that fashion.[30] Halakah occasionally employs the method of haggadic interpretation, but in a manner greatly modified.

Halakah also employs the principle of multiple interpretation; in fact, the principle itself is stated in a halakic context.[31] Halakah presents multiple interpretation of texts when the Rabbis differ on the halakic interpretation of a verse, as they often do. We noticed, for example, that different authorities give different halakic interpretations to Lev. 23:14 and to Deut. 6:7.[32] But this principle, too, is employed by Halakah in a modified manner as compared with its use in Haggadah. In Halakah, a text cannot bear more than one halakic interpretation for the same authority,[33] whereas there is no such limit to haggadic interpretation.

The characteristics of haggadic interpretation, we must remember, are not just peculiarities of style. They are conditioned by the category of significance. Greatly modified,

[30] Scholars sometimes assume that a halakah is based on a haggadah because they have not read the passage correctly. Guttmann so understands a passage in Shabbat 119b which has to do with the interpretation of Gen. 2:1 (op. cit., p. 27). Guttmann's text was faulty. As can be seen from the מסורת הש"ס a. l., the authorities for this particular halakah preceded by several generations the authority for the haggadah, and the halakah is, therefore, older than the haggadah in this instance. Similarly, some medieval scholars have assumed that Ps. 103:3, as interpreted in Yer. Berakot II.3, 4c, conveys the idea that illness purifies the body of sin, and that a certain procedure of R. Yanai's recorded there is based on this haggadic idea — see Ginzberg, Commentary, I, p. 259. But Ginzberg has demonstrated that this entire assumption is erroneous — ibid., p. 265 f. In the light of his explanation, there is no haggadic element in the passage.

[31] Sanhedrin 34a.

[32] Above, p. 125.

[33] See, for example, Sukkah 9a. SEE NOTES, P. 370.

these characteristics are found, frequently enough, in halakic interpretation. If these characteristics are to an extent also found in halakic interpretation, Halakah is certainly at least affected by the category of significance.

This is indeed what we might have expected. Halakot, like haggadot, are concretizations of the value-concepts, and must therefore in one way or another reflect the organismic character of the value-concepts. Halakah reflects that character despite the fact that there is an implicit nexus between the laws, a nexus that becomes more and more explicit. We saw above how Halakah leaves room not only for diversity of opinion, a prime quality of the organismic complex, but for divergence in practice.[34] The characteristics of haggadic interpretation likewise derive from the organismic nature of the value-concepts. By virtue of the manner in which the value-concepts function, each haggadic idea is an independent entity; each haggadic idea therefore has need of a stimulus, and it is thus that the characteristics of haggadic interpretation are called into play. We cannot, of course, expect that Halakah, with its laws connected by an inherent nexus, should exhibit to the full the characteristics of haggadic interpretation; it reflects the organismic nature of the value-concepts if it exhibits some of the characteristics even in modified form. Examples wherein Halakah reflects most clearly the nature of the value-concepts have to do not with halakic discussion or interpretation but with actual practice, and especially with the liturgy. In the latter we often have that interweaving of concepts which is the chief characteristic of the organic complex. The recital, for instance, of the first verse of the *Shema'*, Deut. 6:4, involves at one and the same time the concepts of *Malkut Shamayim*, Torah and *Miẓwot*.[35]

[34] Above, pp. 93–95.

[35] The recital of "Hear, O Israel, the Lord is our God, the Lord is One" (Deut. 6:4) is the affirmation of *Malkut Shamayim* — see TE (above, p. 15, n. 2), p. 60. This is emphasized by an insertion the Rabbis made between Deut. 6:4 and ibid.,

IV. INDETERMINACY OF BELIEF

The category of significance has to do with the element of indeterminacy in thought and action. We described that category as "the category of unitary experiences bearing the imprint of personality."[1] But what makes for that "imprint of personality?" The value-concepts which, in contrast to both the cognitive and the defined concepts, are not objective or definite. Neither are they vague, for every concept has its own distinctive character. They are indeterminate concepts, and they cease to be indeterminate only when concretized in specific situations or in ideas or in laws. A value-concept waits, as it were, to be given different determinate meanings by different personalities or by the same person on different occasions. Thus the indeterminacy of the value-concepts permits them to be the primary channels for the expression of the self. More correctly, their indeterminacy makes it possible for them to cultivate and express the *differentia* of each human personality.

v. 5, the insertion reading: ברוך שם כבוד מלכותו לעולם ועד. It is of course inserted only in the liturgy, not in the text of the Bible. See Baer, op. cit., p. 82. So habitually was this verse taken as a declaration of *Malkut Shamayim* that it is the last verse in the *Malkuyyot* of the *'Amidah* for Rosh Ha-Shanah even though it does not contain any form of the root *mlk*, and thus the ten required "sovereignty" verses are completed. The martyrdom of R. 'Aḳiba, connected with this declaration, is given richer background by Lieberman. The hour for the recital of the *Shema'* had arrived just before his execution which was to have been by the sword; the declaration by 'Aḳiba of *Malkut Shamayim*, a declaration prohibited by decree because of its negation of emperor-worship, caused the method of execution to be changed. "Iron combs were applied to prevent R. 'Aḳiba from his recitation." See Lieberman, The Martyrs of Caesarea, Annuaire de L'Institut de Philologie, VII (New York: Université Libre de Bruxelles, 1939–44), p. 427.

The very term *Ḳeri'at Shema'* indicates that it is not prayer but Torah. The term קרא refers to the study or recital of a passage from the Bible — see OT, p. 39. This, too, is emphasized by the section which leads up to the declaration.

The declaration of the *Shema'* is a *Miẓwah* enjoined, according to the Rabbis, by Deut. 6:7 — see above, p. 125.

[1] Above, p. 113.

Since Haggadah completely reflects the nature of the value-concepts, it will possess certain features characterized by indeterminacy. We depicted one such feature when we analyzed the relation of haggadic interpretation – דרש – to its stimulus in the simple meaning of any biblical text – the פשט. Haggadic interpretation of any particular biblical verse is indeterminate: we speak of *the* פשט but of *a* דרש. In other words, when a biblical verse is given a haggadic interpretation, the element of indeterminacy is still present. Other interpretations are always possible, multiple interpretations, so that there is no limit upon the number that even a single individual may offer. But indeterminacy marks not merely the *number* of interpretations. It is inherent in the very process of haggadic interpretation itself – in the fact that a haggadic interpretation is no more than touched off by a biblical text. A haggadic interpretation is not logically related to the text which it interprets: the text has been a non-determining stimulus. Being non-determining, the text serves afresh as a new stimulus every time it is interpreted haggadically, and its precise effect as a stimulus may therefore be different in every instance. This is to say that, although a single biblical text may touch off many haggadic interpretations, each haggadic interpretation may be different from the others so generated. And if each haggadic interpretation may be different from the others, each haggadic interpretation is obviously independent of the others.

The element of indeterminacy thus informs the category of significance as a whole. Through the indeterminate value-concepts it is a factor in "the imprint of personality," and through the non-determining stimulus it is a factor in the rise of "unitary experiences," or unitary entities, bearing that imprint.

But there is more to the category of significance than the features we have so far depicted. These features stand out more boldly than others, and hence make us aware of the category. They emerge as we analyze the process of interpretation: they are revealed in the course of analyzing the method of interpretation employed by the teachers of the folk. These features — stimulus, multiple interpretation, unitary entities bearing the imprint of personality — all relate to the creative aspects of Haggadah. What of the plain folk who did not create but who were nevertheless affected and molded by Haggadah? To be molded by Haggadah, they had to have some kind of receptive attitude toward it. It is in this receptive attitude, an attitude of mind, that we discern the most subtle feature of the category of significance. A receptive attitude toward Haggadah implies belief in the haggadic statements, but belief of a peculiar kind. The element of indeterminacy which informs the category of significance is also a factor in the attitude of mind toward the products of that category. What we have is indeterminate belief which, on occasion, can harden and become determinate. Nor is this attitude confined to the common people, for it is not simply *another* feature of the category of significance. The category of significance is, at bottom, an attitude of mind, and everyone — teachers and folk alike — shares in that attitude. Indeterminacy of belief is that basic aspect of the category of significance experienced both by the Rabbis and the folk. In that regard, it is like the value-concepts themselves; indeed, it is the attitude of mind that is the climate, so to speak, in which haggadic concretizations of the value-concepts can grow. More literally, it is the attitude of mind of the teacher when he brings forth his haggadic concretizations, and it is also the attitude of the folk when they absorb these teachings.

This indeterminacy of belief is made evident under special circumstances. Thus it may become evident when haggadic interpretations contradict, or disagree with, biblical statements. When R. Isaac was asked by a colleague for a haggadic teaching, he said, quoting R. Joḥanan, "Jacob our father did not die." The colleague objected: "Was it for naught that the wailers wailed, and the embalmers embalmed, and the buriers buried?" (These things are mentioned in the biblical account).[2] Whereupon R. Isaac replied: "I am interpreting a biblical verse. For it says, 'Therefore fear thou not, O Jacob my servant, saith the Lord; neither be dismayed, O Israel; for, lo, I will save thee from afar, and thy seed from the land of their captivity; and Jacob shall again be quiet and at ease, and none shall make him afraid' (Jer. 30:10) – he (i. e., Jacob) is likened (here) to his seed: just as his seed is among the living so is he among the living."[3] Now R. Isaac has in no wise attempted to harmonize the haggadic statement with the biblical account[4]; his reply merely contains the ground for that statement. And yet, despite valid objections that are apparently acknowledged, he persists in his idea. Such persistence surely implies a belief of some kind, but a belief which, in the face of the patent contradictions, is just as surely not unqualified.

The Rabbis sometimes seem to ignore an important segment of a biblical narrative, replacing it with ideas of their own. In the Bible, the defeat at Ai is laid to Israel's sin. "Israel hath sinned . . . they have even taken of the devoted thing; and have also stolen, and dissembled also, and they have even put it among their own stuff" (Josh. 7:11). The Rabbis start with the introductory verse immediately preceding – "And the Lord said unto Joshua: 'Get thee up;

[2] Wailing for Jacob — Gen. 50:10; the embalming of Jacob — ibid., v. 2; the burial of Jacob — ibid., v. 13.

[3] Ta'anit 5b; Malter, ed. major, p. 14; ed. minor, p. 30. See the note on this passage above, p. 117, note 23.

[4] Pseudo-Rashi's attempt at harmonization — a. l., s. v. מקרא — is wholly gratuitous. On the authorship of this commentary, see I. H. Weiss, Dor Dor We-Doreshaw (4th ed., Wilna: Romm, 1904), IV, p. 292 f.

wherefore, now, art thou fallen upon thy face?' " (*ibid.*, v. 10) – and then ignore the subsequent verse, which we quoted, and the entire incident of Achan. They attribute Israel's defeat and the death of "thirty-six righteous men" not to Israel's sin but to something Joshua failed to do. In accordance with Deut. 3:28, it was necessary that Joshua "go over *before* this people," in other words, that he lead them in battle. "But thou," said God according to the Rabbis, "didst send them forth and thou wentest *after* them."[5] The Rabbis have diverged here from the biblical narrative deliberately, a divergence all the more emphatic because they, too, begin with the very verse which introduces the biblical explanation of Israel's defeat. Does the rabbinic explanation represent a clear, hard-and-fast belief? Not in the face of the totally different biblical explanation, from which the Rabbis have consciously diverged. Yet the rabbinic explanation centers on an ideal of noble leadership which Joshua was certainly expected to exemplify, and the explanation was therefore taken with the utmost seriousness. Again, what we have is a belief, but a belief which is not unqualified.

This kind of belief – qualified or modified belief – is indeterminate belief. For it can harden and become determinate not only in affirmation but also in negation. We have some instances of haggadic ideas that are affirmed with vigor, and we have other instances when a haggadic idea is advanced and then, as it were, erased. What kind of belief is this that can go to either extreme? Only the kind of belief that is ordinarily indeterminate.

Vigorous affirmations introduce sometimes a rabbinic statement. "I call heaven and earth to testify for me: whether Gentile or Israelite, whether man or woman,

[5] Sifre to Deut. 3:28. For the rabbinic play on the words *ḳum lak* in Josh. 7:10, see Rashi on Deut. 3:28. A somewhat similar play on these words is to be found in Sanhed. 44a, but the interpretations there do not ignore the incident of Achan.

whether male-slave or female-slave, according to the deed done, thus does the Holy Spirit rest upon him!"[6] A whole group of haggadic interpretations is introduced by affirmations: "He who says that Reuben sinned is in error . . . He who says that the sons of Eli sinned is in error . . . He who says that the sons of Samuel sinned is in error . . . He who says that David sinned is in error . . . He who says that Solomon sinned is in error . . ." In each instance, haggadic interpretation explains away the sin committed according to the biblical account; though it is only fair to add that these interpretations do not represent a consensus, and that they do not set up the men as perfect and without sin.[7] We do not mean to say that a belief which is determinate must always be introduced by an affirmation. Many ideas, especially moral precepts, were implicitly accepted and had no need of affirmation. Similar in style to the statement concerning Gentiles and Israelites, for example, and containing the same phrases, is another statement telling of the recompense for good deeds; and this statement is not preceded by an affirmation.[8]

R. Joḥanan is said to have insisted on unquestioning belief on one occasion. The story is told that a student, listening to a haggadic interpretation by R. Joḥanan, scoffed at it as being highly extravagant and impossible. Some time later on a sea voyage, the student saw angels carving out precious stones of huge size which, they said, were destined for the gates of Jerusalem. This confirmed the haggadah he had scoffed at; and so when he returned and once more heard the master lecture, he voiced his approval and added, "What thou has said I saw taking place." Thereupon R. Joḥanan said to him: "Thou ruffian! Hadst thou not seen, thou wouldst not have believed? Thou scoffest at the words of the *Ḥakamim*." And at a glance

[6] See TE, p. 168.
[7] Shabbat 55b–56b.
[8] See TE, p. 167.

from the master, the student became "a heap of bones."[9] This story is apocryphal, of course, but it is illuminating nevertheless. It is told in a context which warns against disrespect of the Rabbis, and hence it no doubt exaggerates the demand for unquestioning belief in their statements. Accustomed to divergency in interpretation,[10] and even to having their views flatly contradicted by their colleagues,[11] they could not always have insisted that their hearers believe implicitly in every statement they uttered. Moreover, because the prevailing attitude was that of indeterminate belief, outright disbelief was probably not often voiced. This story echoes those infrequent occasions when disbelief was apparent, together with irreverence. It was then natural for the teacher to affirm and demand belief.

In one of the sources in which this story occurs, and but a few pages beyond it, is an instance of haggadot that were advanced and then, as it were, erased. A mishnah names three wicked kings who "have no portion in the World to Come."[12] The Talmud asks why Ahaz, who was so wicked, was not also named with them; and several answers are given, among them two interpretations of Is. 7:3, both of them asserting, in different ways, that Ahaz was ashamed before Isaiah. In the discussion which ensues regarding still another wicked king, however, a general principle is brought forward, a principle involving the concept of the merit of the children. Whereupon the case of Ahaz is reverted to, and the earlier haggadot are dismissed with the statement: "Now that you have come to this (meaning, now that we have this principle), Ahaz also was not named because of (regard for) the honor of (his son) Hezekiah."[13]

[9] Sanhedrin 100a; Baba Batra 75a.

[10] See above, pp. 71–74.

[11] See above, pp. 74–75. "Why do you twist for us the verses?" — see above, p. 117, note 25.

[12] Sanhedrin 90a.

[13] Ibid., 104a. It is also possible that "honor" here is used as a euphemism for the opposite.

This is not just another view, Rashi tells us, but an erasure of the earlier haggadot. He elucidates the talmudic statement by the amplifying comment: "Do not say that (Ahaz) hung his head in shame, but they did not name him because of (regard for) the honor of Hezekiah."[14] Thus, haggadot could actually be taught, biblical texts be supplied with interpretations — and, after a while, teachings and interpretations all be brushed aside merely for a later and more favored idea. What kind of belief is this that can be surrendered so casually, that can accept ideas and stories and then dismiss them so lightly? A belief of this kind can only be an indeterminate belief. Indeterminate belief may become determinate not only in affirmation but also, as in this case, in negation.

Indeterminacy of belief is doubtless a difficult thing for the modern mind to comprehend. It does not seem to be within our ken or within the range of our experience. Indeterminacy of belief is the only climate, as we have said, in which haggadic concretization of value-concepts can freely grow; and the fact that little "Haggadah" clusters around our modern democratic value-concepts testifies to the absence of that climate today. Indeed, the weakness of our modern value-concepts is due as much to this lack of a proper intellectual climate as to the lack of that other factor already mentioned.[15] With both factors absent, the development of anything comparable to the Haggadah is almost impossible today; the development, that is, of a supplementary form of communication that would make our modern value-concepts vivid.[16] To be sure, the modern mind is quite sensitive to another mode of the category of significance, — to poetry and to art in general. But Hagga-

[14] Rashi, a. l.

[15] Above, p. 88 f., and p. 89, note 17 — the interaction between the folk and its spiritual leaders.

[16] See ibid., p. 84.

dah is not poetry, and nothing so clearly demonstrates this as the matter of indeterminacy of belief. Indeterminate belief is bound, on some occasions, to become determinate either in affirmation or in negation. This phenomenon does not occur at all in respect to poetry. "Thou ruffian! . . . thou wouldst not have believed" are words appropriate enough when ascribed to a R. Joḥanan, but not when put into the mouth of a modern poet. Nor is indeterminacy of belief to be associated with "figurative interpretation," a device used down to the present day by religionists. The "figures" are supposed to direct us to the hidden meaning contained in those "figures." Not for naught are these hidden meanings so encased and protected: they represent truths regarded as divine and eternal, and the belief demanded for them is anything but indeterminate.

It was indeterminacy of belief that enabled Haggadah to be so colorful in content. In a later, philosophic age, Naḥmanides described Haggadah as containing many legends, and he maintained that such legends need not be believed.[17] Had they not been believed at all, however, they would never have been told. These legends are usually connected with biblical texts, and hence were presented as interpretations of Scripture, not simply as "serious fiction." But it is also true that ordinarily the Rabbis did not demand belief in these legends and interpretations. Indeterminate belief was sufficient, belief that did not crystallize ordinarily into positive affirmation. This indeterminate belief in the legends allows for the inclusion of material which was at once instructive and colorful. The legends were instructive – more than that, in fact, – because the Rabbis fashioned them into concretizations of the value-concepts. They are colorful, because the Rabbis, besides exercising their own

[17] See S. Lieberman (שקיעין (ירושלים, תרצ״ט, pp. 81–3. This discussion summarizes the views of other medieval authorities, as well as that of Naḥmanides. All of these views more or less concur.

ingenuity, drew on current folktales and even on ancient traditions. For example, as told by the Rabbis, each of the ten plagues visited on the Egyptians becomes a little story in itself which concretizes "measure for measure," a subconcept of God's justice.[18] With genuine art, and ingeniously utilizing both the sound and content of a phrase in Is. 28:10, the Rabbis have the frogs themselves pronounce the reason for descending on Egypt in such swarms. The Egyptians took delight in torturing these creatures, and so the frogs croaked out: "*Ḳaw laḳaw, ḳaw laḳaw*" (measure for measure, measure for measure).[19] A famous example of a folktale is the story of the woman and her seven sons which is found in the Talmud[20] and in many other sources.[21] In all its various versions, this story is a concretization of the concept of *Ḳiddush Ha-Shem*, although in some of the longer versions other concepts are concretized as well.[22] As to legends echoing pre-Israelitic sources, there is the one which says that God has sport with Leviathan, a symbol for Satan.[23] According to Ginzberg, this is reminiscent of the Babylonian myth of Marduk's struggle with Tiamat.[24] These and many other similar stories could be told by the Rabbis — "taught" is the better word — only because their attitude toward them, and their hearers' as well, was that of indeterminate belief.[25]

[18] See TE, pp. 189–90.

[19] Seder Eliahu, p. 41.

[20] Giṭṭin 57b.

[21] See TE, p. 47, notes 69 and 70.

[22] See, for example, ibid., pp. 174–5. This part of the story concretizes God's justice.

[23] 'Abodah Zarah 3b.

[24] See OT, p. 297, note 101. For other vestiges of Babylonian myths in rabbinic literature, see Cassuto, מנח עד אברהם (Jerusalem: Hebrew University Press, 1949), p. 14.

[25] In TE, pp. 76–78, we discussed a number of passages in which qualities of personality — consciousness, emotion and deliberate action — are ascribed to natural phenomena. We expressed ourselves there as being baffled by these

Vividness in concretization is nothing less than the breath of life to the value-concepts. And the more abstract a value-concept is, the greater is the need for vividness in haggadic concretization. The concepts of God's love and God's justice are among the most abstract of all. For them to be experienced in situations, and to be motive-forces for action, a superior sensitivity is required, a sensitivity beyond that required by such concepts as charity or *Mizwot*, or *Derek Erez*, or the study of Torah, all of which act as springs of direct and immediate action. Vividness in haggadic concretization of God's love and God's justice made men also sensitive to these more abstract concepts; and it was indeterminacy of belief that rendered vivid concretizations of that kind possible. The Rabbis trained the folk by means of stories in which God's love and justice were organismically interrelated with concepts like that of charity, deeds of loving-kindness and others so often concretized in day-to-day living. The stories are, therefore, thoroughly and completely anthropomorphic, and they tell of actions done by God and emotions felt by Him in terms entirely human. "He acts as best man at the wedding of Adam and Eve; he mourns over the world like a father over the death of his son when the sins of ten generations make its destruction by the deluge imminent; he visits Abraham on his sickbed; he condoles with Isaac after the death of Abraham; he 'himself in his glory' is occupied in doing the last honors to Moses, who would otherwise have remained unburied, as no man knew his grave; he teaches Torah to Israel, and to this very day he keeps school in heaven for those who died in their infancy; he prays himself, and teaches Israel how

stories and concluded that "the category into which we might place these homilies on nature eludes the modern student." We now recognize that these stories belong to the category of significance, and could be taught by the Rabbis because the attitude toward such nature-anthropomorphisms was that of indeterminate belief, as well as because these stories and episodes are, as we pointed out in TE, concretizations of value-concepts. Cf. ibid., pp. 83–88.

to pray; he argues with Abraham the case of Sodom and Gomorrah not only on equal terms, but tells him, If thou thinkest I acted unworthily, teach me and I will do so."[26] Stories and episodes like these were obviously not crystallized beliefs, but neither were they told with tongue in cheek. Generated in an attitude of indeterminacy of belief, they were received with the same attitude. And they had their effect, as the Rabbis rightly felt. "Wouldst thou come to know Him who spake and the world came to be, then study Haggadah," runs an early rabbinic saying, "for by that means thou dost come to know the Holy One blessed be He and to cleave to His ways."[27]

We have asserted that Haggadah reflects the way in which the value-concepts were concretized in actual life. Our discussion here of indeterminacy of belief modifies that assertion. All the concretizations of the value-concepts, whether in actual experience or in Haggadah, are in the category of significance. The indeterminate value-concepts become determinate in both kinds of concretization,—whether in a living act or event, or in Haggadah. But in Haggadah, the element of indeterminacy still persists, though in another form. There is a difference, for instance, between an actual experience of visiting a sick person, an experience in which the concept of deeds of loving-kindness is concretized, and a haggadic concretization of that concept which tells of God having visited Abraham when he was sick. The haggadah, unlike the actual experience, demands belief of some kind. That kind of belief is itself a reflection of the nature of the value-concepts: it is ordinarily indeterminate belief.

[26] S. Schechter, Some Aspects of Rabbinic Theology, p. 37, and the references there.

[27] Sifre to Deut. 11:22, end.

V. CONCEPTS OF "NATURAL ORDER"

The category of significance is a highly subjective category. It is "the category of unitary experiences bearing the imprint of personality." The *differentia* of each human personality are expressed in that category, and even the changing moods of an individual. Nevertheless, the existence of this subjective category in no wise weakens the capacity to observe and to react to the objective character of the external, physical world.

Paradoxically, the very existence of value-concepts implies that there is a grasp of the objective character of the physical world. A language that contains purely valuational terms, words not used as symbols for objects or for physical qualities and relationships, will necessarily also contain other words that are used as such symbols. Like the valuational terms, these symbols, too, are concepts – cognitive concepts, as we have called them. They add to human perception "the capacity for a more detached and disinterested scrutiny," the capacity, that is, "to perceive the objective relation of things or of persons to each other and to respond, as well, to the elements of the objective world without regard to the particular setting in which they may be at any given time."[1] But this detached scrutiny, this objectification of the environment, is not achieved *despite* the presence of the subjective value-concepts. If anything, the contrary is true. There is little admixture of the cognitive and the valuational when both value-concepts and cognitive concepts are to be found in any culture, and to be found as a generally consistent dichotomy. In fact, that dichotomy is a necessary prerequisite to the development of science, if our interpretation of certain anthropological data is correct.

[1] See above, p. 50 f.

A striking feature of primitive mentality is the way it employs a number of concepts that we should regard as cognitive concepts. Apparently functioning in like manner for the primitives, these concepts nevertheless do not clearly demarcate objects for them as they do for us. "To the Huichol," reports Lumholtz, "so closely are corn, deer, and hikuli (a sacred plant) associated that by consuming the broth of the deer meat and the hikuli they think the same effect is produced, namely, making the corn grow. Therefore, when clearing the fields they eat the hikuli before starting the day's work."[2] What to us are heterogeneous objects are not so to the Huichol. Deer and corn and hikuli are identical. Indeed, the deer's antlers and even the deer itself are also considered as plumes.[3] In the Huichol vocabulary, deer, corn, and plumes and a number of other such concepts do not represent different elements of an objective world, as they do in our vocabulary.

The tendency of the primitives to see "identities" where we do not see them evidently springs from something deeply rooted in their mentality. These "identities" are permanent associations, and are the result neither of accidental resemblances (analogies) nor of temporary fancies.[4] In calling attention to this feature of primitive thought, Lévy-Bruhl calls attention to a fact of first-rate importance to the study of man's mental processes. The theory which he builds upon it bears upon our own inquiry. He accounts for the "identities" by saying that the connections between them are governed by "the law of participation," a law whereby mystic qualities circulate among certain entities, uniting them and identifying them, and that, hence, the connections

[2] C. Lumholtz, Unknown Mexico, ii, p. 45; quoted by Lévy-Bruhl, op. cit., p. 123.

[3] C. Lumholtz, Symbolism of the Huichol Indians, p. 212; cited by Lévy-Bruhl, op. cit., p. 124.

[4] L. Lévy-Bruhl, op. cit., pp. 125–6.

between the "identities" are "preformed."[5] Proceeding from that, Lévy-Bruhl undertakes to indicate how the primitive differs from the civilized mentality in respect to conceptualization. To Lévy-Bruhl true concepts are related to each other in a logical hierarchy, a conceptual hierarchy to be seen at its best in philosophy and science.[6] Concepts of that kind are not to be found in primitive thinking, and he points to the mystic, "preformed" connections for proof. He regards the "preconnections" between the "identities" as classifications of a kind, but as classifications that do not crystallize into concepts. "When the Huichols, influenced by the law of participation, affirm the identity of corn, deer, hikuli and plumes, a kind of classification has been established between their representations, a classification the governing principle of which is a common presence in these entities, or rather the circulation among these entities, of a mystic power which is of supreme importance to the tribe. The only thing is that this classification does not, as it should do in conformity with our mental processes, become compacted in a concept which is more comprehensive than that of the objects it embraces. For them it suffices for the objects to be united, and felt as such, in a complexity of collective representations whose emotional force fully compensates, and even goes beyond, the authority which will be given to general concepts by their logical validity at a later stage."[7]

Lévy-Bruhl overstates his case, and hence his thesis is vulnerable. He overstates his case when he claims that the law of participation makes "itself felt more or less emphatically in all mental operations."[8] Proof to the contrary is not hard to find.[9] "Primitive man by no means lacks the

[5] Ibid., Chaps. II, VI, VII, VIII.

[6] Ibid., pp. 126–8.

[7] Ibid., p. 128.

[8] Ibid., p. 106.

[9] See E. Cassirer, An Essay on Man (New Haven: Yale University Press, 1944), pp. 79–81.

ability to grasp the empirical differences of things."[10] Yet we do not think that Lévy-Bruhl's main thesis has been shaken. What he has demonstrated is not that primitive man has no grasp of the *empirical* differences of things, but that the law of participation does not permit the development of *science*. The linguistic facts that illustrate this thesis have not been called into question.[11]

It is on a different score that fault is to be found with Lévy-Bruhl's thesis. He simply fails to reckon in the least with human personality. For him man at his civilized best is a formulator of logically ordered concepts, and so really nothing but a curiously contrived thinking machine. Modern concepts that possess affective and motor elements – value-concepts, as we should say – are to him but vestiges of primitive mentality.[12] All he can see, therefore, in the mystic "preconnections" of the primitives is their classificatory aspect. To him, they represent merely an early stage of classification, a foreshadowing of that mental process which is to achieve the ordered, hierarchical classifications of philosophy and science.

But there is also another aspect to these mystic "preconnections," if we take human personality into account. The primitive man, too, possesses personality, and that means that he has some kind of valuational life. For him, too, there are situations which are significant and he, too, is

[10] Ibid., p. 82.

[11] These linguistic facts are described in Lévy-Bruhl, op. cit., Chapters IV–V.

For a concise summary of the same linguistic phenomena, see Marett, Anthropology (Henry Holt and Co.), pp. 130–152. Marett does not align himself altogether with Lévy-Bruhl's view. Yet his analysis certainly leads to very similar conclusions. He speaks of the primitive languages as running to "portmanteau" words, to holophrases, and says, "The evolution of language, then, on this view, may be regarded as a movement out of, and away from, the holophrastic in the direction of the analytic" (p. 141). Lévy-Bruhl accounts for the holophrases and shows why abstract concepts, the concepts of science, cannot possibly be formed with a vocabulary of that kind.

[12] See the summary and criticism of these views in OT, pp. 256–7.

moved to actions which convey significance. What makes a situation significant for him and what moves him to acts which convey significance are the "preconnections." Like our value-concepts, the "preconnections" are implicit in a situation or in an act, as in the Huichols' act of eating hikuli before starting on the day's work. But the "preconnections" are not, obviously, purely valuational. They are not value-concepts; in fact they are not concepts at all, for they are not expressed in words or terms. They are expressed in "identities," in what to us are invalid associations, non-objective relations, between cognitive concepts. This admixture of the cognitive and the valuational limits the primitives' grasp of the objective world. The "preconnections" do not apparently affect the empirical grasp of things, but they do prevent the rise of scientific classifications. Societies which utilize scientific classifications have no mystic "preconnections," very little admixture of the valuational and the cognitive.

Modern writers have described and assayed the rabbinic achievements in mathematics, astronomy, medicine, surgery, and the natural sciences.[13] The work in these several fields of science was, naturally, done by the learned class. Is it possible, however, for such work to be done unless a general idea of order in nature is held by the people at large? In the rabbinic period, in any case, the people at large did possess a general idea of regularity and order in the physical world. That general idea is conveyed by the concept *sidre Bereshit*, "orders of *Bereshit*," and also by its alternate, *sidre 'Olam*, "orders of the world." Thus, the regularity of the sun's rising in the east and its setting in the west is referred to by the term *sidre Bereshit*,[14] and so, too, the

[13] For the references, see Strack, op. cit., pp. 182, 193–4. Add to the works on mathematics W. M. Feldman, Rabbinical Mathematics and Astronomy (London: M. L. Cailingold, 1931).

[14] Sanhedrin 108b. The reading in the following reference is סדרי בראשית, and that is also the correct reading here, as can be seen from Rashi a. l., and Yalkuṭ Shime'oni, I, par. 56, and 'En Ya'aḳob. See also Diḳduḳe Soferim, a. l., note.

phenomenon that the milk-producing function is always that of the female and not of the male.[15] In another, and perhaps earlier, version of the first passage cited, *sidre 'Olam* occurs instead of *sidre Bereshit*[16]; and the singular, *sidro shel 'Olam*, "order of the world," elsewhere designates the steady repetition in nature of the number "twelve," — twelve hours in the day, twelve hours in the night, twelve months in the year, twelve constellations.[17] A tannaitic midrash, while not employing either of these conceptual terms, speaks of the fact that natural objects and domesticated animals "do not change their rule or mode" (*middah*) — the sun rises in the east and gives light to the whole world; the earth gives forth its produce after men have sowed, nor does it bring forth barley if wheat has been sown; daily the cow does the threshing and pulls the plow, and the ass is burdened with a load and carries it; the sea keeps to its bounds and does not flood the earth.[18] The midrash goes on to draw a lesson for the folk,[19] so that, obviously, this description of the regularity of the phenomena is not given for its own sake. Rather, the midrash assumes that the folk take the idea of regularity for granted. The concept of *sidre Bereshit* or *sidre 'Olam* was a popular, not an academic, concept.

It is a peculiar concept. Notice that we do not have here merely a habitual adjustment to aspects of regularity

[15] Shabbat 53b. The violations of the order of the physical world described in this and the preceding reference will be dealt with shortly.

[16] Tos. Soṭah X.1, ed. Zuck.-Lieb. p. 314 — סדרי עולם; 'Abot de R. Nathan, Version A, Chap. XXXII, ed. Schechter, p. 93. In the latter reference, the manuscript readings are סדרו של עולם — see Schechter a. l., note. The reading given in the text is סדורו של עולם. SEE NOTES, P. 370.

[17] סדרו של עולם — Pesiḳta de R. Kahana, ed. Buber (Lyck: Meḳiẓe Nirdamim, 1868) p. 126a; Bereshit R. C.9, ed. Theodor-Albeck, II, p. 1294; Tanḥuma, ed. Buber, I, p. 111a; Tanḥuma, Wayeḥi, par. 15.

[18] Sifre to Deut. 32:1.

[19] Ibid. This midrash attributes qualities of personality to natural objects. On this matter, see above, p. 140, note 25.

in nature. We have here an overall concept of regularity, and it is this overall concept that makes for the *awareness* that this or that aspect of the physical world exhibits regularity. By means of the overall concept, it is possible to point to new instances where regularity is exhibited; new, that is, in the sense that previously there had been no real awareness of regularity but merely a habitual adjustment. While everyone doubtless was aware of the regularity of the movement of the sun and of the regularity of other natural phenomena, it may very well have been something new to hear the concept applied to the work traits of the cow and the ass. In this respect, our concept acts quite like a scientific concept, for a scientific concept, too, enables us deliberately to seek out new instances that can be subsumed by the concept. But *sidre Bereshit* is not a scientific concept; it is at best only quasi-scientific. Neither *sidre Bereshit* nor the other term used—*sidre 'Olam*—is defined. There is no definition of the overall concept of regularity; in other words, no description of a general form of regularity or order governing the disparate forms of regularity and related to them as genera to species. Instead, the general concept is a splintered concept; it refers not to a form of regularity but to forms of regularity. This is, indeed, reflected in the very terms *sidre Bereshit* and *sidre 'Olam*, both of them plural terms. We ought, perhaps, to remind ourselves that even after centuries of striving and despite all scientific advances man has not succeeded in arriving at a description of a general order subsuming all known forms of order. Our present-day assumption of a general order in nature is, therefore, like the concept of *sidre Bereshit*, at best only quasi-scientific.

Sidre Bereshit is one of a number of concepts in which the word *Bereshit* is a component of the conceptual term. The other components, including *sidre* in *sidre Bereshit*, are in every case cognitive words. But the word *Bereshit* by itself is a value-concept.[20] Every conceptual term having *Bereshit* as a component – e. g., "the waters of *Bereshit*"[21] – appears, therefore, to be a compound of the cognitive and the valuational. Does the dichotomy of value-concepts and cognitive concepts not hold, then, with respect to these concepts?

There is a group of rabbinic concepts, – man, the world, *Bereshit* – each of which not only has its own connotation but also a connotation in common of universalism. They are overlapping concepts, and hence on occasion may be almost equated with one another. We saw above that such overlapping indicates a special kinship among value-concepts[22]; in our present group of concepts, the kinship consists of the connotation of universalism which they have in common. The concept of man is used in a universalistic sense in a statement such as: "Beloved is man for he was created in the image (of God)."[23] To the Rabbis, the word "man" in Lev. 1:2 is "a term of brotherhood, a term of entreaty, a term of friendship."[24] When man is thus used with a universalistic connotation, it is a concept that is organismically integrated with the other value-concepts,[25] and it is then, too, that we may speak of it as having Israel and the nations of the world for its subconcepts.[26] "World" – *'Olam* – is, obviously, a universalistic concept. As an overlapping concept, it may be closely associated with, practically equated with, the concept

[20] See above, p. 35 f.

[21] See ibid., p. 35, note 2. The term is sometimes used to refer to the ocean — see Levy's Wörterbuch, s. v. בראשית; the reference there ought to read: Yer. Ta'anit 65a.

[22] See ibid., p. 29.

[23] 'Abot III.14.

[24] See OT, p. 137.

[25] See ibid., p. 267 f.

[26] See above, p. 16, note 4. On how Israel, the very concept expressive of nationality, is strongly affected by the quality of universality, see the article on Israel referred to above, p. 15, note 2.

of man. "He that saves a single life (*nefesh*) – Scripture accounts it to him as though he had saved an entire world."[27] Like the concept of man, "world" also has its subconcepts: there are two worlds – *'Olam Ha-Zeh,* this world, and *'Olam Ha-Ba',* the world to come. Our third concept, *Bereshit,* connotes universality in evoking the idea of cosmic creation: "Blessed be He who maketh *Bereshit.*"[28] In a certain sense, it is interchangeable with the concept of world; the latter concept conveys the idea of cosmic creation in the phrase, "the world that was created with ten Sayings"[29] and in similar phrases.[30]

But these concepts may lose their large, universalistic quality. The concept of man may be employed in a strictly limited sense. It may, for example, be a designation for man as one species among other biological species.[31] "World" loses its cosmic connotation when it is a component in a compound term with a cognitive concept as the other component, as in the compound, "fruits of the world" (that is, fruit in general).[32] And the same is true of *Bereshit* occurring as a component of a compound term. Now, when our three concepts lose their cosmic, universalistic quality, they lose their kinship: man can in no way be equated to "fruits of the world," nor the latter to "waters of *Bereshit.*" The loss of kinship and the loss of the quality of universalism are indications that a great change has taken place in the character of the concepts. What we have then are not value-concepts at all, but cognitive concepts. In the compound terms, the cognitive component completely

[27] Sanhedrin IV.5. Also, he who destroys a single life — it is as though he had destroyed an entire world — ibid.

[28] See above, p. 36, note 3.

[29] 'Abot V.1; on "Sayings" see Bertinoro a. l.

[30] "The world was created" — ibid., III.14; Sanhedrin IV.5; and elsewhere. Cf. above, p. 65, note 18.

[31] E. g. "that which is food for man and food for cattle" — Shebi'it VII.1.

[32] Nedarim XI.2.

dominates the compound. Because *sidre Bereshit* and *sidre 'Olam* have the same cognitive component,[33] the terms are absolutely synonymous. The dichotomy of value-concepts and cognitive concepts generally holds throughout, despite these apparent exceptions.

VI. THE CONCEPT OF *NES* ("MIRACLE")

A culture wherein value-concepts and cognitive concepts function as a generally consistent dichotomy will also possess a third conceptual type, that of defined concepts. The Rabbis defined their halakic concepts, we saw above, with care and meticulous exactitude. These halakic definitions may often be concretizations of value-concepts, as in the case of *leḳeṭ, shikḥah,* and *pe'ah.*[1] But is a value-concept itself ever defined? We are not referring to a description of concrete ways in which a value-concept may be realized, to concretizations, but to a general, abstract definition. If a value-concept is never defined, is not at least a characteristic of a value-concept ever given in abstract, general terms?

No rabbinic value-concept is formally defined. There is, however, one value-concept, the concept of *Nes,* which does possess a characteristic described in terms of another abstract concept, that of *sidre Bereshit.* The relation between the two concepts can perhaps best be seen in a passage telling of a man whose wife had died, leaving him with a suckling child for which he was too poor to afford a wet-nurse. But "a *Nes* was done for him": his breast became as a woman's so that he might suckle his child. R. Joseph reacted to this story by saying, "How great this man must have been that such a *Nes* was done for him." Whereupon 'Abaye declared,

[33] *Seder* (construct plural *sidre*) is a cognitive concept expressive of relation. See its use in Rosh Ha-Shanah IV.9; Baba Batra VIII.2; Yoma 73a; and elsewhere.

[1] See above, p. 109.

"On the contrary! How unworthy (גרוע) this man must have been that *sidre Bereshit* were changed in his case."[2]

In telling this story, the Talmud characterizes the change that took place in the man as "a *Nes*." R. Joseph also views it in that light. What is a *Nes*? That we can infer from 'Abaye's statement. The reason for his derogation of the man is not clear,[3] but his description of the event itself is illuminating. This event, characterized as a *Nes,* is described by him as one in which "*sidre Bereshit* were changed." A change in *sidre Bereshit* is, therefore, at least a characteristic of a *Nes.*

Since *sidre Bereshit* is an abstract, quasi-scientific concept, a characteristic of a *Nes* in terms of it is a characteristic in terms of an abstract, nonvaluational concept. Indeed, this description of a *Nes* comes close to being a philosophic description, and we find something corresponding to it in the philosophic idea of a miracle. To believe that nature does not change, says Maimonides, and that there is no departure from fixed norms, is necessarily to disbelieve all signs (i. e., miracles).[4] In accordance with his rationalistic view, however, Maimonides taught that when the norms were created provision was made for specific, miraculous, departures from them.[5] For this teaching, too, support can be found in some rabbinic passages. Maimonides in his

[2] Shabbat 53b.

[3] The word גרוע in his statement is ambiguous, and has been given various interpretations. See I. Heinemann, Die Kontroverse über das Wunder im Judentum der hellenistischen Zeit, Jubilee Volume in Honor of Bernhard Heller (Budapest, 1941), p. 180 and ibid., note 37. On other occasions 'Abaye took an affirmative stand on *Nissim* involving changes in *sidre Bereshit,* as can be seen from his answer to R. Papa (below, p. 158), and from his controversy with Raba (below, p. 165).

[4] Maimonides, Moreh Nebukim, Part II, Chap. 25 — אבל אמונת הקדמות ע"צ אשר יראה אותו אריסט"ו שהוא על צד החיוב ולא ישתנה טבע כלל ולא יצא דבר חוץ ממנהגו הנה היא סותרת הדת מעקרה ומכזבת לכל אות בהכרח. On אות as miracle, see the comment here by Ephodi; on מנהג as norm, see J. Klatzkin, אוצר המונחים הפלוסופיים II (Berlin: Verlag "Eschkol," 1928), p. 212.

[5] Maimonides, ibid., Chap. 29. See below, note 8.

"Guide"[6] quotes one of them: "R. Jonathan said, The Holy One blessed be He imposed a condition on the sea that it be divided before Israel, as it is said, 'And the sea *returned* to its strength when the morning appeared' (Exod. 14:27). R. Jeremiah ben Eleazar said, Not on the sea alone did the Holy One blessed be He impose such conditions but on all that was created in the six days of *Bereshit*, as it is said, 'I, even My hands have stretched out the heavens, and all their host have I *commanded*' (Is. 45:12) — I commanded the sea to divide, the fire not to harm Hananiah, Mishael, and Azariah, the lions not to harm Daniel, and the fish to vomit out Jonah."[7] When Maimonides sums up these statements in philosophical terminology concerning "natural properties" and so on,[8] he uses a terminology that the Rabbis do not use, of course. Yet the rabbinic passage does contain the idea that *sidre Bereshit* are on the whole maintained, and that specific departures from them were ordained from the beginning. That is more or less the theme of another passage also. A mishnah states that a number of things were created on the eve of the (first) Sabbath at twilight, among them being the mouth of the earth that swallowed Korah and his congregation (Num. 16:32), the mouth of the well (ibid., 21:16), the mouth of Balaam's ass (ibid., 22:28), the rainbow, the manna, the rod of Moses, and other matters.[9] The Rabbis

[6] Ibid.

[7] This is the passage as quoted by Maimonides. It is found in Bereshit R. V.5, ed. Theodor, p. 35. For the parallels see Theodor, ibid. Maimonides abbreviated the passage somewhat, leaving out several miracles. The interpretation hinges on לאיתנו ("to its strength") being read as לתנאו, and this has also been omitted by Maimonides. In the version given in Shemot R. XXI.6, the dividing of the sea and elaborations of it related there are designated as *Nissim*.

[8] Maimonides, ibid. שהם אמרו כי כשברא הש״י זה המציאות והטביעו על אלו הטבעים שם בטבעים ההם שיתחדש בהם כל מה שיתחדש מהנפלאות בעת חדושם.

[9] 'Abot V.6. For the identification of the things thus created, see Rashi, a. l. Parallels: Mekita II, pp. 124–5; Sifre to Deut. 33:21; 'Abot de R. Nathan, Version B, Chap. XXXVII, ed. Schechter 48a; Pesaḥim 54a; Targum Yerushalmi to

evidently teach here that these things, while created after *sidre Bereshit,* were still part of the week of Creation. Similar in theme to the passage quoted by Maimonides, this mishnah is elsewhere utilized by him in much the same way.[10]

The affinity between Maimonides' theory and the particular rabbinic passages utilized by him is two-fold. First, these rabbinic passages assume an idea of *Nes* quite like that of Maimonides' idea of a miracle, the idea that *Nes* involves a change in *sidre Bereshit.* Second, these passages imply that such changes in *sidre Bereshit* are exceptional and that they are comparatively few in number, again an idea congruent with Maimonides' theory. This second point of congruence is entirely compatible with the idea of *Nes* as a change in *sidre Bereshit* but not a necessary corollary of it. It represents, rather, a rationalistic tendency on the part of some Rabbis to limit the application of the concept of *Nes* to the biblical period, if *Nes* is to involve changes in *sidre Bereshit.* That may well have been the intent of the later statement of R. 'Asi's — "Esther (ought to be regarded as) the end of all the *Nissim.*"[11] To be sure, the Talmud counters by naming Ḥanukkah, and so it concludes that the statement refers only to the end of the biblical *Nissim.*[12] Whether expressed in this particular statement or no, however, the rationalistic tendency is certainly present in some rabbinic passages, as we have seen. In describing that tendency we were careful to say

Num. 22:28; Pirḳe R. Eliezer, Chap. XIX; ibid., Chap. III. The reading in the last reference is "on the second day," but Luria, in his commentary, rightly takes that to be a misreading of בי"ה"ש, an abbreviation for "the sixth day," that is, just before the Sabbath.

[10] See his Commentary to the Mishnah, a. l.; cf also his Introduction to 'Abot ("Eight Chapters"), Chap. 8. Duran in his commentary to 'Abot (Magen 'Abot), after giving Maimonides' view in the Moreh, Chap. 29, links our mishnah with the passage from Bereshit R. quoted by Maimonides. He goes on, however, to offer an explanation of his own on the meaning of the mishnah.

[11] Yoma 29a.

[12] Ibid.

that it limits changes in *sidre Bereshit* to the biblical *period.* It does not limit them to those specifically depicted in the Bible, but leaves room for such as may be derived by interpretation. For example, according to the full text of the passage quoted by Maimonides, — his quotation is incomplete, — R. Jeremiah ben Eleazer derives from Deut. 32:1 that the heavens stood still at the behest of Moses.[13]

The rationalistic tendency is not a dominant one. The idea of *Nes* as a change in *sidre Bereshit* does not carry with it the implications that these changes must necessarily be few and limited to the biblical period. In point of fact, the stories about *Nissim* that are changes in *sidre Bereshit,* and in which the Rabbis themselves figure, run to a good number.[14] These *Nissim,* as Schechter says, "cover all classes of supernatural workings recorded in the Bible, but occur with much greater frequency."[15] Thus, to mention several, it is told that R. Phinehas ben Ya'ir caused the waters of a river to divide on three occasions[16]; that at the prayer of Naḳdimon ben Gorion the day was lengthened and the sun shone in heaven[17]; that, in answer to the prayer of Ḥoni, the circle-drawer, rain fell,[18] and likewise, at different

[13] Bereshit R. V.5. See above, p. 154, note 7.

[14] See the next note.

[15] The entire context of this statement is relevant: "Starting from the principle that miracles can be explained only by more miracles, an attempt was made some years ago by a student to draw up a list of the wonder workings of the Rabbis recorded in the Talmud and the Midrashim. He applied himself to the reading of these works, but his reading was only cursory. The list therefore is not complete. Still it yielded a harvest of not less than two hundred and fifty miracles. They cover all classes of supernatural workings recorded in the Bible, but occur with much greater frequency" — S. Schechter, Studies in Judaism, Second Series (Philadelphia: Jewish Publication Society of America, 1908), pp. 122–3. Many of the stories, however, belong rather to the literature of mysticism, and among them is the one from the tractate Ḥagigah which Schechter goes on to relate.

[16] Ḥullin 7a.

[17] Ta'anit 19b–20a; ed. Malter — major, pp. 77–9; minor, pp. 141–3.

[18] Ibid., 23a; ed. Malter — major, pp. 96–7; minor, pp. 167–9.

times, in answer to the prayers of others.[19] Some of the Tannaim were said to have been "accustomed to *Nissim*," and this phrase is applied not only to famous teachers like Nahum of Gimzo[20] and R. Simeon ben Yoḥai,[21] but also to the wife of R. Ḥanina ben Dosa.[22] Indeed, it is hardly an exaggeration to state that the presence of *Nissim* was, in a sense, within the expected order of things. 'Abaye felt called upon to answer R. Papa's question as to why a *Nes* should have been brought about for the "former" generations and "not for us."[23] The question apparently was a perfectly legitimate one. And by "former," R. Papa was not referring to the Tannaim but to their own period, that of the 'Amoraim, for he cites R. Judah (bar Ezekiel)[24] who had lived only two generations before. The Talmud does know of *Nissim* that occurred in "later" generations, as well, down to the last generations of 'Amoraim. It tells, for example, that when Mar bar Rabina thirsted when passing through a certain valley, evidently a section known for its lack of water, "a *Nes* was done for him" and a well was created for him.[25] This 'Amora was a younger contemporary of R. 'Ashi, the compiler of the Talmud.[26]

[19] See, for example, the incidents related in ibid., 23b–24b; ed. Malter — major, pp. 100 ff.; minor, pp. 173 ff.

[20] Sanhedrin 109a — דמלומד בנסים הוא.

[21] Me'ilah 17b — שהוא מלומד בנסים.

[22] Ta'anit 25a.

[23] Berakot 20a.

[24] Ibid.

[25] Ibid., 54a.

We ought to mention the singular instance of a *Nes* recorded in the Talmud which is corroborated by a passage in Eusebius giving the report of a witness to the event. Lieberman (The Martyrs of Caesarea, Annuaire de l'Institut de Philologie, VII [1939–1944], pp. 400–402) has shown that the passage in Eusebius refers to the same event which both the Babylonian and the Palestinian Talmud speak of in connection with the death of the great 'Amora, R. 'Abbahu. "When R. 'Abbahu died the pillars of Caesarea shed tears" — Mo'ed Ḳaṭan 25b; Yer. 'Abodah Zarah III.1, 42c. Eusebius connects the phenomenon with the persecution of the Christians. It took place "between the middle of November and that of December 309."

[26] See Strack, op. cit., p. 133 and the reference given there.

A mishnaic introduction which precedes and leads up to the recitation of the Hallel at the Passover Seder contains the phrase, ". . . to Him — *lemi* — who has done all these *Nissim* for our fathers and for us."[27] The word *lemi* in that phrase, says R. 'Ashi, is not ambiguous. "Who does *Nissim*? The Holy One blessed be He."[28] All *Nissim* are thus the work of God, whether they come in response to prayer, or whether, as in the case above of Phinehas ben Ya'ir, they appear to be performed by a human being. If *Nissim* occurred in former generations and do not occur "in ours," declares 'Abaye in answer to R. Papa's question, it is because the former generations were superior in their devotion to God. "The former generations were ready to lay down their lives for *Ḳedushat Ha-Shem*; we are not."[29]

[27] See Pesaḥim X.5. Some regard this as a substitute for the benediction before the Hallel (Kol Bo, commentary on Haggadah) ; others as a substitute for the benediction, "Who has done *Nissim*" (Shibbole Ha-Leḳeṭ, ed. Buber, pp. 92a, 99a). I take it that both these views are disputed by Abigedor Kohen Ẓedeḳ, since he says that a declaration of this kind in place of a benediction is impossible (ibid., p. 99b) .

[28] Berakot 50a.

[29] Ibid., 20a — מסרי נפשייהו. See the use of an equivalent phrase — נתנו נפשן — in Mekilta III, p. 204. On *Ḳedushat Ha-Shem*, see above, p. 44.

Only he who is worthy can be the agent through whom a *Nes* is performed. A similar effect produced by one who is unworthy is regarded by the Rabbis as an act of magic. This has been pointed out by A. Guttmann who cites, in this connection, the story told in Giṭṭin 45a concerning the daughters of R. Naḥman (The Significance of Miracles for Talmudic Judaism, Hebrew Union College Annual, Vol. XX [Cincinnati, 1947], p. 365).

We have here another instance of the exclusion by the value-complex of magic and superstition. The basis for that exclusion lies in the very nature of magical and superstitious practices. They are techniques, and so long as they remain merely techniques they cannot be grasped or interpreted by the value-concepts. See OT, p. 217 f., where we have dealt with this matter.

This theory, it seems to us, is confirmed by conclusions reached by Lieberman. Lieberman has shown how the Rabbis *reinterpreted* a number of practices of magical and superstitious origin (Greek in Jewish Palestine, pp. 97–114). "They drew their material from the vast stores of popular belief; they used it, modified it and offered it to the people in a more suitable form" (ibid., p. 114). What change did rabbinic reinterpretation bring about? The practices remained much the same but their character was changed. They were no longer merely techniques.

But *Nes* regarded as a change in *sidre Bereshit* is only an aspect or phase of the concept of *Nes*. There is another aspect to the concept, and that aspect is true to the nature of value-concepts in general. It is characterized neither in terms of *sidre Bereshit* nor in other abstract terms. It has to do with everyday matters, with unspectacular things – the daily search for bread, the slow recovery from an illness. It also encompasses unusual happenings to the individual and striking events of importance to the nation, but these, too, are such as do not involve any change in *sidre Bereshit*. More correctly, in all these matters the entire question of whether they conform or do not conform to *sidre Bereshit* simply does not enter.

Nissim occur every day in so casual a manner that men are not conscious of them. "Every day Thou doest for us *Nissim* and wonders, and no man knoweth (of them)."[30] Man's daily sustenance is a "wonder" of that kind.[31] Men are saved from dangers of which they are totally unaware – from a poisonous serpent, perhaps, that had waited under the bed and then fled.[32] That there are everyday *Nissim* was recognized not only by those who were especially sensitive. It was a common attitude and was expressed in a daily prayer recited by the people at large. "We will give thanks unto Thee . . . for Thy *Nissim* which are daily with us, and for Thy wonders and Thy benefits which are (wrought) at all times."[33] Do these daily, hourly, *Nissim* involve, or do they not involve, changes in *sidre Bereshit*? The question here is entirely irrelevant.

Joined to this prayer is one that is recited on Ḥanukkah and Purim. "(We thank Thee also) for the *Nissim* and for the redemption and for the mighty deeds and for the saving acts wrought by Thee, and for the wars which Thou

[30] Midrash Tehillim to Ps. 106:2, ed. Buber, p. 227a.
[31] Ibid.
[32] Ibid.
[33] In the *'Amidah*; Daily Prayer Book, ed. Singer, p. 51.

didst wage, for our fathers in days of old at this season."[34] In the paragraphs which follow concerning Ḥanukkah and Purim, and telling obviously of the *Nissim* that had occurred, nothing is mentioned but what is similar to the kind of *Nissim* occurring every day. "Thou didst deliver the strong into the hands of the weak, the many into the hands of the few" are the phrases exemplifying the content of the prayers. These are striking and extraordinary things. Are they "supernatural?" Again, the question is irrelevant.[35]

If our view is correct, everyday *Nissim* cannot be defined as those which do not involve a change in *sidre Bereshit*. That would still be a definition in terms of *sidre Bereshit*, although stated negatively. To be sure, some rabbinic passages might appear at first glance to imply that definition. According to one statement, "the *Nes* wrought" in a sick person's recovery "is greater than the *Nes* wrought for Hananiah, Mishael and Azariah."[36] In other statements it is demonstrated that God's giving sustenance to man is a thing as great, or greater, than the cleaving of the Red Sea.[37] Statements in like vein are made in regard to the giving of rain,[38] an act of God which is a palpable manifestation of His power (*Geburah*) and hence called *Geburot geshamim*.[39] Each of these comparisons assumes

[34] Ibid.

[35] The paragraph on Ḥanukkah closes with: "They children . . . cleansed Thy Temple, purified Thy sanctuary, kindled lights in Thy holy courts, and appointed these eight days of Ḥanukkah in order to give thanks and praises unto Thy great name." The *Nes* regarding the cruse of oil that lasted for eight days is not given here at all; it is a *Nes* involving a change in *sidre Bereshit*. That story is found in Shabbat 21b.

[36] Nedarim 41a. The statement probably refers to recovery from fever, for the comparison is with the fire threatening to consume the three men (Daniel, Chap. 3) .

[37] Bereshit R. XX.9; ed. Theodor, pp. 192–93, and the parallels there. Add to the parallels Midrash Tehillim to Ps. 106.2, ed. Buber, p. 227a.

[38] Bereshit R. XIII.4–6, ed. Theodor, p. 115 f., and the references there.

[39] See Ta'anit 2a — the statement of R. Johanan. "*Geburot* of the Lord" in

that there is a basic contrast between the *Nissim* thus placed one against the other. But the contrast, it seems to us, is not that one *Nes* involves a change in *sidre Bereshit* and the other does not. Rather, the contrast is that one *Nes* is a spectacular thing and the other is not.

The concept of *Nes,* then, has two conceptual phases. But the existence of two distinct phases should not lead us to think that one phase is primary and the other secondary. A conceptual phase acts practically like a subconcept, as we saw above when we discussed other examples of concepts with conceptual phases[40]; and a valuational subconcept is not a secondary aspect of a concept.[41] An organismic complex of value-concepts is not a hierarchical structure with primary and secondary elements.[42] A conceptual phase, however, unlike a subconcept, has no conceptual term of its own; it can only be symbolized by the general conceptual term. That is to say, the general conceptual term can stand for only a phase of the concept, even though the concept is larger than any single phase. The term *Nes* may, therefore, stand for either of its phases. Yet the concept of *Nes* is larger than either of its phases: it contains them both, and neither phase is primary. We may add that, although the concept has biblical antecedents,[43] this larger meaning is rabbinic. In fact, the word itself has a totally different meaning in the

Ps. 106:2 is equated with *Nissim* in Midrash Tehillim to that verse; ed. Buber, 227a.

[40] See above, p. 17.

[41] See ibid., p. 16.

[42] See ibid., p. 25 f.

The Rabbis speak in one place (Baba Meẓi'a 106a, bot.) of a "major *Nes*" and a "minor *Nes*." The "minor *Nes*" here refers to the shepherd being given strength and skill by God to overcome the lion attacking the herd (see Tosafot a. l., s. v. מתיב) . But there is no indication here that a "major *Nes*" is a primary, and a "minor *Nes*" a secondary aspect of the concept.

[43] See below, p. 296.

Bible. There the word *Nes* signifies "sign," "flag," or "mast."[44]

The conceptual phase wherein a *Nes* involves a change in *sidre Bereshit* is a phenomenon unparalleled in the rabbinic value-complex. It is the sole instance, so far as we know, of a characteristic of a value-concept that is described in terms of an abstract concept. Were there not also another conceptual phase – other characteristics – we should have had a value-concept itself given in terms of an abstract concept, in other words, a value-concept defined in abstract terms. As it is, the abstract characteristic comes close, as we have said, to being a philosophical idea. It is similar to the philosophic idea of a miracle. It is a conception underlying some rabbinic statements having a rationalistic tendency, statements that easily lend themselves to the support of a philosophical theory of Maimonides. All this emphasizes the fact that the abstract characteristic is not purely a valuational phase. It is an admixture of a value-concept and an abstract, quasi-scientific concept, the only case of its kind in the rabbinic complex.

If this admixture is different from all the other value-concepts in character or constitution, it ought to be different also in the way it functions. And so it is. Every value-concept, including our abstract phase, is expressed in concretizations of the concept. In contrast to the value-complex as a whole, however, the functioning of our abstract phase is explicitly restricted. The concept is deliberately excluded from functioning in entire areas of human experience.

[44] See Gesenius, Handwörterbuch, s. v. נס.

The rabbinic concept of *Nes* seems to be a subconcept of the concepts of God's love and God's justice. We have other examples of subconcepts not of one but of two separate concepts — see above, p. 27 f. That *Nes* is a subconcept of God's love we can see from the examples given by R. Jeremiah (above, p. 154) and from those of sustenance, etc. (ibid., p. 160) ; that it is also a subconcept of God's justice we can see from 'Abaye's answer to R. Papa (ibid., p. 158) .

The exclusion is stated in the form of a principle. Where there is imminent danger, say the Rabbis, "we do not rely on a *Nes*."[45] This principle is applied even in the case of those who are engaged upon a *Miẓwah*, and it modifies R. Eleazar's dictum that persons so engaged are kept from harm.[46] Similar in spirit to the principle is the aphorism, "Not every day (or, not every hour) does a *Nes* take place," a warning against the taking of undue risks.[47] But we must not forget that the abstract conceptual phase is a genuine element of the value-concept; it possesses, therefore, a drive toward concretization, a drive strong enough to override at times the principle of exclusion. It is told, for example, that Rab and Samuel would avoid passing a crumbling wall in Nehardea, although it had remained standing for thirteen years. But one day they were accompanied by R. 'Adda bar 'Ahabah, and when Samuel suggested going roundabout the wall Rab replied that he was not afraid now that R. 'Adda was with them, since R. 'Adda's merits were very great.[48] On the other hand, the same source continues with another story about the identical R. 'Adda which discourages such an attitude as Rab's. In that story, R. 'Adda quotes R. Yannai's statement: One should never remain in a place of danger and say, "A *Nes* will be wrought for me" — a *Nes* may not be wrought for him; if wrought, it will be detracted from his merits.[49]

Exclusion of the abstract conceptual phase is no less marked in Halakah. The Halakah concretizes this phase in requiring a benediction to be said when one sees a place where *Nissim* were done for Israel.[50] When a *Nes* occurs to

[45] Ḳiddushin 39b — וכל היכא דקביע היזיקא לא סמכינן אניסא.

[46] Ibid. Comp. also Ḥullin 142a; Yoma 11a; Pesaḥim 8b — היכא דשכיח היזיקא.

[47] Pesaḥim 50b; Megillah 7b.

[48] Ta'anit 20b.

[49] Ibid.; cf. Shabbat 32a.

[50] Berakot IX.1. Comp. Berakot 57b, where it is to be noticed that the "places" referred to are a pit of lions and a fiery furnace, things associated with the events

an individual, it was also decided, a benediction ought to be said by the individual affected but not by others.[51] But in Halakah, too, there is exclusion of the abstract phase, and again in the form of a principle. In a number of instances, various authorities – among them Tannaim – bring up *Nissim* involving changes in *sidre Bereshit* as germane to the halakic discussion at hand, only to be challenged with the principle that *Nissim* are not to be taken into account in halakic discussion.[52] Certain *Nissim* mentioned in 'Abot V.5 are apparently disregarded in halakot given elsewhere in the Mishnah, a "contradiction" which the Talmud tends to explain away by invoking the same principle.[53] All these *Nissim* barred by the principle are not signs; but for the principle they would have been germane to the halakic discussions in which they figure. Of *Nissim* as signs in a halakic dispute, we have a solitary report in two fairly similar versions, and here too the majority reject the import of the *Nissim*. To demonstrate that R. Eliezer's stand on a particular halakic matter was the correct one, the report tells us, several *Nissim* occurred, all at R. Eliezer's demand. But his colleagues were unmoved. After each *Nes*, they would declare the *Nes* to be irrelevant so far as halakic proof (ראיה) was concerned; in one case, where the walls of the *bet ha-midrash* slanted and were about to fall, R. Joshua rebuked them, saying, "If scholars (*Talmide Ḥakamim*) are engaged in halakic dispute, what has that to do with you," whereupon another *Nes* occurred, and the walls remained

in Daniel, Chaps. 3 and 6, and hence having to do with *Nissim* involving changes in *sidre Bereshit*.

[51] Berakot 54a.

[52] אין מזכירין מעשה נסים— Yebamot 121b, Yer. Yebamot XVI.4, 15d; Berakot 60a; Ḥullin 43a. In the last reference, Rashi adds to the principle the gloss: להביא ראייה מהן.

[53] See the notes of Z. H. Chajes to Yoma — his comment on Yoma 2a, s. v. רש״י ד״ה ומתקינין לו, and the references there.

standing, slanted as they were.[54] The dominant trend, then, is to exclude *Nes* as a factor in halakic discussion and decision. The same discussions also indicate, however, that some authorities did attempt to inject the consideration of *Nissim* into halakic argument. Indeed, on one occasion this difference in attitude involves a corresponding difference in the actual wording of a mishnah. 'Abaye read a mishnah so as to imply that "we rely on *Nissim*," whilst Raba read it otherwise and in consonance with the attitude that "we do not rely on *Nissim*."[55]

Why is there a dominant trend deliberately to exclude the concept from large areas of experience? It is against the abstract phase of the concept that the excluding principles are directed. That phase employs the concept of *sidre Bereshit* in such fashion as to be in continual conflict with that quasi-scientific concept. *Sidre Bereshit* stands for regularity in nature; the abstract phase of the concept of *Nes* takes this idea and asserts in so many words that it does not apply to particular situations. With respect to those situations, the quasi-scientific concept of *sidre Bereshit* and the abstract phase making this negative use of it are therefore in direct conflict. What we have in the principles of exclusion is an attempt to obviate the conflict in whole areas of experience, and this by giving the quasi-scientific concept the right of way, as it were, in those areas.

In this attempt to restrict the concept, we must not look for consistency. The abstract phase is, after all, a genuine element of the value-complex; it possesses a drive toward concretization which occasionally overrides the principles of exclusion. By the same token, the attitude of individual Rabbis toward the phase is not consistent.

[54] See Baba Meẓi'a 59a; Yer. Mo'ed Ḳaṭan III.1, 81c–d. The two versions have been compared by A. Guttmann, op. cit., p. 374 f.

[55] See Pesaḥim 64b.

Heinemann gives various examples of free concretization and of restriction by the same authorities.[56] Besides, some of the concretizations of the abstract phase, perhaps many of them, are only seemingly in conflict with the quasi-scientific concept. Told or accepted with an attitude of indeterminacy of belief, these concretizations are not downright negations of *sidre Bereshit*. Belonging to this group, very likely, is that singular report of the appearance of the signs in favor of R. Eliezer's view, signs declared to be not relevant.

But the fact remains that the abstract phase is restricted and curbed. It is strongly curbed in the areas wherein the principles of exclusion operate. It is curbed elsewhere too. Do not the statements evincing a rationalistic tendency testify to the curbing of the concept? All this curbing and restriction have very few parallels, and are the result here of the unique constitution of this particular phase. The phase employs a quasi-scientific concept in such a manner as to be in conflict with the latter. In an effort to avoid or lessen the conflict, the phase is restricted and curbed.[57]

[56] Heinemann, op. cit., pp. 184–5. His terminology there differs from ours because his thesis is different. See the following note.

[57] Other explanations have been advanced for the restriction. Heinemann (op. cit., p. 186) attributes it to "die Spannung zwischen rationaler und irrationaler Denkweise, welche in der Kontroverse über das Wunder (und über die Anthropomorphismen) zum Ausdruck kommt." Heinemann's treatment of the subject is suggestive. But although he recognizes that the concept contains what we have called two phases, he fails to notice that one phase is practically defined and the other is not. It is the unique constitution of the defined phase that gives rise to restriction and curbing, not any general tension in the value-complex. The idea of a general tension between rational and irrational thought as a characteristic of the rabbinic value-complex implies a view of the nature of the value-concepts at variance with ours. We have endeavored to demonstrate all along, and especially in this chapter, that the value-concepts are distinctly different from other types of concepts, and that admixture with other types would make it difficult for them to function. "Rational" and "irrational," on the other hand, would mean not that the one type is merely different from the other, but that it is in conflict with the other. According to our analysis, however, a conflict is possible only when there is an admixture. If tension exists, it exists in the concept of *Nes*, or rather in its

The inference is clear. There is no possibility of a conflict of that kind, and consequently no need for restriction, when the value-concept is free from admixture with a concept of a different type. The rabbinic value-complex as a whole functioned easily because, with very few exceptions, it consisted of pure value-concepts.[58]

VII. THE COMMONPLACE AND THE HOLY

The value-concepts are the dominant factors in the category of significance. Situations or actions are significant always only in terms of the value-concepts which are concretized in them. Yet in describing the category of significance, we must also take into account certain objects, natural phenomena, and days. Halakah takes these objects and phenomena, and makes of them occasions for recurrent or fixed concretizations of value-concepts — thereby making them also more or less permanent factors in the category of significance. These objects and phenomena fall into several classes.

One class consists of the ordinary objects and phenomena of everyday existence. Normal, commonplace, everyday situations and actions are for the Rabbis, and for the people they taught, occasions of religious experience. Before eating the first morsel of bread, for example, they uttered the

abstract phase, precisely because that phase is an admixture. That phase alone is restricted and curbed. As to anthropomorphisms, see below, Chap. VII.

A. Guttmann's thesis is that there is "a decline of miracle." "The decline of miracle as regards influencing law and practice goes parallel with the growth of Christianity" — op. cit., p. 405. In the absence of direct evidence, it is difficult to establish that "the imminent danger coming from nascent Christianity" (ibid.) caused the Rabbis to restrict the concept of *Nes*. In any case, the *possibility* for restriction lies in the unique constitution of the abstract phase of the concept.

[58] The other exceptions are taken up below, pp. 232 ff., p. 263.

Berakah (blessing), "Blessed art Thou, O Lord our God, King of the world, who bringest forth bread from the earth."[1] The reciting of the *Berakah* constitutes an act of worship. According to R. Isaac, there is a reference to this *Berakah* in the injunction, "And ye shall serve the Lord your God" (Exod. 23:25).[2]

What evokes this act of worship? It is evoked, for one thing, by the experience of God's love (*Middat Raḥamim*). Our daily bread is given us by God "who feeds the whole world with His goodness, with grace, with loving-kindness and with tender mercy."[3] Present also is the recognition that our sustenance represents a *Nes*, and one that is wrought for us daily.[4] The eating of the first morsel of bread at any meal thus becomes an occasion for religious experience. It becomes a situation in itself, a situation integrated by the concepts of God's love, *Nes*, and *Berakah*, and fraught with their significance. But occasions for religious experience involving these concepts occur when we partake of any kind of sustenance, not of bread alone. Hence an appropriate *Berakah* is to be made before partaking of wine, or of water, or of any sort of food or drink.[5] Nor is the daily experience of God's loving-kindness confined to these occasions. Every new day is itself a manifestation of His love, and so the day's dawning light is the theme of a *Berakah* commencing

[1] See the references in Baer, op. cit., p. 198. "Who bringest forth" etc. is after Ps. 104:14. "Blessing" is not an adequate rendering for *Berakah*, nor "blessed" for *Baruk*. Rabbinic value-concepts are not usually translatable (cf. above p. 77 f.). Here *Baruk* connotes "praise" rather than "blessing." See Baer, p. 36. On the shift from second person to third person in these *Berakot* see below, pp. 267 ff.

[2] Berakot 48b; Yer. Berakot VII.1, 11a; Yer. Megillah IV.1, 75a (in the last two references with R. Nathan as the authority). The play is on the word וברך. The term ועבדתם, "and ye shall serve," is taken as referring to עבודה (*'abodah*), worship or service.

[3] In the first *Berakah* of the grace after meals — Daily Prayer Book, ed. Singer, p. 280; Baer, op. cit., p. 554.

[4] See above, p. 159 f.

[5] Berakot VI.1–4. See also Baer, op. cit., p. 567 f.

the morning service whilst a parallel *Berakah* having the twilight as its theme commences the evening service.[6] These instances, and many more that could be added, are all normal, ordinary happenings which are endowed with valuational significance. The Rabbis apparently sought for every opportunity to transmute the commonplace into the significant. This inclusion of details of living which are repeated day after day made the category of significance steady as well as extensive.

Another class of objects consists of ritualistic objects. They are employed in the performance of what, for want of a better word, we may call "rites" – rites which evoke a consciousness or experience of holiness. Now holiness, *Ḳedushah*, as the Rabbis conceived and experienced it, is not necessarily associated with the unusual and the awesome. On the contrary, it may be centered on personal conduct and be associated with the ordinary and the familiar. It is to this aspect of *Ḳedushah* that the rabbinic rites belong.

The aspect of *Ḳedushah* which is concerned with personal conduct has been dealt with by Schechter in his "Some Aspects of Rabbinic Theology." We shall scarcely do more, in this paragraph, than name some of the ideas developed there, though diverging somewhat from his interpretation. In its broad features, says Schechter, *Ḳedushah* is nothing else than the imitation of God. " 'Ye shall be holy, for I the Lord am holy' (Lev. 19:2). These words are explained by the ancient Rabbinic sage Abba Saul to mean 'Israel is the *familia* (suite or bodyguard) of the King (God), whence it is incumbent upon them to imitate the king.' "[7] More specific is another interpretation by Abba Saul: "*I and He,*

[6] Daily Prayer Book, ed. Singer, p. 39 f. and p. 96; Baer, op. cit., p. 76 f. and p. 164. See the exposition of the *Yoẓer 'Or* in Simon Greenberg, The Ideals of the Jewish Prayer Book (New York: Scopus Publishing Company, 1942), pp. 18–22.

[7] S. Schechter, Some Aspects of Rabbinic Theology (New York: Macmillan, 1910), pp. 199–200. See the notes, ibid., for the sources.

that is like unto Him. As He is merciful and gracious, so be thou (man) merciful and gracious."[8] A second idea, kindred to this, is that the *Mizwot* (commandments) of God are a source of holiness. "With every new *Mizwah* which God (*Ha-Makom*) issues to Israel He adds to them holiness."[9] " 'Be holy' (Num. 15:40) — for as long as you fulfill the *Mizwot* you are sanctified, but if you neglect them, you will become profaned."[10] " 'Ye shall be holy' (Lev. 19:2) — that refers to the holiness (conferred by) all the *Mizwot*."[11] The negative implication of *Kedushah* — the idea of separation or withdrawal inherent in the concept — emerges in matters of conduct in the demand for withdrawal from everything impure and defiling, foremost among which are idolatry, adultery, and the shedding of blood.[12] Such are some of the ideas involving the concept of *Kedushah* which informed daily conduct.

As to the rites, the idea underlying them all is that the *Mizwot* are a source of holiness. The *Berakah* said at a rite begins with the words "Blessed art Thou, O Lord our God, King of the world, who hast sanctified us by Thy *Mizwot*," and then continuing with "and hast commanded us (*we-ziwwanu*)" goes on to mention the particular rite.[13] We shall come soon to the implications of all these phrases. First, however, we wish to discuss the objects employed in the rites, objects which are usually named in the *Berakah*.

Objects employed in the rites are governed by Halakah. There are regulations, for example, covering the construction of a *sukkah* (the booth used during the Festival of Sukkot),[14] the length and condition of the *lulab* (the palm branch

[8] See ibid., p. 201, and the note there.

[9] Mekilta, III, p. 157; cf. Schechter, op. cit., p. 168.

[10] Numbers R. XVII.7, quoted by Schechter, op. cit., p. 208 f.

[11] Sifra to Lev. 20:7. See Schechter, op. cit., p. 208, note 2.

[12] See Schechter, op. cit., pp. 205 f.

[13] See, for example, Baer, op. cit., pp. 56–7.

[14] See the first two chapters of Mishnah Sukkah.

used on that Festival),[15] the makeup of the *ẓiẓit* (show-fringes).[16] Nevertheless, despite all the regulations, these objects and most of the others used in the rites are designated by general cognitive terms. *Sukkah, lulab, ẓiẓit, shofar,* are not words designating specific objects employed in religious rites but are of a general character – *sukkah* meaning a booth, *lulab* a sprout, *ẓiẓit* fringes, *shofar* a horn.[17] And the same thing is true of other objects used in rites.[18] Does this not warrant the conclusion that the objects so designated were regarded as having basically an ordinary character, notwithstanding the central position they occupy in the rites? That conclusion is strikingly confirmed by the Halakah.

Certain things – a *sefer-Torah, tefillin, mezuzot,* and *sefarim* (scrolls of the Prophets or *Ketubim*) – are classified by the Halakah as *Ḳedushah*.[19] Even objects directly used in connection with these holy things, objects which are characterized as *tashmishe Ḳedushah,* such as the receptacles or cases for the holy things, are to be stored away when no longer used, and not just thrown aside carelessly.[20] (This applies all the more, of course, to the holy things themselves.) On the other hand, a second group of objects consisting of those we named above – *sukkah, lulab, ẓiẓit,* and *shofar* – may be thrown away when they can no longer be used,[21] and this applies not only to them but also to "others like them."[22] Classified by the Halakah as *tashmishe Miẓwah,*

[15] Ibid., III.1.

[16] See Maimonides, Mishneh Torah, Hilkot Ẓiẓit, and the references given in the commentaries there.

[17] See Jastrow's Dictionary on these terms.

[18] When the myrtle (used together with the *lulab*) was called *hosha'na'* as well as *'asa'* (Aramaic) — see Sukkah 30b–31a — it was still designated by a "cognitive" word, except that the word was taken from the liturgy. See Rashi a. l., s. v. הושענא קרו.

[19] Megillah 26b.

[20] Ibid.

[21] See ibid. and the commentaries.

[22] See R. Hananel a. l.

the objects in this second group are thus regarded as merely being essential to a particular rite and nothing more. They are not holy in themselves.[23] If, in contrast to *tashmishe Ḳedushah,* they may be finally thrown away, it is because they are basically of an ordinary character.

To our conclusion that general cognitive terms designate things that are not holy in themselves there is one exception. *Sefarim* is the cognitive term for books in general; yet it also refers to scrolls of the Scriptures – sometimes to the Pentateuch alone and sometimes, as in the halakah just quoted, to other books of Scripture[24] – and these scrolls, we saw, are *Ḳedushot.*[25] But the "dual" meaning which this particular term has can be accounted for. In a sense, the general character of the term and its specific reference to books of Scripture coalesced. The books that were most familiar, those which were read and studied over and over again, were the books of Scripture. Sheerly from the point of view of the time lavished upon them, if from no other, they crowded out of consideration such other books as may have been used or known, and of which the Talmud speaks.[26] It is not to be wondered at, therefore, that the word *sefarim* conveyed the idea of scriptural books at least as readily as it conveyed the idea of books in general.[27]

[23] See ibid. — אין בהן קדושה. See also Maimonides, Mishneh Torah, Hilkot Ẓiẓit, III.9. It is true that when the objects are used they are not to be treated with complete casualness. See the discussion in Shabbat 22a on the lights of Ḥanukkah. But in that discussion, too, the point is made that the lights are not holy — וכי נר קדושה יש בה.

[24] See J. Müller's commentary (German) to his edition of Masechet Soferim (Leipzig, 1878), pp. 2–3. When, as in our halakah, both *sefer-Torah* and *sefarim* are mentioned, the latter refers to scrolls of Prophets or *Ketubim.*

[25] Notice Rashi's use of *Ḳedushot* in his commentary — Megillah 27a, s. v. שמכרו. See also 'Erubin III.6.

[26] S. Krauss gives a list of what he describes as "die wenigen profanen oder halb-profanen Schriften" in his Talmudische Archäologie (Leipzig, 1910–12), III, p. 180.

[27] The word *mezuzah* does not offer a parallel case. It simply has two *different* meanings—one meaning being "door-post," and the other the slip of parchment

Aside from this exception, then, the ritual objects designated by general cognitive terms are not holy but ordinary in character. Have the rites performed with such objects anything to do therefore with holiness at all?

We must recall that the Rabbis felt that all the *Miẓwot* are a source of holiness. "With every new *Miẓwah* which God issues to Israel He adds to them holiness."[28] "As long as you fulfill the *Miẓwot* you are sanctified, but if you neglect them, you will become profaned."[29] The holiness conferred by the *Miẓwot*, however, is not experienced in the performance of any and every *Miẓwah*. It is experienced only in the performance of a rite. Any rabbinic rite is, for this purpose, a representative part of the *Miẓwot* as a whole, and it is primarily as such that it has significance. That is why the *Berakah* said at a rite always begins with the statement referring to the sanctifying character of the *Miẓwot* in general – "Blessed art Thou, O Lord our God, King of the world, who hast sanctified us by Thy *Miẓwot*" – and then continues with the phrase *we-ẓiwwanu* ("and hast commanded us"), a phrase which relates the mention of the particular rite to the *Miẓwot* as a whole.[30] To be sure, each rite has its own associations. The background associated with the *sukkah*, for example, is certainly different from that associated with the lights of Ḥanukkah. Nevertheless, at the time the *Berakah* is recited, the experience evoked has to do with the holiness conferred by the *Miẓwot* in general, and the particular rite serves primarily as the representative occasion for that experience. By the same token, the *Berakah*, since it evokes that experience or consciousness, is an integral element of the rite.

containing Deut. 6:4–9 and ibid. 11:13–21 which is fastened to the door-post. Two different objects are thus referred to by the same word, and only the first has an ordinary character. See the references in the Talmudical dictionaries.

[28] See above, p. 170.

[29] See ibid.

[30] See ibid.

There are reasons why the consciousness of holiness could not accompany the performance of any and every *Miẓwah*. The *Berakah*, we have just observed, evokes that consciousness. In the case of many *Miẓwot*, to utter that *Berakah* and to evoke that consciousness would be to obscure the concepts that cause those *Miẓwot* to function. We refer to such *Miẓwot* as those embodying the concepts of charity and deeds of loving-kindness, and to all the other *Miẓwot* governing human relations. How could these *Miẓwot* function were it not for the concepts which are embodied in them, and which act as drives? To add a *Berakah* expressing the concept of holiness would be to obscure the other concepts, concepts not expressed in *Berakot* but, if at all, in action. This consideration does not hold, of course, for the actions — eating, for example — requiring *Berakot*. Some of these actions, as we shall see, may also be rites on occasion and hence have dual *Berakot*. But this is rare, for dual *Berakot* on every occasion would be both cumbersome and confusing. For these reasons, and for others,[31] the consciousness of holiness is evoked only by the rites. The latter serve as representative of the *Miẓwot* in general.

[31] Prof. Saul Lieberman called my attention to the responsum by R. Joseph Ibn Plat on the question as to why many of the positive *Miẓwot* do not require a *Berakah*. Ibn Plat declares that the reasons differ with different groups of *Miẓwot*; among the reasons he gives is that many *Miẓwot*, such as that of charity, depend not alone on him that performs the *Miẓwah* but upon others, e. g., the recipient of charity, as well. See the responsum in ש. אסף, ספרן של ראשונים (ירושלים תרצ"ה) p. 200 ff. For the literature, see ibid., p. 199 f. Prof. Lieberman suggests that *Miẓwot* brought about by the misfortunes of others — visiting the sick, for example — are obviously not of the kind that require a *Berakah*.

He also referred me to the passage in Roḳeaḥ, 366, dealing with this problem. There the rule is laid down that all the *Miẓwot* to which non-Jews are also expected to conform — *Miẓwot* having to do with charity, respect for the aged, and the like — do not require a *Berakah*.

In the Sefer Ha-Pardes attributed to Rashi, ed. H. L. Ehrenreich, pp. 195 ff., is to be found another discussion by Ibn Plat dealing with *Berakot*. There he offers an explanation for the differences in the linguistic forms of the formula after the term *we-ẓiwwanu*.

How does a rabbinic rite differ from other acts which require a *Berakah*? The difference lies not only in the formula of the *Berakah* said at a rite, a formula not employed in other *Berakot*, but also in the act. A ritual act is mandatory — *we-ẓiwwanu*, "and hast commanded us," as we have just noticed, whilst other acts before which a *Berakah* is to be said[32] are not mandatory. This is well illustrated in the matter of eating *maẓẓah* (unleavened bread) on Passover. The eating of *maẓẓah*, even if only a morsel, is mandatory on the first night of Passover alone; for the remainder of the Festival it is merely optional.[33] A man may therefore refrain from eating *maẓẓah* for the rest of the Festival,[34] and so, after the one morsel, have no occasion during that time to say the *Berakah* over bread. The eating of that morsel, however, is mandatory; hence after the *Berakah* over bread, there is also the *Berakah* said at a rite.[35] What we have classified as rites have thus a distinct character of their own. This was recognized by the Rabbis. For the *Berakah* said at a rite they have a special designation, calling it *Birkat Ha-Miẓwot*,[36] a term which implies both that the *Berakah* has a distinctive formula and that the acts before which it is said are mandatory.[37] We have used the term "rites" rather than

[32] In an act requiring a *Berakah*, the latter must *precede* the act — Pesaḥim 7b and the parallels. The one exception is in the case of the ritual of immersion — see ibid., and the commentaries. SEE NOTES, P. 370.

[33] Mekilta, I, pp. 61–3; Pesaḥim 120a; Sukkah 27a.

[34] See Rashi ad Pesaḥim 120a.

[35] See Berakot 39b, and Tosafot there, s. v. הכל מודים בפסח. The *Berakah* over bread is said first because of the principle that what is more frequent or regular precedes — comp. Pesaḥim 114a and the parallels. On the matter of the *Berakot* to be said before the mandatory eating of a morsel of *maror*, bitter herb, and (in the Temple days) of a morsel of the paschal lamb, on the first night of Passover, see the discussion in Shibbole Ha-Leḳeṭ, ed. Buber, p. 100a.

[36] Pesaḥim 104b–105a, Ketubbot 7b.

[37] In regard to the mandatory character of the acts, our rule does not always hold. See Maimonides, Mishneh Torah, Hilkot Berakot XI.2, 3. On the Sabbath light, see Tosafot to Shabbat 25b, s. v. חובה. SEE NOTES, P. 370.

the rabbinic classification because we wished to include in our discussion also the objects with which the acts are performed.

The experience of holiness is a mystical experience. Some have declared it to be an experience entirely separate from any other and something that has no relation whatever to normal experience.[38] This is in keeping with the contention that mysticism constitutes "an entirely separate, completely self-supported kind of human experience."[39] Our study disproves this contention, so far as rabbinic experience is concerned. The concept of *Ḳedushah* has connotations which project it into the sphere of the normal and the practical. It connotes the idea of imitating God in being merciful and gracious; it demands the withdrawal from what is impure and defiling — from idolatry, adultery, and the shedding of blood.[40] On the occasions when the *Birkat Ha-Miẓwot* is recited, these are among the connotations called up by the phrase "who hast sanctified us by Thy *Miẓwot*."

In a rabbinic rite of this type we have what may almost serve as an epitome of the category of significance. On the one hand, there is the mystical consciousness of holiness — subjective and personal, differing in accordance with depth of temperament and of cultural background. On the other hand, there is the object essential to the rite, and without which this mystical experience is not to be had — an object recognized as being of an ordinary, general character, not holy in itself. The most subtle valuational experience goes together with a firm grasp of the impersonal, objective nature of the things that contribute to that experience.

[38] See, for example, Rudolf Otto, The Idea of the Holy (trans. Harvey) (Oxford: Oxford Univ. Press, 1926), especially pp. 5–30.

[39] The phrase is taken from von Hügel's discussion of exclusive mysticism. He regards that kind of mysticism as conducive to error. See The Mystical Element in Religion, second ed. (New York: E. P. Dutton and Company, 1923), Vol. II, pp. 283 f., 304–308.

[40] See above, p. 170.

We now return to the things which are holy in themselves, still another class of objects. The things characterized as holy by the halakah discussed above were a *sefer-Torah*, *sefarim*, *tefillin*, and *mezuzot*.[41] A *sefer-Torah* is a scroll of the Pentateuch[42]; *sefarim* may refer either to that or to other scrolls of Scripture;[43] *tefillin* and *mezuzot* contain certain passages from Scripture on parchment.[44] A *bet ha-keneset*, synagogue, is also characterized as holy,[45] and it is associated with *sefer-Torah* and *sefarim* in a halakah.[46]

The terms which designate these objects are definitely not value-concepts. Value-concepts are never classified by means of another value-concept; every value-concept represents an independent classification. What we have called subconcepts are not subsidiary in any sense, but are "treated in rabbinic literature in exactly the same way as are the 'main' concepts."[47] In contrast, the holy objects *are* classified by the Rabbis as *Ḳedushah*.[48] The terms for these objects, therefore, can only be cognitive concepts, though of a special character. They stand for objects which possess in common the mystic quality of *Ḳedushah*, objects which are thus fixed concretizations of that value-concept.

The mystic qualities which, in primitive thought, were felt to be inherent in certain objects have no designation, are not conceptualized.[49] They are felt as nameless powers circulating among those objects and rendering them identical with each other.[50] The mystic powers could be "utilized":

[41] See above, p. 171.

[42] A *sefer-Torah*, to be holy, must be free from many disqualifying things. Maimonides lists twenty such disqualifying things — Mishneh Torah, Hilkot Sefer Torah X.1.

[43] See above, p. 172.

[44] See Menaḥot 34b (*tefillin*); ibid. 28a and Rashi a. l. (*mezuzot*).

[45] The term *Ḳedushah* is applied to it — e. g. Megillah III.1.

[46] Ibid.

[47] Above, p. 16.

[48] See above, p. 171, note 19, and p. 172, note 25.

[49] See above, p. 144 f.

[50] Ibid.

when the Huichol consume the broth of the deer, they think that the corn is made to grow.[51] All this is a far cry indeed from the mystic quality possessed by our holy objects. Here the mystical quality is designated by a concept, the concept of *Ḳedushah*; the objects possessing it are not identified with each other; it is not a power to be "utilized." Yet the question remains as to whether, after all, this mystical quality is not conceived as having efficacy of a sort. If it is so conceived, it is still not altogether free from primitive vestiges.

We have already noticed a matter that may possibly indicate that efficacy of some sort was attributed to the holy objects. Things used in connection with the latter, those things characterized by the Rabbis as *tashmishe Ḳedushah*, are also to be stored away when no longer used, and not just thrown aside carelessly.[52] This halakah is followed in the Talmud by a statement of Raba's which throws light upon it. Raba declares that at first he took the lectern on which the *sefer-Torah* is placed to be only a *tashmish* of a *tashmish*, an accessory of an accessory, but that he recognized it to be a *tashmish* proper, and hence not to be cast away, when he saw that the *sefer-Torah* was placed upon it directly, and without a cloth intervening.[53] Similarly, he had regarded the curtain outside the ark (containing the *sefer-Torah*) as only a *tashmish* of a *tashmish*, but recognized it to be a *tashmish* proper when he saw that they folded it and placed the *sefer-Torah* on it.[54] An accessory is thus a *tashmish* only if it comes in direct contact with the holy object. Accessories of the same holy object may differ, however, in the grade of holiness. The holy things are graded by the Rabbis in a hierarchy of holiness – a *sefer-Torah* at the top, and then in descending order *sefarim*,

[51] Ibid.

[52] Above, p. 171.

[53] Megillah 26b, and Rashi a. l.

[54] Ibid. "The curtain outside the ark" is in accordance with Tosafot a. l.

the bands used in wrapping the scroll of a *sefer-Torah*, the ark wherein the scroll is kept, a *bet ha-keneset*.[55] In this hierarchy, the band, a *tashmish* of a *sefer-Torah*, outranks in holiness the ark, also a *tashmish* of a *sefer-Torah*, apparently because the former's contact with the scroll is closer. Moreover, both accessories, holy by reason of their direct contact with a *sefer-Torah*, outrank a *bet ha-keneset* which is holy in its own right. An object in which there is *Ḳedushah* seems therefore to be endowed with a power, the power to transmit by direct contact at least a measure of its mystical quality to another object. Almost like a natural power, the power inherent in the mystical quality appears to have its own degrees of effectiveness and its point of limitation. Nor do these halakot reflect merely an isolated instance of the mystical power attributed to holy objects. There are also halakot concerning the sanctifying property of the altar and the vessels of the Temple,[56] whilst gradations in holiness are made frequently.[57] Is not efficacy of some sort, then, attributed to the mystical quality of *Ḳedushah*?

But what actually, according to the Rabbis, does *Ḳedushah* achieve? It is not conceived as having any effect beyond transmitting itself. It is not regarded as having any physical effect, nor as a spiritual agency which, properly applied, can affect the welfare of the individual or of the community. Efficacy without physical or theurgical effect is no efficacy at all. As a matter of fact, it is hardly correct to speak of *Ḳedushah* as possessing a "power." The things to which *Ḳedushah* is transmitted are only such as are ordinarily associated with the holy objects in any event – accessories in the case of our holy objects and, in the case of the altar

[55] See Megillah III.1. Only those things which are public property are named here, and hence *tefillin* and *mezuzot* are omitted.

[56] Zebaḥim IX.1 and 7.

[57] See, for example, the hierarchy of the ten grades of holiness in Kelim I.6–9.

and vessels of the Temple, only what is "fit for the altar" and only what the function of the vessel ordinarily allows it to contain.[58]

Reflected in these halakot is reverence for *Ḳedushah*, rather than any notion of efficacy. The halakot enable this feeling of reverence to be expressed in actions, and as a consequence the feeling is externalized and cultivated. This is the real import of the gradations in holiness. Implicit in all these gradations is a guiding principle of action, namely, that one must act in such fashion that a higher degree of holiness is achieved if possible, and not a lower.[59] The manner in which this principle is applied varies greatly with the circumstances, but in all the circumstances the context is that of reverence.[60] This is the principle which informs the gradations in our holy objects, and in precisely that context. When a holy object is sold by a community, the money received must go toward the buying of an object of a higher grade of holiness; that alone accords with the

[58] See Zebaḥim IX.1 and 7. What is "fit for the altar" — the view of R. Gamaliel.

The halakah that the Holy Scriptures, single Books of Scripture, etc. "make the hands (ritually) unclean" (Yadaim III.2–5, and IV.5) represents a special case, and is not really aligned with the laws of ritual uncleanness, as can be seen from ibid., III.2, nor of course with the laws of *Ḳedushah*. Hence this halakah has to be accounted for on other grounds, and two explanations are given — one in ibid., IV.6, and the other in Zabim, end (and Bertinoro a. l.). SEE NOTES, P. 370.

We shall not enter into a discussion of the concept of *Ṭum'ah* (ritual uncleanness) which is the obverse of the concept of *Ḳedushah*. The last of the six orders of the Mishnah is devoted to this subject, but the laws became largely inoperative shortly after the fall of the Temple. It ought to be remarked, however, that there are stronger grounds for regarding *Ṭum'ah* as a "power" than there are in the case of *Ḳedushah*. *Ṭum'ah* is not only transmitted by contact (Kelim I.1–4) but can also be conducted (e. g. 'Oholot, Chap. VIII), and it "breaks out and ascends, breaks out and descends" (ibid., VII.1). But see Rab's view in Niddah 11a, according to which, in this case, *Ṭum'ah* is not anything resident in the object itself. SEE NOTES, P. 370.

[59] מעלין בקדש ולא מורידין — Menaḥot XI.7; Berakot 28a; Shabbat 21b; Yoma 12b (ibid., 73a, Megillah 9b, Horayot 12b); Yoma 20b; Megillah 21b; Menaḥot 39a.

[60] See the references in the preceding note.

principle.[61] Even the casual act of placing one book on top of another is made into a reverential act when it is done in accordance with the principle: A *sefer-Torah* may be placed on another *sefer-Torah,* it may be placed on a single Book of the Pentateuch, the latter may be placed on Books of Prophets and Hagiographa – but not the reverse.[62] In such acts the feeling of reverence for *Ḳedushah* is externalized. And this also happens when the accessories are given the status of holiness and treated accordingly.[63]

Like the holy objects, the holy days too are fixed concretizations of the concept of *Ḳedushah.* Indeed, the Halakah effectively objectifies or reifies the different character of each of these holy days. This differentiation and objectification is reflected in the gradations in holiness represented in the holy days. The Sabbath, the Day of Atonement, Rosh Ha-Shanah, the Three Festivals, and the Intermediate Days of the Festivals constitute a hierarchy of holiness[64] – each grade in the hierarchy differentiated from the others by the halakot pertaining to it, and especially by those halakot which prohibit anything classified as "labor." The holier the day the more inclusive is the sphere of prohibited "labors."[65] But these halakot not only differentiate one holy day from another; they objectify the days as well. By determining the actions of the individual for the duration of the day, they give the day a definite character. The mystic quality of *Ḳedushah* is thus concretized in days at least as effectively as it is concretized in objects.

[61] כיון דלא מעלי ליה אסור — Megillah 27a. See Rashi, ibid., 26a, s. v. אבל מכרו תורה.

[62] Ibid., 27a.

[63] Some would extend this reverence to speech as well. Those who call the *bet ha-keneset* the "house of the people" (*bet ha-'am*) are strongly disapproved of but so also those who call the holy ark simply "the ark" — Shabbat 32a.

[64] See Pesaḥim 104a and Tosafot, ibid., s. v. בעי למימר. On the holiness of the Intermediate Days, see Mekilta I, p. 68 f.; Sifra, ed. Weiss, p. 102b; Ḥagigah 18a and Tosafot, ibid., s. v. חולו של מועד.

[65] See Pesaḥim 104a and Tosafot, ibid., s. v. בעי למימר.

The problems presented by the holy days are many and complex. Here we shall but deal briefly with the question as to whether the holy days are conceived as having efficacy in themselves. The question arises with regard to the atoning power of *Yom Ha-Kippurim,* the Day of Atonement. One statement in the Mishnah is unequivocal: "He that says 'I will sin and the Day of Atonement will atone' – (In that case) the Day of Atonement does not atone,"[66] since such an attitude implies that there is lacking true repentance. But the Talmud points to a statement by Rabbi Judah the Prince which seems to contradict the mishnah; for Rabbi Judah declares that, except for certain sins, which he names, the Day of Atonement atones for all transgressions whether they have been repented of or not.[67] The two statements are reconciled by the Talmud with the remark that Rabbi Judah, too, would not hold that the Day atones when a man depends upon the Day and continues to transgress.[68] Nor is this idea merely a clever way of getting around a difficulty. It is an idea which is undoubtedly implicit in any rabbinic statement that attributes to the Day of Atonement some atoning power.[69] And if one must not depend on the atoning power of the Day, it is certainly not an outright power. In the liturgy of the Day of Atonement, what is stressed is God's forgiving grace, and the Day appears to be only the occasion of His forgiveness. "Our God and God of our fathers," so runs the prayer of the sanctification of the Day, the *Ḳedushat Ha-Yom,* "pardon our iniquities on this Day of Atonement . . . and purify our hearts to serve Thee in truth; for Thou art the

[66] Yoma VIII.9.

[67] Yoma 87a. Rabbi Judah's full statement is given ibid., 85b.

[68] Yoma 87a, and see Rashi a. l.

[69] Such as the statement that repentance alone atones for light transgressions, whilst that together with the Day of Atonement atone for the grave — Yoma VIII.8. See also Maimonides, Mishneh Torah, Hilkot Teshubah I.3, and the כסף משנה there.

forgiver of Israel and the pardoner of the tribes of Jeshurun in every generation, and besides Thee we have no king who pardoneth and forgiveth."[70] This prayer emanates from the Rabbis[71] and expresses their basic attitude. That attitude is again expressed by R. 'Aḳiba when he exclaims, "Happy are ye, O Israel! Before whom do ye purify yourselves, and who is he that purifies you? Your Father Who is in heaven."[72] And these words are deliberately placed in the Mishnah as the conclusion to the various halakot and statements concerning the Day of Atonement.

We observed above that halakic interpretation is modified or affected by the category of significance.[73] Now we have before us examples of a deeper relation between Halakah and that category. That deeper relation is to be seen in the enormous effect of the Halakah on the category of significance. In this section we have touched — no more than that — on but one segment of the Halakah, that which has to do with recurrent or fixed concretizations of the value-concepts. But it is Halakah that makes these concretizations recurrent or fixed, that makes them concretizations at all. Halakah directs the individual to the commonplace recurrent situations and actions and renders it possible for him to fill them with significance. Again, Halakah enables the individual to experience, in recurrent ritual acts, the mystical consciousness of holiness, and at the same time it makes him clearly apprehend the objective nature of the things that contribute to that experience. Finally, Halakah cultivates reverence for the holiness inherent in certain objects, and objectifies the holiness of certain days, without engendering the notion that these objects and days have mystical efficacy.

[70] Daily Prayer Book, ed. Singer, p. 257.

[71] See the references in Baer, op. cit., p. 412.

[72] Yoma, end.

[73] Above, p. 129 f.

The terms for the holy objects and the holy days are cognitive concepts. Associated with the concept of *Ḳedushah* is another cognitive concept, but of a different sort entirely, the concept of angels. "Angels" is a cognitive term because, in rabbinic literature, it not only stands for beings, but evokes a sense of their physical constitution. Thus a midrash describes the ministering angels as follows: they stand erect, they speak, they see, and they have understanding.[74] The term "angels," in other words, conveys a picture, as it were, of physical beings, and ought therefore to be distinguished from terms like *Ger* (proselyte), *Ẓaddiḳ* (a righteous man), or *Rasha'* (a wicked man). Although the latter, too, refer to beings, human beings, the terms as such convey nothing sensory or physical; rather, they refer to traits of personality or to cognate qualities, and hence are value-concepts.

"Angels" is a cognitive concept of a peculiar kind. If we wish to be fair, we ought to concede that in rabbinic times it is likely that there were some individuals in whose psychical life angels did figure. Stories are told by the Rabbis of persons in rabbinic times who had seen and talked with angels[75]; and these stories doubtless reflect psychical experiences on the part of at least some individuals. By and large, however, it is in rabbinic legends that the angels play their major role.

Angels and demons are often linked together by modern scholars. Ginzberg, for instance, seems to regard them both as "folkloristic" – "a great part if not all of the angelogical and demonological material found in the Babylonian Talmud is folkloristic."[76]

[74] Bereshit Rabba VIII.11, ed. Theodor, p. 64 f. Added features are given in the parallel in Ḥagigah 16a.

[75] See, for example, above, p. 136.

[76] L. Ginzberg, Commentary, English Introd., p. xxxv.

Schechter offers suggestive material on angelology. See Some Aspects of Rabbinic Theology, p. 49, note 2, and the first paragraph on p. 345.

But angels have a function in Haggadah which demons do not have. The concept of demons is limited in rabbinic literature to comparatively few passages scattered here and there. These passages reveal, to be sure, that demons belong to the same conceptual classification as angels. The concept of demons, like that of angels, is a cognitive concept. The concept of demons, too, conveys an idea of beings with a physical constitution, and one that is more tangible than that of angels. According to one statement, for example, demons have some physical features like those of angels and others like those of men.[77] But here the resemblance between angels and demons ends. Demons are malevolent creatures, as the rabbinic terms for them – "the harmful ones,"[78] "evil spirits"[79] – testify. Ever present dangers, diseases for which there was no effective remedy, gave support to the concept, as we can see from a passage wherein incantations against diseases blend with similar incantations against demons.[80] Nor were the Rabbis themselves immune to this popular belief. When an authority prohibited traffic with demons, it was not in order to discourage belief in them but, according to another authority, because of the danger involved, and this danger is illustrated by an incident.[81] Nevertheless, the Rabbis, and presumably the folk in general also, attached but little valuational significance to demons; the latter seldom figure in a situation interpreted by the value-concepts. Occasionally, as in the story about R. 'Aḥa bar Jacob, the supposed presence of a

[77] Ḥagigah 16a. Various descriptions of demons are given in Numbers Rabba XII.3.

[78] E. g. 'Abot V.6.

[79] E. g. Leviticus Rabba XXIV.3. Another rabbinic term for them is *shedim* — e. g., Ḥagigah 16a.

[80] Shabbat 67a.

[81] Sanhedrin 101a. That belief in demons was fairly widespread, even among the Rabbis, can also be gathered from other sources — e. g. from various statements in Numbers R. XII.3.

demon, like the presence of any other danger, may have caused a person to resort to prayer[82]; since prayer is a value-concept, demons were thereby brought into the orbit of the category of significance. Usually, however, demons were not brought into that orbit at all.[83] Incantations – often nothing but mumbo-jumbo – were recommended against demons,[84] and we may safely assume that such incantations, being a specific, were favored by the people at large. Actually, of course, the belief in demons, irresponsible, malevolent creatures, is hardly compatible with the idea of God's loving-kindness. R. Joḥanan and his colleague, R. Simeon b. Laḳish, probably felt this when they declared that, when the Tabernacle was set up, and the *Shekinah* (God) had therefore come "to dwell below, the harmful ones ceased from the world."[85]

In utter contrast, the concept of angels, whenever used by the Rabbis, is used exclusively in concretizations of the value-concepts. We have demonstrated this elsewhere,[86] and have shown how the angels serve as background to bring out the more prominently, in concrete fashion, God's active love for mankind and for the world; how they enhance the

[82] Ḳiddushin 29b.

[83] The attempt at connecting an interpretation of Ps. 20:3 with the story of the demons dwelling in a well, and given in Lev. R. XXIV.3 (Tanḥuma, Ḳedoshim, 9, ed. Buber 39a; Midrash Tehillim, ed. Buber 88b; Yalḳuṭ Shime'oni to Ps. 20:3, par. 680) is instructive in this regard. This is obviously an attempt to utilize a story about demons for ethical purposes, but the point made is indistinct, and the connection with the verse obscure. Such stories simply do not lend themselves to valuational interpretation.

Professor Lieberman called my attention to several passages that are not in line with our treatment of the subject. Two of them — 'Erubin 43a and Pesaḥim 110a — have to do with Joseph the *shed*, and a third — Yebamot 122a — with Jonathan the *shed*. These names may refer to persons versed in the lore of demons, as Rashi suggests explicitly in the case of Jonathan. The instance in Yer. Terumot 46b–c, however, is definitely an exception.

[84] Shabbat 67a.

[85] Numbers Rabba XII.3, end.

[86] TE, pp. 88–98.

vividness with which God's justice is apprehended, both in reward and in punishment; how they serve to underline the vast importance of Torah; how they bring into relief God's concern for Israel; and how they dramatize an aspect of *Ḳiddush Ha-Shem*. In fine, we may say that, with respect to the value-concepts, angelology has the function of supplying them with vivid concretizations. These vivid concretizations consist of stories and legends and, like all the haggadic legends, cultivated sensitiveness to the value-concepts.[87] The attitude to such legends we have described above: it is that of indeterminate belief.[88] Though both angels and demons are cognitive concepts, the kind of belief they inspire is, therefore, not the same. In the case of demons, it is a question simply of whether or not there exist localized "harmful ones" or "evil spirits." In the case of angels, the psychological attitude is much more subtle. Solely an element in many haggadic legends, they inspire the kind of belief that is accorded to haggadic legends in general – indeterminate belief which may harden, on occasion, and become determinate.

The angels are conceived as holy beings.[89] In the very attribution of this quality to the angels, we have another illustration of how angelology acts as background for the value-concepts. Whereas the angels received but one *Ḳedushah*, says R. 'Abun, Israel received two *Ḳedushot*, and this because Israel, unlike the angels, are exposed to the rule of the *Evil Yeẓer*.[90] Here the boon given Israel is made more

[87] See above, p. 141.

[88] Ibid., pp. 131 ff.

[89] See the references to the angels as holy beings in the *Yoẓer* prayer — Daily Prayer Book, ed. Singer, p. 38 f.; and in the *Ḳedushah* of the *Musaf*, ibid., p. 160. The source is Pirke de R. Eliezer, Chap. IV., end — see Baer, op. cit., p. 236. Angels are also referred to in the Talmud as "His holy ones" — Berakot 60b, top, and Rashi a. l. The phrase "and holy ones" in the third benediction of the '*Amidah* refers, according to Baer, op. cit., p. 89, either to Israel or to the angels.

[90] Leviticus Rabba XXIV.8; Yalḳuṭ Shime'oni to Isaiah 6:3, par. 405 (in a

striking by contrasting it with that given the angels. We gather from the parable with which R. 'Abun's statement begins that the two *Ḳedushot* are Israel's reward when they withstand the *Evil Yeẓer* — man's evil impulses, an idea akin to the negative implication of *Ḳedushah* we mentioned above.[91]

The Hebrew term for angel implies that the angels have no power, no efficacy, of their own. In both the Bible and rabbinic literature the term for angel is *mal'ak*, "messenger." And the Rabbis apparently wish to emphasize this meaning of the term. To the verse "Behold I send a *mal'ak* before thee" (Exod. 23:20), a rabbinic comment adds the prayer, "May it be Thy will, O my Father in heaven, that Thou never put us into the hand of a messenger — *shaliaḥ*."[92] All the haggadot in which angels figure retain that implication at bottom, the implication that the angels have no efficacy of their own. Angelology only serves to supply the value-concepts with vivid concretizations, even when angels are described as acting otherwise than just as messengers. Now the angels are conceived as holy beings, a fixed concretization in Haggadah of the concept of *Ḳedushah*. They present an analogy in this regard to the fixed concretizations of that concept to be found in Halakah — the holy objects and the holy days. The analogy goes further. Just as the holy objects and the holy days have no efficacy of their own, so the angels have no efficacy of their own. When the Rabbis attribute the mystical quality of *Ḳedushah* to anything, whether in Halakah or in Haggadah, that mystical quality has nothing in common with the mystical qualities projected by the primitive mind.

slightly different version). In the latter reference, see the preceding midrashim there for other illustrations of angelology making the concept of Israel more vivid.

[91] Above, p. 170.

[92] Seder Eliahu, ed. Friedmann, p. 119.

VIII. SUMMARY

What are the broad features of the category of significance?

It is the category of thought, speech, and action whereby the uniqueness of an individual's personality is expressed. That expression is registered in situations, or projected in actions, each of which is a unitary entity, and each of which is fraught with personality. In these situations or actions, the various types of concepts act in concert; that is, the various types of concepts are fused in such situations or actions, and when an event represents a fusion of various conceptual types, the latter obviously function as a single category. But not all the three conceptual types are necessarily involved at any one time; for an event to express personality, it is only necessary that, among the concepts involved, there be at least one value-concept. In a concrete valuational situation, cognitive concepts are *always* fused with one or more value-concepts, and defined concepts *may* also be involved. Thus in the giving of charity, to use our familiar example, there are, besides the concept of charity motivating the act, factors which are objective and cognitive in character — the objects given and all the material circumstances of the act. The state of poverty entitling a man to take charity has been defined by the Halakah; if this definition has been taken into account, the act of charity will involve, in addition to the value-concept and the cognitive concepts, also a defined concept.

The key-concepts in the category of significance are the value-concepts. Every particular valuational event or experience owes its unitary character to the value-concepts imbedded in it, for these imbedded concepts are the unifying agents in the situation. But they do more. In integrating what may be analyzed out as objective, impersonal elements, the value-concepts endow the situation as a whole with significance. The act of giving away money and food and clothing, to hold to our illustration, can be described purely in "operational" terms; for one who is not acquainted with the concept of charity, however, the act as a whole will have no significance.

The unitary valuational events represent but an aspect of what is achieved by the integrating, unifying function of the value-concepts. An individual's life is certainly not just a staccato series of isolated events. How are those unitary valuational events themselves related? The answer to this question reveals why such events are fraught with personality. The value-concepts are integrative factors in an individual's personality. An organismic complex in constant function, the value-concepts of an individual are nothing less than his personality at the point of self-consciousness, and as the concepts are integrated and dynamic, so is his personality at that point integrated and dynamic. A valuational event is the outward projection of a personality, the fullest projection possible under any given set of circumstances. Another way of stating this fact is to say that a valuational event represents an individual's felt interaction with the immediate environment. Between all the interactions there is an inevitable connection: an event is always strongly affected by the events or interactions which preceded it. A valuational event is thus at least as much the result of past events in an individual's life as it is of the new conditions and stimuli which give rise to it. The valuational events in an individual's life are therefore unitary but not isolated.

Nor is the individual's personality itself an isolated entity. Even the personality of an individual is an aspect of what is achieved by the integrating function of the value-concepts. The individual is related to all the other members of his group by means of the complex of value-concepts which they all have in common. If the value-concepts endow the individual with personality, they also endow the group as a whole with character.

The value-concepts can function in this manner because they are not defined. They are not definite and not objective, but connotative, suggestive, indeterminate. A value-concept ceases to be indeterminate only when it is fused with objective concepts, particularly cognitive concepts, in an event or statement, and this we have called the concretization of the concept. The value-concept is thus characterized, we may say, by a kind of potential determinacy, a determinacy which is realized when the concept acts in concert with other conceptual types. Only this kind of concept is subtle and fluid enough to give full expression to human *differentia* at the same time that it can be fixed, as it were, in an event.

Though the various types of concepts act in concert in any concretization, the conceptual types as such must be distinct. Value-concepts must be distinct from defined concepts. If a value-concept, even a phase of a value-concept, is defined, that phase does not function easily, as we saw in the case of the defined phase of the concept of *Nes*. Again, when cognitive concepts are used in place of value-concepts, the category of significance cannot operate. Instead of value-concepts, primitive societies employ "preformed connections" between certain cognitive concepts, and so manage to have valuational expression without benefit of the category of significance. But this is achieved at heavy cost. The cognitive concepts involved in the "preformed connections" are not clearly demarcated from each other; this linguistic or mental peculiarity so affects the vocabulary as a whole that the language is not analytic; and without an analytic, objective vocabulary there can be no science. On the other hand, the category of significance demands that there be a clear division between value-concepts, cognitive concepts, and defined concepts. Since science consists of systems of defined concepts, this means at the very least that the category of significance need not affect adversely the development of science.

Valuational events represent one mode of the category of significance. There is another mode – aesthetic expression. A work of art, too, is a unitary entity, and it, too, bears the imprint of the personality which achieved it. The difference between a valuational entity and an aesthetic entity is reflected in the respective ways in which the unitary character of the entity is produced. The unitary character of a valuational entity is due to the value-concepts embodied; the unitary character of an aesthetic entity is the result of balance, rhythm, form.

Haggadah is a literary expression of the valuational mode of the category of significance. It consists of discrete ideas or statements, each of which, like a valuational event, is a unitary entity wherein the unifying factors are value-concepts. In order to overcome the atomic character of the haggadic statements, something the Rabbis were obliged to do in their sermons and discourses, the discrete statements were often built up into larger structures by means of various compositional forms; in these instances, however, what gave the discourse its unity was the compositional form, an art form, not the valuational content. But a haggadic statement is, after all, a literary product, and hence presents aspects and gives rise to attitudes not associated with a nonliterary valuational event. These aspects and attitudes are matters which themselves belong to the category of significance – to the category of significance as it affects Haggadah. Thus, a haggadic statement usually takes its departure from a biblical verse, the biblical verse acting as a stimulus to the haggadic idea. Now any number of haggadic ideas can be touched off by the same biblical verse; the biblical verse acts therefore as a non-determining stimulus, and this is possible only because the element of indeterminacy is, by virtue of the indeterminate nature of the value-concepts, a characteristic of the category of significance. The same prime characteristic of the category of significance accounts for the attitude of mind in which the haggadic ideas are entertained. Haggadic statements inspire indeterminacy of belief that, on occasion, can harden and become determinate. This indeterminacy of belief allows room for legends and anthropomorphism.

Halakah is not a literary expression of the category of significance in the same sense as Haggadah. The halakot, the laws, are not discrete, independent entities, but are connected by an implicit nexus which becomes more and more explicit. Again, halakic interpretation of biblical verses is affected only to a degree by the category of significance. Nevertheless, the halakot play a very large rôle in the category of significance. They are concretizations of the value-concepts in their own right, and they enter into valuational events. It is due to the laws that a great many valuational acts take place at all, and hence the laws enter into these events much as defined concepts do; indeed, the laws include many defined concepts. Moreover, Halakah enlarges the category of significance by the way it treats certain objects and natural phenomena. It takes these objects and phenomena – all of them designated by cognitive concepts – and makes them more or less permanent factors in the category of significance.

CHAPTER VI

Normal Mysticism

To judge by rabbinic religious experience, the modern emphasis on the personal experience of God is only partly sound. From almost every page of the rabbinic texts it is evident that the Rabbis *experienced* God, and that this experience was profound and unique. But rabbinic religious experience is not the kind that is conditioned by pure "solitariness," nor has it so little of a social character as to be divided into numerous "varieties." The actual experience of God is personal; the ways or modes of experiencing God, however, are common to the group as a whole. Being common to the entire group, the modes of God-experience are expressed in value-concepts, among them such concepts as prayer, repentance, the study of Torah. The personal experience of God through the modes crystallized by these and other value-concepts can be characterized, we expect to show, as normal mysticism.

I. CONCEPTUAL TERMS FOR GOD

At first glance it would seem that the Rabbis employ *'Eloah* and *'El*, biblical terms for God,[1] in more or less the same way as they do conceptual terms. A conceptual term is always classificatory, that is, it puts particular instances into a single classification. This would seem to be true, as well, of the way in which the Rabbis employ the words

[1] See Gesenius, Handwörterbuch, on these terms.

'Eloah and *'El*. Both are used as generic terms, and either may refer to pagan deities as well as to God. A third biblical word for God which the Rabbis use is *'Elohim*,[1] and this word too has its conceptual aspect.

The word *'Eloah* is used as a general term. In a passage, for example, where the contrast is drawn between God, who hears prayer, and idols, *'Abodah Zarah*, which cannot, the word is to be found twice – first in a specific reference to idols and later in a generic sense, but where the application is to God. When speaking of an idol, the passage says, " *'Eloho* – his god, i. e., the idolater's god – is with him in the house," and when speaking of God who hears prayer though it be only whispered, the passage asks, "Can you have a God – *'Eloah* – nearer than that?"[2] *'Eloah* is used in a generic sense, and yet with reference to *God* in the following statement: "He that dwells in the Land of Israel can be considered as he who has a God – *'Eloah* – and he that dwells outside the Land can be considered as he who has no God – *'Eloah*."[3] On the other hand, in the statement "A graven image becomes a god – *'Eloah* – as soon as it has been made," (that is, even before it has been worshipped),[4] the word as used in a generic sense is applied to idols.

It is usually this term for God – *'Eloah* – that the Rabbis employ in a generic manner. But the word *'El* also occurs as a generic term, although rather infrequently. It refers to God in the dictum "One God – *'El* – gave them"[5]; and it refers to *'Abodah Zarah*, the idol of the golden

[2] Yer. Berakot IX.1, 13a. The reference to idols is an elaboration of Is. 46:7, and the reference to God is associated with Deut. 4:7.

[3] Ketubbot 110b (comp. Tosefta 'Abodah Zarah IV [V].3, 5, ed. Zuck.-Lieb., p. 466) — דומה כמי שיש לו אלוה. For the negative of this expression, also given here, see 'Abodah Zarah 17b and Rashi's comment there.

[4] 'Abodah Zarah 52b. Other examples of the term as used in a generic sense are also to be found there.

[5] Ḥagigah 3b, and see Rashi a. l.

calf, when *'El* is taken as a separate word in a play on "Nahaliel" (Num. 21:19).[6] As to the word *'Elohim,* it refers only to God when it is not inflected and used as a singular noun. Nevertheless, this word too has its conceptual aspect, and that is expressed in the possessive forms of the word. Possessive forms of the word *'Elohim* are used not only when the reference is to God but also when the reference is to a pagan deity. When referring to God, the Rabbis will often use the expression *'Elohenu,* our God, as when R. Joshua b. Ḳorḥa, for example, exclaims, "How long will you continue to hand over the people of our God for slaughter?"[7] But there are also instances where a possessive form of the word *'Elohim* in the singular has reference to a pagan deity. Thus, for example, the Rabbis say that no nation is smitten but what "her god — *'eloheha* — is smitten with her"[8]; and here the singular of the verb "smitten" indicates that the possessive *'eloheha* is also in the singular. The possessive forms of *'Elohim* evidently imply, then, a generic idea.

But what generic idea do the various terms convey? How can there be a classification which would include both God and the pagan deities, both God and *'Abodah Zarah*? Of one thing we may be certain, namely, that a truly inclusive classification here is out of the question. God and *'Abodah Zarah* could, under no circumstances, be given a common status.

'Abodah Zarah was, of course, abhorrent to the Rabbis, and many are the laws and prohibitions that are concerned with it.[9] Most of these laws relate, directly or indirectly, to the matter of worship — "strange" and wrong worship, as the name *'Abodah Zarah* indicates. If, therefore, what was

[6] Midrash Tehillim to Ps. 5:1, ed. Buber 25a–b; Yalḳuṭ Shime'oni, Ḥuḳḳat, par. 764.

[7] Baba Meẓi'a 83b.

[8] Sukkah 29a. See Edeles' remarks on Rashi's comment a. l.

[9] Tractate 'Abodah Zarah.

an idol of any kind is definitely no longer an object of worship, it no longer has the odium of *'Abodah Zarah.* But when can it be said that an idol is definitely no longer worshipped? When its pagan worshipper demonstrates, by some action upon the idol, that he has ceased to regard it as a god.[10] He thereby "cancels" (*mebaṭṭel*) the idol.[11] The converse of "cancelling" is the acknowledgment or acceptance of an object as a god. Grouped together are he who worships an idol in accordance with its particular form of worship, or else with a form of Temple-worship, and he who "accepts it as a god (*le-'Eloah*) upon himself or says to it, 'Thou art my god (*'Eli*).' "[12]

Now we have met before with the idea of acknowledgment or acceptance. We saw above that Israel, according to the Rabbis, early in its career accepted *Malkut Shamayim*, the Kingship of God. This took place in Egypt, according to one opinion,[13] whilst others say that it occurred at Sinai.[14] The acceptance of *Malkut Shamayim*, however, is not something that happened on only one or another occasion in the past. There is acceptance of *Malkut Shamayim* daily by the individual, morning and evening, when he recites the *Shema'*.[15] This acceptance of God's Kingship is really obligatory upon all of mankind; the time will come when "the idols will be utterly cut off" and when all the inhabitants of the world "will accept the yoke of Thy Kingship."[16] Since the idea of acceptance or acknowledgment is applied to idols as well, however, we have here a generalizing idea. The Rabbis

[10] 'Abodah Zarah, 53a and 49b. Also by an action with regard to it — ibid., 53b.

[11] Ibid., 52b.

[12] Sanhedrin 60b. See also Mechilta de R. Simon, ed. Hoffmann, p. 105. And see the remarks of Maharam of Lublin on Sanhedrin 61a, beg. רמי ליה.

[13] See above, p. 20 f.

[14] Ibid., p. 21.

[15] See ibid., p. 130 and note 35 there.

[16] The *'Alenu* prayer — Prayer Book, ed. Singer, p. 77; see Baer, op. cit., p. 132; and comp. above, p. 19.

convey that generalizing idea when they employ the possessive forms of the word *'Elohim*, and when they use the terms *'Eloah* and *'El* in a generic sense. Our instances of the acceptance of *Malkut Shamayim* are based on biblical verses, and it is noteworthy that the terms for God in those verses are all possessive forms of *'Elohim*.[17]

Yet these terms are not genuine generic terms. The expression "other gods" in Exod. 20:3 causes the Rabbis to ask, "But are they gods (*'Elohot*)? Has it not been said, 'And have cast their gods into the fire; for they were no gods'" (Is. 37:19)? Various explanations are then offered for the expression "other gods" — among them that others (i. e. the pagans) call them gods; that they act like "others," strangers, toward those who worship them; that they are always being made over into new and other gods, since he that has one of gold and then needs the gold makes one of silver, and he that has one of silver and then needs the silver makes one of copper, and so on.[18] What these and the rest of the explanations amount to is, in every case, a negation of "other gods." Such negation, explicit as in the passage just discussed or else implied in the contexts, accompanies our "generic" terms whenever they refer to *'Abodah Zarah*. They are therefore not really inclusive of *'Abodah Zarah*, and this on the very occasions when they have reference to it. More accurately, the generic terms first include and then immediately negate "other gods."

In the passage above, the Rabbis employ the word *'Elohot*, gods, plural of *'Eloah*. This plural is found often enough elsewhere. Thus we are told that sectarians asked R. Simlai,

[17] The verses are: in regard to Egypt — Exod. 20:2; to Sinai — Lev. 18:2; the *Shema'* — Deut. 6:4.

The expression "acknowledge My Godhead" (*'Elohuti*) is apparently equivalent to "acknowledge My Kingship" — see Bereshit R. XLVI.9, ed. Theodor, p. 466; similarly Canticles R. I.13.

[18] Mekilta, II, pp. 239–241; ed. Horovitz-Rabin, pp. 223–4, and the notes there.

"How many *'Elohot*, gods, created the world?"[19] Again, in another passage, the Rabbis interpret Ezek. 33:24 as an attempt on the part of the inhabitants of "the waste places in the land of Israel" (ibid.) to draw a contrast in their favor between Abraham, "who worshipped only one God (*'Eloah*)," and themselves, "who worship many gods (*'Elohot*)."[20] Obviously, this plural is employed only when *'Abodah Zarah* is in mind, not God,[21] and that fact is further evidence that *'Eloah* is not a genuinely generic term. A true generic term does not possess a form that is not generic.

We may say, then, that the generic terms are not really classificatory, do not represent a true classification. This observation is borne out by another way in which the terms are used. They are sometimes used as though they were proper nouns, names, while still clearly retaining a conceptual connotation. For example, in reference to him who greets his fellow man before the morning *Tefillah*, Samuel applies Is. 2:22 to mean, "With what right didst thou pay thy regard to him and not to *'Eloah*?"[22] Again, quoting Ben Sira the Rabbis say, "*'Eloah* made drugs come forth out of the earth" so that men may be healed of wounds.[23] Similarly, the term *'Elohim* is used as a proper noun, though with a conceptual connotation, in what Epstein has described as "didactic *derashot*"; he calls attention to the frequent occasions when it occurs in place of the term "the Holy One blessed be He" in such Midrashim as the Pesiḳta R., Exodus R., and in the other Yelammedenu passages or collections.[24] We cannot tell for sure in every instance,

[19] Bereshit R. VIII.9, ed. Theodor, p. 62, and the parallels given there.

[20] Tosefta Soṭah VI.9, ed. Zuck.-Lieb., p. 305. For the expression "many *'Elohot*," see also Ḥullin 60b, Sanhedrin 101b.

[21] The plural *'Elohot*, gods, must not be confused with *'Elohut*, Godhead. The latter is used with reference to God — see above, p. 198, note 17. Levy, Wörterbuch, s. v. אלהות, apparently confuses the two terms; see the references there.

[22] Berakot 14a.

[23] Bereshit R. X.6, ed. Theodor, p. 78.

[24] A. Epstein, מקדמוניות היהודים (Wien, 1887), pp. 62–3; see also L. Ginzberg

however, whether it is the nominal or the conceptual element which predominates. Certainly when the terms are found in a phrase like "*Ha-'El* (O, God) our salvation and our help,"[25] the conceptual element is strong, and so, too, when occurring in a statement like, "(Both) these and these are the words of (the) living God (*'Elohim*)."[26] In any case, the nominal element is also present, as it is when we use, in a completely analogous manner, the term "God" and capitalize the first letter. When the generic terms, all of them synonymous, are thus restricted into a name, they have no generic character, even while retaining a conceptual connotation. In other words, they spell not "god" or "gods" but "God." By and large this holds also for the generic terms for God in the Bible.[27]

What kind of concept, then, is the rabbinic (and biblical) concept of God? It is a concept *sui generis*. It cannot, in the first place, be classed as a defined concept. To be sure, occasionally a statement here and there may look like a definition, but not on closer scrutiny. R. Ḥananiah ben Antigonos, for example, calls attention to the literal meaning of the name *Molek* – "ruler" – in Lev. 18:21; and he draws the conclusion that it stands for "anything at all which you declare as ruling over you, even if it be a chip of wood or a potsherd."[28] But this definition patently refers to idols only; the definition is, therefore, like the other statements in that passage, a negation of "other gods." As a matter of fact, the rabbinic concept of God is simply not amenable to definition. In the case of a defined concept, the definition is all-important and the conceptual term something quite secondary.[29] Here, on the contrary, the

Genizah Studies, I, p. 28, and the selection there on pp. 37 ff.; also ibid., p. 51, and the selection on pp. 52 ff.

[25] In the '*Amidah* — Prayer Book, ed. Singer, p. 53.

[26] 'Erubin 13b; Giṭṭin 6b.

[27] See below, p. 300, note 57.

[28] Mekilta, II, pp. 240–1, and the references there.

[29] See above, p. 46.

term is essential to the concept, whether the term is used generically or whether it is used as a proper noun. Despite this essential character of the conceptual term, however, the concept of God is not a value-concept. A value-concept is always a classifying term,[30] and we have shown that the conceptual terms for God do not represent a classification. By the same token, since cognitive concepts, too, are classifying terms, the concept of God is not a cognitive concept.

The rabbinic concept of God, hence, is neither a cognitive, nor a valuational, nor a defined concept. Again, a generic term for God can also serve as a proper noun. What does all this imply?

II. THE EXPERIENCE OF GOD

"The world of each of us," says de Laguna, "is not completely objectified, but retains a privacy which is inexpressible to ourselves and incommunicable to others."[1] De Laguna has reference here to our sense perceptions, to our "immediate and incommunicable recognition of the 'rightness' of the look and feel of textures and consistencies and combinations."[2] But any living experience, not only sense perceptions, has an *aspect* to it which is purely private, incommunicable. Is there any experience that *as a whole* is essentially incommunicable? The mystics have insisted that this is true of the mystical experience of God. Indeed in the words "a privacy which is inexpressible to ourselves

[30] See ibid., p. 36 — the example of *Derek Ereẓ*, and ibid., p. 38 — the example of *'Abot*. In *Malkut Shamayim*, the classifying aspect is in the idea of "accepting *Malkut Shamayim*," and the instances thus classified may be either in Israel's past or the individual's daily experience — see above, p. 197, and TE (see above, p. 15, n. 2), p. 60 f.

[1] G. de Laguna, op. cit., p. 290.

[2] Ibid., p. 291.

and incommunicable to others," we have an apt characterization of mystical experience. Is this not also what the rabbinic concept of God comes to? It is neither cognitive, nor valuational, nor defined — that is to say, nonexpressible to oneself, noncommunicable to others. The rabbinic concept of God stands for mystical experience, experience like none other.

Yet the rabbinic experience of God is not *altogether* ineffable, is not *exclusive* mysticism. Always there is a personal relationship to God that enables man to address God as "Thou," especially in a *Berakah*. That is why a generic term for God can also serve as a proper noun, a symbol that stands not for a generalizing idea but for a unique relationship; and when an experience permits the expression of a relationship, it is at least to that extent not ineffable.[3] Moreover, we shall find that certain concepts are associated with this mystical experience, after all. The concept of God by itself, indeed, points to the essentially private character of the mystical experience; there are other concepts, however, through which that experience does become, to a degree, communicable.

At present we shall not deal directly with the communicability of the mystical experience of God, but with the various ways of experiencing Him. These ways of experiencing God are crystallized in a large group of value-concepts — in concepts like *Middat Ha-Din, Middat Raḥamim, Nes,* prayer, repentance, Torah, *Miẓwot, Yir'at Shamayim, Ḳiddush Ha-Shem* and a number of others. Each of these concepts has a character of its own, a connotation not shared by any other concept, as is true of all value-

[3] The mysticism of the Buddhist is a way of salvation in which the attempt is made to escape from the world. This is another way of saying that there is an attempt to escape from all relationships. Hence, he "has no god to thank, as he had previously no god to invoke during his struggle." See H. Oldenberg, Buddha, trans. Hoey (London, Edinburgh: Williams and Norgate, 1882), p. 314.

On exclusive mysticism, see the reference above, p. 176, note 39.

concepts.[4] Nevertheless, in one way or another, all of them refer to God and are thus but different ways of experiencing Him. It often happens, therefore, that several concepts of that kind will bear on a single situation at once, reinforcing each other and rendering the experience of God all the stronger. We may recall, for example, that the concepts of *Middat Raḥamim* (God's love), *Nes*, and *Berakah* are all involved when a morsel of bread has been eaten.[5]

We can perhaps now begin to recognize why the rabbinic experience of God can be thought of as normal mysticism. The ordinary, familiar, everyday things and occurrences, we have observed, constitute occasions for the experience of God. Such things as one's daily sustenance, the very day itself, are felt as manifestations of God's loving-kindness, calling forth *Berakot*.[6] *Ḳedushah*, holiness, which is nothing else than the imitation of God, is concerned with daily conduct, with being gracious and merciful, with keeping oneself from defilement by idolatry, adultery, and the shedding of blood.[7] The *Birkat Ha-Miẓwot* evokes the consciousness of holiness at a rabbinic rite, but the objects employed in the majority of the rites are nonholy and of general character, while the several holy objects are nontheurgic.[8] And not only do ordinary things and occurrences bring with them the experience of God. Everything that happens to a man evokes that experience, evil as well as good, for a *Berakah* is said also at evil tidings.[9] Hence, although the experience of God is like none other, the *occasions* for experiencing Him, for having a consciousness of Him, are manifold, even if we consider only those that call for *Berakot*.

[4] See above, pp. 38 ff.

[5] Above, p. 168 f.

[6] Ibid.

[7] Ibid., p. 169 f.

[8] Ibid., pp. 170 ff.

[9] Berakot IX.2, 5. This *Berakah* extols "the true Judge," and is thus a concretization of God's justice. SEE NOTES, P. 371.

The everyday situations and events bring with them the consciousness of God because these events are made significant by value-concepts. This means that every man, in the course of his everyday activities, has some experience of God. For the value-concepts, including the concepts representing the ways of experiencing God, not only give the group as a whole a special character, but integrate the personality of every individual within the group.[10] In reacting merely to the normal events or demands of the environment, therefore, events such as those mentioned in the preceding paragraph, every individual is bound to have, at least in some degree, experience of God. Of course, individuals who are particularly sensitive, or who possess other advantages of temperament, will apprehend more than those who are less gifted or perhaps less well trained. But every member of the group, by being given the value-concepts, is thereby already given training and sensitivity. In this kind of mysticism, normal mysticism, the ordinary man closely approaches the gifted man.

A matter directly associated with the normal mysticism of the Rabbis has been strangely misinterpreted by some recent writers. Instead of the conceptual terms for God, the Rabbis usually employ appellatives or epithets for God – the Holy One blessed be He, the *Maḳom* (Space or Place), Heaven, Above, the *Dibbur* (Word), the Name, Father in heaven, the King of the kings of kings, and a number of others.[11] Some recent writers profess to see in such epithets, and especially in the terms Heaven, *Maḳom,* Above, the Name, and the like, evidence that to the Rabbis God was remote, cold, unapproachable. This view is disproved by

[10] See above, pp. 76 ff.

[11] See A. Marmorstein, The Old Rabbinic Doctrine of God, I, The Names and Attributes of God (London: Oxford University Press, 1927), pp. 54–107, for a long list of all these appellations. (See also TE, pp. 49 ff.). Marmorstein takes up ibid., pp. 17 ff., the question of the Tetragrammaton in rabbinic times. We do not deal with this problem, since our concern here is with the terms for God in common use.

passage after passage in rabbinic literature, indeed by the very passages which contain even such abstract appellatives as *Maḳom* and Master of the world. To quote several instances from those cited by Schechter: "Beloved are Israel, for they are called children of Space (*Maḳom*)," as it is said, "Ye are children unto the Lord your God"[12]; "Israel (on the waters of Marah) was supplicating and praying to their Father in Heaven, as a son who implores his father, and a disciple who beseeches his master, saying unto him: Master of the world, we have sinned against Thee, when we murmured on the sea."[13] Passages like these, depicting a warm personal relationship to God, but reflect the normal mysticism which the Rabbis, and the people as a whole, experienced in everyday life. And in the expression of that normal mysticism, the appellatives and epithets themselves are an important factor. They are used as names for God, names applied to Him out of feelings of unbounded reverence and love[14]; they are, in fact, just so many tributes of reverence and love, and hence their multiplicity. Being thus names alone for God, not generalizing concepts, the appellatives represent a personal relationship to God, the sheer consciousness of Him, more poignantly perhaps than do the names for God that are also conceptual terms. This is true regardless of whether a particular epithet originated with the Rabbis or in some Alexandrine schools; as used by the Rabbis, it is always a reverential name for God, never a designation for an emanation or an intermediary. In other words, when the Rabbis speak of the *Dibbur* or the *Memra'*, they always "mean God."[15] They "mean God" because

[12] 'Abot III.18; cited by Schechter, Some Aspects of Rabbinic Theology, p. 34.

[13] Mekilta 45b, ed. Friedmann; ed. Lauterbach, II, 93; cited by Schechter, op. cit., p. 34, and his note there. The translation of these two passages is Schechter's. See also his entire treatment of the matter, pp. 21 ff.

[14] See TE, p. 56 f.

[15] "The Rabbi may speak of the *Dibbur* or the *Memra* but means God; the

God to them was an experience, heartfelt and personal, and the epithets, the names, stand for the singularity of that experience, for a relationship so unique as to be symbolized by reverential names rather than by a general idea.

The appellatives or epithets are used as names for God, then, in the same way as are the conceptual terms for God. Similarly, another term, a value term, performs another function of the conceptual terms for God. The latter negate heathen gods, "other gods," but so also does the concept of *'Abodah Zarah,* the rabbinic concept which connotes the idea that all heathen worship is "strange," wrong and abhorrent.[16] Functions of the conceptual terms for God are thus also the functions of other terms in the rabbinic vocabulary, and it is, therefore, not surprising to find the use of the conceptual terms themselves to be fairly limited. The terms *'El, 'Eloah,* and *'Elohim* – our conceptual terms – are in the main limited in rabbinic literature, Guttmann has pointed out, to five contexts. They occur when the difference between God and *'Abodah Zarah* is emphasized; in interpretations of biblical verses containing these terms; in texts of rabbinic prayers; as a kind of oath or vow (*'Elohim*) which is really but a strong affirmation or negation; in discussions with Gentiles or in statements attributed to Gentiles.[17]

Why should the conceptual terms occur in just these contexts and so seldom elsewhere? Every usage here, we think, can be accounted for. The conceptual terms, we have said, first include and then immediately negate "other gods"; hence these terms add point in a context where the difference between God and "other gods" is emphasized. In statements attributed to Gentiles, the use of the con-

Hellenist may speak of God, but means the *Dibbur* or the *Memra*" — Schechter, op. cit., p. 43, note.

[16] See above, p. 196.

[17] Michael Guttmann, מפתח התלמוד, Vol. III, Part I (Breslau, 1924), pp. 3 ff., and the references there.

ceptual terms reflects the fact that a similar generic idea is known to the Gentiles and is represented by terms in their vocabularies. This would also account for the presence of the conceptual terms in discussions with Gentiles. When commenting on biblical verses containing the conceptual terms, the Rabbis must obviously use these terms if the comment is to be recognized as bearing on the verse. The wide prevalence of the conceptual terms in the prayers is also an aspect of the influence of the Bible. Rabbinic prayers are studded with phrases adapted from the Bible, and even with whole verses, and hence the style of the prayers has a definite biblical quality.[18] Thoroughly in keeping is the prevalence in the prayers of the conceptual terms for God, since these terms, too, are biblical. The oathlike form of affirmation and negation appears likewise to have come down from prerabbinic times, and to have been an ingrained speech habit. In all these contexts, then, there were reasons for using the conceptual terms for God. Aside from such contexts, however, the Rabbis usually refer to God in appellatives or epithets; the latter not only suggest a warm personal relationship to God but have also the added advantage of being expressions of reverence and love. Again, whenever the Rabbis refer to "other gods," aside from the special context just mentioned, it is usually by means of the value-concept of '*Abodah Zarah*; not only is that term a designation for "other gods" but at the same time it also stigmatizes and negates them.

What we have in normal mysticism is not a logically conceived idea of God but, far more than that, an awareness of Him. How poignant was this mystical consciousness of God, and what care was taken to cultivate it, are illustrated particularly well in the case of prayer. Evoking, accompanying rabbinic prayers, whether petition or praise, was a

[18] The Daily '*Amidah* is an especially good example — see Baer, op. cit., pp. 87 ff., and his commentary. See also C. Tchernowitz, קצור התלמוד, Vol. I, Introd., p. xxvi. SEE NOTES, P. 371.

sense, more than physical, of God's nearness. "Can you have a God nearer than that?" ask the Rabbis in telling of how God hears even a whispered prayer.[19] This sense of God's nearness to a man in prayer allows an authority to put into a rule what must long have been a matter of practice. "He that prays ought to regard himself as though *Shekinah* (God) were in front of him, as it says 'I have set the Lord always before me'" (Ps. 16:2).[20] The same practice apparently informs Rab's dictum that a *Berakah* (benediction) ought always to begin with, "Blessed art Thou, O Lord," a dictum which is again based on the verse, "I have set the Lord always before me."[21] A practice of another kind is reported of the "*Ḥasidim* (pious men) of the former generations." In order to fix their mind (lit., their heart) upon God (*Maḳom*), it was their custom to wait and concentrate for an hour, and only then to pray.[22] A different tannaitic report has it that there was also a similar period of waiting after the prayer.[23] Practices like these are practices of men whose consciousness of God is fundamentally a mystical one, of men who trustfully expect to have experience of Him, and to have it as a concomitant of "ordinary" prayer, prescribed prayer.

These and similar rules or practices were not confined to

[19] See above, p. 195.

[20] Sanhedrin 22a — כנגדו.

[21] Midrash Tehillim on Ps. 16:2, ed. Buber, p. 61b, and Buber's note there. Yalḳuṭ Shime'oni on that verse emphasizes that the verse is the basis for Rab's opinion and not for Samuel's. The rule or practice and Rab's dictum are linked in Maḥzor Vitry, par. 88, ed. Hurwitz, p. 56. "Blessed art Thou, O Lord" itself is taken from Ps. 119:12.

[22] Berakot V.1 — כדי שיכונו את לבם למקום. The mishnah in the Gemara has לאביהם שבשמים — Berakot 30b. The reference to God does not occur in the phrase as found in the Mishnah of Talmud Yerushalmi, and hence Tosefot Yom Tob on Ber. V.1 says that the practice may have had the purpose only of concentration on the saying of the prayers. But he cites R. Jonah Girondi who (in his commentary on Alfasi a. l.) insists that it is for the purpose of concentrating ברוממות השם. In any case, the Babylonian tradition here is unequivocal. And what of the baraita that there was a period of waiting *after* prayer (see the following note)?

[23] Berakot 32b; Yer. Berakot V.1, 8d.

the spiritual leaders, although undoubtedly originating with them. The Halakah made of such aids to prayer the practices of the people as a whole. Rab's formula for a *Berakah* was accepted as the standard.[24] Even the difficult practice of "the *Ḥasidim* of the former generations" appears to have been taken as an example and followed in a modified form.[25] The idea of "the whispered prayer," to mention only those matters already touched upon, was likewise incorporated in a halakic practice. It is forbidden for a person to cause his voice to be heard when he prays.[26] "He that causes his voice to be heard when he prays," declares a baraita, is among those of little faith, (and) he that raises his voice when he prays is among the false prophets.[27] It was expected that the people at large cultivate a sense of the immediate nearness of God.

The experience of God was intrinsic to rabbinic prayer. Besides the types of *Berakot* we have referred to, there are the Eighteen *Berakot* of the daily *'Amidah*, the *Berakot* of the *Shema'*, the special Sabbath and Festival *Berakot*,[28] and others,[29] each with its own theme and character. Repeated

[24] See, for example, the list of *Berakot* in Baer, op. cit., p. 566 f. Rab's dictum is given in another form in Berakot 12a, 40b. Saadia Gaon characterizes the formula as "a fundamental rule" — Siddur R. Saadie Gaon (Jerusalem: Meḳiẓe Nirdamim, 1941), p. 83; see also note 7 ibid.

[25] It is so understood by the codists. See Ṭur, Oraḥ Ḥayyim, par. 93; Maimonides, Mishneh Torah, Hilkot Tefillah IV.16, and the commentaries there. See also Berakot 32b — the statement of R. Joshua b. Levi and the baraita following it.

[26] Berakot 31a, bottom. Cf. Tosefta Berakot III.9; Yer. Berakot IV.1, 7a. See Ginzberg, Commentary, III, p. 7, and references there regarding the reading of להגביה.

[27] Berakot 24b, top. Rashi a. l. adds in a gloss on "those of little faith" — "As though the Holy One blessed be He does not hear a whispered prayer."

[28] See Baer, op. cit., and the references: Daily *'Amidah*, pp. 87 ff.; *Berakot* of the *Shema'*, pp. 76 ff.; Sabbath Berakot, p. 187 f., p. 198 f., p. 219; Festival *Berakot*, p. 348 f., p. 366.

[29] For example, for *Hallel* — ibid., p. 328, p. 332; for the new month — ibid., p. 334 f. According to R. Me'ir a man ought to recite a hundred *Berakot* every day— Menaḥot 43b.

each time, "Blessed art Thou" gains in meaning from every additional theme, and the consciousness evoked by "Thou" becomes richer and deeper. Nor do the *Berakot* alone make for the mystical apprehension of God through prayer; it is an experience evoked by the language and content of rabbinic prayers in general. God's relation to man, tender and majestic at once, becomes in prayer a felt reality. "O our Father, merciful Father, ever compassionate, have mercy upon us."[30] "Forgive us, O our Father, for we have sinned; pardon us, O our King, for we have transgressed."[31] The language of prayer is often the language of poetry, but this is not, in rabbinic prayer, a deliberate intention. Rather, it is the breaking through into words of the awareness of God. "Though our mouths were full of song as the sea, and our tongues of exultation as the multitude of its waves, and our lips of praise as the wide-extended firmament; though our eyes shone with light like the sun and the moon, and our hands were spread forth like the eagles of heaven, and our feet were swift as hinds, we should still be unable to thank Thee and to bless Thy Name, O Lord our God and God of our fathers, for one thousandth or one ten thousandth part of the bounties which Thou hast bestowed upon our fathers and upon us."[32]

Rabbinic prayer illustrates how Halakah, the product of

[30] Singer Prayer Book, p. 39; Baer, op. cit., p. 80.

[31] From the Daily *'Amidah* — Singer's Prayer Book, p. 46; Baer, op. cit., p. 90.

[32] From the *Nishmat* prayer — Singer P. B., p. 125 (Singer's translation); Baer, p. 207. See Baer's commentary, p. 206. This part of the *Nishmat* is referred to in Berakot 59b, and quoted in such fashion as to indicate that it is of earlier origin and well known. According to Davidson, there are three parts to the *Nishmat* prayer, and the selection we have given consists of the second part and was composed during the 'Amoraic period in Palestine — Israel Davidson, אוצר השירה והפיוט (New York: Jewish Theological Seminary of America, 1930), Vol. III, p. 231. A few words in our selection are apparently later interpolations to make the meaning clearer; they are "of song," "of exultation," "of praise," "shone with light," "spread forth," "swift" — see Seder R. Amram Gaon, ed. Frumkin, Vol. II (Jerusalem, 1912) p. 23a, and the references there. The original version is more powerful and more suggestive, certainly in the Hebrew.

the spiritual leaders, facilitates the expression of the value-concepts. Halakah gives regularity and steadiness to the drive toward concretization possessed by the concept of prayer, enlarges the scope of its expression, and supplies the means for its expression. The drive for concretization functions best when it is touched off by a stimulus, as is true of the haggadic expression of the concepts.[33] But it is due to Halakah that instead of being haphazard the stimuli are regular and steady. It is Halakah that makes of every occasion on which a person eats or drinks a stimulus for prayer. Not only that, but Halakah sensitizes a person to stimuli for prayer otherwise barely perceptible – for example, to the different periods of the day as occasions for morning, afternoon and evening prayer.[34] And besides thus enlarging enormously in these and other ways the scope of prayer, Halakah supplies the individual with the *Berakot* and prayers themselves, with means of expression developed by the creative minds and spirits. At the same time Halakah encourages spontaneous prayer and private petitions, and especially the adding of such prayers to appropriate sections of the Eighteen *Berakot*.[35]

Is it, then, so surprising that the ordinary man and the gifted man should have had the same kind of experience of God? Through the agency of Halakah, the gifted man shared his finest achievements with the ordinary man, the spiritual leader brought the common man up to his own level.[36] This is most noticeable in prayer, but it also holds,

[33] See above, pp. 113 ff.

[34] Tanḥuma, Ḥayye Sarah, par. 5 – "How many *Tefillot* ought a man to pray during the day?" The answer by Rabbi Samuel b. Naḥman. See also above, p. 128, notes 28 and 29.

[35] 'Abodah Zarah 8a. The several statements there given in the name of Rab. See also Rashi, ibid., s. v. מעין כל ברכה. (Comp. Berakot 31a). Notice the statement of Rabba and R. Joseph in Berakot 29b. See also Soṭah 32b.

[36] The interaction between the spiritual leaders and the folk is a matter developed above, pp. 84 ff., where we described how the spiritual leaders trained the folk by means of Haggadah.

in a great degree, with regard to the other ways of experiencing God characteristic of normal mysticism.

We have spoken before of the acknowledgment and acceptance of God's Kingship by the individual. This "acceptance of the yoke of *Malkut Shamayim*"[37] is by itself sufficient indication that we have to do not with a formulated concept of God but with mystical experience of Him. And again that mystical experience is achieved by every man, and again through the agency of Halakah. Integrating into the morning and evening liturgies a unit composed of two sections from Deuteronomy (6:4–9 and 11:13–21) and one from Numbers (15:37–41), Halakah designates the first verse in that unit as an affirmation of *Malkut Shamayim*.[38] But although powerfully suggestive, the verse – "Hear, O Israel, the Lord is our God, the Lord is One" – contains the idea of God's Kingship only by implication. To make that idea explicit, the Rabbis inserted after the verse in the liturgy a kind of response taken from Temple usage.[39] Now the sheer reading or reciting of the *Shema'*, as the unit composed of the three biblical sections is called, is not enough. The reciting of the *Shema'* requires *Kawwanah*, a term as untranslatable as most of the rabbinic value terms but perhaps best conveyed in this connection by such words as intention, devotion, concentration; and the *Kawwanah* required extends to the entire section, according to the opinion of R. 'Aḳiba.[40] The first verse, however, the declaration or affirmation of *Malkut Shamayim*, is distinguished

[37] Berakot II.2; Berakot 13b — in reference to Rabbi (Judah the Prince).

[38] See above, p. 125 and notes 15, 16 and 17, and Berakot 13b.

[39] See above, p. 130, note 35, and the references in Baer, op. cit., p. 82. The response is recited in an undertone, *belaḥash*, in order to indicate that it is not part of the scriptural section — see the כסף משנה on Maimonides, Hilkot Ḳeri'at Shema', I.4. Finkelstein points out that originally the response did not contain the idea of God's Kingship — "The Meaning of the Word פרס," Jewish Quarterly Review, XXXIII, no. 1 (The Dropsie College, 1942), pp. 36–38. On the association of God's Kingship with the Tetragrammaton, see Roḳeaḥ, par. 363.

[40] Berakot 13a–b. Other opinions limit it to the first two or the first three verses. On R. 'Aḳiba's opinion, see Tosafot, ibid., s. v. אשר אנכי. A study of *Kawwanah* has been made by H. G. Enelow, Selected Works (1935) IV, pp. 252 ff.

by special instructions with respect to *Kawwanah*. Pure mysticism characterizes these halakic practices. The last word of the declaration, *'eḥad* (אחד), is to be lengthened in enunciation, and lengthened in such a way as to permit one "to make Him King above and below and in the four directions of heaven."[41] What can this be but a mystical experience, even if we take the literal "to make Him King" in the sense of "apprehend His Kingship"?[42] Indeed, this is the highest point in the liturgy, the exalting apex of devotion, the moment when man is so attuned as to experience the boundless majesty of God.

The study of Torah can be a means of experiencing God. Study of Torah was regarded by the Rabbis as a form of worship, and as parallel in that respect to prayer. One interpretation of Deut. 11:13 takes "and to serve Him" to refer to prayer — "Just as the service of (*'Abodat*) the altar is called *'Abodah* so is prayer called *'Abodah*"[43]; another interpretation, and given first in the passage, takes the phrase to refer to study of Torah — "Just as the service of the altar is called *'Abodah* so is study called *'Abodah*."[44] When the Rabbis thus equate study with prayer and call them both *'Abodah*, worship, they do so as a result of deep inward experience. Prayer requires that a man fix, direct, his mind or heart upon God; this was the purpose, we saw, of the quietistic practice of "the pious men of former generations."[45] But the proper study of Torah, too, requires that a man direct his mind and heart to God, that he have *Kawwanah*. Applied to the study of Torah is the statement that "it matters not whether much or little, if only a man directs (a verb form of *kwn*) his heart to Heaven."[46] Intel-

[41] Berakot 13b — כיון דאמליכתיה.

[42] So Enelow, op. cit., p. 259.

[43] Sifre Deut. on that verse; ed. Friedmann, p. 80a (and the reference there to Ta'anit 2a).

[44] Ibid.

[45] Above, p. 208.

[46] Berakot 5b. The statement in its original setting — Menaḥot 110a — has to do with Temple offerings.

lectual activity here is an aspect of the inward life, a direct means for mystical experience, and it is just that quality which gives the study of Torah its special character. We have a reflection of this mystical experience, it seems to us, in the familiar saying found in Pirḳe 'Abot: "If two sit together and interchange words of Torah, *Shekinah* (God) abides ('rests') between them, as it is said, 'Then they that feared the Lord spake one with the other, and the Lord hearkened and heard' (Mal. 3:16)."[47] "Words of Torah" were the intellectual occupation of every literate man in the community, and hence the dictum cannot refer to scholars alone. "It matters not whether much or little, if only a man directs his heart to Heaven."[48]

The rabbinic consciousness of God exemplified in all these instances is undeniably mystical in character. What gives rise to this mystical awareness of God? Daily events and daily activities, as we have observed. But this is only one of the characteristics of normal mysticism, and we shall now depict another. The rabbinic experience of God is a phenomenon associated with the organismic integration of the value-concepts, in other words, with the normal functioning of the value-concepts. For example, when an individual accepts the Kingship of God by reciting the *Shema'* in his daily prayers, not only is the concept of *Malkut Shamayim* involved but also those of *Miẓwot* and Torah.[49] A similar case in point is martyrdom. By his readiness to suffer martyrdom, a man brings home to others an awareness of God, and hence his act is characterized as *Ḳiddush Ha-Shem,* sanctification of the Name[50]; but in the instance

[47] 'Abot III.2.

[48] See TE, p. 61, for the association between the acknowledging of *Malkut Shamayim* and the studying of Torah.

[49] See above, p. 130 and note 35 there.

[50] See OT (see above, p. 15, n. 2), p. 7.

of martyrdom given above, *Ḳiddush Ha-Shem* is integrated with the concept of *Miẓwot*.[51] Figuring most often in such combinations of concepts, however, are the concepts of God's love and His justice. What is a *Berakah* if not an acknowledgment of God's love or His justice, as the case may be? The very reliance on prayer assumes God's love[52]; the very ability to repent — repentance being another way of experiencing God — is a manifestation of that love[53]; and so, too, is the capacity for studying Torah.[54] In fact, since the concepts of God's love and His justice are fundamental concepts, they interweave with all the concepts in the complex. There is no concept in the entire value-complex that may not be integrated, at some time or other, with a concept symbolizing mystical experience. Far from being a rare or peculiar experience, the mystical awareness of God was, therefore, a steady aspect of the valuational life as a whole, an aspect of the normal valuational life of the individual.

The concepts of God's love and God's justice, which play so large a rôle in normal mystical experience, render it an experience that is expressible, communicable. First of all, it is important to recognize that the rabbinic terms for these concepts do not contain any word for God. *Middat Ha-Din* and *Middat Raḥamim* are the rabbinic terms most frequently used in order to designate, respectively, God's justice and God's love. A midrash declares, for example, that the world was created in accordance with both *Middat Raḥamim* and *Middat Ha-Din*, and that the world could not have endured had either of these alone entered into

[51] See above, pp. 80–1. Notice also how *Ḳiddush Ha-Shem* is integrated with *Malkut Shamayim* — OT, p. 7.

[52] See TE, p. 137 f.

[53] See ibid., pp. 119 ff. Because of this relationship of prayer and repentance to God's love, we have taken the former to be subconcepts of God's love.

[54] See OT, p. 45 f.

it creation.[55] Conspicuous by its absence is any conceptual word for God in these terms, or any of the appellatives for Him; (and this is true as well of other terms that refer to God's justice, terms apparently representing subconcepts of *Middat Ha-Din*).[56] Since the meaning of *middah* in this connection is "quality", our terms in their bare, literal sense thus refer only to "the quality of justice" and to "the quality of love." As conceptual terms, therefore, *Middat Ha-Din* and *Middat Raḥamim* stand for concepts in their own right, concepts sufficiently individualized to merit their own distinctive symbols. This explains, it seems to us, why the Rabbis can sometimes personify *Middat Ha-Din* and speak of it as though it were distinct from God and addressing Him.[57] So far as sheer conceptual terminology is concerned, *Middat Ha-Din* and *Middat Raḥamim* are actually distinct from the concept of God. They are genuine concepts, classifying events, situations, or actions; they endow those events and actions with significance, and hence are value-concepts.[58] On the other hand, the several conceptual terms for God are not, as we saw, really classifying terms at all, not being either cognitive, or valuational, or defined concepts.

Containing neither a conceptual term for God nor an appellative for Him, *Middat Ha-Din* and *Middat Raḥamim* nevertheless do convey the ideas of *God's* justice and *God's* love. How could this be? Here we have to do with a matter that indicates, perhaps more strikingly than anything else can, how widespread among the people as a whole was at

[55] Bereshit R., XII.15, ed. Theodor, p. 112 f. Similarly in the creation of man, ibid., XXI.8, ed. Theodor, p. 202, and the references there.

[56] See below, p. 219, note 73.

[57] E. g. Shabbat 55a — אמרה מדת הדין לפני הקב"ה. See also TE, p. 165.

[58] The thirteen *middot* of God which the Rabbis discover in Exod. 34:6–7 are not concepts, even though referred to as *middot*. They are qualities which, when taken as a whole, spell *Middat Raḥamim* — see TE, p. 114. Notice that they are not noun forms as are *Middat Raḥamim* and *Middat Ha-Din*, and value-concepts in general, but adjectives and adjectival phrases.

least an acquaintance with the Bible. It is a rule of the Rabbis that the Tetragrammaton in the Bible refers to *Middat Raḥamim*, as in Exod. 34:6, and that *'Elohim* in the Bible refers to *Middat Ha-Din*, as in Exod. 22:8.[59] Passages in the Bible which do not seem to conform with this rule are interpreted by the Rabbis in such a fashion as to be in harmony with it,[60] so firmly was the rule itself held. Since the people at large heard the reading of scriptural lections at least once a week,[61] and since the Rabbis always interpreted the lections on the Sabbath and the Festivals,[62] is it not most likely that the people in general were familiar with the rule, and not only the learned? *Middat Ha-Din* was thus not simply "the quality of justice" but God's justice, and *Middat Raḥamim* not "the quality of love (or mercy)" but God's love (or mercy).[63] When either of these concepts made a situation significant for an individual, therefore, he was made aware of God, whether through a sense of God's love or His justice. Yet these concepts are not merely ways of experiencing God such as we had noticed in the case of prayer, or repentance, or study of Torah. They are that and more. Prayer refers to an action by man; here it is *God's* love, *God's* justice. The awareness of God remains mystical, but it is now expressible, communicable, no longer a purely private experience. *Middat Ha-Din* and *Middat Raḥamim* are thus really concepts wherein the mystical experience of God rises to expression. Nor do they violate the formal requirement which prevents the mystical experience of God from being expressed in a

[59] Sifre Deut., par. XXVII, ed. Friedmann, p. 71a; see also Bereshit R., ed. Theodor, p. 112 f. and the reference there.

[60] See Bereshit R. XXXIII.3, ed. Theodor, p. 308. The harmonization here has been called attention to by Marmorstein, The Old Rabbinic Doctrine of God, I, pp. 43 f.

[61] See above, p. 79.

[62] See ibid., p. 86.

[63] *Middat Raḥamim* and *Middat Ha-Din* are not, of course, subconcepts of God. The conceptual terms for God "included," we must remember, idols as well.

generalizing concept. Formally, *Middat Ha-Din* and *Middat Raḥamim* are genuine, classifying concepts; only by a rule of interpretation are they identified with terms for God.

Modern students have a tendency, in their representations of rabbinic thought, to oversimplify the rabbinic concept of God's justice. It is true that, according to this concept, good is meted out to every individual for his good deeds and evil for his misdeeds.[64] It is also true that, aware of how often those who suffer may be righteous men and those who prosper may be wicked, the Rabbis declare that a full accounting is reserved for the world to come.[65] But these ideas alone by no means completely express the reaction of the Rabbis to the presence of evil in the world. There is the subconcept of *Yissurin*, chastisements, which interprets misfortunes as chastisements that are sent so as to purify and ennoble men.[66] And there is also the conceptual phase of corporate or collective justice, a phase of the concept of God's justice having its own subconcepts in merit of the fathers,[67] merit of the children,[68] and vicarious atonement.[69] Underlying these subconcepts of collective justice is not only the idea of corporate responsibility but also of corporate personality. In this view, an individual shares in a larger personality, be it that of his family, his people, or mankind, and hence is involved with that larger personality both in reward and punishment.[70]

[64] See TE, pp. 166–179.

[65] See, for example, Bereshit R. XXXIII.1, ed. Theodor, pp. 288–9, and the references there — the statement of R. 'Aḳiba: the righteous are punished in this world for the few bad deeds they have committed, but are given tranquility and reward in the world to come; the wicked are rewarded by tranquility in this world for the "light" *Miẓwot* they observed, but are punished *Le'atid Labo*, in the future; see also TE, p. 208.

[66] See TE, pp. 194 ff.

[67] See ibid., p. 182 f., 191 f.; also ibid., p. 133.

[68] See ibid., p. 184.

[69] See ibid., p. 134. Vicarious atonement may also be regarded as a subconcept of atonement, *Kapparah*, and it is thus that we have spoken of it above, p. 15.

[70] See TE, pp. 179 ff., p. 206 f.; OT, p. 268, note 31.

Rabbinic thought is dominated, however, by the idea of God's love rather than by the idea of His justice. When the Rabbis tell us to imitate God, to walk "in the ways of Heaven," they have in mind primarily the imitation of various aspects of God's loving-kindness — mercy and compassion, graciousness, patience, forbearance.[71] Their reliance upon prayer and repentance, we noticed above, assumes God's love. They speak again and again of God's forgiveness, of His readiness to receive repentant sinners, of how His mercy tempers His judgment.[72] Even when God dispenses justice, it is God's love that predominates, according to the Rabbis. His reward is always in greater measure than His punishment.[73] So dominant is the concept of God's love in the outlook of the Rabbis that they will interpret in its light matters which the Bible describes in terms of justice. For example, in the Bible stern justice is meted out to Adam after his disobedience; but the Rabbis transform the decree into an expression of God's love and into a promise of everlasting life.[74] Similarly, the statement "visiting the iniquity of the fathers upon the children . . . unto the third and unto the fourth generation" (Exod. 34:7) is interpreted in such a way as to render it evidence of God's love.[75] All this is of a piece with the significance that the numerous ordinary, everyday events and situations have for the Rabbis. To the Rabbis, these are most often

[71] See OT, p. 142 f.

[72] See TE, pp. 114 ff., 209 f.

[73] מדה טובה מרובה and מדת הפורענות מעוטה — e. g. Mekilta I, 55, 103. (Lauterbach's rendering of these terms is not correct.)

Middah Ṭobah and *Middat Pur'anut* are apparently subconcepts of *Middat Ha-Din*. Notice how they are used, for example, by R. Me'ir who declares that just as one ought to say a *Berakah* over the good so ought one to say a *Berakah* over an evil that may befall one, (for) "He is thy Judge in every act of justice dispensed to you, whether *Middat Ha-Ṭob*, or whether *Middat Pur'anut*" — Tos. Berakot (ed. Lieberman) VI (VII).1, p. 33; Berakot 48b.

[74] See TE, p. 111.

[75] See ibid., p. 115.

manifestations of God's love, occasions for *Berakot* and prayers of gratitude.[76]

God's love and God's justice are value-concepts and are represented in rabbinic literature by genuine conceptual terms. But ideas like God's omniscience, God's omnipotence, God's omnipresence, no matter how often they occur, are not represented by conceptual terms. This is not, we found above, simply a linguistic deficiency but a reflection of the way these ideas are employed in rabbinic literature. They are not value-concepts but are among what we have characterized as auxiliary ideas.[77] They are "usually in the service, so to speak, of a true concept, broadening the range of the latter's manifestations or else placing the concept into bolder relief."[78] This fact, namely, that the ideas of God's omniscience, God's omnipotence and the like lack abstract conceptual representations in rabbinic literature, is highly indicative of the nature of rabbinic religion. Were rabbinic religion a kind of religious philosophy, there would have been an attempt to coordinate all ideas, including the auxiliary ideas, a task that medieval Jewish philosophy did indeed set for itself. It endeavors to coordinate, for example, the idea of God's omniscience with that of His justice.[79] Such a task demands that the auxiliary ideas too be represented by abstract conceptual symbols[80] – witness also our own need when we must refer to them here. But rabbinic religion, not being a religious philosophy, had no occasion to speak of these ideas in any abstract manner. We may recall, for instance, that in telling of how God hears even a whispered prayer, the Rabbis ask, "Can you have a God nearer than that?"[81] This rhetorical question obviously

[76] The topics of God's love and God's justice are dealt with at length in TE, Chapters V and VI.

[77] See above, pp. 53–55.

[78] Ibid., p. 54.

[79] See, e. g. Maimonides, Moreh Nebukim, Part III, Chaps. 16–24.

[80] As, for example, ידיעת האלוה (God's omniscience) in ibid., Chap. 16.

[81] Above, p. 195.

contains the idea of God's omnipresence; but the theme is God's nearness in prayer, not the abstract idea of God's omnipresence. Rabbinic religion was experiential. God's love, His justice, prayer, are all aspects of that normal mystical experience. Ideas about God that are not represented by conceptual terms are often essential to the various aspects of religious experience, but are never additional experiences in themselves. It is only in religious philosophies that those ideas, now become the subject of speculation, are supplied with conceptual terms.

To treat the auxiliary ideas in rabbinic literature as though they were ideas in themselves is, then, to do violence to rabbinic thought. This applies, in the first instance, to the attempt to conceptualize these ideas. It applies, moreover, to renderings of particular midrashim that take the auxiliary ideas there out of their contexts. Basing itself on Ps. 103:1 — "(A Psalm) of David. Bless the Lord, O my soul" — a midrash asks why David saw fit to praise the Holy One blessed be He with his soul. One answer given is: "The soul fills the body and the Holy One blessed be He fills His world, as it says 'Do I not fill heaven and earth?' (Jer. 23:24). Let the soul come that fills the body and praise the Holy One blessed be He who fills the whole world."[82] Modern scholars, with their philosophic bias, often point to this midrash as an expression of the Stoic doctrine that God is the soul of the universe. Even Schechter, despite his usual insight, so paraphrases this passage as almost to give it this turn. "In another place," he says referring to this passage, "God is compared by a Rabbi to the soul 'filling the whole world, as the soul fills the body.' "[83] Does the passage actually compare God to the soul of the world? Supposing the passage to contain this idea, is it the theme of the midrash? We take the theme to be that

[82] Leviticus R. IV.8. See Midrash Tehillim, ed. Buber, p. 217a, for the parallels. SEE NOTES, P. 371.

[83] S. Schechter, Some Aspects of Rabbinic Theology, p. 27.

it is appropriate for the soul to praise God, a theme involving the concept of prayer, and we regard the idea of God's filling the world, or His omnipresence, as an auxiliary idea.[84] One is almost bound to misconstrue a passage, it seems to us, if an auxiliary idea there is treated as a subject in itself. From the very outset, the idea is torn out of its context.

Philosophy conceptualizes what it regards as attributes of God, ideas that lend themselves to speculation. The concepts of rabbinic religion, on the other hand, are not the result of deliberate conceptualization but of experience. This is conclusively evident in the case of the concept of *Ḳedushah*, holiness, which we discussed at some length above.[85] Holiness is not something that is the product of intellectual ratiocination; it is either felt, experienced, or it is nothing. In rabbinic religion, holiness is a mystical experience, and we recognized also that it is a normal mystical experience.[86] The fact that holiness, *Ḳedushah*, is a concept does not detract from the purely experiential character of the phenomenon it represents. The concept of *Ḳedushah* is a value-concept, not the type of defined concept with which philosophy must operate. What is true of *Ḳedushah* is in every respect also true of the other concepts expressive of normal mysticism in rabbinic religion.

III. REVELATION OF *SHEKINAH* (GOD)

Although everyday experience of God was normal mystical experience, the Rabbis left room for experience of God of a different order. That other form of mystical experience emerges as we study the several ways in which

[84] There are kindred ideas regarding God's omnipresence — e. g. the idea that God is the *maḳom* of the world, and cited by Schechter, l. c. — that we shall take up at the end of our discussion of *Shekinah*.

[85] Above, pp. 169 ff.

[86] Ibid., p. 203.

the Rabbis employ the term *Shekinah*. At the same time, there is also brought to light an important feature of normal mysticism.

Shekinah is a name for God. This was not the view of medieval philosophers like Yehudah Ha-Levi and Maimonides; they insisted that *Shekinah* was created by God and is not to be identified with God Himself.[1] But Naḥmanides attacks Maimonides most vehemently on this matter, and declares that "among the words of the Rabbis many things demonstrate that the name *Shekinah* is indeed (that of) God."[2] Though Naḥmanides himself does not support his assertion with proof from Talmud and Midrash, such proof is to be had almost every time the Rabbis employ the word *Shekinah* in their homilies. For their statements concerning *Shekinah*, they bring as warrant biblical texts that speak of God, *Shekinah* being thus absolutely equated to the biblical word for God. "Whenever Israel is enslaved, *Shekinah*, as it were, is enslaved with them . . . 'In all their affliction He was afflicted' (Isaiah 63:10)."[3] Similarly: "When Israel went down to Egypt, *Shekinah* went down with them, as it says, 'I will go down with thee into Egypt' (Gen. 46:4); when they came up from Egypt, *Shekinah* came up with them, as it says, 'And I will surely bring thee up again' (ibid.); . . . when they went into the wilderness, *Shekinah* was with them, as it says, 'And the Lord went before them by day' (Exod. 13:21)."[4] In these and all other instances, *Shekinah* is unmistakably

[1] Yehudah Ha-Levi, Kuzari, II, 4, 7; cf. also ibid., IV,3. Maimonides, Moreh Nebukim, I, 25.

[2] Naḥmanides, Commentary to Pentateuch, Gen. 46:1. Naḥmanides takes issue here with the opinion of Maimonides that in Targum Onkelos and Targum Jonathan there is an attempt to do away with the anthropomorphisms of the Bible. See below, p. 326 f.

[3] Mekilta, I, p. 113.

[4] Ibid., II, p. 27. "And I will surely bring thee up again" (Gen. 46:4) is the rendering of the *peshaṭ*. The Rabbis apparently take the words גם עלה as referring to God Himself.

equated to the word for God in the supporting biblical text.[5]

Moreover, we find the Rabbis using *Shekinah* interchangeably with other rabbinic terms for God, names for God about which there can be no dispute whatever. After the famous statement of R. Me'ir that *Shekinah* cries out when a man (i. e., a malefactor) suffers punishment, the Mishnah immediately continues with: "If God (the *Makom*) thus suffers over the blood of the wicked which is spilled, (He suffers) over the blood of the righteous *a fortiori*."[6] In another passage, *Shekinah* is identical with the Holy One blessed be He,[7] again a common rabbinic name for God. Here we ought to point out that the phrase, "My *Shekinah*" also refers to God Himself. It is identical with the Holy One blessed be He in the following passage: "At that hour (when the Temple was burnt) the Holy One blessed be He wept, saying 'Woe is Me! What have I done! I had caused My *Shekinah* to dwell below for the sake of Israel, but now that they have sinned I have returned to My original (dwelling) place."[8]

Finally, the very deeds and attitudes which the Rabbis ascribe to *Shekinah* they also ascribe to God. We have learned that *Shekinah* shares the afflictions of Israel. But we also read that Israel's troubles are, as it were, God's troubles and their joys, His joys[9]; and that Israel's enemies are God's enemies[10]; and that he who helps Israel, it is as though "he helps Him who spake and the world came to be."[11] These and other parallels we might have cited indicate once more that *Shekinah* is another rabbinic name for God.

[5] See TE, p. 53 f., for other examples.

[6] Sanhedrin VI.5.

[7] See TE, l. c.

[8] 'Ekah Rabbati, Petiḥata, 24, ed. Buber, p. 13a. We shall soon explain what else the phrase "My *Shekinah*" connotes.

[9] Mekilta, II, p. 160.

[10] Ibid., II, pp. 42, 45.

[11] Ibid., II, p. 45.

In sum, the use of the word *Shekinah* by the Rabbis rather than by their medieval interpreters indicates that it stands for God Himself. Medieval philosophers place an interpretation on this, as upon other rabbinic ideas, of a kind totally at variance with rabbinic thought.

Shekinah is one of the reverential appellatives for God.[12] The circumspect, reverential nature of these appellatives is often apparently emphasized by the use of the definite article — *Ha-Maḳom,*[13] *Ha-Geburah,*[14] *Ha-Dibbur.*[15] Similarly, the word *Shekinah* is often preceded by the definite article — *Ha-Shekinah*[16] — so as to give additional emphasis, it would seem, to its reverential nature. The note of circumspection is still stronger when our term is used with a genitive, as in the case of "My *Shekinah*" in place of "I". It was doubtless this quality of circumspection possessed by *Shekinah* and other rabbinic appellatives for God that determined the view taken of them by medieval Jewish philosophy. Influenced by an aversion to anthropomorphism, the medieval Jewish philosophers construed the circumspection involved in the term *Shekinah* to mean that *Shekinah* was not to be identified with God. But the philosophic problems associated with the idea of anthropomorphism, the very terms, including the word "anthropomorphism" itself, which philosophy employs in order to express these problems, were simply not within the rabbinic universe of discourse.

Unlike most of the reverential appellatives for God, the name *Shekinah* is used in a special context. It is employed as a name for God only when the Rabbis speak of God's nearness to man. "Primarily," declare the Rabbis in a midrash often met with, "primarily *Shekinah* was (here) below." Because of man's sins, *Shekinah* became more and

[12] On these appellatives, see above, p. 204 f.

[13] E. g., Sanhedrin VI.5.

[14] E. g., Shabbat 87a, 88b.

[15] E. g., Yebamot 5b.

[16] E. g., Mekilta, II, p. 274.

more distant, retiring to the first firmament when Adam sinned, ascending to the second when Cain sinned, and continuing to ascend in every sinful generation to higher firmaments until, when the Egyptians of Abraham's day sinned, it rose to the seventh and highest firmament. Offsetting the sinners, however, was the succession of seven righteous men, beginning with Abraham, each of whom brought it to a lower firmament until finally Moses brought it down to the earth (when he set up the Tabernacle).[17] *Shekinah* "dwelt" or "rested" (*sharetah*) in the Tabernacle[18] and in the Temple.[19] When the Temple was destroyed, God withdrew His *Shekinah* and went up to His former dwelling place.[20] Nonetheless, God is never really absent from His world. Not one but a number of Rabbis make the statement that "*Shekinah* is in every place," the point of this statement being, it would seem from the instance of R. Sheshet, that one may stand in prayer facing any direction.[21] The opinion that *Shekinah* is always in the west[22] also seems to refer to one's direction when standing in prayer; in this opinion, too, God is always here and near.

For the moment we shall ignore the apparent contradiction between the idea that God withdrew His *Shekinah* and the idea that *Shekinah* is everywhere. We wish merely to point out at present that the name *Shekinah* is used only in contexts having to do with God's nearness. Even the statement that God withdrew His *Shekinah* is made in such a context.

But what is normal mysticism if not the experience of

[17] Bereshit R. XIX.13, ed. Theodor, pp. 176–7. For the parallels see Theodor's note there.

[18] Numbers R. XII.5.

[19] Sifra on Lev. 24:3, ed. Weiss 103d.

[20] 'Ekah Rabbati, l. c.

[21] Baba Batra 25a. See, however, the discussion by Ginzberg, Commentary, III, pp. 384 ff.

[22] Ibid.

God's nearness? *Shekinah* is therefore often the name for God in statements reflecting normal mystical experience. Thus it is used in statements concerning prayer. We may recall the rule that one who prays "ought to regard himself as though *Shekinah* were in front of him"[23]; and we have just quoted the dictum that "*Shekinah* is in every place," again a statement made with regard to prayer. "Wherever ten persons assemble in a synagogue," the Rabbis also say, "*Shekinah* is with them."[24] Study of Torah, too, can lead to normal mystical experience, and so the Rabbis speak of *Shekinah* as "resting" on two persons who interchange words of Torah,[25] and as being even with one person who may be studying alone.[26] The awareness of God's love and compassion can be a profound experience, and this experience is evidently at the basis of the idea that *Shekinah* shares, as it were, the affliction of the community and even of the individual.[27] The figure of Israel gathered, when worthy, "under the wings of the *Shekinah*"[28] reflects another normal mystical experience, that of *Ḳedushah*, holiness. It is a figure used particularly in regard to proselytes, the proselytes being often characterized as having been brought "under the wings of the *Shekinah*."[29] That this figure is associated with *Ḳedushah* is apparent from a mishnah dealing with the children of proselytes. A child born to converts after they had been converted, says this mishnah, is born "in *Ḳedushah*."[30]

[23] See above, p. 208.

[24] Mekilta, II, p. 287.

[25] 'Abot III, 2.

[26] Mekilta II, p. 287. The midrash starts with "ten," a congregation, goes on to speak of "three," a court, then of "two" and finally of "one." "Two" and "one" refer to persons studying Torah, as is evident from the proof texts. Does the reference to the court of justice reflect the sense of rightness in judgment?

[27] Ibid., I, p. 113 f.

[28] Seder Eliahu, ed. Friedmann, p. 104.

[29] תחת כנפי השכינה — See, for example, Mẹkilta, II, p. 186; Sifre on Deut. 6:5, ed. Friedmann 73a and the references there.

[30] Yebamot XI.2; cf. ibid., 97b, 98a.

Again, we have seen that it was the fulfillment of *Mizwot* that made for the experience of holiness.[31] An act of transgression, therefore, must result in a loss of holiness. How is this loss depicted? By the figure of "crowding off the feet of *Shekinah*." He that commits an *'Aberah* (transgression) in secret, declares R. Isaac, "it is as though he crowds off the feet of *Shekinah*."[32]

In mystical experience, it is God's nearness that is experienced. *Shekinah* is a name for God used only in statements having to do with God's nearness. It is therefore to be found in statements and ideas that reflect normal mystical experience, in statements and ideas about prayer, study of Torah, God's love, *Ḳedushah*.[33]

There is, however, another use of the word *Shekinah* that is consistent with the idea of God's nearness. The word *Shekinah* also forms part of the conceptual term of *Gilluy Shekinah*, revelation of *Shekinah*, and this concept stands for the occasions when, according to the Rabbis, God manifested Himself either to man's sight or to some other human sense. Hence the Rabbis frequently use the name *Shekinah* when telling of God's revelations of Himself to man's senses.

The concept of *Gilluy Shekinah* interweaves, as do all the concepts in the value-complex, with the four fundamental concepts. Seven groups of righteous men (*Ẓaddiḳim*) will greet (or receive) the presence of *Shekinah* (lit., the face of *Shekinah*), the righteous being classed in accordance with the shining glory of their countenance[34]; here our concept

[31] Above, pp. 170 ff.

[32] Ḳiddushin 31a — כאלו דוחק רגלי שכינה.

[33] On prayer as a means of experiencing God — see above pp. 207 ff.; on study of Torah as such a means — see ibid., p. 213 f.; on God's love as expressing God-experience — see ibid., pp. 215 ff.; on *Ḳedushah* as normal mystical experience — see ibid., p. 222 and the references there.

[34] Leviticus R. XXX.2 להקביל פני שכינה. Yalḳuṭ Shime'oni to Ps. 16:11 has לראות פני השכינה, "to see the face of the *Shekinah*." See also above, p. 30.

interweaves with that of God's justice. The tribe of Levi diminished in numbers (cf. Num. 3:39 and Ezra 8:15), say the Rabbis, "because they saw the *Shekinah*"; "in the world to come, however," the Rabbis have God say, "when I shall return My *Shekinah* to Zion, I shall reveal Myself in My Glory to all Israel, and they will see Me and live forever, as it says, 'For they shall see eye to eye, the Lord returning to Zion' (Is. 52:8)."[35] We take this passage to be an interweaving of our concept with the concepts of God's love and Israel. In fact, in the majority of the passages on *Gilluy Shekinah* that concept is associated with the concept of Israel, as we may notice in the ensuing discussion. *Gilluy Shekinah,* finally, is associated with the concept of Torah. He that goes out of the *bet ha-keneset* (synagogue) and (immediately) enters the *bet ha-midrash* and engages in (the study of) Torah merits and greets (or receives) the presence of *Shekinah.*[36]

We saw in an earlier chapter that the value-concepts are often employed without recourse to the conceptual terms. Being mental habits of the people in general, the concepts were embodied in concrete situations and events, in concretizations of the concepts, and there was no need for the conceptual terms to act as labels.[37] This is true of *Gilluy Shekinah* as well; it is not even necessary to use the name *Shekinah* when referring to God in statements embodying this concept. A midrash on Exodus 15:3 declares that "He revealed Himself at the (Red) Sea," when he punished the Egyptians, "as a mighty hero doing battle," and at Sinai when He gave the Ten Commandments, "as an old man full of mercy." (He revealed Himself in these two opposite ways) "so as not to give an excuse to the nations of the world to say that there are two Powers . . . He was in

[35] Tanḥuma, ed. Buber, IV, p. 9b; Yalḳuṭ Shime'oni, Numbers, par. 691.

[36] Berakot 64a; Mo'ed Ḳaṭan 29a.

[37] Above, p. 51 f.

Egypt, He was at the (Red) Sea; He was in the past, He will be in the future (*Le'atid Labo*); He is in this world, He will be in the world to come."[38] Rabbi Judah's comment on the same verse (Exod. 15:3) contains more elaborate and more graphic figures. "He revealed Himself to them (i. e., to Israel) with all the implements of war" – as a mighty hero girded with a sword, as a horseman, in a coat of mail and a helmet, with a spear, with bow and arrows, with shield and buckler. Rabbi Judah bases himself on scriptural verses, of course, but neutralizes the anthropomorphisms by adding that God has no need of any of these measures – "He wars by means of His Name. Scripture merely means to tell that when Israel is in need of such measures, God (*Ha-Maḳom*) fights their battle for them."[39] Incidentally, *Gilluy Shekinah* is not necessarily associated with a particular act of God, with a *Nes*, as it is in these passages about the Red Sea and the giving of the Ten Commandments. A number of passages already discussed depict *Gilluy Shekinah* as taking place not in conjunction with any particular act.

The concept of *Gilluy Shekinah*, then, not only interweaves with the fundamental concepts but also exhibits another characteristic of the value-concepts – it is imbedded in its concretizations, not named. Furthermore, like the other value-concepts, our concept allows for various, and sometimes contradictory, concretizations. *Gilluy Shekinah* at Sinai is depicted in various ways[40]; one authority declares that there was *Gilluy Shekinah* when God gave Israel the

[38] Mekilta, II, pp. 31–2; ibid., pp. 231–32. Horovitz-Rabin (Mechilta d'Rabbi Ismael, Frankfort a. M., 1928–31), p. 129, note 16, deletes וכשנגאלו . . . לטוהר, and with good reason. The verses from Daniel then follow properly, for they refer to the "Ancient of Days" and to "fire," the latter a symbol for Torah to the Rabbis, hence the giving of it on Sinai.

[39] Mekilta, II, pp. 30–1. The scriptural verses are: Ps. 45:4; ibid., 18:11; Is. 59:17; Hab. 3:11; ibid., 3:9; II Samuel 22:15; Ps. 91:4.

[40] See above, p. 74. See also Mekilta, II, pp. 220, 221–2, 275.

manna whilst another apparently denies it[41]; opinions differ as to whether *Shekinah* dwelt in the Second Temple.[42]

But in an important respect *Gilluy Shekinah* is certainly not typical of the value-concepts. Value-concepts do not refer to things perceived through the senses, to definite phenomena in sensory experience.[43] *Gilluy Shekinah*, however, involves man's senses, especially those of sight and hearing. According to the passages we have cited, *Shekinah* was seen and will again be seen by Israel. Other rabbinic texts are equally as explicit, if not more so. "A maid-servant saw at the (Red) Sea what Isaiah (?) and Ezekiel and all the rest of the prophets never saw . . . when the Holy One blessed be He revealed Himself at the (Red) Sea . . ."[44] In a number of passages, the Rabbis employ the phrase "enjoying the effulgence of the *Shekinah*" — *neheneh mi-ziw Ha-Shekinah* — to describe the bliss of sensory experience of *Shekinah*. They employ this phrase, for example, in reference to Moses,[45] and to the people of Israel present at Solomon's dedication of the Temple.[46] The phrase has to do with visual experience, as we can tell from several contexts.[47] Sensory experience of *Shekinah*, as described by

[41] Mekilta, II, p. 102. Rabbi Joshua and R. Eleazar interpret Exod. 16:4 differently, and so also subsequent verses — ibid., p. 106.

[42] See below, p. 253, note 131.

[43] See above, pp. 50 f. and 107 f.

[44] Mekilta, II, pp. 24–5. There is no proof text from Isaiah but there are texts from Hosea and Ezekiel. Prof. Louis Ginzberg therefore suggests that originally the passage read: ". . . what Ezekiel and all the rest of the prophets never saw;" and this was followed by the verses from Hosea and Ezekiel. A copyist then indicated on the margin that the first text was from Hosea by merely writing "Hosea". The word "Hosea" crept into the passage and was changed to "Isaiah," for Isaiah like Ezekiel had a vision of God (cf. Is. 6:1 ff.). Comp. Mekilta II, p. 212.

[45] Exodus Rabba III.2.

[46] Mo'ed Ḳaṭan 9a.

[47] Nadab and Abihu "feasted their eyes on the effulgence of the *Shekinah*" — Exodus R., loc. cit. The "eyes" of the sun and moon "are dim from the effulgence of the *Shekinah*" — Leviticus R. XXXI.7.

The *ziw Ha-Shekinah* also "fills" the Tent of Meeting (Pesiḳta de-Rab Kathe Rabbis, may also be in the nature of locutions. When R. Jose declared that "neither Moses nor Elijah went up to heaven, nor did the Glory come down to earth," he added: Scripture merely teaches "that God (*Ha-Maḳom*) said to Moses, 'Behold, I shall call you from the top of the mountain and you will (then) ascend (it).' "[48] The *Shekinah*, another passage says, used to beat like a bell before Samson.[49] In *Gilluy Shekinah* the Rabbis thus possessed a concept capable of expressing experience accompanied by sense phenomena, mystical experience similar in that regard to the kind studied by modern psychologies of religion. What place, if any, had this sort of mysticism in the actual, personal and immediate religious experience of the Rabbis? To put the question differently, to what extent is the character of the concept of *Gilluy Shekinah* compatible with the character of the rabbinic value-complex as a whole?

In the preceding chapter,[50] we found that only when there is no admixture of value-concepts with cognitive concepts can there be a grasp of the objective character of the physical world. The two types of concepts must exist side by side as a generally consistent dichotomy. Now the Rabbis and the people at large had a grasp of the objective character of the physical world; they even possessed concepts — *sidre Bereshit* and *sidre 'Olam* — indicative of a general idea of order in nature.[51] So consistently did the Rabbis maintain the dichotomy of value-concepts and cognitive concepts that it extended to the domain of ritual, the great majority of the objects used in rites being nonholy and the few holy objects being nontheurgic.[52] All this does

hana I, ed. Buber, p. 2b); so also the palaces of the kings of the nations when God uttered "I am the Lord thy God" (Mekilta, II, p. 233). In the latter instance, the kings were terrified by the phenomenon.

[48] Mekilta, II, p. 224. See also above, p. 74.

[49] Soṭah 9b.

[50] Above, pp. 143 ff.

[51] Ibid., pp. 147 ff.

[52] Ibid., pp. 170 ff.

not mean, nevertheless, that there cannot ever be an admixture of the valuational and the cognitive. It does mean that, in view of the character of the complex as a whole, such an admixture will not function as readily as do the other concepts; that it may, indeed, function rarely or with difficulty. In the single instance of an admixture of a value-concept with an abstract, quasi-scientific concept, we found that the resultant conceptual phase was actually restricted and curbed.[53]

The concept of *Gilluy Shekinah* is an admixture of the valuational and the cognitive. On the one hand it exhibits, we have recognized, a number of features characteristic of value-concepts. But on the other hand, it involves, like a cognitive concept, sense phenomena. That the concept of *Gilluy Shekinah* did function is obvious from the many passages in which it is imbedded. It did not function, however, in the same way as did the value-concepts in general.

Some Rabbis had the expectation of actually experiencing *Gilluy Shekinah*. R. Jose b. Ḥalafta tells his son, R. Ishmael, "(Do) you want to see the face of *Shekinah* in this world? Engage in (the study of) Torah in the land of Israel."[54] R. Jose was a Tanna of the second century, but the Talmud also tells, in one place, of later Babylonian 'Amoraim who experienced *Gilluy Shekinah*, apparently in the form of locutions.[55] We also take two references to vivid experience of *Gilluy Shekinah* on the part of High Priests of the Second Temple as evidence that there was some expectation of this experience in rabbinic times. In one instance, R. 'Abbahu declares that it was the Holy One blessed be He who was "the old man" that, according to the story, always entered

[53] Ibid., pp. 153 ff.

[54] Midrash Tehillim on Ps. 105:1, ed. Buber, p. 224b. "Strength" in the proof text refers to Torah, as Buber points out. Cf. Mekilta, II, p. 234.

[55] Megillah 29a. The passage is explicit only in the case of R. Sheshet.

with Simeon the Righteous into the Holy of Holies[56]; in the other instance, a "baraita" reports R. Ishmael b. Elisha as saying that once upon entering the Holy of Holies to offer incense, he saw " 'Akatriel, Lord (יה), the Lord of hosts" as He was "sitting upon a throne high and lifted up," a statement patterned in part after Is. 6:1.[57]

But the passages just cited, and the few more of like character that are perhaps to be found, are decidedly not representative of the bulk of the passages on *Gilluy Shekinah*. In most of those passages, the various instances of *Gilluy Shekinah* are, with respect to the rabbinic period, depicted as being either in the past or in the future. This alone would imply a denial by the Rabbis of *Gilluy Shekinah* in their own day; in any event, it certainly indicates that the Rabbis, by and large, refrained from applying the concept to their own times. And we have more explicit evidence. "In this world," says a midrash, "as the result of our sins neither any prophet nor the Holy Spirit is with us, as it says, 'We see not our signs; there is no more any prophet' (Ps. 74:9). Not these alone but the *Shekinah* as well, as it

[56] Yer. Yoma V.3, 42c. See also the version in Pesikta de R. Kahana, ed. Buber, p. 178a, and in Lev. R. XXI.11, where an additional statement by R. 'Abbahu is given. מתנות כהונה on Lev. R. a. l. suggests that this additional statement may represent a retraction by R. 'Abbahu that angels were not permitted in the Holy of Holies. Lauterbach says that R. 'Abbahu may not himself have held that God actually appeared in the guise of an old man, and he takes the additional statement to support that contention — J. Z. Lauterbach, A Significant Controversy Between the Sadducees and the Pharisees, Hebrew Union College Annual, IV (Cincinnati, 1927), p. 189, note 16. The question of the presence of angels in the Holy of Holies is again raised in Yer. Yoma I.5, 39a, and again R. 'Abbahu has an explanation, but the commentators differ as to its meaning.

In Tosefta Soṭah XIII.8, ed. Zuck.-Lieb., p. 319, Yoma 39b, and Menaḥot 109b, the story alone regarding Simeon the Righteous is given.

[57] Berakot 7a. Zunz regards this passage as post-talmudic (and hence an interpolation) — op. cit., p. 164, note. But see G. Scholem, Major Trends in Jewish Mysticism (Jerusalem: Schocken, 1941), p. 352, note 3. He regards the passage as kindred to the material in Hekalot Rabbati, and hence as belonging to the *Merkabah* literature. On this material, see below, p. 260.

says, 'But your iniquities have separated between you and your God' (Is. 59:2). In the future, however, — *Le'atid Labo* — He will reveal Himself to them, as it says 'And the glory of the Lord shall be revealed, and all flesh shall see it together' (ibid., 40:5); and they will see Him, as it says, 'For they shall see eye to eye, the Lord returning to Zion' (ibid., 52:8)."[58] From the second half of this midrash it is clear that *Shekinah* here means *Gilluy Shekinah,* and from the statement that "in this world" there is "neither any prophet nor the Holy Spirit" it is evident that in this instance the term "this world" refers to the Rabbis' own day. *Gilluy Shekinah,* the midrash declares, will take place *Le'atid Labo* but does not take place in the present. Statements in the same vein by early Tannaim, and based on the verse "For man shall not see Me and live" (Exod. 33:20), go even further. In a version of these statements found in a passage of the Sifra,[59] a tannaitic Midrash, R. Dosa interprets the verse to mean that men cannot see God during their lifetime but will see Him upon their death; R. 'Aḳiba interprets it to mean that the Holy *Ḥayyot* bearing the throne of Glory also do not see the Glory; R. Simeon adds to R. 'Aḳiba's interpretation the idea that the angels, too, who live forever, do not see the Glory. *Gilluy Shekinah* in visual form, according to all these views,[60] never takes place in the lifetime of any man; nor was Moses an exception,[61] since

[58] Agadat Bereshit, ed. Buber, p. 47. The conclusion is reminiscent of, and no doubt affected by, the midrash we quoted above, p. 229.

[59] Sifra on Lev. 1:1, II.12, ed. Weiss, p. 4a; Numbers R. XIV, end.

[60] Both R. 'Aḳiba and R. Simeon take וחי as referring to others, since "man" has already been mentioned — R. 'Aḳiba refers it to *Ḥayyot* and R. Simeon to *ḥayyim.* See the commentary of R. Abraham b. David in the Sifra a. l. Abraham Geiger in המקרא ותרגומיו (Hebr. trans.), p. 221, says that R. 'Aḳiba was anxious lest Exod. 33:20 be understood to mean that a man can see God but must die at the sight; and that therefore he interprets וחי as having reference not to man at all but to the *Ḥayyot.*

[61] A variant of R. Dosa's statement specifically includes Moses — see Midrash Agadah, ed. Buber, I, p. 184.

the verse here interpreted begins with "Thou canst not see My face," and it is the full verse that the Rabbis are interpreting.

Another version of these statements, differing in a few details but with substantially the same content, is found in the Sifre, also a tannaitic Midrash.[62] In the Sifre, the passage begins with an anonymous comment on a word in Numbers 12:8, — *mar'eh,* a word ordinarily meaning sight or vision.[63] The comment, nevertheless, declares that *mar'eh* here must refer to *mar'eh Dibbur* and not to *mar'eh Shekinah,* the sight (or vision) of *Shekinah*; and that it cannot refer to *mar'eh Shekinah,* that is, the seeing of *Shekinah,* because of Exod. 33:20 — "Thou canst not see My face, for man shall not see Me and live." (That verse, in turn, now brings in its train the same interpretations of it given in the Sifra).[64] *Dibbur* alone is a rabbinic synonym for prophecy,[65] more specifically, God's utterance to prophets[66]; it is a form of *Gilluy Shekinah,* for the idea of God's "revealing Himself" is associated with it.[67] *Mar'eh Dibbur* we take to mean "revelation of *Dibbur,*" since the literal meaning of "sight" is here excluded. It would thus be an aspect of *Gilluy Shekinah,* the revelation of *Shekinah,* an aspect, according to our passage, that was experienced only by Moses. In any case, *mar'eh Dibbur,* too, was obviously not possible in the Rabbis' own day nor, as we shall see later, was *Dibbur.*[68] Incidentally, the version in the Sifra makes a

[62] Sifre on Numbers 12:8, par. 103, ed. Horovitz, p. 101. See the notes there.

[63] Ibid. The text in the Sifre here reads במראה whereas the Massoretic text of the Bible has ומראה. Is the Sifre text merely a scribal slip because of Num. 12:6?

[64] Ibid.

[65] See Bereshit R. XLIV.6 ed. Theodor, p. 429 and the parallels there.

[66] Notice the use of the word in Sifra on Lev. 1:1, I.2–7, ed. Weiss, p. 3c. There was also the instance of "the *Dibbur* at Mt. Sinai" to all Israel — ibid.

[67] As, for example, Bereshit R. LII.5, ed. Theodor, p. 544 f., and the parallels there — the distinction between the prophets of Israel and the prophets of the nations.

[68] See below, p. 250 f.

similar distinction, though in its own way, between the seeing of *Shekinah* and the *Dibbur* experienced by Moses.[69]

We have been obliged, in our discussion, to use the term *Gilluy Shekinah* rather frequently. In doing so, however, we have departed from rabbinic usage. The term *Gilluy Shekinah* occurs but a single time in the whole rabbinic literature — and that single time in a very old section of the Passover Haggadah, so old as even to have been assigned to the prerabbinic epoch.[70] Reading *ubemora' gadol* (Deut. 26:8) as *ubemar'e (h) gadol* — "and with a great sight (or vision)" — that early passage explains the phrase by saying, "This refers to *Gilluy Shekinah* (revelation of *Shekinah*)."[71] Thus, in one brief comment only do the Rabbis give utterance to the conceptual term. This does not mean that our frequent use of the term is unjustified. When the Rabbis say that "He revealed Himself" or that "the Holy One blessed be He revealed Himself," they use the word *niglah*, a verb form of the noun *gilluy*; similarly, when they speak of "seeing" *Shekinah*, or use a circumlocution for that (e. g., to greet the face of *Shekinah*), again the reference is to *Gilluy Shekinah* — witness how the Rabbis identify *Gilluy Shekinah* with the word "sight" in Deut. 26:8. Instances of both kinds occur often enough, and it was

[69] In the Sifra passage, the interpretations of Exod. 33:20 immediately follow expository comments concerning God's speaking to Moses, *Dibbur*, and they also immediately precede other comments depicting the circumstances of God's communications to Moses. The three interpretations of Exod. 33:20 are therefore undoubtedly interjected here, and interjected for the purpose of contrasting the seeing of God, which is not possible in this world, and God's speaking to Moses. The latter consists of *Dibberot*, and *Dibberot* were experienced by Moses alone, except for those given on Sinai, according to this text — see the reference in note 66 above. The Rabbis even interpret away biblical verses saying that God spoke to both Moses and Aaron — ibid., II.1–4. Other sources, however, have Aaron too experiencing several *Dibberot* — Mekilta, I, p. 1, and the references there.

[70] See Louis Finkelstein, The Oldest Midrash: Pre-Rabbinic Ideals and Teachings in the Passover Haggadah, The Harvard Theological Review, Vol. XXXI, no. 4 (October, 1938), pp. 291–317.

[71] See ibid., p. 297, note 16; also ibid., p. 310, notes 38 and 39.

from these that we drew our examples of *Gilluy Shekinah*. Nevertheless, the fact remains that, in decided contrast to all the other value-terms,[72] the term *Gilluy Shekinah* is mentioned only once by the Rabbis themselves. Can this be mere accident? Does it not seem likely that the Rabbis wished to withdraw the term from general circulation, as it were, and is this not of a piece with the denial of the possibility of *Gilluy Shekinah* in their own day?

The concept of *Gilluy Shekinah* is not fully in keeping with the character of the rabbinic value-complex as a whole. Standing for the revelation of God to human senses, particularly to the sense of sight, it represents a mixture of the valuational and the cognitive, and it is therefore not a pure value-concept. A concept of that kind does not function easily, as we saw in the case of the defined aspect of the concept of *Nes*, where the admixture was that of a value-concept and an abstract, quasi-scientific concept.[73] There the conceptual phase was restricted and curbed by means of definite and stated principles.[74] The concept of *Gilluy Shekinah* was likewise restricted, but by what was common usage rather than by stated principles. The type of mysticism the concept stands for was apparently very rarely experienced in rabbinic times. The conceptual term itself seems to have fallen practically into desuetude. Moreover, outstanding authorities, among them R. 'Aḳiba, denied the possibility of this type of mystical experience when they insisted that even the angels could not see God. Obviously other authorities did not go that far, since the Haggadah contains numerous instances of *Gilluy Shekinah*; yet here, too, the concept is restricted, its concretizations being generally confined, with respect to the rabbinic period, to the past and future. Seldom concretized in actual life, the concept of *Gilluy Shekinah*, it appears, was largely merely

[72] See above, p. 52 f.

[73] Above, pp. 153 ff.

[74] Ibid., p. 162 f.

a haggadic concept, that is to say, a concept utilized mainly for haggadic interpretations — and haggadic interpretations, we may remember, were often subject to indeterminacy of belief.[75] At the same time, although restricted in its functioning, the concept was a component part of the rabbinic value-complex. Individuals so inclined by temperament could, therefore, at least expect or hope for an actual experience of *Gilluy Shekinah.*

While the concept of *Gilluy Shekinah* was used mainly in Haggadah, it also figured, on a few occasions, in Halakah as well. A consideration of these halakic instances reveals that the general attitude is the same as that found in the Haggadah. Nor do we need many instances, in the case of Halakah, in order to discover the general attitude. The latter can be discerned from a halakic statement containing the majority opinion, and hence designated as being that of the *Ḥakamim*[76] or that of *Rabbanan*[77]; or else from an anonymous mishnaic statement, the anonymity being an indication of general concurrence.[78]

One of our halakic instances is concerned with Exodus 23:17 — "Three times in the year all thy males shall appear (lit., shall be seen) before (lit., to the face of) the Lord God."[79] "Shall appear," or more literally, "shall be seen," is the rendering of the word *yera'eh,* a passive form, and is in accordance with our received Massoretic text. It is also in accordance with the old versions, among them the Septuagint; the reading *yera'eh,* therefore, was the estab-

[75] See above, pp. 132 ff., p. 142.

[76] E. g., Berakot I.1 — the opinion of the *Ḥakamim* as opposed to that of R. Eliezer. In Ḥullin 85a, it is stated that because Rabbi Judah the Prince (the editor of the Mishnah) approved of the opinion of R. Me'ir in one instance and of that of R. Simeon in another, he designated those opinions as being those of the *Ḥakamim.*

[77] E. g., Pesaḥim 10a — in the instances there, notice how the term *Rabbanan* is an alternate to the term *Ḥakamim.*

[78] See above, pp. 93–94.

[79] "God" here is the Tetragrammaton.

lished reading well before mishnaic times.[80] The same is true of the word *yera'eh* occurring in that part of Deut. 16:16 which is a parallel to Exod. 23:17. Now the text in the scrolls of the Bible gives only the consonants, and so non-Massoretic readings, too, based on the consonantal text, were utilized for rabbinic interpretations, even for halakic interpretations at times.[81] This was the case with the halakic interpretation of our word *yera'eh*. Subjecting the phrases of Exod. 23:17 to halakic interpretation, the Mekilta of R. Simeon takes *yera'eh* to teach that the blind man is excluded, "for he cannot see."[82] But the word can have this implication only if it is read *yir'eh* "(he) shall see," the consonantal text remaining the same yet so vowelized as to render it an active form and not the passive of the Massoretic text. "Three times in the year all thy males shall see the face of the Lord" was the reading given to Exod. 23:17 in this interpretation, and therefore the blind man is to be excluded, "for he cannot see." The reading of the Massoretic text, however, may also have entered into this interpretation. This we can infer from another tannaitic work, the Sifre on Deuteronomy, the halakic section of which stems from the same school as does the Mekilta of R. Simeon.[83] In the passage on Deut. 16:16 found in that section, a passage that closely parallels our passage in the Mekilta of R. Simeon, the comment on

[80] See Geiger, op. cit., p. 337 (in the supplement written by him in Hebrew and edited by Poznanski, Warsaw, 5670). On Geiger's theory, see below, p. 243, note 92.

[81] For example, the interpretations of R. 'Aḳiba in Sanhedrin 54b; also the instances given ibid., 4a–b, among which is a version we shall take up soon of the halakic interpretation of *yera'eh* in Exod. 23:17 that utilizes also the non-Massoretic reading of the word. An example of haggadic interpretation of that kind was given above, p. 118, and the note there.

[82] Mechilta de Rabbi Simon, ed. Hoffmann, p. 159.

[83] David Hoffmann, לחקר מדרשי התנאים (Hebrew trans.), in מסלות לתורת התנאים ed. Rabinowitz (Tel Aviv, 5688), p. 67. Both tannaitic works are from the school of R. 'Aḳiba — ibid., p. 68. Notice how R. 'Aḳiba is given to halakic interpretations based on non-Massoretic readings of consonantal texts — above, note 81.

yera'eh is: "As he comes 'to be seen', so does he come to see."[84] "To be seen" obviously refers to the Massoretic *yera'eh* and "to see" can refer only to the non-Massoretic *yir'eh*.[85] A man is duty bound to appear before the Lord, this interpretation has it, but he must also come to see. Is it not to be understood, therefore, that the blind man is excluded, since he cannot see? Moreover, the kinship of the sources and the parallel character of the two passages argue a similar derivation of the halakah. Was this derivation so well known that it had only to be hinted at? In the Mekilta of R. Ishmael, all that is given in comment on *yera'eh* is the phrase, "to exclude the blind,"[86] without any further explanation. It is also possible, of course, that the derivation here is only from the non-Massoretic *yir'eh*, "shall see"[87]; since the blind cannot see, they are to be excluded. At all events, the three sources have in common the idea that the pilgrims who went up to the Temple in Jerusalem went up to see God. In other words, they assume that the pilgrims could experience *Gilluy Shekinah*.[88]

[84] כדרך שבא ליראות כך בא לראות — Sifre on Deuteronomy, ed. Friedmann, par. 143, p. 102b. We take the reading of the mss. — see Friedmann's note there — although the reading in Friedmann's text simply inverts the clauses. Notice there the derivation of R. Hillel b. Eliakim which we give immediately. On the phrase "to be seen," see below, p. 244, note 98.

[85] See the preceding note regarding the derivation by R. Hillel.

[86] Mekilta, III, p. 182. See Horovitz-Rabin, p. 333, note 3, as to the verses from Deut. in this passage.

[87] From Midrash Tannaim, p. 95, it would also seem that the exclusion of the blind in the anonymous statement there rested only on the non-Massoretic *yir'eh*; but the baraita following it was probably edited by the Rabbis of the Talmud — see below, p. 244 and note 99. The haggadic interpretation of *yera'eh* by R. Joshua b. Levi in Yer. Ḥagigah I.1, 76a, does indicate, however, that the non-Massoretic *yir'eh* could by itself be the basis for interpretation. Yet it is not taken literally by R. Joshua. He says of him "who observes the *Miẓwah* of *re'iyyah* (i. e., the pilgrimage to the Temple — ראיה)" that it is "as though he greets (or receives) the presence of *Shekinah*," and derives this from the non-Massoretic *yir'eh*. On ראיה see below, p. 244, note 98.

[88] If R. 'Aḳiba was consistent in his view on *Gilluy Shekinah* — see above, p. 235 — the teaching on *yera'eh* emanated from pupils who employed his methods

The Mishnah rejects that assumption, namely, that the pilgrims could experience *Gilluy Shekinah*, at the same time that it teaches the halakah that the blind are to be excluded. That halakah was inserted by the *Ḥakamim*; in the Mishnah as edited by Rabbi Judah the Prince, there was no mention of the blind in the list of those excluded from appearance at the Temple. We shall find that the manner of that insertion enables us to discern the attitude of the *Ḥakamim* – that is, the general attitude – toward *Gilluy Shekinah*.

The Tosefta in Ḥagigah I.1 begins by saying that he who is ritually unclean is free from the obligation of appearance in the Temple. It then continues as follows: "Joḥanan b. Dahabai says in the name of R. Judah, 'The blind man also; for it says (Exod. 23:17) *yera'eh* – (thus) excluding the blind man.' Rabbi (Judah the Prince) argues against the words of Joḥanan b. Dahabai (in the name of R. Judah), but the *Ḥakamim* decided in favor of the words of R. Judah."[89] Obviously, the Tosefta here does not give the full list of those who are excluded from appearing at the Temple; it intends merely to add two classes to the list in the mishnah of Ḥagigah I.1. There is, in fact, no mention in that mishnah of him who is ritually unclean. Nor did that mishnah as edited by Rabbi mention the blind man; the Tosefta plainly states that Rabbi was opposed to the halakah which would exclude the blind; further, the word "also" in the phrase "the blind man also" clearly indicates that the mishnah had not mentioned the blind. The halakah on the blind man, doubtless an old tradition, was inserted

of textual interpretation but who may not have agreed with him on *Gilluy Shekinah*. A teaching on *yera'eh* related to ours is given in the name of R. Judah b. Tema, according to Sanhedrin 4b, and he may have been a pupil of R. 'Aḳiba. His time, however, has not been fixed — see Frankel, op. cit., p. 213.

[89] Tosefta Ḥagigah I.1, ed. Zuck.-Lieb., p. 231–2; (comp.: Yer. Shabbat III.3, 17b; ibid., Ḥagigah I.1, 76a; ibid., Yebamot VIII.1, 9a). השיב ר׳ על דברי יוחנן בן דהבאי is omitted in the Erfurt ms., but is found in the Vienna ms. and in the editio princeps.

into the mishnah by the *Ḥakamim*, since they had "decided in favor of the words of R. Judah." But the manner of its insertion is tantamount to an announcement that, while the *Ḥakamim* accepted the halakah, they rejected its *derivation* from *yera'eh*, and thus also, the idea that the pilgrims could experience *Gilluy Shekinah*. As the mishnah reads now, the persons at the end of its list of those excluded are "the lame man, and the blind man, and the sick man, and the old man, and he that cannot ascend with his feet."[90] Evidently the mishnah groups these persons as a unit. A baraita brought by the Talmud in explanation supplies the reason for that grouping, the reason being that all of them are prevented by a disability from making the pilgrimage without extraneous physical help.[91] According to the mishnah, then, what disqualifies the blind man is his physical incapacity to make the pilgrimage without help. This means that the derivation from *yera'eh*, and hence also the idea associated with it, were not acceptable to the *Ḥakamim*.[92] And that general attitude is reflected in the discussions of both the Palestinian Talmud and the Babylonian Talmud on our mishnah. When either Talmud brings derivations from the Bible in support of the disqualifications enumerated in our mishnah,[93] it utilizes the relevant derivations found in the tannaitic Midrashim.[94] The one such

[90] Ḥagigah I.1.

[91] Ḥagigah 4a, bottom; see Rashi a. l.

[92] Geiger's theory is as follows: The original reading was *yir'eh*, then it was fixed by the Soferim as *yera'eh*, and then the attempt was made to revert to the original reading, and finally it was again established as *yera'eh* — Geiger, op. cit., pp. 337–40. He has not taken account of the derivations in the tannaitic Midrashim — Sifre on Deut., Mekilta, and Mekilta of R. Simon; (he speaks only of the passage in Sifre on Deut. — op. cit., p. 339, note —and evidently does not think it refers to the blind man). But he was the first to point out that the mishnah of Ḥagigah I.1, as edited by Rabbi, did not mention the blind, though his proof for that is not the same as ours.

[93] Yer. Ḥagigah I.1, 76a; and Ḥagigah 4a.

[94] Mekilta, III, p. 182 f.; Mechilta de R. Simon, p. 159; Sifre on Deut., par. 143, ed. Friedmann, p. 102b.

derivation they do *not* utilize is the derivation from *yera'eh* that would disqualify the blind. This is hardly accidental, for most of these tannaitic derivations, including the one from *yera'eh*, are interpretations of different parts of the same biblical verse.[95]

There remains another baraita to be considered. Found in a number of places, this is a baraita in which Joḥanan b. Dahabai says in the name of R. Judah that blindness in one eye disqualifies a man from appearing in the Temple.[96] Both the Massoretic *yera'eh* and the non-Massoretic *yir'eh* enter into the derivation here, as they do in the interpretations of the Mekilta of R. Simeon and the Sifre on Deuteronomy according to our inference, except that here the interpretation disqualifies even a man who is blind in one eye.[97] As in those passages, our baraita also says in so many words that a pilgrim could have an experience of *Gilluy Shekinah* — "he comes to see."[98] Still greater is the resemblance of our baraita to the Tosefta in Ḥagigah I.1, since not only is the derivation similar but the authorities are identical. Indeed, Geiger insists that our baraita is based on the passage in the Tosefta, and it may well be.[99]

[95] Nor can the omission of the blind in the mishnah as edited by Rabbi be the cause. The insertion of the halakah on the blind was made by the *Ḥakamim*, that is, by the Tannaim, and hence it was made before the days of either Talmud.

[96] Ḥagigah 2a; ibid., 4b; Sanhedrin 4b (R. Judah b. Tema); 'Arakin 2b.

[97] See the references in the preceding note.

[98] Tosefot Yom Ṭob to Ḥagigah I.1, s. v. והסומא, says that all the passages in the Talmud read: כדרך שבא ליראות כך בא לראות.

We feel that, in any case, "to be seen" was used as a cliché by the Rabbis to refer to the appearance at the Temple, and was not meant in the literal sense taken by Rashi in his comments on the baraita. Notice how הראייה is used as such a cliché in Ḥagigah II.2; and again that הראיון is so used in Pe'ah I.1. See also above, p. 241, note 87.

[99] According to Geiger, the Rabbis of the Talmud, having before them the mishnah as amended by the *Ḥakamim*, explain by means of our baraita the now "superfluous" addition in the Tosefta of the halakah on the blind — loc. cit., p. 339. But see Midrash Tannaim, p. 95, where our baraita is also found, and where it is directly preceded by the comment, "*yera'eh* — to exclude the blind man."

In any case, in our baraita no mention at all is made of the *Ḥakamim*. The interpretation of *yera'eh* affirming *Gilluy Shekinah* is here definitely associated only with individuals, with R. Joḥanan and his teacher R. Judah.

Our conclusions from the Haggadah are, therefore, confirmed by the Halakah in this instance. There is a general attitude toward *Gilluy Shekinah* and there is also the attitude taken by individual authorities. While the *Ḥakamim* accept the halakah on the blind man, they reject the derivation of that halakah from *yera'eh*, a derivation affirming that the pilgrims experience *Gilluy Shekinah*. Being the attitude of *Ḥakamim*, that rejection represents the crystallized attitude in this instance. We have thus another illustration of the restriction of the concept of *Gilluy Shekinah*. Yet the concept is, after all, a component element of the value-complex. This allows individual authorities to concretize the concept, on occasion, in Halakah too, not only in Haggadah; and hence the various halakic passages, some of them actually naming their authors, where the interpretation of *yera'eh* assumes that the pilgrims could experience *Gilluy Shekinah*.

A controversy between the Sadducees and the Pharisees raised another halakic issue that involved the concept of *Gilluy Shekinah*. Centering apparently on a detail of ritual practice in the Temple, this controversy really brought to a focus a doctrinal difference. The practice in dispute had to do with the offering of incense in the Holy of Holies on the Day of Atonement. The Sadducees maintained that the High Priest must put the incense on the censer "full of coals of fire" (Lev. 16:12) whilst he was still outside the curtain, in other words, that the censer carried by the High Priest into the Holy of Holies must already contain the incense.[100] They argued: "If it is done thus before

[100] Sifra, Aḥare, III.11, ed. Weiss 81b; Yer. Yoma I.5, 39a–b; (Midrash Ha-Gadol on Lev. 16:13, ed. Rabinowitz, p. 418).

(a man of) flesh and blood — before God (*Ha-Maḳom*) *à fortiori!* And it says, 'For I appear — *'era'eh* (lit., also, 'I will appear') — in the cloud upon the ark-cover' (Lev. 16:2)."[101] The biblical verse justifies, for the Sadducees, their claim that when the incense is placed in the Holy of Holies, it is placed before God. Their argument is simply that, since God appears "in the cloud upon the ark-cover" in the Holy of Holies, it is not seemly that the incense be put on the censer in His presence; this is not done even when incense is offered to a man, "flesh and blood."[102] To be sure, the controversy took place in the period of the Second Temple, probably some time after the Maccabean Revolt,[103] and in the Second Temple there were no ark and no ark-cover.[104] The absence of the ark-cover, however, certainly did not signify to the Sadducees that God no longer appeared in the Holy of Holies. Because there was no longer an ark-cover, there was no longer a cloud, but He was present in the Holy of Holies nevertheless; it is His presence within the veil or curtain that the verse refers to with the word *'era'eh*. In such a connection forms of this word, as we have noticed, were taken to indicate *Gilluy Shekinah*, and the word was so taken by the Sadducees here. God is manifest immediately within the veil, the Sadducees argued, and it is unseemly that the offering of incense be not given at once. When the censer is brought into the Holy of Holies, therefore, it must already contain the incense.[105]

[101] Ibid.

[102] Incense was used in triumphs by the Romans — see Encyc. Brit., 13th ed., Vol. 14, p. 351a.

[103] Finkelstein points out that the ritual practice insisted on by the Sadducees "must have come into vogue before the Maccabean Rebellion" — The Pharisees, Vol. I (Philadelphia: Jewish Publication Society of America, 1940), pp. 120–1.

[104] See Yoma V.2.

[105] Malbim, in his commentary to the Sifra, a. l., regards the verse — Lev. 16:2 — as constituting a *second* argument by the Sadducees. His view of the way the Sadducees interpret the verse has been determined apparently by the version of

The Pharisees, designated in this controversy by the term *Ḥakamim*,[106] taught differently. They answered the Sadducees by pointing to the order of the actions prescribed by Lev. 16:12–13. "And he shall take a censer full of coals of fire from off the altar before the Lord, and his hands full of sweet incense beaten small, and bring (them) within the veil (v. 12). And he shall put the incense upon the fire before the Lord, that the cloud of the incense may cover the ark-cover that is upon the testimony, that he die not (v. 13)." The *Ḥakamim* taught that the consecutive verses prescribe consecutive actions. Holding the censer and the incense, the High Priest is first to "bring (them) within the veil"; after having done so, "he shall put the incense upon the fire before the Lord."[107] The High Priest, then, must put the incense on the fire-containing censer *after* he has entered the Holy of Holies, not before. What of the seemliness, however, of such an act? Does it not say "For I will appear — *'era'eh* — in the cloud upon the ark-cover" (Lev. 16:2)? But this verse does not have the same meaning for the *Ḥakamim* that it has for the Sadducees. According to the *Ḥakamim*, the words "in the cloud" refer to the cloud of incense. The verse "teaches that he must put into it (that is, into the incense) *ma'aleh 'ashan*,"[108] a certain herb which, as its name "smoke-raiser" implies, causes the incense smoke to rise in a cloudlike column.[109] Proof that the word "cloud" in v. 2 indeed refers to the cloud of incense they find in the actual term "the cloud of the incense" in v. 13 of the same passage. "And whence do we know that he must put into it *ma'aleh 'ashan* (so that the smoke will rise like a column of cloud)? Scripture teaches, 'That the *cloud of*

the controversy given in the Babylonian Talmud, and we shall deal with that version soon.

[106] See the references above, p. 245, note 100.

[107] See ibid.

[108] Ibid.

[109] See the baraita quoted by 'Abaye in Yoma 53a.

the incense may cover the ark-cover that is upon the testimony, that he die not' (v. 13)."[110] The verse "For I will appear in the cloud upon the ark-cover," therefore, does not have the meaning given it by the Sadducees. It does not mean, as the Sadducees would have it, that God manifests Himself immediately within the veil, that in the Holy of Holies there is always *Gilluy Shekinah.* What the verse teaches is that there is *Gilluy Shekinah* only after the incense has been made to rise.

This controversy shows that restriction of the concept of *Gilluy Shekinah* was a characteristic of rabbinic thought even early in the rabbinic period. The *Ḥakamim* here deny that there is permanent or steady *Gilluy Shekinah* in the Holy of Holies. So strongly were they opposed to the idea that they imposed an oath on the High Priest, the purpose of the oath being to uproot the Sadducean practice which involved that idea.[111] The *Ḥakamim* also teach, it is true, that God does reveal Himself in the Holy of Holies after the rising of the incense. But it is quite possible they assumed merely that *Gilluy Shekinah* might take place at such time, not that it necessarily would take place. The sheer rising of the cloud of incense in the Temple could not have been, for them, a phenomenon inevitably associated with *Gilluy Shekinah.* Incense was offered on the golden altar in the *Hekal* twice daily,[112] and this incense, too, contained *ma'aleh 'ashan,* the "smoke-raiser"[113]; yet that incense cloud was unquestionably not associated with *Gilluy Shekinah.*

The baraita which tells of the controversy is found in several versions. We have based our discussion on the

[110] See the references above, p. 245, note 100. That the *Ḥakamim* bring in v. 13 — "the cloud of the incense" — in order to prove that the word "cloud" in v. 2 refers to the smoke of the incense is a point made by Malbim, l. c., toward the end of the comment.

[111] See Tosefta Yoma I.8, ed. Zuck.-Lieb., p. 181; Yoma 19b.

[112] Menaḥot IV.4.

[113] Yoma 53a; Keritot 6a.

version common to the Sifra[114] and to the Palestinian Talmud.[115] The version in the Babylonian Talmud,[116] though the one best known, represents a distinctly defective tradition. Omitting the argument of the Sadducees, it gives only the verse they use, and this as if the verse itself contained the details of their practice. As a result, the "Sadducean" interpretation of the verse resembles that of the *Ḥakamim* and the doctrinal difference is thus obscured. We mention this version and its difficulties because it has always determined the view taken of the controversy.[117]

Both Haggadah and Halakah reveal, we are led to conclude, the same general attitude with regard to *Gilluy Shekinah.* The general tendency is to restrict the concretization of the concept, a tendency evidenced in the case of very few other concepts. This is the point we have been emphasizing in the present discussion. We ought, however, to enlarge somewhat on a matter we touched on only incidentally — the association of *Gilluy Shekinah* with prophecy.

[114] Sifra, Aḥare, III.11, ed. Weiss 81b.

[115] Yer. Yoma I.5, 39a–b.

[116] Yoma 53a. See also the version in Tosefta Yoma I.8, ed. Zuck.-Lieb., p. 181.

[117] The Babylonian version (Yoma 53a), after telling of the Sadducean practice, asks מאי דרוש, and answers by quoting, "For I will appear in the cloud upon the ark-cover" (Lev. 16:2). "Cloud" therefore must be understood to refer to the incense, as it does in the interpretation by the *Ḥakamim*. See Rashi's gloss a. l. Apparently influenced by this version, Malbim, as we pointed out in a previous note (above, p. 246, note 105) takes the verse to represent a second argument by the Sadducees, and he struggles with its interpretation. Lauterbach, op. cit., also regards the verse as a second argument, and hence he also, we must say, has difficulty in explaining the position of the Pharisees. He enlarges, incidentally, on the idea that the incense smoke served the purpose of screening the visible manifestation of God from man's vision. According to him, this is why the Sadducees insist that the High Priest enter the Holy of Holies with the smoke already rising from the censer (op. cit., pp. 195 f.). But do not the Sadducees plainly tell their reason? The incense is an *offering*—and, say the Sadducees, similar offerings may be made to men, to kings. Is incense offered to men so that their faces may be hidden? Lauterbach may have been influenced here by Ibn Ezra's explanation — see Ibn Ezra on Lev. 16:2. But Ibn Ezra is attempting to explain the *peshaṭ* of the verse, whereas Lauterbach endeavors to depict the mental attitude of the Sadducees.

Gilluy Shekinah is associated with prophecy in two ways. It may refer to God's communication to the prophet, to *Dibbur*, as we mentioned above.[118] Thus, because the Rabbis explain away " (the case) of those prophets with whom He did speak — *shenidbar* — outside the land (of Israel)," they can affirm "that the *Shekinah* does not reveal itself outside the land."[119] Again, R. Joḥanan in the name of R. Jose b. Ḳisma tells of how hospitality "caused *Shekinah* to rest on prophets of Baal," the proof being, "And it came to pass, as they sat at the table, that the word of the Lord came unto the prophet that brought him back" (I Kings 13:20).[120] The occasions when God "speaks with" the prophets, when "the word of the Lord" comes upon them, are then regarded as revelations of *Shekinah*. Besides, there is also the assumption that all of the prophets had visions of God, as in the passage where reference is made to "what Isaiah and Ezekiel and all the rest of the prophets . . . saw."[121] But the experience of this aspect of *Gilluy Shekinah* is rather minimized by the Rabbis, so far as the prophets are concerned: "a maidservant at the Red Sea"[122] and "all the people" at Sinai saw "what Isaiah and Ezekiel and all the rest of the prophets never saw."[123] What did make for the special character of the prophet's message? That other aspect of *Gilluy Shekinah* wherein the revelation of God consisted of His communication to the prophet, of His utterance or *Dibbur*.[124] For the Rabbis, it is ultimately this experience of the prophet that gives authenticity and authority to the prophet's words.

The Rabbis insisted that prophecy was no longer possible. "When the last prophets, Haggai, Zechariah and Malachi

[118] Above, p. 236.

[119] Mekilta, I, pp. 5–7.

[120] Sanhedrin 103b–104a; Seder Eliahu, pp. 60–1.

[121] Mekilta, II, pp. 24–5. See above, p. 231, note 44.

[122] Mekilta, II, p. 24.

[123] Ibid., p. 212.

[124] See above, p. 236.

died," they declare, "the Holy Spirit – *Ruaḥ Ha-Ḳodesh* – ceased out of Israel."[125] In this statement, *Ruaḥ Ha-Ḳodesh* stands for God's utterance through the medium of a prophet, in effect, for prophecy. Now if *Ruaḥ Ha-Ḳodesh* has ceased, then *Dibbur* has ceased, too, and also that aspect of *Gilluy Shekinah* characteristic of prophecy and associated with *Dibbur*; the three concepts are overlapping concepts.[126] The concept of *Gilluy Shekinah* is, therefore,

[125] Tosefta Soṭah XIII.2, Sanhedrin 11a and the parallels there. The statement goes on to say that afterwards a *Bat Ḳol* made pronouncements; we shall take up *Bat Ḳol* shortly. On the cessation of prophecy see E. E. Urbach, מתי פסקה הנבואה, in Tarbiẓ, XVII, pp. 1 ff.

[126] On overlapping concepts, see above, p. 29 f. To give specific examples of the overlapping of our concepts: *Dibbur*, the noun form, is associated with *Gilluy Shekinah* in Bereshit R. LII.5, ed. Theodor, p. 544 f. and the parallels there; *Ruaḥ Ha-Ḳodesh* and *Gilluy Shekinah* are, on occasion, interchangeable—where Tosefta Soṭah XIII.3, 4 twice has "fit for *Ruaḥ Ha-Ḳodesh*," the parallel in Sanhedrin 11a twice reads, "fit that *Shekinah* should rest upon him," and in Seder Eliahu, pp. 60–1, the terms are interchanged in a single passage.

Although overlapping, each of these concepts, like all rabbinic concepts (see above, pp. 38 ff.), has its own individuality. *Dibbur* refers specifically to God's communication to the prophets; *Gilluy Shekinah* stands, in addition, for non-prophetic revelation of God to man's senses; and *Ruaḥ Ha-Ḳodesh* is a term used in a number of ways — see Bacher, ערכי מדרש (Hebr. trans.), pp. 123–4, 290–4. *Ruaḥ Ha-Ḳodesh* is also used in an extended sense, that of divine inspiration in rabbinic times. On the occasion when Hillel fell back on the popular practice, he said, "Let them (the people) be. The Holy Spirit (rests) on them. If they are not prophets, they are the sons of prophets"—Tosefta Pesaḥim IV.2, ed. Zuck.-Lieb., p. 163. See also OT, pp. 37–8.

As used by Naḥmanides, the concept of *Ruaḥ Ha-Ḳodesh* affords another example of the way a medieval philosopher deviated from rabbinic thought. Naḥmanides tells us that *Ruaḥ Ha-Ḳodesh* was a lower grade than prophecy, and higher than *Bat Ḳol* (Com. to the Pentateuch, Exod. 28:30). He speaks, again, of "prophecy and the degree which is lower than it," meaning by the latter *Ruaḥ Ha-Ḳodesh*, and so has the category of prophets and also that of "men of *Ruaḥ Ha-Ḳodesh*" (ibid., Num. 22:23). An example of such men of the Holy Spirit is Daniel (ibid.). In one place, however, the Rabbis definitely put Daniel among the forty-eight prophets mentioned by name in the Bible and bracket him with Ezekiel, both of them being referred to in Scripture by the phrase "son of man" — see Seder 'Olam R., Chap. XX, end; comp. R. Ḥananel on Megillah 14a. Elsewhere, it is true, the statement is made that Daniel was not a prophet — see Megillah 3a. In any case, the Rabbis have no such concept as "men of *Ruaḥ Ha-Ḳodesh*," and the entire idea of *Ruaḥ Ha-Ḳodesh* as a "grade" in itself is foreign to rabbinic

restricted in rabbinic times at best to the nonprophetic revelation of God to man's senses, and the general tendency, as we concluded, is to negate the application of the concept altogether. And it is well to remember another thing; authority derives only from that aspect of *Gilluy Shekinah* which characterized prophecy,[127] from an experience, that is to say, which is no longer possible. Those who may have experienced *Gilluy Shekinah* in rabbinic times could claim no special authority as the result of such experience.

If the concretization of *Gilluy Shekinah* is restricted, even negated, what is the character of the experience of God that the Rabbis took such pains to cultivate? Experience of God as manifest in His love, His justice, His holiness, was something without which life was unthinkable. It was cultivated and felt in *Berakah* and prayer, in repentance, in study of Torah, in the practice of the *Miẓwot*, in everyday life and on the holy days. On all these occasions, what was the character of the experience of God? Since that which the Rabbis in general experienced, and the folk as well, was not *Gilluy Shekinah*, it was experience of God *unaccompanied* by psychic phenomena such as visions or locutions. Here, then, is another feature of normal mysticism. In order to achieve that kind of mysticism, a person must develop habits of action that are at the same time habits in sensitivity, but this is largely a matter of cultivation, of training. The psychological equipment required

thought. Furthermore, Naḥmanides' description of the experience of these "men of the Holy Spirit" seems to reflect medieval thought. In this description, he aptly applies phrases from Job 4:14–15 and Daniel 10:8, but he also emphasizes that the experience occurs בהתבודדות, when these men are apart from society — see his Commentary to the Pentateuch, Num. 23:4. Pertinent in this connection is the study by Prof. A. J. Heschel, על רוח הקודש בימי הבינים, תדפיס מתוך ספר היובל לכבוד אלכסנדר מארכס (נוירק, תש"י).

[127] That authority did not mean that a prophet could either introduce or abrogate a law. "Forty-eight prophets and seven prophetesses prophesied unto Israel, and they neither took away from nor added to what is written in the Torah, except for the reading of the *megillah* (on Purim)" — baraita in Megillah 14a.

is only the sort called for also in ordinary, day-to-day living, not that of any unusual temperament. This feature of normal mysticism is in accord with those already observed. We noticed that normal mystical experience is occasioned by daily events and daily activities[128]; and we recognized, too, that it is associated with the integration of the concepts as a whole, that it is a steady aspect of the normal valuational life of the individual.[129] The grasp of daily events, the normal valuational life — do these call for anything more than the ordinary psychological equipment? Persons whose psychological constitution allows them to see visions and hear locutions are certainly not excluded; in fact, in the concept of *Gilluy Shekinah* the value-complex gives room for such extraordinary phenomena. But that very concept, we found, is not completely in keeping with the nature of the value-complex as a whole.

This third feature of normal mysticism has been brought into relief by an analysis of the contexts of the word *Shekinah*. As Ginzberg has pointed out, the word can hardly have been used in an identical way in all the various rabbinic statements containing it.[130] It seems to us, however, that its use can usually be discerned from the context. To be more precise, the word is used in either of two contexts; in one context it refers to *Gilluy Shekinah* and in the other it reflects normal mystical experience.[131] Statements on *Shekinah*

[128] Above, p. 203.

[129] Ibid., pp. 214–215.

[130] See Ginzberg, Commentary, III, pp. 395–7.

[131] Thus, in the passages cited by Ginzberg, ibid.: (A) The term *Shekinah* refers to *Gilluy Shekinah* in (a) the statement by R. Jose (Mekilta, II, p. 224) and which we took up above; (incidentally, *Kabod* refers to *Gilluy Shekinah* also in Mekilta, II, p. 162, as the word in the proof text, Ps. 29:9 indicates; comp. ibid., II, p. 233; see also Louis Finkelstein, The Transmission of Early Rabbinic Tradition, H. U. C. Annual, XVI, 117–121); (b) the statements regarding *Shekinah* in the Temple. Those who say that *Shekinah* did not dwell in the Second Temple refer obviously only to *Gilluy Shekinah*, or to the possibility of *Gilluy Shekinah* there; others could and did differ with them on this point. (B) The

that appear to be contradictory, hence, may not really be so at all. For example, the statement that God withdrew His *Shekinah* when the Temple was destroyed, and the statement, in a context of prayer, that *Shekinah* is everywhere,[132] do not really contradict each other; the former refers to *Gilluy Shekinah* whereas the latter reflects normal mystical experience. Again, the word *Shekinah* can be used in both contexts because of something common to both contexts, namely, the idea of God's nearness. A teaching explicitly stating this common idea may, therefore, be applicable in both contexts. We have a case in point in the teaching, just alluded to, that *Shekinah* is everywhere. This statement is made in a context of prayer, a context reflecting normal mysticism. Yet practically the same teaching, given in a negative form, occurs in a context of *Gilluy Shekinah*. When R. Gamaliel was asked why the Holy One blessed be He revealed Himself in a bush (to Moses), the answer was: To teach you there is no place on earth not occupied (*panuy*) by the *Shekinah*,[133] that is, there is no place on earth where the *Shekinah* cannot reveal itself. In regard to statements on *Shekinah*, contradictions may be only apparent contradictions, and the same is true of similarities. The question to be asked in every instance is: Does the passage speak of a revelation of God to man's senses? If

term *Shekinah* reflects normal mystical experience in (a) the statements concerning the study of Torah; (b) the statement that *Shekinah* "dwells" among a gathering of ten (congregation). There remains only the statement of R. Gamaliel, and we shall deal with it shortly.

We advanced the idea that *Shekinah*, as a term, was to be found in two contexts, that of *Gilluy Shekinah* and that of normal mysticism, some years ago in an article (Bulletin of the Rabbinical Assembly, V, no. 1, June, 1942). Our thesis there was that there are two concepts, *Gilluy Shekinah* and *Shekinah*. We were wrong, of course, in speaking of *Shekinah* as a concept, although we did say that it was also a name.

[132] See above, p. 226.

[133] Pesiḳta de R. Kahana, I, ed. Buber, 2b (and the parallels there); cited by Ginzberg, l. c.

it does, the passage deals with *Gilluy Shekinah*; if it does not, it reflects normal mystical experience.

Before closing this discussion, it is well to reckon with a view of *Shekinah* held today. *Shekinah* is generally taken today to be the rabbinic term which expresses the idea of the immanence of God. What is meant by this idea? If "immanence of God" means that God is present *within* man or *within* any place as a kind of permanent inherent principle, we have to do with an idea foreign to rabbinic thought, with a philosophical conception. Only when statements are taken out of context, or not checked against other passages, do they at all imply this conception.

There can certainly be no implication of the "immanence of God" in the context of *Gilluy Shekinah*. In that context, God is depicted as revealing Himself to man's sight or hearing, and not as a "principle," or as "inherent." For example, the dictum that there is no place on earth not occupied by the *Shekinah* does not imply "immanence," despite its seeming aptness. It is a reply by R. Gamaliel to a question on *Gilluy Shekinah*; it teaches that there is no place on earth where the *Shekinah* cannot reveal itself. Nor can we possibly attribute to the Rabbis belief in an immanance of a kind that breaks forth, occasionally, into *Gilluy Shekinah*. *Gilluy Shekinah*, we noticed, was primarily associated with the Temple. Yet the Rabbis did not conceive even the Temple-site itself as inevitably the "abode" of *Shekinah*. In the wilderness, before the First Temple was built, *Shekinah* "rested" in the Tabernacle[134]; and there is the opinion which plainly states that *Shekinah* did not "dwell" (or "rest") in the Second Temple.[135]

Nor does *Shekinah* stand for a divine principle permanently inherent *within* Israel. The Rabbis do say, it is true, that *Shekinah* is *with* Israel. They speak of *Shekinah*

[134] Numbers R. XII.5; Sifra on Lev. 9:1, ed. Weiss, p. 44c.

[135] Yoma 9b–10a.

as sharing, as it were, the exile of Israel and the affliction of the people[136]; and as being with a congregation at prayer, with persons engaged in the study of Torah, with a court at its session.[137] Such statements reflect the normal mystical experience of the Rabbis and of the people as a whole. But the Rabbis never take it for granted that *Shekinah* is inevitably associated with Israel. As a matter of fact, they do dissociate *Shekinah* from Israel. When the people sin, *Shekinah* leaves Israel. Whenever Israel surrenders itself to sexual licentiousness, says a midrash, *Shekinah* goes away.[138] Indeed, it is one thing to say that *Shekinah* is usually with Israel and quite another to regard *Shekinah* as a divine principle permanently immanent *within* the people, as a residing principle which is neither distinct, nor to be dissociated, from the people. And on this score, it seems to us, the figures which the Rabbis use with respect to *Shekinah* are conclusive; even though metaphorical, figures are always consistent with the idea. But how can *Shekinah* represent the immanence of God *within* Israel when it is Israel who is gathered "under the wings of *Shekinah*?"[139] Or how can the idea of a permanent inherent principle be conveyed by such a figure as "crowding off the feet of *Shekinah*?"[140] Once more we are bound to conclude that *Shekinah* does not represent the philosophical conception of immanence.

One rabbinic passage appears to have been affected by the conception of immanence, but it is not a passage on *Shekinah*. The Holy One blessed be He is called *Maḳom* (another appellative for God), says R. Huna in the name of R. 'Ammi, because He is the *maḳom* — locus — of His

[136] See above, p. 223.
[137] See ibid., p. 227.
[138] Numbers R. VII.10.
[139] See above, p. 227.
[140] See ibid., p. 228.

world; R. Jose b. R. Ḥalafta concludes from the words *maḳom 'itti* in Exod. 33:21 that the Holy One blessed be He is the locus of His world, whereas His world is not His locus; and R. Isaac concludes from the word "dwelling-place" in Ps. 90:1 that the Holy One blessed be He is the dwelling-place of His world whereas His world is not His dwelling-place.[141] Were these statements, which are not very clear, influenced by the philosophical conception of immanence? They may have been, but if so, the figure with which the passage closes shows that the idea of immanence was soon eliminated. The passage closes with a parable drawn by R. 'Abba bar Judan from Hab. 3:8, of a hero riding on a horse – "the horse is secondary to the rider, the rider is not subservient (lit., secondary) to the horse."[142] God controls, governs the world, says this parable, which makes at the same time the strongest of demarcations between God and the world. The parable affirms not a philosophic conception but *Malkut Shamayim*, and this is quite likely also true of the statements on *maḳom* and "dwelling-place."[143]

Normal mysticism is experience of God without visions or locutions or other sense phenomena. It is not the special prerogative of particular individuals qualified by an unusual aptitude of temperament; it calls for no more than the psychological equipment required in everyday living. What makes normal mysticism possible is the rabbinic value-complex. We demonstrated that the experience of God is associated with the integration of the value-concepts. But the process of the integration of the value-concepts is also the

[141] Bereshit R. LXVIII.9, ed. Theodor, pp. 777–8, and the parallels and notes there.

[142] Ibid. On *Maḳom*, see the references and remarks in Schechter, Some Aspects of Rabbinic Theology, p. 27, note 1.

[143] Another midrash, wrongly summarized in some such epigram as "God is the soul of the universe," has also been taken to express immanence. We dealt with it above, on p. 221 f.

process of the integration of the self.[144] The awareness or experience of God is thus a phenomenon associated with the integration of the self. What stimulates the awareness of the self also stimulates the experience of God. Just as dreams or visions are not the means of bringing about awareness of the self, so are dreams and visions not the means of bringing about awareness of God. By the same token, just as the concretizations of the value-concepts do make poignant the awareness of the self, so the concretizations of the value-concepts make poignant the awareness of God.

In the paragraph above, we have stressed the relation of normal mysticism to the integrative process of the value-complex as a whole. It is also true, however, that certain concepts in that complex represent ways of experiencing God; and that only when these concepts are concretized can there be poignant awareness, or poignant experience, of God. The effective cultivation of these concepts constitutes a remarkable achievement on the part of the Rabbis. Through the medium of Halakah, daily living, even the physical aspects of it, and even the literal day itself with its morning, afternoon and evening, everything yielded experience of God. All this was possible providing the concepts representing ways of experiencing God were always fresh and vivid. It was the function of Haggadah to keep them so. The value-concepts in general, not being objective like the cognitive concepts or definite like defined concepts, had need of Haggadah, the supplement to ordinary communication, in order to remain vivid. This was doubly true of the concepts of God's love, His justice, *Malkut Shamayim*, *Ḳedushah*. Indefinite and suggestive merely, as were the others, they had also to evoke the experience of God without the aid of sense phenomena. It was here that Haggadah played its most striking rôle — living words depicting in

[144] See above, p. 81.

story, suggesting in parable, drawing on legend, always embodying, in one form or another, the concepts of God-experience. Naturally, such Haggadah teems with "anthropomorphisms," but it has its own way, as we shall see, of neutralizing them, its own nonphilosophic correctives. The Haggadah, undeniably, lacks the poetry and power of the prophets' utterances, but then Haggadah is in no wise prophecy. It is not the outcome of *Dibbur*, and prophecy is. But in the sensitivity required by normal mysticism, in the ability to inculcate in others a similar receptivity, in the genius for "storing" this sensitivity, as it were, in folkwide regimen and habit, the Rabbis were certainly never surpassed and probably never equaled. Of course, the Rabbis possessed in the Pentateuch and the Prophets and the rest of the Bible a foundation for all their work. Let us not forget, however, that it was none other than the Rabbis who made the Bible an institution.

The attitude of the Rabbis toward *Gilluy Shekinah* has a parallel in their attitude toward another mystical phenomenon of the same order. We have discussed elsewhere instances in which the prophet Elijah is said to have appeared to individual Rabbis and instructed them in specific haggadic and even halakic matters.[145] "Such a source of haggadic or halakic interpretation did not lend to the latter any added prestige in the eyes of the Rabbis, however. On the contrary, the Rabbis gave the preference to the cooperative method of the study of the Torah pursued 'every day continually' — to the normal interpretations of texts and laws by means of inferential reasoning."[146] The general attitude here corresponds to the attitude toward *Gilluy Shekinah*. Normal mysticism is the rule; although a few persons seem to have experienced *Gilluy Shekinah*, they acquired no special authority as a result.

[145] See OT, pp. 238–9, and the references there.

[146] Ibid., p. 239, and the references.

Relevant in this connection is also the Rabbis' attitude toward the study of *Ma'aseh Bereshit* and *Ma'aseh Merkabah*. The former refers to mystic lore associated with the chapter on Creation, the latter to mystic lore associated with Ezekiel's vision of the Chariot. Such matters, if taught at all, were taught privately to a few chosen students, and it was forbidden altogether to speak on these things in public.[147] Scholem suggests that by late Talmudic times there may have already existed a school of *Yorede Merkabah*, but characterizes them as "a school of mystics who are not prepared to reveal their secret knowledge, their 'Gnosis' to the public."[148] Obviously, the true concern of the Rabbis as a whole was with what we have called normal mysticism, and not with these byways of religious thought.

Does the experience of the *Yorede Merkabah* have anything in common with the concept of *Gilluy Shekinah*? Scholem, who takes *Shekinah* to express the idea of immanence, says that this idea plays practically no part at all in *Merkabah* mysticism.[149] We have tried to demonstrate that the entire idea of the immanence of God is foreign to rabbinic thought, and have depicted *Gilluy Shekinah* as a concept in itself. It does not seem at all likely, however, that the Rabbis had *Merkabah* mysticism in mind when they spoke of *Gilluy Shekinah*. In *Merkabah* mysticism, the visionary had to pass through heavenly *Hekalot*, or palaces, in the seventh of which he saw the rise of the throne of divine glory[150]; in preparation for this vision, there were ascetic practices, and then special bodily actions and postures, and finally the ecstasy of the trance[151]; the visionary used secret names of God and those of the angels

[147] See Zunz, op. cit., p. 163, and the references there.

[148] G. Scholem, op. cit., p. 46. SEE NOTES, P. 371.

[149] G. Scholem, Major Trends in Jewish Mysticism, p. 54.

[150] See ibid., p. 44.

[151] See ibid., pp. 48–9.

and archons[152] which had certain theurgic powers;[153] the visionary sensed a metamorphosis wherein his flesh turns into fire.[154] None of these characteristics of *Merkabah* mysticism is even hinted at in the passages which speak of *Gilluy Shekinah.* The Rabbis even seem to be opposed, as Scholem points out, to the prayers or hymns of the *Merkabah* mystics.[155] In the light of *Merkabah* mysticism, the mysticism represented by the concept of *Gilluy Shekinah* thus appears remarkably restrained; and this, in turn, was no doubt due to the fact that generally what the Rabbis experienced was normal mysticism, mysticism devoid of sense phenomena.

IV. *BAT ḲOL*

The Rabbis say that upon the death of the last of the prophets, Haggai, Zechariah and Malachi, "the Holy Spirit departed from Israel," but, they add, resort was had to the *Bat Ḳol.*[1] Lieberman has described the means used when the *Bat Ḳol* was resorted to.[2] At times the Rabbis speak also of "a *Bat Ḳol* from the heaven."[3] A view expressed in Tosafot accounts, in these instances, for the word *Bat,* "daughter," by saying that it was a derivative sound — what was heard was not directly a voice from heaven but

[152] See ibid., pp. 50, 56. One of these secret names is 'Akatriel, and hence Scholem regards the passage in Berakot 7a, referred to above, p. 234, as having to do with *Merkabah* mysticism.

[153] See, for example, Hekalot Rabbati, Chap. 30, in Bet Ha-Midrash, ed. Jellinek (2nd ed.: Jerusalem: Bamberger and Wahrmann, 1938) III, p. 107.

[154] See Scholem, op. cit., p. 51.

[155] Ibid., p. 59.

[1] Sanhedrin 11a, Yoma 9b, Soṭah 48b; Tos. Soṭah XIII.2, ed. Zuck.-Lieb., p. 318. See the next note.

[2] S. Lieberman, Hellenism in Jewish Palestine (New York: Jewish Theological Seminary of America, 1950), pp. 194 ff. On the reading היו משתמשין בבת קול, see ibid., p. 194 f.

[3] For example, Sanhedrin 11a.

a derivative sound issuing from that voice, something like an echo.[4] It is this kind of *Bat Ḳol*, obviously, that Blau refers to in the following statement: "The characteristic attributes of the *Bat Ḳol* are the invisibility of the speaker and a certain remarkable quality in the sound, regardless of its strength or weakness."[5]

Neither kind of *Bat Ḳol* had any association whatever with experience of God. When the Rabbis assert that resort was had to a *Bat Ḳol*, they also declare at the same time that upon the death of the last prophets, the Holy Spirit had departed from Israel. In other words, the Rabbis say that the aspect of *Gilluy Shekinah* characteristic of prophecy could not be experienced in rabbinic times,[6] and hence they imply that the *Bat Ḳol* is an entirely different phenomenon. Moreover, the statement contains another implication. It is the prophet's experience of *Ruaḥ Ha-Ḳodesh* (the Holy Spirit) or *Gilluy Shekinah* that gives authority and authenticity to the prophet's words; by the same token, the *Bat Ḳol* apparently lacks authority. That the *Bat Ḳol* does indeed lack authority is evidenced by the fact that it is rejected, on a number of occasions, in Halakah.[7] This lack of authority is a sure indication that it was not associated with any experience of God.[8]

[4] Tosafot, ibid., s. v. בת קול.

[5] L. Blau, Jewish Encyclopedia, Vol. II, art. *Bat Ḳol*, p. 588a.

[6] See above, p. 250 f.

[7] It is rejected in Baba Meẓi'a 59b (and parallel), and in Tosefta Shebu'ot III.8. It is rejected by Bet Shammai and accepted by Bet Hillel in Yebamot 122a (and parallels), and it is accepted in an anonymous mishnah in Yeb. XVI.6 (and parallel); but these are instances where every effort is made to permit a woman to re-marry — comp. Maimonides, Mishneh Torah, Hilkot Gerushin XIII.29. A *Bat Ḳol* declares the law always to be according to Bet Hillel (Yer. Berakot 3b and parallels), but the Talmud has R. Joshua applying here too the principle, "A *Bat Ḳol* is not to be taken into account" (Berakot 52a and parallels); moreover, Tos. Yeb. I, end (and parallel) declares that the law must always be according to Bet Hillel but does not mention a *Bat Ḳol* at all.

[8] To be sure, the *Bat Ḳol* is sometimes identified with the Holy Spirit. Blau reckons with that — see op. cit., p. 589b. As we have indicated above, p. 251,

Only value-concepts that are not pure value-concepts are restricted or curbed. *Bat Ḳol* belongs to this small group, together with the concepts of *Nes* and *Gilluy Shekinah.* In fact, *Bat Ḳol* is less a pure value-concept than the other two, for it alone is also used as a cognitive concept, although most likely in a borrowed sense. It is used in one place in the sense of sound — "as oil has no *bat ḳol*" (that is, gives no sound),[9] and in another place in the related sense of echo — "if a man calls to his fellow, his voice has a *bat ḳol,* but the voice which issued from the mouth of the Holy One blessed be He had no *bat ḳol.*"[10] If *Bat Ḳol* was thus also employed occasionally as a cognitive concept, its function as a value-concept could not have been otherwise than weak. To this, its rejection in Halakah gives testimony.

V. THE RELATIONSHIP TO GOD

In normal mysticism, the ways of experiencing God are expressed in a number of value-concepts. Most of these concepts, like the other value-concepts, refer to actions or attitudes on the part of man, as in the case of prayer, for example, or repentance, or *Ḳiddush Ha-Shem.* Two, however — God's love and God's justice — stand for qualities of God. A third, *Ḳedushah,* likewise a quality of God, connotes also the imitation of God by man. Although there are thus various modes of experiencing God, all of them are

note 126, the term *Ruaḥ Ha-Ḳodesh* (the Holy Spirit) is used in several ways. It is thus used instead of an appellative for God sometimes when a statement is attributed to God — see the example in TE, p. 50 f.; hence it is sometimes also identified with *Bat Ḳol.* But *Ruaḥ Ha-Ḳodesh,* as associated with prophecy, has other connotations.

[9] Song of Songs R. I.21 (on Song of Songs 1:3).

[10] Exod. R. XXIX, end (comp. XXVIII, end). This and the previous reference are cited by Blau, op. cit., p. 588a.

crystallized in concepts. Yet one thing is not expressed by means of any concept. The consciousness of relationship to God is expressed, we shall see, in another manner.

Being value-concepts, the concepts of normal mysticism are in themselves not objective or definite, but merely connotative, indeterminate. They do not, in themselves, involve sense perception, unlike the cognitive concepts. They are made determinate when they are concretized in situations or events, in other words, when they act in concert with cognitive concepts.[1] Nor does the indeterminate character of the abstract value-concept render concretization difficult, but just the contrary. The indeterminacy of the value-concept gives the concept flexibility, and thereby renders it amenable to all sorts of concretizations, no matter how diverse. A concept like God's love, for example, can be associated with the possession of a morsel of bread no less than with the dawning of the day. Hence, if the normal experience of God is mediated by concepts these must be value-concepts. Only value-concepts can be vehicles for normal mysticism, for mystical experience associated with all the variegated phenomena of daily life. By the same token, normal mysticism, the experience of God expressed in value-concepts, is devoid of any sensory experience of God. Value-concepts do not involve sense phenomena in themselves.

The Rabbis also possess a concept representing mysticism of a different kind, the concept of *Gilluy Shekinah* (revelation of *Shekinah*). This concept does involve sensory phenomena and, like the few other value-concepts lacking the quality of indeterminacy, is restricted and curbed. The Rabbis, by and large, deny that *Gilluy Shekinah* is possible in their own day. Indeed, they apparently avoided the use of the conceptual term itself for it is found in only a single, very early passage. This attitude of the Rabbis

[1] See above, pp. 97, 107–111, 131.

toward *Gilluy Shekinah* confirms our conclusion that the God-experience of the Rabbis was, generally, normal mysticism. The Rabbis' negation of *Gilluy Shekinah* in their own times implies that their own experience of God was devoid of sensory phenomena. Since the general attitude of the Rabbis is actually formulated in Halakah, we took pains here to establish each halakic instance.

It must not be assumed, from our description, that the experience of God was sporadic, now stimulated by one occasion and now by another. Experience of God that is altogether sporadic is not possible. It would mean that a person, stimulated by an occasion, could summon up almost at will, as it were, an experience of God. At any rate, the rabbinic experience of God was not really occasional or sporadic. It was in the nature, rather, of a constant, felt relationship to God, a relationship more acutely apprehended when the concepts of normal mysticism were concretized. Even the rare experience of *Gilluy Shekinah*, an experience that was certainly sporadic, would have been impossible without this constant consciousness of a relationship to God.

Particularly in normal mysticism is there a steady consciousness of a relationship to God. We cannot actually depict that consciousness; at best, as we shall see, it can only be suggested. But we can indicate — in fact, we have already indicated — that it is something steady, as steady as the integrative process of the self. We have demonstrated above that the experience of God is associated with the integration of the value-concepts, and that the process of the integration of the value-concepts is also the process of the integration of the self.[2] If the integration of the self cannot be other than steady, constant, neither can the consciousness of God. Both are phenomena associated with the same process and they are thus allied phenomena. So

[2] See above, p. 81, pp. 214–15, and p. 257.

long as the steady integration of the self goes on, so long, and as steadily, is there a consciousness of a relationship to God.

In the endeavor of the Rabbis to express this sense of relationship to God, we have once more an approach characteristic of normal mysticism. They address God as "Thou" in *Berakot* and prayers. "Blessed art Thou, O Lord our God" is the opening phrase characteristic of the *Berakah*.[3] "We therefore hope in Thee, O Lord our God," reads a famous prayer, "that we may speedily behold the glory of Thy might, when Thou wilt remove the abominations from the earth, and the idols will be utterly cut off, when the world will be perfected under the Kingship of the Almighty, and all the children of flesh will call upon Thy Name, when Thou wilt turn to Thyself all the wicked of the earth."[4] "For Thou dost pardon and forgive," "for Thou art a mighty Redeemer" are typical phrases from the Daily *'Amidah*.[5] These are examples taken from the prayers almost at random, and many others might have been given instead. All of them illustrate that the relationship to God is felt as to someone who is near, who listens, whom you can face directly. It is a warm, personal relationship, so intimate and direct as to allow one to use such words as "thou," "thee," "thy."

But the consciousness of the relationship to God, nevertheless, cannot be equated to a sense of intimacy. In our discussions thus far, we seem to have assumed that it can; that impression, however, results from our having tried not to make more complicated an analysis that is already complicated enough. Now that we have presented various features of normal mysticism, we can discuss to better

[3] See ibid., p. 168, and note 1 there.

[4] The *'Alenu* prayer — Prayer Book, ed. Singer, pp. 76–7 (and his translation); see Baer, op. cit., pp. 131–2.

[5] Prayer Book, ed. Singer, pp. 46, 47; Baer, op. cit., pp. 90, 91, and his introduction to the Daily *'Amidah*, pp. 87–8.

advantage another important feature — the consciousness of the relationship to God.

That consciousness, as we have said, cannot be equated to a sense of intimacy. Such a feeling is present, of course, but so is another and an opposite feeling. In the *Berakah*, both rise to expression at the same time, as it were. Let us take, as an example, the first part of the *Berakah* said at a rite. A coherent translation of that part, and one that we have used in our discussions, would be: "Blessed art Thou, O Lord our God, King of the world, who hast sanctified us by Thy *Mizwot*."[6] This is a coherent but not an exact translation, for an exact or correct translation is impossible. There is a shift from the second to the third person here so that the reference is to "(Him) He (that) sanctified us by His *Mizwot*." Further, the next word is *we-ziwwanu*, "and He commanded us." "Thou" and "He," both, refer to God, and are thus apparently successive attempts to express, in the same statement, a consciousness of the relationship to God. This is true of other types of *Berakot* also, not only of the *Birkat Ha-Mizwot*. One of the *Berakot* over foods, for example, ends with "everything exists through His word"[7]; it begins, of course, with "Blessed art Thou." The *Berakot* in the daily prayers afford a number of striking examples. Before the *'Amidah* in the morning service, for instance, there is the *Berakah*, "Blessed art Thou, O Lord (who) (He) has redeemed Israel"[8]; and, to give another example, there is the *Berakah* at the beginning of the evening service — "Blessed art Thou, O Lord our God, King of the world, who at His word brings on the evening twilight."[9]

[6] אשר קדשנו במצותיו — see above, p. 170.

[7] שהכל נהיה בדברו — see Baer, op. cit., p. 567. This *Berakah* is said before the eating of cheese, fish, meat, etc., and all liquids except wine.

[8] גאל ישראל — Singer's Prayer Book, p. 44; see Baer, op. cit., p. 86, and the notes there.

[9] אשר בדברו מעריב ערבים — Singer, p. 96; Baer, p. 164.

A characteristic of many *Berakot,* this shift from the second to the third person is also to be found, occasionally, in the body of the prayers. "His children beheld His might," reads a section of the evening service, "they praised and gave thanks unto His Name and willingly accepted His Kingship: Moses and the children of Israel sang a song unto Thee with great joy, saying, all of them, 'Who is like unto Thee, O Lord' (Exod. 15:11)."[10] Similarly, a section of the morning service reads, "His words are living and enduring, faithful and precious, forever and to all eternity, as for our fathers so also for us, for our children and future generations, and for all generations of the seed of Israel Thy servants."[11] Nor are these the only examples.

What we have just observed can all too easily be dismissed as a stylistic peculiarity; but then so can all matters often enough expressed in a repetitive way. On the other hand, it seems to us that the explanations given by the medieval authorities are not sound either. According to Naḥmanides, the third person is used as a mark of respect after the mention of God's Kingship in a *Berakah,* whether in the *Birkat Ha-Miẓwot* or in any other *Berakah* apparently, whereas the second person is used when the idea of God's Kingship is not mentioned; in the first part of the *'Alenu* prayer, he adds, the reference to God is in the third person for the same reason — in that section we have the phrase, "before the King of the kings of kings."[12] A glance at our examples, however, will indicate that Naḥmanides' rule does not always apply. There are some *Berakot* which close with a reference to God in the third person, but which do

[10] Singer, p. 99; Baer, p. 166.

[11] Singer, p. 42, and P. Birnbaum, Daily Prayer Book (New York, 1949), pp. 79–80; Baer, p. 84. SEE NOTES, P. 371.

[12] Naḥmanides, Commentary on the Pentateuch, Exod. 15:26, toward the end. The background of his explanation here is mystical, but it is a mysticism developed in medieval times.

not mention God's Kingship.[13] Other authorities say that when we use the second person we refer to the character of God as revealed through His activity or deeds, and that when we use the third person the reference is to His Godhood or essence, hidden and beyond knowledge.[14] A view with a sounder basis in rabbinic thought is the one given in the Maḥzor Vitry. Here the use of "Thou" in the *Berakah* is linked with a rabbinic rule, the rule that a man in prayer "ought to regard himself as though *Shekinah* were in front of him"[15]; and it is this rule or practice, we may remember, which apparently informs Rab's dictum that a *Berakah* ought always to begin with, "Blessed art Thou, O Lord."[16] But the explanation in Maḥzor Vitry, too, goes on to associate the sudden change to the third person with a specific idea.[17] The attempt to make an idea specific when the Rabbis have not done so often results, as we have learned, in the misinterpretation of a rabbinic idea. This is again illustrated by the explanations we have mentioned here.

The Rabbis themselves offer no explanation for the sudden change from "Thou" to "He." Why? Because their apprehension of God is not rationalistic or quasi-philosophical but mystical. When the medieval authorities discuss the *Berakah*, they take "Thou" and "He" to be two distinct and different forms of address, and hence must account for them by associating each of them with a different idea. But the authorities disregard an essential fact, namely, the fact that a relative pronoun, *'asher*, connects the reference to God in the second person with the reference to God in the third person. We have to do with a unit, that is, with

[13] See above, p. 56, note 11, and p. 267, note 8.

[14] See the opinions cited in Frumkin, Seder R. Amram, I, p. 24a, and in Baer, op. cit., p. 36.

[15] Maḥzor Vitry, par. 88, ed. Hurwitz, p. 56.

[16] See above, p. 208.

[17] Maḥzor Vitry, l. c. The forced explanation involves a gratuitous harmonization of Ps. 16:2 with Ezek. 3:12.

a consciousness of relationship expressed as a unitary attitude. When we regard the two forms of address as distinct from one another — and this we must do on all other occasions — we break up that unity. That is why the consciousness of relationship expressed here can only be characterized as a mystical consciousness. It is a consciousness of relationship like none other, expressible to a point, but in a manner in which no other relationship is expressible. The *Berakah* formula thus enables the Rabbis and the people as a whole to express their consciousness of relationship to God, and also to evoke, to make more acute, that consciousness. It was nothing short of religious genius first to have achieved the *Berakah* formula, and then to have made it the basic element of the prayers. Two forms of address representing two different relationships — normal relationships — are so conjoined as to express a unitary consciousness of mystical relationship.

The mystical consciousness of relationship to God is expressed, again, in terms of *various* human relationships. Besides the oft-used phrase "Father in heaven,"[18] other terms of relationship are used as well. It is none other than God who is referred to as "thy Friend" in Prov. 27:10, according to the Rabbis.[19] They interpret ibid., 17:17 as referring to God who is the "Brother" helping Israel in their adversity.[20] In depicting the giving of the Torah on Mt. Sinai, they speak of God as the "Bridegroom" and of Israel as the bride.[21] These terms of relationship are, of course, metaphorical expressions of God's love as the Rabbis sensed it. But do the Rabbis intend merely to give

[18] See, for example, above, pp. 183, 205.

[19] Exod. R. XXVII.1. "'Thy friend' (Prov. 27:10) — that is the Holy One blessed be He."

[20] Mekilta, I, p. 221.

[21] See Ginzberg, Legends of the Jews, III, p. 92 and VI, p. 36, note 200.

A play on the word *wayegaresh* (Gen. 3:24) enables the Rabbis to say that God gave Adam "a divorce as (is done) with a woman" — see TE, p. 110.

an impression of God's love, and no more? Are the Rabbis not striving to express a consciousness of a relationship in their very attempt to tell of God's love? The terms they use are not only metaphorical expressions of God's love but, at the same time, metaphorical expressions of a sense of relationship. That consciousness of relationship can be expressed only metaphorically because it is a mystical consciousness. To express this mystical consciousness of relationship to God, the Rabbis again employ terms representing normal relationship, now giving such terms a metaphorical character.

Finally, the mystical consciousness of relationship to God is expressed also in the use of the appellatives for God. The appellatives or epithets are names, and hence they signify a consciousness of relationship.[22] These names or appellatives, we may remember, are used far more frequently than the generic terms for God – indeed, the generic terms are limited to only a few contexts, and such contexts can be readily accounted for.[23] Does not this fact testify as to the character of the rabbinic "idea" of God? If the Rabbis so often resort to names for God rather than to a generic term, are they not expressing thereby a consciousness of relationship rather than a generic idea? Furthermore, the Rabbis' use of the generic terms is perfectly consistent with their use of the appellatives. The generic terms themselves are sometimes used as proper nouns, as names.[24] They are, in fact, not really classificatory terms at all, being neither defined, nor cognitive, nor valuational terms; they point, instead, to a private experience, that is to say, to a mystical experience of God.[25] If the appellatives express a sense of mystical relationship to God, the generic terms, therefore, do practically the same thing, whatever else they may do.

[22] See above, p. 204 f.

[23] See ibid., p. 206 f.

[24] See ibid., p. 199 f.

[25] See ibid., pp. 198–202.

The consciousness of relationship to God, which is mystical and therefore incommunicable by itself, thus becomes something that can to a degree be expressed, or, more correctly, suggested. It rises to expression, particularly, when concepts such as God's love, His justice, *Ḳedushah* and the like are concretized in *Berakot* and prayers. The rabbinic *Berakot* and prayers, hence, play a tremendous rôle in the spiritual life. They enable the ordinary man as well as the spiritual leader to express the mystical consciousness of relationship to God, but they also do more than that. They may even be said to evoke that consciousness. The recitation of a prayer or, on the appropriate occasion, of a *Berakah*, has the effect of making that consciousness more acute, and in that sense evokes it.[26]

Normal mysticism, then, is characterized by three main features. It is experience of God in various modes, all of them crystallized in value-concepts; and, since value-concepts do not involve sense phenomena in themselves, it is therefore experience of God devoid of any sensory perception of God. Second, since value-concepts are concretized in everyday situations, it is experience of God that makes significant everyday phenomena and situations, not only unusual occasions. Lastly, the awareness of God in normal mysticism is a mystical consciousness of relationship to God; a consciousness that rises to a degree of expression in the *Berakot* and the prayers; a steady consciousness that becomes acute and poignant in these and in the other concretizations of the value-concepts of normal mysticism.

These features of normal mysticism made it possible for the spiritual leader and the common man to have the same *kind* of experience of God, provided that the common man, too, received the necessary training. Through the agencies of Halakah and Haggadah, the Rabbis supplied that training.

[26] See the discussion above, p. 209 f.

CHAPTER VII

This Side of Philosophy

The Rabbis were not philosophers. This is something taken for granted in modern studies of rabbinic thought. Yet there seems to be the feeling also that, in several specific matters, the Rabbis are nevertheless influenced by considerations akin to philosophic principles. When the Rabbis appear to ask certain questions, those questions are taken to be strictures on anthropomorphisms; when they express certain attitudes, those attitudes are taken to be doctrines of a creed. We expect to show, however, that such questions and attitudes are entirely in accord with the complex of rabbinic thought as a whole. They arise as the result of normal mysticism, and not from any speculative tendency or from any attempt to formulate a creed.

I. THE QUESTION OF ANTHROPOMORPHISM

In the questions just referred to, the Rabbis apparently object to biblical statements about God that appear to limit Him. It will suffice to give the following examples from the Mekilta. " 'And the Lord went before them by day' (Exod. 13:21) — is it possible to say so? Has it not been said: 'Do not I fill heaven and earth, saith the Lord' (Jer. 23:24)? And it is written: 'And one called unto another, and said: Holy, holy, holy, is the Lord of hosts; the whole earth is full of His glory' (Is. 6:3). And it also says: 'And, behold, the glory of the God of Israel came from the way of the east; and His voice was like the sound of many waters; and the earth did shine with His glory' (Ezek. 43.2). How then can Scripture say 'And the Lord went before them by day'?"[1] A parallel instance is to be found in the comment on Exod. 15:3. Here the same question is raised again: " 'The Lord is a man of war' (Exod. 15:3) — is it possible to say so?" Quite as in the previous passage, the three verses from the Prophets are then set off against the limiting verse.[2] In another passage, the question is raised in a different form. " 'And He rested on the seventh day' (Exod. 20:11) — and is He subject to such a thing as (lit., is there before Him) weariness? Has it not been said: 'The Creator of the ends of the earth fainteth not, neither is weary' (Is. 40:28)? And it says: 'He giveth power to the faint' (ibid., v. 29). And it also says: 'By the word of the Lord were the heavens made, and all the host of them by the breath of His mouth' (Ps. 33:6)."[3]

In all the passages the questions raised certainly imply an apprehension of some kind on the part of the Rabbis. The questions are more pointed than the general thought of the verses which support them; they voice an apprehension against depicting God as lighting the way at the head of Israel, as being "a man of war," as working and resting from work. But has this apprehension anything to do with the philosophers' objection to anthropomorphism?

The answers the Rabbis give indicate no concern with the problem of anthropomorphism. Is it possible to say that "the Lord went before them by day?" Rabbi (Judah the Prince) replies by telling of how Antoninus would him-

[1] Mekilta, I, p. 185 — איפשר לומר כן.

[2] Ibid., II, p. 34. On the verses, see also Friedmann's edition a. l., and the note there.

[3] Ibid., II, p. 255.

self take the torch and light the way for his sons in the darkness, and that he would say to the notables who offered to perform that service: "It is not that I have no one to take the torch and light the way for my sons. But it is thus that I make known to you how beloved my sons are to me, so that you should treat them with respect." And Rabbi adds, "In like manner, the Holy One blessed be He made known to the nations of the world how beloved Israel is to Him: He Himself went before them, so that they (the nations) should treat them with respect."[4] Obviously, no attention is paid here to the problem of anthropomorphism. But why was there any apprehension in the first place if the limiting verse is only affirmed?

The answer to the question in the second passage, though more circumspect, is similar. "How then can Scripture say, 'The Lord is a man of war'? Because of My love for you and because of your holiness I sanctify My Name in you (*ba-kem*), as it says, 'For I am God, and not man, the Holy One in the midst of thee' (Hosea 11:9) – I sanctify My Name in you."[5] If we take Schechter's view of this statement, the limiting verse is definitely not explained away. "The words, 'The Lord is a man of war' are contrasted," says Schechter, "with 'For I am God, and not man,' and explained to mean that it is only for the love of Israel that God appears in such a capacity."[6] Thus here, too, the Rabbis express apprehension and yet affirm, though with circumspection, the limiting verse.

To the question in the third passage, two answers are given, although our source contains only one. Our source declares that God "caused it to be written about Him that

[4] Ibid., I, pp. 185–6.

[5] Ibid., II, p. 35; Horovitz-Rabin, p. 131. We have taken the reading in the latter; the variations are slight.

[6] S. Schechter, Some Aspects of Rabbinic Theology, p. 36. For a different view, see Weiss, in his edition of the Mekilta, p. 45b, note 60.

He created His world in six days and rested on the seventh"; and it draws the inference that "if He who is not subject to weariness caused it to be written about Him that He created His world in six days and rested on the seventh, all the more should man, of whom it is said, 'But man is born unto trouble' (Job 5:7) (rest on the seventh)."[7] Our source then, in this case, does explain away the limiting verse. A different source, however, also raising the question of how it is possible to speak of God as needing rest, gives another answer first, and this answer is found in a number of parallels as well. "Why, then, does it say, 'And He rested on the seventh day?' In order to exact penalty from the wicked who are destroying the world that was created with trouble and labor."[8] As is true of our passages above, in this source too and in the parallels, the Rabbis express an apprehension and nevertheless proceed to affirm the limiting verse.

Statements like "the Lord went before them by day," to repeat, are preceded by questions indicating an apprehension on the part of the Rabbis, but such statements are nevertheless affirmed. Do those questions or apprehensions qualify the affirmations? If so, the Rabbis have a more direct way of qualifying some of their statements about God. Sometimes they preface an interpretation by saying, "Were it not for the scriptural verse, it would be impossible to say this." We shall have occasion later on to give examples of midrashim in which this expression occurs.[9]

At the same time, rabbinic literature abounds in similar statements about God that are not qualified in any way whatsoever. Thus, in a summary of midrashim about God

[7] Mekilta, II, pp. 255–6; Horovitz-Rabin, p. 230.

[8] Mekilta de R. Simon, p. 109. The parallels are: Bereshit R. X.9, ed. Theodor, pp. 85–6; Tanḥuma, ed. Buber, I, p. 4a; Pesiḳta Rabbati, 3rd pisḳa on *'Aseret Ha-Dibberot,* 5.

[9] Below, p. 309.

quoted in a previous chapter, practically all of those striking rabbinic anthropomorphisms are unqualified.[10] The instances there are concretizations of the concepts of God's love and His justice. None of them, however, is more striking in its unqualified anthropomorphism than a statement on the holiness of God, a passage in which an authority finds warrant in scriptural verses for saying that His speech, His walk, His way, His sitting, the baring of His arm, are all with *Ḳedushah*, holiness.[11] From another version of the statement, it is evident that the intention here was to emphasize the ideal of holiness in man's everyday conduct, the connotation of *Ḳedushah* being the imitation of God by man. That version begins by saying, "'Be ye holy, for I am holy' (Lev. 19:2) — the Holy One blessed be He said to Israel: Be ye holy just as I am holy in every thing."[12] Nevertheless, the fact remains that the anthropomorphisms involved are not only bold but unqualified. How is it that there are so many statements in which the anthropomorphisms remain unqualified while similar anthropomorphisms in other statements are qualified?

Marmorstein attempts to solve all these problems with the hypothesis that there were two schools among the Rabbis — allegorists and literalists.[13] By qualifying an anthropomorphism, the allegorists wish to convey the idea, according to Marmorstein, that the anthropomorphism is to be taken allegorically[14]; and the questions raised by the Rabbis represent a means on the part of the allegorists, according to him, of overcoming biblical anthropomorphisms.[15] On the other hand, the literalists, he says, not

[10] See above, p. 141 f.

[11] Yer. Berakot IX.1, 13a; Midrash Tehillim, ed. Buber, p. 14a.

[12] Tanḥuma, ed. Buber, III, p. 37a, and the notes there. On the connotation of *Ḳedushah*, see above, p. 169 f.

[13] A. Marmorstein, The Old Rabbinic Doctrine of God, II, Essays in Anthropomorphism (London: Oxford University Press, 1937), pp. 29 ff.

[14] Ibid., pp. 107 ff., p. 123 f.

[15] Ibid., pp. 29 ff.

only take the biblical anthropomorphisms literally but enlarge upon them and add to them.[16] He also regards a number of anthropomorphic passages as an endeavor to reply to the polemics directed against Israel in the rabbinic period.[17]

But if there are two schools, allegorists and literalists, what *do* the allegorists intend to convey by means of their allegories? Ought there not be somewhere a statement of what the allegories point to? When the Rabbis themselves interpret the Song of Songs as an allegory, they tell us the meanings of the allegory.[18] And so do Maimonides and other philosophers when they declare that certain biblical passages are to be taken as allegories.[19] Nor is it possible to say that the questions raised by the Rabbis are a means of overcoming biblical anthropomorphisms; those anthropomorphisms, as we saw, are actually affirmed. The whole hypothesis, indeed, falls to the ground as soon as we examine its central thesis — the division into two schools. In the attempt to maintain this division, Marmorstein is forced, in a number of instances, to change around the proponents of opinions, often solely on the basis of his thesis.[20]

A less elaborate explanation imputes to the Rabbis the ideas of the immanence of God and His transcendence. According to this explanation, when the Rabbis leave the anthropomorphisms unqualified, they stress God's immanence and when they qualify them they stress His transcendence. But we saw above that the very idea of immanence

[16] Ibid., p. 131 f.

[17] Ibid., p. 71 f., p. 76 f.

[18] Since Haggadah is characterized by multiple interpretations of biblical verses (see above, p. 120), there is no consistency in the rabbinic interpretation of the Song of Songs either. But, in each case, the interpretation here too indicates what the particular passage, taken as an allegory, points to. See I. Heinemann, Darke Ha-Agadah. p. 137 f.

[19] See, for example, Philo's approach as depicted by Heinemann, op. cit., p. 157 f. On Maimonides, see above, p. 102 f.

[20] See Marmorstein, op. cit., pp. 42 ff.

is foreign to rabbinic thought.[21] Moore says the same thing about the idea of transcendence, declaring that the "Palestinian masters" were innocent "of an 'abstract' or 'transcendent' — or any other sort of a philosophical — idea of God."[22] He rightly characterizes the imputation to the Rabbis of the idea of transcendence as an abuse of philosophical terminology.[23]

Another explanation in vogue among modern scholars, and one often resorted to, involves undeclared assumptions. The stereotype phrases or terms employed in connection with some anthropomorphisms, say a number of scholars, weaken or mitigate those anthropomorphisms. Bacher, for one, states that the term כביכול is always employed where there is "a strong expression" concerning God, as a way of apology for that bold expression.[24] Schechter, for another, speaks of "the marked tendency, both in the Targumim and in the Agadah, to explain away or to mitigate certain expressions in the Bible investing the deity with corporeal qualities."[25] Now these authorities also point out time and again that the Rabbis were not philosophers,[26] and hence would be the last to impute to the Rabbis philosophic ideas. But what of the aversion to "investing the deity with corporeal qualities?" If this is not the same as the philosophers' objection to anthropomorphism, it is certainly very much akin to it. It assumes a principle on the part of the Rabbis, namely, that corporeal qualities must not be attributed to God *because* they are corporeal. Being only a "marked tendency," this is not conceived as a thoroughgoing principle, to be sure, but its kinship with philosophical thought nevertheless cannot be gainsaid. Implied by the principle

[21] See above, p. 255 f.

[22] G. F. Moore, op. cit., I, p. 421.

[23] Ibid., p. 423.

[24] W. Bacher, ערכי מדרש (Heb. trans.) I, p. 50 and II, p. 200.

[25] S. Schechter, op. cit., p. 35.

[26] See, for example, Schechter, ibid., pp. 11 ff. and p. 39.

is some idea about God which negates anthropomorphism or corporeal qualities, whereas the philosophers go further and supply such an idea. We have only to speak of "mitigating" anthropomorphisms to be swept, without being aware of it, into the stream of philosophic thought.

The fact is that the Rabbis and the philosophers simply do not inhabit the same universe of discourse. Whatever the Rabbis do, they do not really qualify or mitigate either biblical anthropomorphisms or their own. The very problem of anthropomorphism did not exist for them. Value-concepts like God's love and His justice are basically anthropomorphic or anthropopathic even as abstract concepts; but their character as value-concepts render them necessary elements in the organismic complex.[27] On the other hand, it is wrong to say that the Rabbis affirmed the corporeality of God as a principle. Such a principle would hardly be compatible with what we recognized to be the normal religious experience of the Rabbis, since that form of mystical experience, normal mysticism, is devoid of sensory experience of God; more, it would certainly not be compatible with the restriction of the concept of *Gilluy Shekinah,* the concept standing for sensory experience of God, and that restriction, as we saw in the last chapter, is a genuine characteristic of rabbinic thought. To ascribe to the Rabbis any sort of stand on anthropomorphism is to do violence, therefore, to rabbinic thought. Indeed, this entire discussion only shows that when we employ the terms of classical philosophy even in an attempt to clarify rabbinic ideas, we are no longer within the rabbinic universe of discourse. Rabbinic statements about God arise as a result of interests entirely different from those of philosophic thought, represent human experiences that have nothing to do with speculative ideas. In other words, unless we emancipate ourselves from philosophic influences,

[27] See above, p. 28.

we shall struggle in vain to comprehend what the Rabbis said or felt about God. Or, to put it more fairly: Only on the occasions when we are free from philosophic influences can we sense the authentic rabbinic experience of God.

Postrabbinic Jewish thought confirms our contention, it seems to us. The vantage point of the Rabbis was lost everytime a stand was taken on anthropomorphism. This happened not only when a thinker avowedly undertook to harmonize philosophy with Rabbinic Judaism, as was the case with Saadia, Maimonides and so many others. It happened also when those who took a stand on anthropomorphism regarded themselves as opponents of philosophy, as in the case of Yehudah Ha-Levi, and also, we must say, when some medieval authorities made a principle of corporeality.

Yehudah Ha-Levi is opposed to the method, the theories, and the conclusions of the philosophers. Their method, which is that of rational demonstration, or rational proof, leads only to wrong and destructive ideas,[28] he declares, and accordingly their theories are either open to grave doubts, as with their notion of the four elements, or else wholly fallacious, as with their notion of the soul.[29] The conclusions of the philosophers, namely, that God does not know man, does not listen to his prayers, or know his movements and thoughts,[30] are utterly repugnant to Ha-Levi.[31] Central in Ha-Levi's thought, on the contrary, is the relationship to God, a relationship he depicts in his famous theories on Israel, prayer, *Mizwot*.[32] And yet, all this notwithstanding, he remains a medieval philosopher, and takes a stand on anthropomorphism, the philosophers' stand. The Second Commandment spells for him a prohibition

[28] Kuzari IV, 3.

[29] Ibid., V, 14.

[30] Ibid., I, 1.

[31] Ibid., IV, 3.

[32] See the sensitive treatment of I. Heinemann, טעמי המצוות בספרות ישראל, I (Jerusalem: Obadiah, 1949), pp. 48–54.

against attributing to God any corporeal or anthropomorphic qualities.[33] He interprets away such an attribute as mercy or compassion when applied to God and, like other medieval philosophers, he too advances the theory of negative attributes.[34] He has a conception of God, therefore, quite like that of the medieval Jewish philosophers who attempt to harmonize philosophy with Judaism.[35]

In depicting the relationship to God, Ha-Levi also diverges from rabbinic thought in an important respect. He defines the Holy Spirit "as a 'subtle spiritual substance' from which by the will of God are formed those 'spiritual forms' which 'appear to the prophets' during their prophetic experience."[36] The "spiritual forms" arise from the "subtle spiritual substance" through the action of "Divine Light," a term not found in either biblical or rabbinic literature.[37] Both the idea of a "subtle spiritual substance" and the idea of "Divine Light," Wolfson points out, correspond to ideas of Plotinus.[38] Not only are these ideas not biblical and not rabbinic, but the entire conception comes perilously close, it seems to us, to positing intermediaries between God and man.[39]

A number of medieval talmudic authorities, in obvious reaction to the philosophic movement, made a principle of corporeality, although some only went so far as to

[33] Kuzari, I, 89.

[34] Ibid., II, 2. See D. Kaufmann, Geschichte der Attributenlehre (Gotha, 1877), p. 152 f., and compare I. Husik, A History of Mediaeval Jewish Philosophy (New York: Macmillan, 1918), pp. 161–2.

[35] See the references in the preceding note.

[36] H. A. Wolfson, Hallevi and Maimonides on Prophecy, Jewish Quarterly Review, Vol. XXXIII, no. 1 (July, 1942), p. 50.

[37] Ibid.

[38] Ibid., p. 52.

[39] Despite his recognition of the kinship of these ideas with a Neoplatonic view, Wolfson apparently feels that they are also rooted in rabbinic thought: "In the vague utterances about the 'Holy Spirit' and the 'Shekinah' in talmudic literature there is indeed sometimes the undoubted implication that they are real beings created by God" — ibid., p. 57.

ascribe form to God, and others were even more cautious.[40] Ezekiel Kaufmann, who cites these views in his *Toledot Ha-'Emunah Ha-Yisre'elit,* cites them as evidence that the problem of anthropomorphism was foreign to indigenous Judaism.[41] Kaufmann means by this, however, that biblical and Rabbinic Judaism had not achieved an abstract conception of God, and that, while Rabbinic Judaism refined the conception of God, the basic anthropomorphisms are to be found there as well.[42] But it is no accident that Kaufmann has to resort to the talmudic authorities of the Middle Ages in order to present a stand on anthropomorphism, a stand that arises in opposition to, and that is influenced by, philosophical theory. The problem of anthropomorphism is indeed foreign to indigenous Judaism, but foreign in a far more radical manner than Kaufmann conceives it to be. Such problems are not in any sense within the rabbinic universe of discourse, not even by implication, and are not to be injected there even for the purpose of analysis.

There is another matter to be settled before we can attempt to describe the Rabbis' own attitude to "anthropomorphism." It has been widely assumed that medieval Jewish philosophy represents a development in Judaism, and especially in respect to the idea of God. We shall try to indicate, first, that the idea of God in medieval Jewish philosophy does not represent a development of rabbinic thought. Second, we shall try to describe briefly an authentic line of development in Judaism, that which leads from biblical to rabbinic thought, and also to suggest

[40] See Ezekiel Kaufmann, Toledot Ha-'Emunah Ha-Yisre'elit, Vol. I, Book II (Tel-Aviv: Dvir, 1938), pp. 240–1, and the notes there. The last phrase in the famous remark by R. Abraham ben David of Posquières, omitted in Kaufmann's quotation, indicates that he himself did not subscribe to the principle of corporeality; see his criticism in Maimonides, Mishneh Torah, Hilkot Teshubah, III.7; comp. Albo, 'Iḳḳarim, ed. Husik, Vol. I (Philadelphia: Jewish Publication Society of America, 1929), p. 53.

[41] Ezekiel Kaufmann, ibid.

[42] Ibid., pp. 226–238.

how that authentic development affected the experience of God.

Kaufmann is among those who hold that the philosophical idea of God advanced by the Jewish thinkers of the Middle Ages represents a development in the Jewish idea of God. He sees implications of the abstract, philosophical idea of God in Jewish tradition itself. Anthropomorphic figures, he argues, were only necessary symbols incident to prophecy and vision, symbols of the God who acts, commands, and judges; they could not be other than merely symbols, since in Judaism there is no mythology, no history of God, no subjection of God to matter or to an order of things.[43] Other things, too, imply the transcendence of God over the world – the implicit idea, for instance, that God alone is primary, since the Bible contains no notion of primal or original matter.[44] There was no awareness in Jewish tradition, however, that anthropomorphism limits God to space, to the laws of space.[45] When such an awareness did arise through the influence of Greek thought, Judaism accepted the idea that God was abstract as an idea wholly in accord with its own concept of God, and thus added a necessary element to its conception that God was free and supreme.[46]

In the course of this argument, Kaufmann touches on a subject which he enlarges upon subsequently in a detailed study. He asserts that all pagan religions, that is, all religions except Judaism and its daughter faiths, Christianity and Islam, possess a ground in common.[47] What is that common ground which is the stamp of paganism? The belief, either expressed or implicit, in a primordial or pre-existent order of things to which the gods, too, are subject.[48]

[43] Ibid., p. 250.
[44] Ibid., pp. 250–1.
[45] Ibid., p. 252.
[46] Ibid., pp. 252–3.
[47] Ibid., pp. 297–8.
[48] Ibid.

This *motif*, Kaufmann shows, is to be found in the idea that the gods are subject to Fate, in the ascribing of reproduction to gods, in the idea that the world was created from primordial matter, and in other aspects of pagan mythology[49]; and he also demonstrates that it is a basic *motif* in the pagan notions of magic, of divination, and of worship.[50] Now this essential characteristic of paganism, Kaufmann points out, is characteristic of Greek philosophy as well. Greek philosophic thought achieved the concept of monotheism, and further, the concept of an abstract monotheism, but it remained pagan thought nonetheless – for, according to it, God remains subject to law, to nature, to "Fate".[51] Neither in pantheism, where the world is conceived as a "garment" of God, nor in Platonism where it is conceived as a reflection of God, nor in Neoplatonism where it is conceived as an emanation of God, nor in Aristotelianism where it is conceived as the result of a process beginning with the First Cause, is God regarded as free from the world and its laws.[52] When Jewish thought in the Middle Ages took over the idea of an abstract God, adds Kaufmann, that idea was entirely purged of its pagan character.[53]

Kaufmann himself goes on to say that the rose thus plucked from pagan thought "is not without its thorns." Tension remains, he says. The anthropomorphic God of prophecy and Haggadah is more suited to the practical aspirations of Judaism; the entire philosophic approach creates a new and most complex problem: wherein has it helped and made for the completion of the religious idea, and wherein has it been the source of "heresy" and denial (of God)?[54]

The truth is, and hence these grave doubts of Kaufmann's,

[49] Ibid., pp. 299 ff.

[50] Ibid., pp. 350–416.

[51] Ibid., p. 248.

[52] Ibid., pp. 248, 250.

[53] Ibid., p. 253.

[54] Ibid.

that the new idea was not really absorbed into Judaism. Kaufmann's analysis but helps us to realize afresh that rabbinic thought is not in the same world of discourse as philosophic thought. Philosophic thought retains the essential characteristic of paganism, and its conclusions about God are therefore bound to be different from the concepts of rabbinic thought. In proof, we need only recall Yehudah Ha-Levi. Influenced by philosophic thought despite his rejection of it, he actually attempts to explain away, as we saw, the concept of God's mercy.[55]

To our mind, Kaufmann commits an error when he assumes that what informs Jewish tradition is an *idea* of God, a *concept* of God. He declares that the religion of Israel did not result from this or that historical event, or from a covenant, or from political and military successes, or from the shocks of defeat and destruction, and in proving these and many cognate matters he makes a contribution of immense importance.[56] He takes the source of the religion, however, to be an idea, "a new religio-metaphysical idea,"

[55] The view that medieval Jewish philosophy does not represent a development of Jewish tradition was advanced also by S. D. Luzzatto. See his מחקרי היהדות (וורשה, תרע"ג) I, pp. 159–185, II, pp. 243 ff., and also Shalom Spiegel, Hebrew Reborn (New York: Macmillan, 1930), pp. 85–89 and the references there on pp. 446–7. Solomon Goldman, in a penetrating study on Maimonides (The Jew and the Universe) (New York: Harper and Bros., 1936), maintains that "the differences between Maimonides and historic Judaism are only on the surface" (p. 128), and that "Aristotle may have provided Maimonides with a method, but certainly not with the ideology" (p. 131).

Although not bearing on our own thesis, which has a different orientation, it is a fact that the classic philosophic stand on anthropomorphism is being challenged today on the grounds of science itself: "Every scientific explanation of a natural phenomenon is a hypothesis that there is something in nature to which the human reason is analogous; and that it really is so all the successes of science in its application to human convenience are witnesses. They proclaim that truth over the length and breadth of the modern world. In the light of the successes of science to my mind there is a degree of baseness in denying our birthright as children of God and in shamefacedly slinking away from anthropomorphic conceptions of the universe" — C. S. S. Peirce, op. cit., Vol. I, pp. 158–159.

[56] See the analysis, for example, in op. cit., Vol I, Book I.

out of which in the course of generations an entire world-outlook was born.[57] This idea, he says, the idea of monotheism, was a concept of God[58] arrived at not by speculation about the world but through intuition.[59] We feel that Kaufmann's great contribution in no wise depends on his theory that at the beginning there was an idea. That theory only leads him to regard as a true development of Jewish thought the postrabbinic attempt to incorporate into Judaism a philosophic idea.

What characterizes Judaism is the *experience* of God rather than a God-concept, we saw in the last chapter. The generic terms for God do not really function as conceptual terms. There are, it is true, a number of concepts which have to do with the experience of God, but they are of a nature altogether different from that of philosophic concepts. Being value-concepts, they are, unlike the philosophic concepts, always undefined; and that is why they cannot be aligned with a philosophic concept. These things, to be sure, we have demonstrated only with respect to rabbinic thought, since we have not undertaken an analysis of the Bible. But perhaps, for our purposes, so detailed a study is not absolutely necessary at this point. We expect to show, instead, that a close bond unites rabbinic thought with the Bible, that rabbinic thought is a development out of the Bible. That bond and that development will also be discernible, we believe, in regard to the experience of God — and if so, we shall have enough warrant for assuming that the Bible, too, reflects experience of God rather than a concept of God. Nor are we engaging in this discussion entirely for its own sake. It will have direct bearing on the problem with which we started this chapter, the attitude of the Rabbis toward "anthropomorphisms."

[57] Ibid., Vol. I, Book II, p. 254.
[58] Ibid., p. 253.
[59] Ibid., p. 244.

II. ORGANISMIC DEVELOPMENT

How can we demonstrate that rabbinic thought represents a development out of biblical thought? Such a development ought to be reflected, obviously, in the value-concepts. Do the rabbinic value-concepts differ in any way from biblical ideas, or do they merely constitute a repetition of biblical thought? If there is a difference, are the rabbinic concepts nevertheless akin to those of the Bible? Granting the kinship, what are our criteria for regarding the rabbinic concepts as a development and not as a retrogression?

Rabbinic value-concepts do differ from biblical concepts. On the other hand, there is no rabbinic concept that does not have its roots in biblical thought. What are our criteria for regarding as a development the changes represented by the rabbinic concepts? The changes that have taken place have either made the rabbinic concept more applicable than its biblical antecedent, or else have given the rabbinic concept greater range and universality.

There are three types of rabbinic concepts, so far as their relationship to the Bible is concerned. One type consists of concepts having conceptual terms that are not to be found in the Bible. But this does not mean that such concepts are not represented in the Bible in any manner at all. In many instances, they are at least foreshadowed there by complete ideas, and these ideas are congruent with the rabbinic concretizations of the concepts. So close is the relation, in fact, that the Rabbis are able to use the biblical statements as proof texts in apt support of their own concretizations. Thus, to give several examples, the terms *Ḳiddush Ha-Shem* and *Ḥillul Ha-Shem*, *Malkut Shamayim*, *Teshubah*, *Middat Ha-Din* and *Middat Raḥamim* are conceptual terms, noun forms, that are purely rabbinic and not to be found in the Bible. Notice, however, the proof texts which the Rabbis employ as biblical warrant for some of their own concretizations of these concepts. For a rabbinic statement on *Ḳiddush Ha-Shem*, sanctification of the Name, the biblical warrant is, "But I will be hallowed among the children of Israel" (Lev. 22:32)[1]; for one on *Ḥillul Ha-Shem*, profanation of the Name, it is, "And ye shall not profane My holy Name" (ibid.)[2]; and for one on *Malkut Shamayim*, the Kingship of God, it is, "And the Lord shall be King over all the earth" (Zech. 14:9).[3]

Similarly, for a rabbinic statement on *Teshubah*, repentance, the biblical proof text is, "Take with you words and return (*we-shubu*) unto the Lord" (Hos. 14:3)[4]; for another on *Middat Raḥamim*, God's mercy and love, it is, "The Lord, the Lord, God, merciful (*raḥum*) and gracious, long-suffering, and abundant in goodness and truth" (Exod. 33:19)[5]; for still another on *Middat Ha-Din*, God's justice, it is, "For the arms of the wicked shall be broken" (Ps. 37:17).[6] In every example here, there is an intimate connection between biblical verse and rabbinic concept. That is why these proof texts are so apt.

The presence of the conceptual terms in the rabbinic complex, however, spells a certain development as against the antecedents in the Bible. Symbolized by an abstract term, the concepts can now be used to abstract and to classify; as a result, they are now more applicable, have a wider function, inform and interpret everyday phenomena. *Ḳiddush Ha-Shem* not only characterizes an act of martyrdom,[7] which is itself a nonbiblical usage of the idea, but also points to the effect of daily actions, as does *Ḥillul Ha-Shem*.[8] *Malkut Shamayim* is accepted by the individual twice daily, when he recites the *Shema'*.[9] *Teshubah* informs the New Year and the Day of Atonement and the days

[1] Sanhedrin 74b.
[2] Ibid., 74a.
[3] See above, p. 19.
[4] See TE (above, p. 15, n. 2), p. 127.
[5] See ibid., p. 114.
[6] See OT (above, p. 15, n. 2), p. 148.
[7] See above, p. 214.
[8] See TE, pp. 69–70.
[9] See above, p. 212.

between them.[10] Manifestations of *Middat Raḥamim* and *Middat Ha-Din,* especially of the former, are seen in the many daily occasions that call for *Berakot.*[11] None of these various concretizations is other than rabbinic.

We cautioned, in an earlier chapter, against using conceptual terms that are not rabbinic as a means of representing or symbolizing rabbinic ideas.[12] What we have just observed serves to reinforce that warning. The Rabbis themselves introduce new conceptual terms that may well stand as symbols for biblical ideas. But the new conceptual terms are more than just epitomes of the biblical ideas. They represent what are really new concepts, concepts with concretizations that are different from the "concretizations" in the Bible. Here the new conceptual terms reflect a conceptual development. When conditions make such a development impossible, or when there is a conscious attempt in postrabbinic times to formulate or to epitomize rabbinic ideas, the new conceptual terms introduced are bound to be out of line with rabbinic thought.

In another type of rabbinic concept, the conceptual term is the same as the biblical but with wider, more universal, connotations. Again we shall illustrate with only several examples out of a larger number. Our examples are the concepts of *Ger,* Israel, and *'Olam.*

A noun formed from the root *gur,* to sojourn, the word *Ger,* as used in the Bible, means a sojourner. A *Ger* is a non-Israelite who came to dwell in the land, and who, in the course of time, took over the customs and culture of Israel.[13] Although recognized as a non-Israelite, he could even participate in the eating of the sacrifice of the paschal lamb, provided he became circumcised.[14] Because the

[10] See ibid., p. 79, note 2.

[11] See ibid., pp. 203–204 and p. 209, note 29.

[12] Ibid., pp. 57–58.

[13] See Ezekiel Kaufmann, Golah We-Nekar I (Tel-Aviv: Dvir, 1929), pp. 227 ff.

[14] See ibid., p. 231.

process of assimilation was a gradual one, there were also "sojourners" who were only partly assimilated, and it would appear that the Bible classifies them too as *Gerim*.[15]

A new, universalistic note is struck by the prophets. The word *Ger* by itself, to be sure, still connotes a non-Israelite who comes to dwell in the land, and this is the case even in Isaiah 14:1.[16] But the attitude of "the *Ger*" there is that of one who comes by choice, and not by force of circumstances merely. After saying that God, in His compassion, will "set them (Israel) in their own land," the prophet declares: "and the *Ger* shall join himself with them, and they shall cleave to the house of Jacob" (ibid.). The same note is struck more clearly in Isaiah 56:6–7, in reference to aliens (*bene ha-nekar*). They are "the aliens that join themselves to the Lord, to minister to Him," that keep the Sabbath, that hold fast by His covenant. "Even them will I bring to My holy mountain, and make them joyful in My house of prayer . . . For my house shall be called a house of prayer for all the peoples" (ibid.). All this is in accord with the vision in which "all nations" and "many peoples" say, "Come ye, and let us go up to the mountain of the Lord, to the house of the God of Jacob; and He will teach us of His ways, and we will walk in His paths" (ibid., 2:3).

It is the universalistic idea of the prophets that is embodied in the rabbinic, as distinguished from the biblical, concept of *Ger*. True to the spirit of that universalistic idea, the concept of *Ger* is now dissociated from the idea of dwelling in the land. The *Ger* is now a convert, and he

[15] See ibid., and the references there.

The errors in the view on the biblical idea of *Ger* held by many modern scholars are pointed out by Kaufmann, ibid., p. 228 f., and the notes on p. 228. These scholars all assume that Leviticus is post-exilic; but Kaufmann has demonstrated that it is pre-exilic. He has done this in his Toledot Ha-'Emunah Ha-Yisre'elit, I, Chaps. V, VI, and VII. It would seem that this work has not yet come to the attention of non-Jewish scholars.

[16] See ibid., Golah We-Nekar, I, p. 237.

becomes so through a ritual of conversion. For the male, among the requirements of that ritual are circumcision and immersion, (and, in the days of the Temple, also the bringing of a sacrifice).[17] "When he has come up from immersion, he is like an Israelite in every respect."[18] This change in the meaning of the concept, as Moore points out, is reflected in the language. "For living as a resident alien in the land of Israel the verb is *gur*, 'sojourn'; for conversion to Judaism and adoption into the people as well as the religion a new form was needed and created, the denominative *nitgayyer*, 'become a proselyte,' with a corresponding active denominative, *gayyer*, convert some one to Judaism, make a proselyte of him."[19] What Moore does not make clear, however, is that these new forms are not biblical but purely rabbinic.[20] Just as these forms are rab-

[17] See B. J. Bamberger, Proselytism in the Talmudic Period (Cincinnati: Hebrew Union College Press, 1939), p. 42 f. Bamberger's work is a careful study of both the Halakah and the Haggadah on *Gerim*, and contains also a survey and critique of the literature on the subject. On the reception of the prospective convert, and the instructions during conversion, see ibid., p. 38 f.

[18] Yebamot 47b; for the implications, see Bamberger, op. cit., p. 60. A few vestigial disabilities remain, such as the prohibition of marriage between a female convert and a *kohen*, priest. But the daughter of a *kohen* is permitted to marry a convert. Actually the convert is a complete Israelite, as Maimonides declares. "There is no difference between us and you," he says to a convert. See Kaufmann, Golah We-Nekar, I, p. 249 and the note there.

[19] G. F. Moore, op. cit., I, pp. 329–30.

[20] For *gayyer*, see, for example, Bereshit R. XXXIX.14, ed. Theodor, pp. 378–9, and the further instances given in the parallels there; for *nitgayyer*, see, for example, Tos. Ḳiddushin V.11.

Moore (loc. cit.) links the word *hityahed* with these forms, saying that it means "turn Jew." It is found only in Esther 8:17. Taking the prevailing critical view (see above, p. 291, note 15), Moore also depicts *Ger* in Is. 14:1 as "the converts" (op. cit., p. 328). Since he thus finds ideas of conversion in the Bible, he prefers apparently to be noncommittal as to the rabbinic origin of *gayyer* and *nitgayyer*. See now Ezekiel Kaufmann, Toledot Ha-'Emunah Ha-Yisre'elit, Vol. IV, Book I (Jerusalem: Dvir, 1956), pp. 44 f., 47 f. He regards *hityahadut* as a process which took place in the Babylonian exile. Non-Jews voluntarily associated themselves with Israel, acquired belief in God and forsook idolatry; but this process constituted a problem since there was as yet no ritual of

binic beyond any question, so is the concept of *Ger* rabbinic in its new meaning of proselyte or convert.[21]

Obviously, if a *Ger* "is like an Israelite in every respect," the concept of Israel, too, has undergone a change. A universalistic element has entered into the concept. True, the dividing line between Israel and the nations still remains, and is as deeply sensed as in earlier times,[22] but a non-Jew anywhere, if he wishes, can cross that line. Another change to be noticed in the concept is in the same spirit. "The rabbinic concept of Israel widens the biblical ideal of Israel as a priest people until the demarcation between the priest class and the rest of Israel is all but eliminated."[23] The concept of Israel in rabbinic literature is hence another example of conceptual development.[24]

Still another such example is the rabbinic concept of *'Olam*. *'Olam* is a biblical word, but it is not until the rabbinic period that it is used in the sense of "world." This was first pointed out by the medieval Jewish exegetes and philosophers. Thus, both Ibn Ezra and Naḥmanides distinguish between the word *'Olam* in rabbinic literature, where it means "world," and its use in the Bible where it ordinarily refers to "time,"[25] and also to "eternity," according to Ibn

conversion. Kaufmann bases himself on Is. 56:3, 6–7, takes account of Esther 8:17, and refers to Is. 14:1. The problem is reflected in Is. 56:3.

[21] The new *Ger* received from the ancient *Ger* only the name, but the concept is entirely new — Kaufmann, Golah We-Nekar, I, p. 236. This is not quite correct. Circumcision of the *Ger* is biblical, as we saw, and the biblical *Ger*, too, was equal before the law — see Lev. 19:33 f., 24:22. What we have is a development of the biblical concept. On semi-proselytes, see Bamberger, op. cit., Chap. VII, and also above, p. 39, note 11.

[22] Thus in the *Habdalah* service (Prayer Book, ed. Singer, p. 216), one of the divisions is between Israel and the nations.

[23] See OT, p. 222 f.

[24] See also Aspects of the Rabbinic Concept of Israel, H. U. C. Annual (1946), pp. 57–59.

Notice also that the word "Israel" designates, in rabbinic literature, the members of the people individually as well. This is not the case in the Bible. See above, p. 55 and ibid., note 8.

[25] Ibn Ezra in his comment on Koh. 3:11; Naḥmanides on Gen. 21:33.

Ezra.[26] Modern authorities take the biblical word to stand either for an indistinct and unimaginable past or else for a distant future.[27] We ought to add that the original, biblical meaning of the word is not altogether lost in rabbinic literature. There, too, *'olam* still refers to time in various connections: *'olam* designates the fifty years between the jubilees,[28] and *le'olam* often means "always" or "forever".[29]

'Olam in its new, universalistic connotation of "world" is associated with the concept of man, that is, with mankind in general, as we may remember from an earlier chapter.[29a] Now in the case of *Ger*, the change in connotation is reflected in the language. Here, too, there is a linguistic change, but the change is in the character of the word itself. This is illustrated by a midrash on Ps. 119:160: "And forever – *ule'olam* – (endureth) all Thy righteous ordinance." R. Isaac interprets this verse to mean: "Thy creatures" acknowledge the righteousness of each of Thy dispensations (that is, of Thy punishments).[30] All the factors implied in the new connotation of *'Olam* are contained in this interpretation. By retaining the consonants but by changing the vowels, the midrash reads *ule'olam*, "forever," as though it were *wela-'Olam*, "and to the world," hence "Thy creatures." But the change in the meaning here involves also a change in the linguistic character of *'Olam*. *Ule'olam* is an adverb; *wela-'Olam* is a substantive, the word now taking the definite article, *Ha-'Olam*. A nonmidrashic

[26] Ibn Ezra, loc. cit. — על זמן ונצח. But he differentiates between *le'olam* and *le'olam wa-'ed*; the former refers to limited periods — Ibn Ezra on Gen. 3:6. Albo, too, argues that *'olam* is often applied to periods of limited time — *'Ikkarim*, III, 16, ed. Husik, p. 139 f.

[27] Gesenius, Handwörterbuch, s. v. עולם.

[28] E. g., Ḳiddushin 15a.

[29] E. g., Yeb. 46a. H. L. Ginsberg, Commentary on Ḳohelet (Hebrew) (Tel Aviv-Jerusalem: M. Newman, 1961), p. 33, shows how *'olamim* differs from *'olamot*.

[29a] See above, p. 150.

[30] Bereshit R. I.7, ed. Theodor, p. 4. The passage (see Theodor's notes, ibid.) is not free from textual difficulties.

example is to be found in the *Berakah* formula. There the phrase *Melek Ha-'Olam*, "King of the world," with *'Olam* as a noun taking the definite article, reminds us of the biblical *Melek 'olam*, "everlasting King" (Jer. 10:10), where *'olam* is a modifier.[31] When the Rabbis used *'Olam* in the sense of "world," therefore, they really coined a new term. It is a value-term, having a universalistic connotation that embraces all of mankind as a unit.

With regard to the conceptual kinship with the Bible, there is still one more type of rabbinic value-concept. This last type is quite similar to the one just discussed. In this type, too, the conceptual term is a biblical term; but there is no definite connection in the concepts of this type between the biblical terms and the same terms as used by the Rabbis. The words are identical but their meanings are entirely different.

As our examples, we shall point to several concepts discussed here in earlier chapters – the concepts of *Goy*, *Nes*, and *Ẓedaḳah*. In the Bible, the word *Goy* means "nation," and is applied both to Israel and to other nations, yet the same word has come to stand in rabbinic literature for the individual non-Jew.[32] The rabbinic word, in contradistinction to the biblical, connotes a status, and hence there is also the abstract rabbinic form *Gayyut*, "gentile status."[33] But this status need not be a permanent one: an individual who becomes a convert is no longer a *Goy* but a *Ger*.[34] The two concepts, *Goy* and *Ger*, are thus related to each other.

[31] In the New Year liturgy, the phrase *harat 'olam* from Jer. 20:17 is taken over intact, and the definite article is not prefixed to *'Olam*. But again the word is changed from a modifier to a noun, and is used in the rabbinic sense of "world." *Harat*, according to the second explanation of it in the Shibbole Ha-Leḳeṭ, ed. Buber, p. 138a, means "judgment" in its liturgical setting here.

[32] See above, p. 40 f. Notice that the word does not necessarily have the connotation of "pagan."

[33] Ketubbot 11a; see Jastrow, Dictionary, s. v. גיות.

[34] See Ketubbot 11a, and Rashi, ibid., s. v. יכולין למחות. A minor who has been converted can retract on reaching maturity, and can thus revert to *Gayyut*.

The concept of *Goy* may well be taken to be the obverse of the universalistic concept of *Ger*.[35]

Despite the fact that the biblical meaning of the word *Nes* is totally different from the rabbinic,[36] the rabbinic concept of *Nes* has biblical antecedents. The Bible speaks, for example, of God who "does wonders" (*'oseh fele'*),[37] and of "wondrous works (*nifla'ot*) in the land of Ham,"[38] of catastrophic, spectacular acts of God in behalf of Israel or in punishment of the wicked. At the same time, according to the Bible, the sustenance of living things, commonplace though it be, is also the work of God — "The eyes of all wait for Thee, and Thou givest them their food in due season."[39] Rabbinic literature, likewise, sees the hand of God in both the spectacular and the commonplace happenings, but now these two different things are but different phases of a single concept, the concept of *Nes*. Moreover, paradoxically, though the spectacular and catastrophic, on the one hand, and the commonplace, everyday things, on the other hand, are now included within the same concept, they are also more clearly differentiated. There are *Nissim* involving a change in the natural order, more correctly, a change in *sidre Bereshit*,[40] and there are everyday *Nissim*.[41] Uniting both conceptual phases is the idea of God's steady and direct intervention. That idea is expressed by the rabbinic concept of *Nes* more succinctly than it had been expressed before.[42]

[35] On concepts that are related by being obverses of each other, see above, p. 26 f. Of course, the concept of Israel is also an obverse of the concept of *Goy*, but two concepts can have the same obverse — see above, p. 40, note 12.

[36] The biblical word signifies "sign," "flag," or "mast" — see above, p. 162.

[37] Exodus 15:11.

[38] Ps. 106:22.

[39] Ibid., 145:15.

[40] See above, p. 152 f.

[41] See ibid., p. 159 f.

[42] The Rabbis continue to use sometimes various forms of the biblical root פלא when they wish to emphasize that something is astonishing or marvellous — see

The words formed from the root *ẓdḳ*, as found in the Bible, have been the subject of much careful study in recent times. The conclusion is that all such words have a common ground in the idea of "right".[43] In rabbinic literature, however, the word *Ẓedaḳah* does not mean the same as it does in the Bible, as Ibn Ezra has pointed out, although he has not gone on to give the rabbinic usage.[44] We have demonstrated elsewhere that in rabbinic usage *Ẓedaḳah* and *Gemilut Ḥasadim* (deeds of loving-kindness) are overlapping concepts,[45] and that *Ẓedaḳah* in the rabbinic sense not only refers to acts of charity but has the wider connotation of love.[46] This conceptual change, we also observed, reflects a tendency in rabbinic thought to emphasize love and compassion.[47]

But have we not, in this discussion of conceptual changes, been discussing also other rabbinic emphatic trends? If rabbinic concepts are more applicable, more pointed, than their biblical antecedents, does not this, too, reflect a certain emphasis on the part of the Rabbis? What is reflected by such rabbinic concepts is an emphasis on the ordinary, everyday events and actions, and the significance that these can yield. Likewise, when a rabbinic concept has a greater universality than does the same word in the Bible, what is reflected in that rabbinic concept is an emphatic

I. Heinemann, Die Kontroverse über das Wunder im Judentum der hellenistischen Zeit, Jubilee Volume in Honor of Bernhard Heller (Budapest, 1941), p. 171.

[43] See I. Heinemann, Darke Ha-Agadah (Jerusalem: Hebrew University Press, 1949), p. 114 and the references there.

[44] Ibn Ezra on Gen. 15:6.

[45] See OT, pp. 138–9. Notice the interpretations given in Yebamot 79a and in Ketubbot 8b of the word *Ẓedaḳah* as it occurs in Gen. 18:19. On overlapping concepts, see above, p. 29.

[46] See the references above, p. 110, note 9. Heinemann, loc. cit., takes a rather similar view of *Ẓedaḳah* in rabbinic usage. He says, however, that *Ẓedaḳah* in the sense of compassion and mercy is already to be found in Joel 2:23 and in Proverbs.

[47] See OT, p. 225. Comp. also Heinemann, op. cit., pp. 92, 114.

rabbinic trend toward universality.[48] Nor do these represent the only emphatic trends to be found in rabbinic literature. We are dealing with an emphatic trend when we depict normal mysticism, and in a previous work we dealt with the emphasis on the individual[49] and the emphasis on the ethical.[50] There is hardly any need to demonstrate with regard to most of these trends that they, too, have their biblical antecedents.[50a] We have to do with an organismic complex that has grown out of the Bible, that is a development out of the Bible.

A living bond unites the Bible with rabbinic thought. Even though rabbinic thought possesses its own concepts, it remains in a state of continuous dependence on the Bible. We have seen above that the texts of the Bible usually act as a stimulus to haggadic ideas, and hence that

[48] This emphatic trend — all the emphatic trends — are not only reflected in the rabbinic concepts. They are expressed as well in the interplay of the concepts. Thus we have shown how the element of universality is given expression in the interplay of the concept of Israel with the other fundamental concepts — see the article referred to on p. 293, note 24.

[49] See OT, p. 223 f. See also Heinemann, op. cit., p. 87 f. and the references there.

[50] See OT, p. 245 f.

[50a] One of the fundamental errors in modern biblical scholarship is its view of the rôle of the individual in the Bible. It is assumed that we have to do here with a religion still bearing the stamp of primitive Semitic origins, and that hence its subject is always the group, not the individual; according to this view, it was only after the exile first of Israel and then of Judah, and the period of national or group disintegration which ensued as a consequence, that there was an emergence of the individual.

This neat theory is an excellent illustration of how a wrong approach can make one blind to the facts. There is the double assumption here that a good part of the Bible is the product of a primitive society, and that in primitive society the individual has not yet emerged. We dealt with the latter fallacy above, p. 82 f. Further, there is the assumption that social ideas or values can be traced to definite events, a fallacy dealt with ibid., p. 48 f. The thing to do is to let the Bible speak for itself, and again it is Kaufmann who allows it to do so. Kaufmann shows that attention was paid to the individual in the Bible throughout — in the early stories, in the narrative sections, in the legal sections. See his Toledot Ha-'Emunah, Vol. II, Book II, pp. 533–543.

the Bible plays a never ending rôle in the development of rabbinic thought.[51] But the Bible could never have had this function were it not for the conceptual kinship between the Bible and rabbinic thought, a basic, intrinsic, kinship. To be sure, the midrashic method permits the exploitation of even the faintest connection between the biblical text and a rabbinic interpretation[52]; only in this wise could the texts of the Bible have provided a constant stimulus to the development of new rabbinic ideas. On the other hand, however, we have noticed also that in many instances the biblical proof texts in support of rabbinic ideas genuinely confirm those ideas. Obviously, then, the bond between the Bible and rabbinic thought is stronger at some points than at others. It is in respect to the Prophets that the bond is strongest. Thus, the rabbinic concept of *Ger*, we may remember, has its antecedents in the Pentateuch, but it has a still closer kinship with the universalistic vision of the Prophets.

We cannot enter now into a discussion of the relation of rabbinic Halakah to the Bible, nor even to attempt to summarize the more inclusive investigations of that intricate subject.[53] Nevertheless, it is apparent, from matters already touched on here, that Halakah is still more dependent on the Bible than Haggadah. Halakah makes it possible for the new rabbinic concepts to be concretized in daily life as we have frequently indicated. But how are the halakot derived? Often by means of hermeneutic rules, that is, rules for interpreting the Bible.[54] What is merely faint sequence does not suffice; the hermeneutic rules of halakic interpretation include logical procedures such as inference

[51] Above, p. 114 f.

[52] Ibid., p. 118 f.

[53] The most recent is C. Tchernowitz, Toledot Ha-Halakah, Vols. I–IV (New York, 1934–1950).

[54] See above, p. 123 and the references there. On the relation of the oral Torah to the written Torah, see also OT, pp. 34–5, and the analogies quoted there.

and analogy, and also literary considerations. The dependence of the Halakah on the Bible is such, indeed, that the dichotomy of *derash* and *peshaṭ*, rabbinic interpretation and the simple meaning of the biblical text, so basic in the Haggadah, does not hold for the Halakah.[55] And again it is in regard to the Prophets that the bond between the Bible and the Halakah is strongest, and that the kinship is closest, and this not only in the ethical but in the ritual sphere. In the ritualism of paganism everywhere, the dominant element was that of magic; but rabbinic Halakah, as Kaufmann points out, eliminated every vestige of this element from the ritual, achieving what prophet after prophet had striven for.[56]

The rabbinic complex, then, is a development out of the Bible, but its relation to the Bible goes even further. There is a living bond between rabbinic thought and the Bible. This can only mean that the character of rabbinic thought and the character of biblical thought are not essentially different. Specifically, it means that if in Rabbinic Judaism there is *experience* of God rather than a God-concept, this must also be true of the Bible.[57] As a matter of fact, the rabbinic emphasis on the experience of God is related to the Bible in the same way as are all the other emphatic trends. Normal mysticism, too, is a development out of the Bible and has its antecedents in the Bible.

A mystical relationship to God is taken for granted by the Bible. "And thou shalt love the Lord thy God with

[55] See above, p. 124 f.

[56] See Kaufmann, Toledot Ha-'Emunah, I, pp. 532 ff., especially, 537–8. The Rabbis also interpret the sacrifices symbolically, removing them, in a way, from the sphere of Temple ritual to the sphere of personal ethics, and they negate the belief that the sacrifices are a means of propitiation — see TE, p. 129 f.

[57] Although the term *'Elohim* in the Bible has undoubtedly, at times, a genuine conceptual connotation, it is more often used there as the Rabbis later use it, namely, as a proper name. Cassuto says that though the term was originally a concept, the people of Israel used it as a proper name because of their recognition that there is but one God — מאדם עד נח, (Jerusalem: Hebrew University Press, 1944), p. 46.

all thy heart, and with all thy soul, and with all thy might" (Deut. 6:5). This is a message for the people as a whole, and does not apply only to those who are specially endowed; it reflects what we have called normal mysticism. We are wont to stress today the ethical aspect of the prophets' teachings, but do not the prophets demand at the same time the establishing of a relationship to God? "Seek righteousness, seek humility," says Zephaniah, but this only follows upon, "Seek ye the Lord" (Zeph. 2:3). Similarly, and earlier: "Seek ye Me, and live" (Amos 5:4). The call to repentance is not merely a call to righteous action: "Return, O Israel, unto the Lord thy God; for thou hast stumbled in thine iniquity" (Hosea 14:2). Is it not steady experience that inspires the Psalmist's faith? "Yea, though I walk through the valley of the shadow of death, I will fear no evil, for Thou art with me" (Ps. 23:4).

The rabbinic experience of God is the same kind of experience, but there is now a development, a new emphasis. The inward life is now consciously cultivated. We need only recall some of the ways in which Halakah achieves that purpose. Through the agency of Halakah, prayer becomes the thrice-daily practice of the people as a whole[58]; *Berakot* are now the means, on innumerable occasions, of evoking a consciousness of God,[59] and also, in the case of the *Birkat Ha-Miẓwot*, of evoking the experience of holiness;[60] the call to *Teshubah*, repentance, becomes the function of annually recurring days,[61] indeed, it is embodied in the Daily *'Amidah.*[62]

Here the development consists in making it possible for everybody to have steady experience of God. Some of the aspects of normal mysticism, however, represent a develop-

[58] See above, p. 211.

[59] See ibid., p. 167 f.

[60] See ibid., p. 173 f.

[61] See ibid., p. 79, and note 2 there.

[62] In the Fifth *Berakah* — see Baer, op. cit., p. 90, and the notes there.

ment of a different character – an enlargement of the rôle of a particular idea, and hence a development that represents, in a sense, a departure from the Bible. We indicated above, for example, that rabbinic thought is dominated by the idea of God's love rather than by the idea of His justice.[63] There is thus an emphasis on God's love, and this is of a piece with that general emphasis on love and compassion that we have just noticed. Now the idea of God's love is, of course, a biblical idea. "The Lord, the Lord, God, merciful and gracious, long-suffering, and abundant in goodness and truth" (Exod. 33:19). "When Israel was a child, then I loved him" (Hos. 11:1). "The Lord is good to all; and His tender mercies are over all His works" (Ps. 145:9). But in rabbinic thought the idea of God's love becomes a dominant theme. It is an idea that is assumed in prayer and repentance, that informs numerous *Berakot*, and that gives direction to the imitation of God.[64] This emphasis represents, in a sense, a departure from the Bible, the Rabbis at times interpreting in terms of God's love matters which the Bible describes in terms of justice.[65] Such interpretations were made deliberately, and with full awareness of the implications. According to Resh Laḳish, the verse, "And I will take you one of a city, and two of a family" (Jer. 3:14), is to be understood literally – "Construe the biblical words as they are written." But R. Joḥanan declared that this rendering of His words is displeasing to God; instead, the verse is to be taken to mean that one person of a city protects the entire town, and that two persons of a family protect the entire family.[66] The Talmud repeats this discussion word for word, but with different proponents.[67] In both cases, the one who suggests the

[63] Above, p. 219 f.

[64] See ibid.

[65] See ibid.

[66] Sanhedrin 111a — see Jastrow, Dictionary, s. v. זכה.

[67] Ibid.

literal rendering is the pupil; in both cases, the master reproves him, and gives, instead, a haggadic, and a much kindlier, interpretation.

Related to the Bible in a similar manner is another aspect of normal mysticism. It is this aspect that brings us back to the problems posed at the beginning of this chapter. Those problems have nothing to do, we have shown, with the question of anthropomorphism. What they are really concerned with is the emphasis of normal mysticism on the otherness of God.

III. THE OTHERNESS OF GOD

One of the prime characteristics of normal mysticism is the consciousness of a relationship to God. It is a consciousness of relationship like none other, expressible, we may recall, in a manner in which no other relationship is expressible.[1] Indeed, being a mystical consciousness, it can be conveyed only by suggestion, or, at best, through metaphors.[2] But this consciousness of a relationship to God is a steady consciousness, as steady as is the integration of the self.[3] It underlies, as it were, the more communicable modes of the experience of God that are expressed through value-concepts.[4] Every experience of God, therefore, brought with it the recognition that God is like none other. It is this recognition of the otherness of God that the generic terms for God point to; they are like no other terms, being neither defined, nor cognitive, nor valuational terms[5]; they are thus, in a sense, the rabbinic terms for the otherness of God. Furthermore, the entire character of normal

[1] See above, p. 269 f.

[2] See ibid.

[3] See ibid., p. 265.

[4] See ibid., p. 270 f.; cf. ibid., p. 215 f.

[5] See ibid., p. 198 f.

mysticism leads toward the recognition of the otherness of God. It is mysticism that does not involve sense phenomena, and this in itself would tend to demarcate the experience of God from other experience.

Like all the other elements of the organismic complex, the recognition of the otherness of God needs to be cultivated. Sometimes, however, it is cultivated, given expression, and yet at the same time serves only as background to another idea. This is the case with the passages cited at the beginning of this chapter.

Those passages affirm, first of all, the otherness of God. It is amazing that such passages were ever thought to be strictures on anthropomorphisms. True, the Rabbis appear to be apprehensive with regard to a verse like, "And the Lord went before them by day" (Exod. 13:21); they ask, "Is it possible to say so?" But are not the verses they bring in "negation" also anthropomorphic? One of them reads: "And, behold, the glory of the God of Israel came from the way of the east; and His voice was like the sound of many waters; and the earth did shine with His glory" (Ezek. 43:2). Are not the ideas that God "came from the way of the east" and that "His voice was like the sound of many waters" anthropomorphic ideas? Again, one of the verses brought in "negation" of "And He rested on the seventh day" (Exod. 20:11) reads: "By the word of the Lord were the heavens made, and all the host of them by the breath of His mouth" (Ps. 33:6).[6] Can there be anything more anthropomorphic than the phrase, "the breath of His mouth?"

But one verse is not the negative of another. The verses are placed side by side for *contrast*. In contrast with the idea of God's going at the head of Israel, and lighting the way, is placed the idea of His glory appearing from the east and the whole earth shining with His glory; in contrast

[6] On these passages, see above, pp. 273 ff.

with the idea of God's resting, as though from labor, is placed the idea that He created without labor, merely "by the breath of His mouth." The contrasts serve to indicate the otherness of God. He has no need, really, to light the way; He has no need, really, to labor. Such things are done by human beings; God is other. That God did engage in these things, however, is not negated; it is affirmed, as we saw above: He did these things for special reasons.[7]

The idea of the otherness of God is a biblical idea. In one of the passages just discussed, the Rabbis quote the verse, "For I am God and not man" (Hos. 11:9).[8] The idea is given more generalized expression in the following verses, also from the Prophets: "To whom then will ye liken Me, that I should be equal? saith the Holy One" (Is. 40:25); "To whom then will ye liken God? Or what likeness will ye compare unto Him" (ibid., v. 18). Our last verse here, and the subsequent verses on the futility of images (ibid., vv. 19–20), reveal a distinct kinship with the Second Commandment (Exod. 19:4) and its prohibition of image making. The Second Commandment can thus be regarded as a biblical halakah embodying the idea of the otherness of God. That note is struck again in the verse, "Take ye therefore good heed unto yourselves—for ye saw no manner of form on the day that the Lord spoke unto you in Horeb out of the midst of the fire" (Deut. 4:15); and also in the verses following, with their detailed injunctions against image making and against the worship of heavenly bodies (ibid., vv. 16–19).

Despite the vividness of the idea in the Bible, it can nevertheless be said that the Rabbis accent it still more strongly. As found in rabbinic thought and law, the idea of the otherness of God represents a foliation, a development, of the antecedent biblical idea. An entire rabbinic tractate,

[7] See ibid., p. 274 f. We shall take up these affirmations soon.

[8] See above, p. 275, and note 5 there.

the tractate of *'Abodah Zarah,* is devoted to laws and prohibitions with regard to every aspect of idol worship; it endeavors to preclude the remotest contact with idolatry.[9] As a sheer idea, however, the otherness of God stands out more prominently in the Haggadah. Not only do the Rabbis often take account of the otherness of God in their own statements and interpretations, but they occasionally call attention to biblical passages that seem to them not in harmony with that idea, attempting, at the same time, of course, to explain away such passages. All these matters, which we shall take up shortly, indicate that here, too, just as in the concepts and trends previously discussed, rabbinic thought represents a development out of biblical thought. We ought to notice, in fact, that the passages already cited reflect that development. In those passages, it is the Rabbis who, by their apprehensive questions, suggest the idea of the otherness of God in the first place; further, by bringing in other verses as contrasts, the Rabbis contribute in no small degree to the full emergence of the idea.

But though these passages express the idea of the otherness of God, and hence do cultivate it, they do not stress it. The idea, in these instances, only serves as background, and against that background are stressed God's love and His justice. God made known "how beloved Israel is to Him" when, notwithstanding His otherness, He did go at the head of them and light the way.[10] Similarly, to quote Schechter: "The words, 'The Lord is a man of war' are contrasted with 'For I am God, and not man,' and explained to mean that it is only for the love of Israel that God appears in such a capacity."[11] Again, it was in order to stress God's justice that "He rested on the seventh day,"

[9] See, for example, 'Abodah Zarah, Chap. I. Cf. above, p. 196.

[10] See above, p. 275.

[11] See above, p. 275 and the note there.

notwithstanding His otherness – "in order to exact penalty from the wicked who are destroying the world that was created with trouble and labor."[12]

From our analysis, it would appear that, in the self-same statement, the Rabbis both do and do not hold to the idea of the otherness of God. Partly, this is the result of our having introduced a factor, for the purpose of analysis, not to be found in rabbinic texts – namely, the term "otherness of God." It is our own term, and it is justified to the extent that it is helpful in analysis. But it stands for an idea that, however suggested or expressed, is never epitomized by the Rabbis in a single term. At the same time, it is not an auxiliary idea either[13]; we shall notice that expression is given to the idea in its own right.

We must bear in mind two things with regard to what we have called the otherness of God. Of the very essence of the God-experience of the Rabbis, implicit in their very consciousness of a relationship to God, the otherness of God relates to the deeply private aspect of that experience. That is why it cannot really be crystallized in a single conceptual term of any kind[14]; and that is why, too, the nearest approach to such a term consists of the generic terms for God themselves. But the deeply private experience of God, we must also remember, is only one aspect of God-experience, and it is this fact that is central in normal

[12] See ibid.

[13] On auxiliary ideas, see above, pp. 53–55, and pp. 220–222.

[14] It is precisely at this point that the difference between normal mysticism and certain other forms of mysticism is most marked. Because of their extreme emphasis on the otherness of God, those forms of mysticism do have terms for that idea — expressions like "beyond," "that which is nothing." "By this 'nothing' is meant not only that of which nothing can be predicated, but that which is absolutely and intrinsically other than and opposite of everything that is and can be thought" — R. Otto, op. cit., p. 30. Notice his use of the term, "wholly other" — ibid., p. 28. Cf. above, p. 202. On "Nothing" in Kabbalah, see G. Scholem, op. cit., pp. 25, 213 f., 217.

mysticism. The *Berakot*, for example, express not only the consciousness of the otherness of God[15] but, together with that, the consciousness of holiness, or of God's love, or of His justice.[16] Normal mysticism thus contains at once an element that is private and elements that are shared with others; it refers to an experience which contains at once something not expressible in a single concept of any kind and matters expressible in commonly shared value-concepts. This is what is reflected in the haggadic passages we have considered, except that, having a didactic interest, the passages stress God's love or His justice at the expense, as it were, of the non-conceptualized element, – at the expense of what we have called the otherness of God.

The idea of the otherness of God has been expressed, in the instances so far given, through structural stereotypes. Is not the expression of that idea in the *Berakah* achieved by a structural stereotype, the stereotype consisting of the *Berakah* formula?[17] In the passages with which we began this chapter, the idea is likewise conveyed through a structural stereotype, but of a different kind. All such passages are constructed in the same manner – first, a biblical verse; then, an apprehensive question ("Is it possible to say so?") by the Rabbis; then, the contrasting of the verse in question with other biblical verses, the contrast implying that the Rabbis' apprehension is in reference to the idea of the otherness of God; and finally the affirmation of the verse in question. Actually, the stereotypes convey the idea merely by suggestion rather than by complete expression: the idea is only implied in the *Berakah* formula,[18] and, once more, the idea is only implied in the contrasts set up by the Rabbis.

[15] See above, pp. 267–270.
[16] See ibid., p. 203, and the references there.
[17] See above, pp. 267–270.
[18] See ibid.

There is a third structural stereotype that conveys the idea of the otherness of God, and again only by intimating or suggesting it. This stereotype generally contains the expression, "Were it not for the scriptural verse, it would be impossible to say this"[19]; usually following that introduction is a concretization of God's love or of His justice which is decidedly not in harmony with the idea of the otherness of God. An example of such a stereotype is R. Joḥanan's interpretation of Exod. 34:6–7. Beginning with, "Were it not for the scriptural verse, it would be impossible to say this," he goes on to interpret the verse as hinting (מלמד) that God wrapped Himself in a cloak like the leader in prayer and demonstrated to Moses the order of prayer (for forgiveness of sin).[20] The hint he refers to, be it noted, is by no means present in the text itself, but is the result of a word play.[21] In an example we have given elsewhere, the expression "Were it not for the scriptural verse" etc., or rather a slight variation of it, is placed at the end of the interpretation.[22] That interpretation is based on a word play employing the method of analogy.[23] Whatever be the warrant in the Bible, it remains true that the interpretation and the expression placed either at the beginning or at the end, in all such instances, form a structural stereotype. Like its kindred stereotypes, this one also has a dual function. In the very process of making a statement that con-

[19] אלמלא מקרא כתוב אי אפשר לאומרו. For variations in the expression see TE, p. 43, notes 55 and 56.

[20] Rosh Ha-Shanah 17b.

[21] Instead of ויעבֹר (Exod. 34:6), he reads ויעבִיר, apparently. This seems to be the derivation suggested by Edeles in his comment a. l. Edeles calls attention there to the fact that the hint is not contained in the simple meaning of the verse. Rabbi Phineas Kadushin explains the derivation in a manner that does not involve a change in the last vowel of ויעבר, — as a play on עבר, the word being part of the expression (see Berakot V. 3; ibid., V.4; 'Erubin III.9, and frequently elsewhere in the Mishnah) that refers to leading in prayer.

[22] See TE, p. 43.

[23] See ibid., and OT, p. 204.

cretizes God's love or His justice, it suggests or intimates His otherness.[24] By suggesting the idea of God's otherness — "Were it not for the scriptural verse, it would be impossible to say this" — this structural stereotype, like the others, cultivates the idea.

But we must not lose sight of the difference between the *Berakah* formula and the other two structural stereotypes. The *Berakah* performs its dual function in the context of an actual experience. An event or an act becomes an occasion for an experience of holiness, or of God's love, or of God's justice, and a *Berakah* is the means for expressing that experience. Now this experience of God's love, or of His justice, or of holiness, is one that does not involve any sensory experience of God. It is in complete accord with the consciousness that God is like none other, also expressed in the *Berakah* formula. The structural stereotype, in this instance, stresses neither aspect of the experience at the expense of the other. This cannot be said of the other two structural stereotypes. For they are haggadic stereotypes — not a means for expressing an experience in actual life, but only a reflection of such experience. As haggadic stereotypes, they are a didactic device, and, whilst suggesting the idea of the otherness of God, they concretize God's love or His justice at the expense of that idea. This we indicated a little earlier with regard to the stereotype characterized by "an apprehensive question." It is equally true of the structural stereotype we have just discussed. When the Rabbis say, "Were it not for the scriptural verse, it

[24] Because the structural stereotypes have the same dual function, the same idea can be expressed by two different stereotypes. Thus, in comment on "And the Lord went before them by day" (Exod. 13:21), R. Jose the Galilean says, "Were it not for the scriptural verse, it would be impossible to say this — like a father who carries the torch before his son and like the master who carries the torch before his servant" (Mekilta de R. Simon, ed. Hoffmann, p. 40). Here the same idea is expressed, and the same analogy employed as in the other stereotype characterized by contrasting verses, and found in the Mekilta passage quoted above, pp. 273, 275.

would be impossible to say this," what precedes or follows is a concretization of God's love or of His justice not in keeping with the idea of His otherness.

The primary function of the haggadic stereotypes, then, is to stress concretizations of God's love and justice. If Haggadah is to be an effective agency for cultivating the value-concepts, the haggadic concretizations must be vivid. Can the concretizations of God's love and justice be more vivid than against the background of the idea of the otherness of God? While the haggadic stereotypes do suggest the idea of the otherness of God, therefore, their more immediate function is to stress God's love and justice over His otherness.[25]

Do the Rabbis teach the idea of God's otherness, not incidentally, but as an idea in its own right? They do, and it is then that, instead of being merely intimated, the idea is given explicit expression. To be sure, the Rabbis do not possess a conceptual term that would epitomize the idea. This is due, as we have pointed out, to the nature of the rabbinic experience of God. But the absence of such a term is somewhat compensated for. In place of a single term used repetitiously, the Rabbis express the idea in a number of different ways.

[25] The word כביכול is used occasionally together with the expression, "Were it not for the scriptural verse, it would be impossible to say this"—e. g. 'Erubin 22a, Exod. R. XXX.21. Frequently, however, the word כביכול in the sense of "as it were" is found by itself. We have not dealt with the word because there is good evidence that later scribes were wont to insert it into the texts, as the following communication from Prof. Saul Lieberman indicates:

בענין „כביכול" בבבלי יומא ג׳ ב׳ אין ספק לדעתי שיש כאן הוספה של סופרים חסידים. בספרי בהעלותך פיס׳ ע"ב וכן בבבלי מנחות כ"ח ב׳ (בכת"י ובדפוסים ישנים) ליתא ונוספה בבבלי שם על פי רש"י, כמו שהעיר בדק"ס במקומו. וכן היה דרכם של המלקטים החסידים להוסיף מלה זו במובן „כאילו". עיין לדוגמא במה"ג בראשית ויצא עמ׳ תק"ה שו׳ 9: כביכול שקפלה כפינקס ונתנה תחת ראשו. במקור (במדרש רבה שם) אינה נמצאת מלה זו בשום כת"י. וגם כאן אין כאן כינוי כלפי מעלה, אלא „אם אפשר לומר כן" שכל הארץ נתקפלה תחתיו.

Lieberman's theory above, it seems to us, is also borne out by a comparison of Canticles R. I.48 with Midrash Tehillim, ed. Buber, p. 72a.

A passage in the Mekilta[26] affirms that the phrase "as the smoke of a furnace" (Exod. 19:18) is not to be taken literally. Scripture only intended "to soothe the ear (so as to make it listen to) what it can hear,"[27] meaning, Scripture speaks in a manner that is within man's ken.[28] The passage continues as follows: "Similarly, 'The lion hath roared, who will not fear? The Lord God hath spoken, who can but prophesy?' (Amos 3:8). And who has given strength and power to the lion? Is it not He? We compare Him, however, to His creations[29] merely to soothe the ear (so as to make it listen to) what it can hear." Ezek. 43:2 is cited next as another example: " 'And, behold, the glory of the God of Israel came from the way of the east; and His voice was like the sound of many waters.' And who has given strength and power to the waters? Is it not He? We compare Him, however, to His creations merely to soothe the ear." Comparison of anything about God to phenomena in this world, says this passage, is not a true comparison. God is other.

A variant[30] of the same passage expresses the idea a shade differently. "Is it possible that He is like His creations?[31] But (it is only that) the ear is made to listen to what it can hear." Question and answer are applied not only to Ezek. 43:2 and to Amos 3:8, as in the passage above, but also to Ps. 24:8.[32] Most of the fairly numerous

[26] Mekilta, ed. Horovitz-Rabin, p. 215 and the parallels there (Mekilta, II, ed. Lauterbach, p. 221).

[27] So Schechter translates לשכך האוזן מה שהיא יכולה לשמוע, in Some Aspects of Rabbinic Theology, p. 35. This is in accordance with the suggestion of Bacher, op. cit., p. 2, s. v. אזן. See the entire discussion in Bacher, ibid., and the notes there.

[28] Notice that Rashi on Exod. 19:18 explains the phrase by נותן לבריות סימן הניכר להם. On לשבר את האזן there see the note in ed. Berliner, p. 65a.

[29] אלא הרי אנו מכנין אותו מבריותיו.

[30] Mekilta de R. Simon, ed. Hoffmann, p. 100–1.

[31] אפשר לבריותיו כמותו — This is undoubtedly a euphemism, for the comparisons are the other way around.

[32] This passage in the Mekilta de R. Simon ends differently from our first pas-

variants and parallels, however, express the idea of God's otherness in the manner of our passage in the Mekilta.[33]

Biblical verses that "liken the Creator to His creation"[34] are regarded by the Rabbis as only poetic, or rather prophetic, license. "Happy are the prophets," declares Hezekiah bar Ḥiyya, "for they liken the Creator to His creation and the Planter to His plant."[35] Examples given are "For the Lord God is a sun and a shield" (Ps. 84:12) and the recurrent ones of Amos 3:8 and Ezek. 43:2; and the statement concludes with "But (it is only that) the ear is made to listen to what it can hear and the eye is made to behold what it can see."[36] Based on this statement, according to Theodor, is another that has many parallels in midrashic literature. "R. Judan said: Great is the power of the prophets, for they liken the Creator to His creation — 'And I heard the voice of a man between the banks of Ulai' (Dan. 8:16); (whereupon) R. Judan the son of R. Simon said: We have another verse more clear than that (i. e., a better instance) — 'And upon the likeness of the throne was a likeness as the appearance of a man upon it above' (Ezek. 1:26)."[37] The point here is that the phrases "the voice of a man" and "a likeness as the appearance of a man," both of which

sage, concluding with the comparison of Torah to rain in Deut. 32:2, and saying that in that comparison, too, "the ear is made to listen to what it can hear." The same formula is also applied earlier in this source (p. 94) to "And how I bore you on eagles' wings" (Exod. 19:4); this constitutes another affirmation of God's otherness.

[33] These variants and parallels are: Tanḥuma, Yitro, 13; Mishnat R. Eliezer, ed. Enelow, p. 25; Abot de R. Nathan, I, Chap. 2, and II, Chap. 3, ed. Schechter, p. 7a; Yalḳuṭ Shime'oni, Deut., par. 942; ibid., Ezek., par. 382; Leḳaḥ Ṭob, ed. Buber, II, p. 66a. Of all these, only Abot de R. Nathan does not express the idea of God's otherness. Schechter regards the text as defective — see his note there.

[34] See the next note.

[35] Midrash Tehillim, ed. Buber, p. 3a. שהן מדמין את הצורה ליוצרה ואת הנטיעה לנוטעה — again a euphemism. See Buber's note.

[36] Ibid. — ומראין את העין מה שיכולה לראות.

[37] Bereshit R. XXVII.1, ed. Theodor, pp. 255–6, and the notes and the parallels there.

refer to God, are to be attributed to prophetic license. Having established this point, R. Judan proceeds to interpret Ecclesiastes 2:21 in the same light. According to R. Judan's interpretation, the words "a man whose labour is with wisdom" refer, by prophetic license, to God.[38] The examples from Dan. 8:16 and Ezek. 1:26 serve as warrant that these words, too, are to be regarded as an instance of prophetic license.

Whenever the Rabbis interpret "man" in any biblical verse as referring to God, they most likely assume the word to be an instance of prophetic license. This holds, we believe, even if the assumption is not stated or any warrant offered. Thus, in several of the parallels to R. Judan's interpretation of Ecc. 2:21, no mention is made of what we have called prophetic license[39]; it is apparently so taken for granted that it need not be specifically stated. In a number of interpretations, "man" (*'ish*) in Exod. 15:3 – "The Lord is a man of war" – is likewise apparently assumed to be prophetic license. The Rabbis contrast this verse, we may recall, with Hosea 11:9 – "For I am God, and not man"[40]; elsewhere, too, the Rabbis use the latter verse to stress that God "is not man."[41] Is it likely, then, that they would use "man" in Exod. 15:3 as warrant for man in the ordinary sense? Is it not more likely that, regarding the word here as an instance of prophetic license, they use it as a warrant for taking another verse in the same way?[42] Moreover, the wording in some of the passages seems to indicate that God is only *called* "a man." One passage, for example, speaks

[38] Ibid.

[39] Pesiḳta R., Addition, Chap. 2; Tanḥuma, ed. Buber, I, p. 12b — here one of the verses constituting the warrant is given, but it is introduced by: "And whence do we know that He is called 'a man?' "

[40] Above, p. 275.

[41] Sifre Deut., par. 306, ed. Friedmann, p. 130b; Midrash Tannaim, ed. Hoffmann, p. 181. The latter reference also employs Num. 23:9 — "God is not a man."

[42] See Bereshit R. XCII.3; Tanḥuma, ed. Buber, IV, p. 15b; Numbers R. IX.1; ibid., 54; Tanḥuma, ed. Buber, III, p. 25a; Soṭah 42b; ibid., 48a.

of "the Holy One blessed be He who is *called* 'a man' (in Exod. 15:3)" and of "her husband (i. e., the husband of the suspected wife) who *is* 'a man.'"[43]

The otherness of God is emphasized when the Rabbis discuss the Temple sacrifices. Does God Himself need the sacrifices? "There is no eating and drinking with (lit., before) Him," says an early text, quoting these verses from Ps. 50: "I know all the fowls of the mountains; and the wild beasts of the field are Mine. If I were hungry, I would not tell thee; for the world is Mine, and the fullness thereof. Do I eat the flesh of bulls, or drink the blood of goats?" (Ps. 50:11–13).[44] What then is the purpose of the sacrifices? They are for man's sake.[45] A parallel elaborates: You are not to say, "I will do His will that He may do my will" – you are not offering sacrifices for My benefit, but for yours, (that you may fulfill My *Miẓwot* and obtain atonement thereby).[46]

Other texts, teaching that "there is no eating and drinking with Him," marshal argument after argument in support of that teaching.[47] Such special emphasis was apparently necessary. "That your (*Evil*) *Yeẓer* not mislead you to say there is eating and drinking with Him – who brought Him sacrifices before Israel existed?"[48] The apprehension here – namely, lest the *Evil Yeẓer* incite the thought that God eats and drinks – is voiced again in other arguments.[49] Evidently the Rabbis intended to counteract with these arguments a possible pagan influence, the common pagan

[43] Numbers R. IX.1; comp. ibid., 54.

[44] Sifre Numbers, par. 143, ed. Horovitz, p. 191–2. Here verse 12 is given first.

[45] Ibid.

[46] Menaḥot 110a and Rashi a. l. The Rabbis also interpret the sacrifices symbolically, removing them thus, in a sense, from the sphere of Temple ritual to the sphere of personal ethics — see TE, p. 129 f.

[47] See Pesiḳta de R. Kahana, pisḳa 6, ed. Buber, and the parallels given there on p. 57a, note 2. A similar type of argument is in Tosefta Menaḥot VII.9.

[48] Tanḥuma, 'Emor, par. 15; Tanḥuma, ed. Buber, III, p. 48b and the notes there.

[49] Ibid.

belief being that sacrifices and libations were food and drink for the gods. To counteract such influence, it was necessary to stress the otherness of God. He has no need of food or drink. He is other. Nor was the need to stress God's otherness in this particular manner obviated by the fact that the Temple had been destroyed. It was the daily expectation that the Temple would be rebuilt and that the sacrifices would be reinstituted.

The light of the candlestick in Tabernacle (Num. 8:2) and Temple likewise furnished an opportunity for teaching God's otherness. "Not because I have need of the lamps (prepared by men) of flesh and blood have I commanded concerning the lamps, but in order to cause them, (i. e., the people) to have merit (לזכותם). And thus it says, 'And the light dwelleth with Him' (Dan. 2:22). And it also says, 'Even the darkness is not too dark for Thee, but the night shineth as the day; the darkness is even as the light' (Ps. 139:12)."[50]

Sometimes, indeed, it was not only this or that aspect of Temple ritual that caused the question of God's otherness to be raised, but the very fact of the sanctuary itself. "R. Judah the son of Simon said in the name of R. Joḥanan: Three things did Moses hear from the Might that made him start back with astonishment. (The first was) when He said, 'And let them make Me a sanctuary, that I may dwell among them' (Exod. 25:8). Moses said to (lit., before) the Holy One blessed be He: Master of the world, 'Behold, heaven and the heaven of heavens cannot contain Thee' (I Kings 8:27), and Thou hast said, 'And let them make Me a sanctuary.' "[51] We ought to give here also the next command that caused Moses to start back with astonishment. It was: "My food which is presented unto Me for

[50] Tanḥuma, Beha'aloteka, par. 2; Cf. Tanḥuma, ed. Buber, II, p. 49a and the references there. Compare also Tanḥuma, 'Emor, par. 17.

[51] Pesiḳta de R. Kahana, ed. Buber, p. 20a, and the parallels in the notes there.

offerings made by fire, of a sweet savour unto Me, shall ye observe to offer unto Me in its due season" (Num. 28:2).[52]

A comment on the phrase "of a sweet savour unto the Lord" in Num. 28:8, a few verses below the one just quoted, represents still a different way of teaching the idea of God's otherness. By a word play, *reaḥ niḥoaḥ*, "a sweet savour," is interpreted to mean *naḥat ruaḥ*, "pleasure" — "pleasure before Me that I spoke and My will was done."[53] No actual mention is made of the idea of God's otherness, but it is present here nonetheless, whilst the literal biblical meaning is, in effect, interpreted away. Word play is, of course, not necessarily a characteristic of this method of teaching the idea. An instance without it is a comment in the Mekilta on a phrase in Exod. 12:13. " 'And the blood shall be to you for a token upon the houses where you are' — to you for a token and not to Me."[54] The comment inserts the idea of God's otherness, for the verse itself continues with, "And when I see the blood, I will pass over you" (ibid.). But now how are these words — "And when I see the blood" — to be taken? Do they not seem to indicate that God needs the token, and hence to contradict the idea of His otherness?

Two interpretations are given, and the second one,[55] in another form of word play, treats the words "I see" almost purely as a symbol. "And when I see the blood" means, according to this interpretation, "I see the blood of the

[52] Ibid. The third thing to cause Moses to be astonished was God's saying, "Then shall they give every man a ransom for his soul" (Exod. 30:12).

[53] Sifre Numbers, par. 143, ed. Horovitz, p. 191. See also ibid., pp. 110, 140 — the phrase as it occurs in Num. 15:10 and again in ibid., 18:17 is interpreted in precisely the same way.

[54] Mekilta, I, p. 56. The implication here is that the blood was on the inside of the house, as R. Jonathan (or Nathan) maintains, ibid., p. 44 — see ed. Horovitz-Rabin, p. 24 and the note there.

[55] Mekilta, I, pp. 57, 87–8. This interpretation is not dependent on the first; it is introduced in a number of sources by the term "another interpretation" — see Horovitz-Rabin, pp. 24, 39.

sacrifice (lit., the binding) of Isaac." That is, God says that He will pass over and not smite the Israelites for the sake of the sacrifice of Isaac. This interpretation is derived by placing "And when *I see* the blood" in conjunction with Gen. 22:14, the verse telling that Abraham called the place of the sacrifice by the name "The Lord *will see*" (Adonai-jireh). Corroboration is had from another event: " 'And as he was about to destroy, the Lord *saw* and He repented Him of the evil' (I Chron. 21:15). What did He see? He saw the blood of the sacrifice of Isaac, as it is said: 'God will Himself *see* the lamb for a burnt offering, my son' (Gen. 22:8)." Once more, then, a word play interprets away a verse that would seem to contradict the idea of God's otherness. Again the idea is not actually mentioned but is nonetheless present and taught.

What does "the blood of the sacrifice of Isaac" refer to? In a brilliant study, Shalom Spiegel demonstrates that our passage is one of numerous rabbinic vestiges of a very ancient legend, a legend that Isaac's blood was shed, that Isaac was really sacrificed by Abraham and then revived by God.[56] Sometimes the Rabbis used the legend to concretize the concept of *Zekut 'Abot*, the merit of the fathers, and sometimes to concretize that of *Kapparah*, vicarious atonement, as we can gather from Spiegel's treatment and from the passages he quotes.[57] Our passage, since it contains no

[56] Shalom Spiegel, מאגדות העקדה, offprint from ספר היובל לכבוד אלכסנדר מארכס (נויורק, תשי״א). Our passage is discussed on pp. 23 ff., in the offprint.

[57] Ibid., pp. 55–6. Since the Rabbis speak of the sacrifice of Isaac now in terms of merit of the fathers and now in terms of vicarious atonement, we conclude that the two concepts overlap. (On these two concepts, see above, p. 218 and the references there, and on overlapping concepts, see ibid., p. 250 f. and the references).

Spiegel also demonstrates here that the sacrifice of Isaac is by no means regarded by the Rabbis as the sole instance of vicarious atonement. The death of every righteous man effects atonement for his generation; not only that, but a righteous man may "be taken" by God in order to be atonement for a sinful generation. (See also other instances of vicarious atonement in TE, p. 134). All this has an important bearing, it seems to us, on the question of the relation of value to

reference to sin, is a concretization of *Zekut 'Abot*. It is an excellent example of how the Rabbis exploit an ancient legend for the purpose of teaching their own concepts and ideas.[58]

In its first interpretation of "And when I see the blood," the Mekilta counters the verse by asserting God's omniscience. "R. Ishmael used to say: Is not everything revealed before Him, as it is said, 'He knoweth what is in the darkness and the light dwelleth with Him' (Dan. 2:22)? And it also says, 'Even the darkness is not too dark for Thee' (Ps. 139:12). What then is the purport of the words, 'And when I see the blood?' "[59] The answer then given implies that the blood is no token for God, and, accordingly, the word *ufasaḥti* is interpreted not as "I will pass over" but as "I will protect," another possible meaning. "In reward for the *Miẓwah* being performed" by the Israelites, this interpretation says, God will protect them.[60] It is noteworthy that the verses quoted here in proof of God's omniscience are the verses quoted elsewhere in proof of God's otherness[61]; it is also noteworthy that there is no rabbinic

dogma. So long as the value-concept of vicarious atonement has many concretizations, it is not a dogma. Like the other value-concepts, the concept of vicarious atonement is indeterminate, and it becomes determinate only when concretized. New concretizations thus testify to its indeterminate character. But when the concept of vicarious atonement is given one concretization, and one only, it is no longer indeterminate but fixed. Its entire character has been changed. The fluid quality of the value-concept is gone, and there is now only a static belief in a single concretization.

In another matter, as well, Spiegel's study bears on our theory. We have attempted to depict the interaction of the Rabbis with the folk (above, pp. 85 ff.). An aspect of that interaction is to be found in the Rabbis' use of folklore and legend for purposes of concretization (ibid., p. 139 f.). The use of the ancient legend of the sacrifice of Isaac is an illustration in point.

[58] See the preceding note.

[59] Mekilta, I, pp. 56, 87.

[60] Ibid. This meaning is given to ופסחתי through comparison with the same root in Is. 31:5. See Lieberman, op. cit., p. 50 f.

[61] See above, p. 316.

term for God's omniscience, or for any auxiliary idea,[62] just as there is no rabbinic term for the idea of God's otherness. God's omniscience, and most likely some of the other auxiliary ideas, implicate the idea of God's otherness. That is why they can, as in this instance, teach the idea of God's otherness.

We have been depicting here various ways in which the Rabbis expressed the idea of God's otherness. It is this idea that the Rabbis express, and not an aversion to anthropomorphism. Mark what the Rabbis say — "We *compare* Him to His creations merely to soothe the ear." Mark, too, the examples. They object not to saying that God has a voice; they object to *comparing* His voice to "the sound of many waters." "And who has given strength and power to the waters? Is it not He?" Again, in speaking of prophetic license, do the Rabbis object to the notion that God has a likeness? Some of the parallels read: "Great is the power of the prophets, for they liken the likeness of Might above to the likeness of man"[63] (or, "to the form of man").[64] And this may well be what all the texts imply, if Theodor is right. He says that R. Judan takes Ezek. 1:26 to liken the likeness of God to the likeness of man.[65] The claim that the Rabbis opposed anthropomorphism as such cannot be upheld.

We have been obliged to reckon with the claim that the Rabbis opposed anthropomorphisms as such. Having raised the question of anthropomorphism, however, we have been swept, willy-nilly, into the stream of foreign, philosophic thought. Can we say that the Rabbis accept anthropomorphism in principle? If we do say so, how can we then say that they emphasized the idea of the otherness of God?

[62] On auxiliary ideas, see above, pp. 220–222.

[63] Pesiḳta de R. Kahana, ed. Buber, p. 36b; Pesiḳta Rabbati, Parah, Chap. 10.

[64] Tanḥuma, Ḥuḳḳat, par. 6; Numbers R. XIX.3.

[65] Bereshit R., ed. Theodor, p. 255, note to line 9. See also ibid., p. 230, and the commentary quoted there in the note to line 2.

The fact is that the philosophic problem of anthropomorphism and the rabbinic idea of God's otherness belong in two entirely different worlds of discourse. The rabbinic idea is not merely a less strict version of the philosophic idea. On the score of anthropomorphism, one would hardly single out for objection verses that are obviously nothing but metaphors, pure and simple. We refer to a verse like, "For the Lord God is a sun and a shield" (Ps. 85:12),[66] or to a verse like, "And how I bore you on eagles' wings" (Exod. 19:4).[67] But these verses do involve a *comparison* of God to phenomena in this world, and hence do violate the idea of God's otherness. The Rabbis single such verses out because of their own standpoint, a standpoint arising out of their own non-sensory mystical experience, and one that has nothing to do with philosophy.[68]

What all the passages here teach, then, is the idea of God's otherness. That idea represents nothing less than an emphatic trend. Like all the emphatic trends, it is rooted in the Bible; and this is evidenced not only by the biblical verses we quoted at the outset of this discussion, but also by verses quoted in the rabbinic passages we have discussed. The idea of God's otherness, however, is accented much more strongly in rabbinic literature than it is in the Bible, again like all the rabbinic trends. The Rabbis teach the

[66] See above, p. 313.

[67] See above, p. 312, note 32.

[68] Ezekiel Kaufmann (op. cit., Vol. I, Book II, pp. 231–238) also deals with what we have called expressions of the idea of God's otherness. He, too, points out that such rabbinic sayings do not imply that the Rabbis opposed anthropomorphism. But his approach remains philosophic. According to him, such rabbinic sayings have for their purpose the exalting of God, for the Rabbis did not arrive at an abstract concept of God. See below, p. 330, note 27.

Kaufmann calls attention to Maimonides' use of the rabbinic dictum, "The Torah speaks according to the language of man," in the Moreh, I, Chap. 26. This dictum has nothing to do with the problem of anthropomorphism; and Kaufmann cites Geiger and others who have shown that the saying refers solely to halakic derivations. See Kaufmann, op. cit., I, p. 236, note 20, where he also deals with Maimonides' use of R. Judan's statement.

idea in various ways, each an endeavor to overcome biblical verses that seem to contradict the idea. Besides raising the question of God's otherness by means of the structural stereotypes, they declare that Scripture intends in some verses only "to soothe the ear," they attribute to the prophets what we have called "prophetic license," they reinterpret the sacrifices and other aspects of Temple ritual, and sometimes they even interpret verses away. Whilst basically biblical, the idea of God's otherness is thus more accented, more emphasized, by the Rabbis. It may hence be regarded, like all the emphatic trends, as a development out of the Bible.

But if the idea of God's otherness is truly an emphatic trend, how are we to account for a great number of rabbinic statements about God? In these statements, apparently no cognizance at all is given to this trend. As Schechter says, "A great number of scriptural passages, when considered in the light of rabbinic interpretation, represent nothing else but a record of a sort of *Imitatio hominis* on the part of God."[69] For illustration, he gives a list, already quoted here, of some of those interpretations: "He acts as best man at the wedding of Adam and Eve; he mourns over the world like a father over the death of his son when the sins of ten generations make its destruction by the deluge imminent; he visits Abraham on his sickbed; he condoles with Isaac after the death of Abraham"; and so on.[70] Obviously, interpretations like these cannot be reconciled with any aversion to anthropomorphism. Are they out of harmony, as well, with the idea of God's otherness?

God's otherness is a very indefinite idea. It has no real power of generalization. A possible generalization is the principle that God must not be compared in any manner to "His creations." But this principle may be violated in

[69] S. Schechter, op. cit., p. 37.

[70] Ibid. Quoted above, p. 141.

order "to soothe the ear;" further, it is applied very unevenly – a metaphor about God is questioned whereas the ascription of "a likeness" to Him is not. Nor can the biblical verses used by the Rabbis in support of the idea supply a clue for a generalization. Here, too, there is no consistency; in the structural stereotypes, Ezek. 43:2 supports the idea,[71] whereas in other instances the same verse is called into question.[72] Were there a rabbinic term for the idea of God's otherness, the idea would have been a value-concept perhaps, and hence have had the generalizing power of a value-concept. But the idea is not conveyed by a conceptual term, and it is not a value-concept. Of all the rabbinic ideas, this is, without a doubt, the most indefinite.

This does not mean, however, that it is an idea that has little in common with the general character of rabbinic thought. On the contrary, the indefinite character of the idea is in accord with the entire midrashic approach. In the midrashic approach, as we may recall, an extremely important rôle is played by the element of indeterminacy. A biblical text may touch off any number of haggadic interpretations; the biblical text, therefore, acts as a non-determining stimulus.[73] More to the point here, the atmosphere of belief in which the haggadic interpretations are given and received is that of indeterminate belief, an indeterminacy which, on occasion, can harden and become determinate.[74] But if the idea of God's otherness is an indefinite idea, it is subject from the outset to indeterminacy of belief. While it is firmly upheld on occasion, inconsistencies and exceptions are also permitted. Among the interpretations eliciting indeterminacy of belief, therefore, none are more striking, or more easy to identify, than some of the

[71] See above, p. 274.

[72] See ibid., p. 312.

[73] Above, p. 132.

[74] Ibid., pp. 133 ff.

interpretations involving the idea of God's otherness. We refer especially to the structural stereotypes. They strongly suggest the idea of God's otherness; at the same time, they concretize God's love or His justice in a manner thoroughly out of keeping with that idea. Such interpretations imply an attitude of indeterminate belief, an attitude that permits of shadings in belief.

Interpretations such as those in the list given by Schechter are really no different in character. They, too, concretize God's love, or His justice, or His holiness, and in such fashion as apparently to contradict the idea of His otherness. But they no more ignore the idea of God's otherness than do the haggadic stereotypes, if that idea represents an emphatic trend. They, too, like the stereotypes, therefore, imply an attitude of indeterminate belief. Interpretations depicting "a sort of *Imitatio hominis* on the part of God" are not dogmatic statements. They are all instances of a belief that is indefinite, of an attitude of mind that is left uncrystallized.

It is impossible so to coordinate the haggadic elements here as to produce a clear-cut, logical system. By the same token, they are all reflections of actual experience. Haggadic concretizations of the concepts of God's love and justice derive from the daily experience of God's love and justice in the world. The idea of God's otherness is indefinite because the consciousness of His otherness is mystical, private, all but inexpressible. Indeterminacy of belief refers back to the category of significance, to the creative and nondeterminate aspects of the valuational life, and that in turn goes back to the unpredictability and novelty characteristic of organismic function.[75] No static ideational principle unites these elements. Expressions of an organismal mental and cultural complex, they interweave and interact in a dynamic and subtle manner of their own.

[75] See above, p. 23 f.

IV. ANTHROPOMORPHISM AND TARGUM ONKELOS

Medieval philosophers found support for their attitude toward anthropomorphism in the Aramaic versions of the Bible, and especially in Targum Onkelos on the Pentateuch.[1] The discussion that has ensued has continued down to our own day. A consideration of some of the problems involved will, we believe, bring into stronger relief the difficulties inherent in the philosophic approach. It will also enable us to take up a phase of the idea of God's otherness, or rather a matter closely associated with that idea, that we have not dealt with heretofore.

Onkelos made it his task, says Maimonides, to oppose the belief in God's corporeality; hence, any expression in the Bible that might imply this belief Onkelos paraphrases in accordance with its true meaning.[2] Now motion implies corporeality. Any reference to motion by God is therefore interpreted by Onkelos to mean the revelation or appearance of a (Divine) Light created (for the occasion), namely, *Shekinah* or Providence.[3] "Thus he translates 'The Lord will come down' (Exod. 19:11) – 'The Lord will reveal Himself'; 'And the Lord came down' (ibid., v. 20) – 'And the Lord revealed Himself.' "[4] Nor is Gen. 46:4, although rendered literally, a real exception, for that verse is in the context of a prophetic dream and does not relate an actual occurrence.[5] Maimonides also calls attention to other passages which, according to him, Onkelos so translates as to

[1] This goes back to Saadia, the first medieval Jewish philosopher. See his Ha-'Emunot Weha-De'ot, II, 9 end. Cf. H. Malter, Saadia Gaon (Philadelphia: Jewish Publication Society of America, 1921), p. 144, note 311. On Targum Onkelos, see above, p. 101.

[2] Maimonides, Moreh Nebukim, Part I, Chap. 27; ed. Ibn Samuel (J. Kaufman) (Tel-Aviv, 1935), I, p. 114. See Ibn Samuel's commentary there.

[3] Ibid. (On "Divine Light," see above, p. 282, where we spoke of it in connection with the views of Yehudah Ha-Levi).

[4] Ibid.

[5] Ibid. Maimonides adds that Onkelos may have understood the verse to refer to an angel.

avoid any implication of anthropomorphism, such as Exod. 17:15, where the expression "The hand upon the throne of the Lord" is paraphrased by Onkelos.[6] Again, where the term "to hear" is applied to God, Onkelos translates, "It was heard before the Lord," or, where there is a reference to prayer, as in Exod. 22:22, "I will surely accept."[7] Finally, Maimonides seeks for a consistent principle in the renderings of the term "to see" as applied to God, since Onkelos sometimes translates "The Lord saw" and sometimes "It was revealed before the Lord."[8]

Naḥmanides is opposed to every detail of this thesis. He asserts that "among the words of the Rabbis many things demonstrate that the name *Shekinah* is indeed (that of) God,"[9] and for this assertion, we saw above, there is ample support in Talmud and Midrash.[10] He argues that Maimonides is utterly unwarranted in taking the rendering "The Lord will reveal Himself" to refer to a revelation of a Divine Light.[11] Do Onkelos' deviations from a literal rendering stem from a desire to remove any implications of anthropomorphism? If so, why does he translate literally when the term "to speak" is applied to God? As to the term "to see," Onkelos employs a consistent principle, to be sure, but not the one attributed to him by Maimonides. When "seeing" is used by the Bible in the sense of "understanding," Onkelos translates accordingly, but otherwise the translation is literal, and this, examples show, whether the term "to see" refers to God or to men. Nor are there lacking other examples of literal translations of anthropomorphisms. "The Lord thy God is He who *goeth over* before

[6] Ibid., Chap. 28.

[7] Ibid., Chap. 48.

[8] Ibid. He encounters a number of exceptions to the principle, and suggests that those exceptions are textual errors.

[9] Naḥmanides, Commentary to the Pentateuch, Gen. 46:1.

[10] See above, p. 223 f.

[11] Naḥmanides, l. c.

thee" (Deut. 9:3) is translated literally, although the verse applies motion to God, and so is the verse, "Behold I will *stand* before thee on the rock in Horeb" (Exod. 17:16). Likewise translated literally are the verses "written with the *finger* of God" (Exod. 31:18, Deut. 9:10); "Thy *right hand*, O Lord, glorious in power, Thy *right hand*, O Lord, dasheth in pieces the enemy" (Exod. 15:6); "Thou stretchedst out Thy *right hand*" (ibid., v. 12); "Thy strong *hand*" (Deut. 3:24); "by a mighty *hand* and by an outstretched *arm*" (Deut. 5:15, ibid., 26:8); ". . . and My *hand* take hold on judgment" (ibid., 32:41); "the *eyes* of the Lord thy God are always upon it" (ibid., 11:12). These and other examples are given by Naḥmanides as evidence that Onkelos was not troubled by the problem of anthropomorphism.[12] What did guide Onkelos, according to cryptic allusions by Naḥmanides, is known to men versed in the secrets of Kabbalah.[13]

Why does Maimonides try to establish a consistency in Onkelos' deviations from literal rendering? Because he holds that Onkelos is teaching that God is incorporeal, and the idea of the incorporeality of God involves a consistent philosophic system. Any anthropomorphism in Onkelos, therefore, is only apparently one, and can be accounted for. In turn, the accounting for such apparent anthropomorphisms brings forth further philosophic aspects of the idea of God's incorporeality. When Isaac Abarbanel reckons with the anthropomorphisms listed by Naḥmanides he finds it necessary to enlarge on the philosophic structure provided by Maimonides; in his first answer, for instance, he distinguishes between anthropomorphisms that imply a change in God, such as motion, and anthropomorphisms that refer to God's will or decree, such as "speaking."[14]

[12] Ibid.

[13] Ibid. וסודם ידוע למשכילים and דברים ידועים בקבלה וסודם ליודעים חן. SEE NOTES, P. 371.

[14] Isaac Abarbanel, Commentary to Moreh Nebukim, I,27. In this argument

We are calling attention here to the character of the idea thus attributed to Onkelos. When an aversion to anthropomorphism is attributed to Onkelos, what is really attributed to him is an idea with numerous philosophic implications, an idea wholly and completely within the philosophic universe of discourse.

A curious fallacy seems to have developed in regard to the philosophic idea of God's incorporeality. If the more subtle implications of that idea are avoided, some scholars seem to say, the idea itself is not really philosophic. These scholars declare that their approach to Onkelos is nonphilosophic, yet their explanations for the renderings of Onkelos include the idea of God's incorporeality. Now, however, that idea accounts only for certain deviations; they assign other reasons for the remaining deviations or for the nondeviations. The explanatory scope of the idea of God's incorporeality has been curtailed. But if the philosophic approach is wrong, it does not become right when the renderings so accounted for are fewer in number.

Isaac Arama's theory is a case in point. To account for the renderings of Onkelos, Arama declares, we need resort neither to philosophy, that is, Maimonides' thesis, nor to the mysticism of Naḥmanides.[15] When Onkelos departs from the literal sense of a verse, according to Arama, he does so for one of several reasons, not because of an inclusive general principle.[16] Thus, Onkelos uses the expression "*Yeḳara*' (Glory) of the Lord," in reference to God's coming, or appearing, or standing, or going up, as, for example, "And the *Yeḳara*' of the Lord went up," instead of "And

he bases himself on the thought in the Moreh I, 55. In some of his other arguments, he speaks of differences between his texts of Onkelos and that of Naḥmanides. Our texts, so far as I can discover, agree with those of Naḥmanides on the disputed points.

[15] Isaac Arama, עקדת יצחק, Gate 31, comment on Gen. 46:3 (at the end of this comment).

[16] Ibid.

God went up" (Gen. 17:22); and he uses this expression out of respect or reverence for God, just as in addressing the nobility men use terms like "your honor," "your highness," and the like.[17] Arama in this explanation is nonphilosophic, but it is the only one in which he is clearly so. Of the other reasons he gives for Onkelos' deviations, one is "the removal of anthropomorphisms," and a second is "the removal of (expressions implying) a change (in God)."[18] Examples are lacking, unless he means those in his discussion on *Memra'* and *Shekinta'*. But the principles he employs in that discussion are very unclear.[19]

A great modern scholar, S. D. Luzzatto, quotes Arama with warm approval.[20] An outspoken opponent of the philosophic school,[21] he agrees with Arama that Onkelos' deviations are not to be explained by a single inclusive principle. Luzzatto analyzes these deviations anew,[22] and we shall have occasion soon to draw upon some of his many valuable contributions. But he, too, does not free himself altogether from the philosophic approach. Among the categories into which he divides Onkelos' deviations, there is one couched in philosophic terms. A number of deviations are made, he says, lest "attributes, actions, and changes in nature (i.e., affections) be ascribed to God that might lower His honor and His glory in the mind of the masses."[23] Since the criterion is God's honor, he adds, some deviations

[17] Ibid.

[18] Ibid. — ההתפעלות.

[19] Ibid. Onkelos uses *Memra'*, he says, for God's Providence, while for its steady continuance he uses *Shekinta'*. But if so, there are occasions when he should have used *Shekinta'* instead of *Memra'* in the very examples cited, e. g., Gen. 28:15, ibid., v. 20; moreover, there are verses where such an explanation of *Memra'* is not possible even in a forced interpretation, e. g. Lev. 26:14; ibid., v. 18.

[20] S. D. Luzzatto, אוהב גר (Cracow, 1905), Introd. p. XI.

[21] See the references above, p. 286, note 55.

[22] S. D. Luzzatto, op. cit., Part I.

[23] Ibid., pp. 3, 8, 11, 19 — להרחיק התארים, הפעולות, וההתפעליות, אשר יחוסן אל הבורא יוכל למעט כבודו והדרתו בלב ההמון.

merely replace one anthropomorphism by another but a more dignified one — such as "And with a word of Thy mouth" in place of "And with the blast of Thy nostrils" (Exod. 15:8),[24] and "under the throne of His Glory" in place of "And under His feet" (ibid., 24:10).[25]

But is God's honor the sole criterion? Is there not also the apprehension lest "attributes, actions and affections be ascribed to God," a philosophic apprehension? To be sure, the apprehension concerns only expressions that might appear gross to the common folk; but are the common folk affected by philosophic considerations? It is Luzzatto's own contention that philosophical considerations have no place in religion. His use of philosophical terms has led him here to a conclusion from which he himself dissents.

When an aversion to anthropomorphism is attributed to Onkelos, after the manner of Maimonides, what is attributed to Onkelos is an intricate philosophical idea. Attempts so far at a more simple explanation of his deviations, however, have not been wholly successful. The approach has remained in part philosophic, and as a result the explanations attempted are not free of contradictions. Since Targum Onkelos is a rabbinic version,[26] it is once more evident that philosophy and rabbinic thought are two distinct and different worlds. To employ *any* philosophic criterion in an approach to Targum Onkelos leads us nowhere. We cannot speak of Targum Onkelos, therefore, as making a principle either of the incorporeality of God or of the corporeality of God.[27]

[24] Ibid., p. 8.

[25] Ibid., p. 11.

[26] See above, p. 101 and the references there. The Rabbis speak of Targum Onkelos as "our Targum" — Ḳiddushin 49a.

[27] Ezekiel Kaufmann (op. cit., p. 232 f. and the notes) holds that Targum Onkelos reflects the belief in the corporeality of God. The deviations are for the purpose of imparting an idea of the sublimity of God. This accords with his thought that the Rabbis in general held that God is corporeal. See above, p. 282 f. Kauf-

Targum Onkelos, like rabbinic literature in general, teaches the idea of the otherness of God. That is why the Targum, instead of translating literally expressions in which seeing, hearing and the like are applied to God, often employs circumlocutions of one kind or another. On the other hand, as Naḥmanides and others have pointed out, many such expressions *are* translated literally. The Targum, then, is not consistent. But now we are not called upon to account for every deviation and nondeviation, for consistency here is not to be expected. The idea of God's otherness is a very indefinite idea; it permits of exceptions and it ignores inconsistencies.[28] This is the case, we saw, when the idea is applied in halakic as well as in haggadic sections in the Midrash, and Targum Onkelos may be considered as part of midrashic literature. Despite being largely a literal translation, it also teaches many rabbinic ideas and laws.[29] Among the rabbinic ideas taught by Targum Onkelos is the idea of God's otherness.

In teaching that idea, the Targum often employs the terms *Memra'*, *Yeḳara'*, and *Shekinta'*.[30] Some examples out of many are: "And I will make My covenant between My *Memra'* and thee" for "And I will make My covenant between Me and thee" (Gen. 17:2); "And the *Yeḳara'* of the Lord went up" for "And God went up" (ibid., v. 22); "Is the *Shekinta'* of the Lord among us" for "Is the Lord among us" (Exod. 17:7).

mann's approach here is entirely philosophical. Teaching the sublimity of God, or the exalting of Him, he says apparently, is an intermediate step in the direction of removing God from any contact with matter (op. cit., p. 232).

[28] For the basis of this statement, see the discussion above, pp. 322–324.

[29] See Luzzatto, op. cit., pp. 8, 9, 17, 22. Luzzatto's category here consists of deviations because "of the oral Torah and the interpretations of the Rabbis." But many more deviations belong in this category, although he reckons with them under some of his other categories. See OT, p. 318, note 177, where a number of such deviations are cited.

[30] For these terms Luzzatto (op. cit., p. 13) avoids an explanation and simply quotes what Arama says on them.

Memra' means the word, *Yeḳara'* means the honor or the glory, and *Shekinta'* has the connotation of "abiding."[31] These terms are often used in special connections, as Moore has shown,[32] and hence are certainly not interchangeable. And yet it is fair to say that their character is due less to their individual meanings than to their common function.[33] Moore gives to *Memra'* the function of being, in many contexts, "a buffer-word," introduced "where the literal interpretation seemed to bring God into too close contact with his creatures."[34] *Yeḳara'* and *Shekinta'*, he adds, are also "buffer-words."[35] It is hard to see how Moore can say this and also emphasize, as he does, the "accessibility of God"[36] and "the intimacy of the religious relation."[37] The terms introduced by the Targum have indeed a common function, but it is not that of being "buffer-words." They have the purpose not of interposing any distance between God and His creatures but that of cultivating an awareness of His otherness, an awareness that He is other than His creatures.

The *Memra'*, *Yeḳara'*, and *Shekinta'* of the Lord have much in common with epithets for God, such as the *Maḳom*, the Holy One blessed be He, and the like. These epithets or appellations, found so profusely in the Talmud and Midrash, are not indications, as some have supposed, that to the Rabbis God was remote and unapproachable; that notion, as we saw, is disproved by passage after passage.[38] On the contrary, being reverential *names* for God, the appellatives reflect a mystical experience of relationship to

[31] See the next note.

[32] See Moore, Judaism, Vol. I, p. 417 f.

[33] Moore, ibid., p. 418, note 1, quotes Strack-Billerbeck who conclude that *Memra'* is "ein inhaltsloser, rein formalhafter Ersatz für das Tetragramm."

[34] Ibid., p. 419.

[35] Ibid., pp. 434–5.

[36] Ibid., p. 423 f.

[37] Ibid., p. 442.

[38] See above, p. 204 f.

God, a poignant sense of closeness to Him.[39] But this consciousness of relationship is unique, it is fraught with the awareness of the otherness of God, and hence the appellatives are expressions of that awareness. Much of what applies to the appellatives applies as well to *Memra'*, *Yeḳara'* and *Shekinta'*; in fact, *Ha-Dibbur, Ha-Kabod,* and *Shekinah,* the Hebraic forms, are appellatives for God in the Talmud and the Midrash,[40] and *Shekinah* is used on just those occasions when the Rabbis wish particularly to stress God's nearness to man.[41] Like the appellatives, the Targum terms, then, are reverential expressions for God, and they, too, reflect a consciousness of relationship to Him. The Targum terms differ from the appellatives, however, in one respect; they are used in special connections, whereas the appellatives are, for the most part, interchangeable. To be used in special connections means to be used with a specific intention. What is that specific intention? It cannot be that of interposing any distance between God and His creatures, as we have seen, yet the terms are reverential terms. In view of the rabbinic emphasis on the otherness of God, we must say that the Targum terms are used with the intention of cultivating an awareness of God's otherness.

Mention of reverential terms for God brings us to the discussion of another word frequently used in order to express reverence. "And Cain said before the Lord" (Gen. 4:13), "And Abraham prayed before the Lord" (ibid., 20:17),[42] "And Moses returned before the Lord" (Exod. 5:22) — in these and in many other places Targum Onkelos has "before" instead of "unto."[43] This usage is undoubtedly

[39] See ibid.; also ibid., p. 271.

[40] See the reference ibid., p. 204, note 11.

[41] See ibid., pp. 225 ff.

[42] Onkelos usually interprets *'Elohim* as the Tetragrammaton where the word represents the name of God — see Luzzatto, op. cit., p. 28, and S. B. Schefftel, Biure Onkelos (Munich, 1888), p. 3.

[43] A similar usage is characteristic of rabbinic literature in general. "Instead

an expression of reverence, as can be seen from an analogous use of "before" in the Aramaic of the Book of Daniel: "The Chaldeans answered before the king" (Dan. 2:10), and "None other that can declare it before the king" (ibid., v. 11).[44]

But what are reverence and honor if not a recognition of otherness? When expressions of honor are used with regard to a king, are they not a means of marking him off from his subjects? Analogously, similar expressions of honor and reverence are used in regard to God, but now the otherness is no longer a matter of degree or comparison. Reverence for God and the recognition of God's otherness go together, therefore, and expressions of reverence often convey also the suggestion of His otherness. This is true of certain usages of the term "before," of which only one type will be given here. The Targum renders "And when it was heard before the Lord" for "And when the Lord heard it" (Num. 11:1); again, "And it was heard before the Lord" for "And the Lord heard it" (ibid., 12:2). In these, and in many similar renderings, the introduction of "before," indicative of reverence, also makes it possible to avoid saying "the Lord heard"; reverence is expressed here, but there is also an emphasis on God's otherness.

Deviations or circumlocutions that can be attributed to reverence for God also teach the idea of His otherness. "And the Lord smelled the sweet savour" (Gen. 8:21), for example, is rendered, "And the Lord accepted his sacrifice with pleasure"; similarly, "And with the blast of Thy nostrils" (Exod. 15:8) is rendered, "And with a word of Thy mouth." Particularly in the second instance, one anthropomorphism is substituted for another; and hence all that motivates these changes, according to Luzzatto, is reverence

of the natural expression, 'Moses said to Him', the Rabbis employ the circumlocution: 'Moses said before Him (לפניו)' " — TE, p. 44.

[44] Luzzatto, op. cit., p. 12.

for God.[45] Do they not also teach, however, that such expressions as "smelling a sweet savour" and "blast of Thy nostrils" cannot really be applied to God – that God is other?

Two schools of thought have attempted to account for the marked inconsistencies in Targum Onkelos. Attributing an aversion to anthropomorphism to the Targum, the philosophers find in the apparent inconsistencies only further elaborations of that basic philosophic idea. The anti-philosophic school endeavors to find more simple explanations, the clearest by far being that of Luzzatto. According to him, anthropomorphisms that might lower the honor and glory of God in the eyes of the masses are removed or softened; otherwise anthropomorphisms are translated literally, and hence the inconsistencies. But Luzzatto, who is an opponent of the philosophic school, has taken his criterion from philosophy after all. The aversion to anthropomorphism, "to ascribe to God attributes, actions and changes in nature," is still a philosophic aversion, even if it is only an aversion to a degree.

From our standpoint, the inconsistencies are to be expected. Targum Onkelos, so authentically rabbinic as to be characterized by the Rabbis as "our Targum,"[46] emphasizes the idea of God's otherness. That idea is an emphatic trend in rabbinic literature, but it is at the same time very indefinite, not even being epitomized in a conceptual term, and it permits inconsistencies and exceptions. Undoubtedly reverence to God, deference to His honor, also have much to do with the deviations to be found in the Targum; but reverence for God and the emphasis on His otherness go together. In fact, the emphasis on God's

[45] Luzzatto, op. cit., pp. 3, 8. "Sweet savour" in reference to sacrifice is always similarly rendered — e. g. Num. 28:2; ibid., v. 6, etc.

[46] See above, p. 330, note 26.

otherness may be regarded as the criterion for the changes made out of reverence for Him; that is to say, the honor of God demanded that a change be made that would teach the idea of His otherness.[47] Instead of a philosophic criterion, the criterion was authentically rabbinic, a reflection of the normal mysticism of the Rabbis.

V. SUMMARY

Rabbinic thought and philosophic thought constitute two different universes of discourse. Problems like that of anthropomorphism, ideas like that of the incorporeality of God, are philosophic problems and ideas. The incorporeality of God is an idea in a coordinated system of ideas, a system built up by ratiocination, a speculative system. But rabbinic thought is not speculative; it is organismic. Rabbinic ideas are not built up by ratiocination; they refer back directly to experience, and hence the integration of thought here is not a matter of design but of the interpenetration of concepts.

It is wrong, therefore, to attribute to the Rabbis any aversion to anthropomorphism as such. Implied in that aversion is the idea of the incorporeality of God, a philosophic

[47] We have not dealt here with the "corrections of the Soferim." These are changes made in the text of the Bible itself, the alteration generally being limited to a single letter. The justification for these corrections, according to Lieberman, is very likely the rabbinic dictum: "It is better that one letter be removed from the Torah than that the Divine name be publicly profaned." See his Hellenism in Jewish Palestine, pp. 28–37, where new light is shed on the entire problem.

The corrections of the Soferim, we may add, have nothing to do with the deviations in Targum Onkelos. The corrections of the Soferim were made simply on the ground that the original expressions were irreverent, derogatory; no other criterion was necessary. But this is not the case with the paraphrases in Targum Onkelos. Why should an expression like "the Lord heard" be regarded as in need of paraphrase? Obviously, some criterion must have been in mind. For the philosophic school, the criterion is an aversion to anthropomorphism. The criterion we attribute to Targum Onkelos is the idea of God's otherness.

idea. On the other hand, it is equally wrong to say that the Rabbis had not developed an abstract conception of God. To say so would be to imply that rabbinic thought is an undeveloped, or a partially developed, form of philosophic thought. *Any* attempt to depict rabbinic thought in philosophic terms is bound to do violence to rabbinic thought.

Certain apprehensive questions and expressions in rabbinic literature, however, present a problem. For example, after quoting "And the Lord went before them by day" (Exod. 13:21), the Rabbis ask, "Is it possible to say so?" Some present-day scholars see in such a question an aversion to anthropomorphism. Others contend that it does not yet indicate the development of a abstract conception of God. Both theories obviously employ philosophic standards and terms. If neither theory is correct, how then are we to explain these rabbinic questions and expressions?

All these questions and expressions of the Rabbis have reference to definite statements in the Bible. They are characteristic of a development in Judaism, not a development in the direction of philosophy, but of an indigenous development, namely, that of rabbinic thought out of the Bible. Medieval Jewish philosophy is neither a continuation of that development nor in line with it. Rabbinic thought alone has its roots firmly in the Bible, and it alone remains united with the Bible in a living bond.

There are three types of rabbinic concepts, so far as their relationship to the Bible is concerned. One type consists of concepts having conceptual terms that are not found in the Bible; despite this, such concepts are in many instances at least foreshadowed in the Bible. In the second type of concept, the conceptual term is the same as the biblical but with wider, more universal, connotations. In the third type, too, the conceptual term is a biblical term, although there is no definite connection in the concepts of this type between the biblical terms and the same terms as used by the Rabbis; nevertheless, this group of rabbinic concepts also has biblical antecedents. Rabbinic value-concepts, then, have biblical antecedents. The changes that have taken place have either made the rabbinic concept more applicable than its biblical antecedent, or else have given the rabbinic concept greater range and universality.

The rabbinic complex of concepts is thus a development out of the Bible, but its relation to the Bible goes even further. There is a living bond between rabbinic thought and the Bible. By acting as a stimulus to haggadic ideas, the Bible plays a never ending rôle in the development of rabbinic thought. But even more dependent on the Bible than Haggadah is Halakah. The dependence of Halakah on the Bible is such, indeed, that the dichotomy of *derash* and *peshaṭ*, rabbinic interpretation and the simple meaning of the biblical text, so basic in Haggadah, does not hold for the Halakah.

Rabbinic thought is marked by certain major trends, trends that rise to expression in the rabbinic concepts. These trends, like everything else in rabbinic thought, are rooted in the Bible, but in rabbinic literature they are given much greater emphasis. To be reckoned among these great emphatic trends in rabbinic thought is the emphasis on normal mysticism. A mystical relationship to God, taken for granted in the Bible, is now consciously cultivated, and hence attains a new development, a new emphasis. Some of the aspects of this normal mysticism are, indeed, so strongly emphasized, particular ideas being given so great a stress, as to constitute, in a sense, a departure from the Bible.

An idea stressed in this manner is the idea of the otherness of God. In rabbinic literature, the idea is not epitomized in a conceptual term; the phrase "the otherness of God" is our own, and it is justified only to the extent that it is helpful in analysis. Nor could that idea have been crystallized in a term. Of the very essence of the God-experience of the Rabbis, implicit in their very consciousness of a relationship to God, the otherness of God relates to the deeply private aspect of that experience. The nearest approach to such a term consists of the generic terms for God themselves.

Though the idea is vividly expressed in the Bible, the Rabbis accent it still more strongly. As found in rabbinic thought and law, the idea of the otherness of God represents a foliation, a development of the antecedent biblical idea. An entire rabbinic tractate, the tractate of *'Abodah Zarah,* is devoted to laws and prohibitions with regard to every aspect of idol worship; it endeavors to preclude the remotest contact with idolatry. As a sheer idea, however, the otherness of God stands out more prominently in midrashic literature. There the idea is given expression in a number of different ways. Statements in the Bible that seem to compare God to His creatures, say the Rabbis, have merely a pedagogic purpose – "to soothe the ear." Again, biblical verses that "liken the Creator to His creation" are regarded by the Rabbis as only poetic, or rather prophetic, license. Further, the Rabbis reinterpret the sacrifices and other aspects of Temple ritual, and sometimes they even interpret verses away. Various means are thus employed to teach the idea of God's otherness, each an endeavor to overcome biblical verses that seem to contradict the idea.

The idea of God's otherness is also expressed through structural stereotypes. One such stereotype begins with quoting a verse like "And the Lord went before them by day" (Exod. 13:20), a verse which causes the Rabbis to ask, "Is it possible to say so?" What follows, however, is an affirmation of the verse in question. All the haggadic stereotypes are constructed in the same manner. The idea of God's otherness is suggested, no more; the primary function of the stereotypes is to stress concretizations of

God's love or of His justice at the expense of His otherness, as it were. How could the Rabbis at the same time both teach and not teach the idea of God's otherness?

Despite being an emphatic trend, the idea of God's otherness is a very indefinite idea. Not epitomized in a conceptual term, it has no real power of generalization. It allows exceptions and permits inconsistencies. It is therefore an idea that is subject from the outset to indeterminacy of belief, and it is that kind of belief that is evoked by the structural stereotypes. They are instances of a belief that is indefinite, of an attitude of mind that is left uncrystallized.

Targum Onkelos represents still another means of teaching the idea of God's otherness. Paraphrases and circumlocutions in the Targum are not the result of an aversion to anthropomorphism. Often they are indicative of reverence for God, but expressions of reverence and the idea of otherness go together. Reverence for God demanded paraphrases be made that would teach the idea of His otherness.

The idea of God's otherness, though not a rabbinic value-concept, is nonetheless characteristic of rabbinic thought. Unlike a philosophic idea, it is not clearly defined, and it does not fit into a nicely articulated system of ideas. The idea of God's otherness refers back to experience, to a deeply private aspect of experience. Not spun into a speculative idea, it remains, for all the emphasis laid upon it, not really crystallized, not wholly generalized, indefinite.

VI. RABBINIC DOGMA

In their own fashion, the Rabbis crystallized several of their beliefs into dogmas. But these dogmas differ widely in their character from the dogmas of medieval Jewish thought, and they do not constitute a creed.

If there is any definitely dogmatic element in rabbinic thought, it is associated with the words מודה, "acknowledge" or "admit," and כופר, "deny." These terms are employed in the Halakah[1]; they are not confined to the Halakah, however. Our concern here is with those contexts where acknowledgment or denial indicates that we have to do with a belief or with what appears to be a belief.

Once more we must distinguish between the philosophic approach and the rabbinic approach. Maimonides devotes the first four of his Thirteen Articles of Faith to the dogmas of the existence and incorporeality of God[2]; the first chapter of his code deals with the same theme[3]; in his *Guide*, he sets forth the twenty-six propositions of Aristotle in proof of the existence and incorporeality of God, discussing them and finding fault only with the one concerning the eternity of the universe.[4] But even the phrase, "the existence of God,"[5] a phrase so characteristic of the approach of Maimonides and other philosophers, is not to be found in rabbinic literature. Normal mysticism does not call for a systematic demonstration of God's existence. True, the Rabbis speak of acknowledgment of God and of denial of God. What the Rabbis refer to, however, is not a philosophic doctrine. The background of acknowledgment or denial, as some of the statements reveal, is experience of God.

Rabbi Ṭarfon finds the idolaters' denial of God less reprehensible than that of *Minim*, Jewish sectarians. "For the worshippers of *'Abodah Zarah* (idolaters) do not know Him and deny Him; but these (the sectarians) know Him and deny Him, and it is of them that Scripture says, 'And

[1] As in the case, for example, where the plaintiff claims the debt to consist of both vessels and landed estate, and the defendant *admits* the debt concerning vessels but *denies* it as to landed estate — Shebu'ot VI.3.

[2] Maimonides, Commentary to the Mishnah, Sanhedrin, Introd. to Chap. X.

[3] Ibid., Mishneh Torah, Hilkot Yesode Ha-Torah, Chap. I.

[4] Ibid., Moreh Nebukim, II, Introduction; Chaps. 1, 13–19.

[5] מציאות השם. For its use see the three preceding references.

behind the doors and the posts hast thou cast thy memory (of Me)' (Is. 57:8)."[6] The entire context of this statement abounds in points of interest, but we shall restrict ourselves to the phrase that the sectarians "know Him and deny Him." When the expression מכירין אותו is used with respect to human relationship, it refers to direct personal acquaintance, to immediate "knowledge,"[7] and it must have therefore a similar connotation here. The idea thus conveyed is made still more explicit by the supporting text from Scripture. According to our passage, then, the sectarians have deliberately put away the memory of Him whom they have known in their actual experience. In other words, denial of God is nothing else than willful rejection of God.

Even when the Rabbis use the more general ידע in speaking of knowledge of God, it is not a matter of doctrine that they have in mind. In a comment on Lev. 26:4 – "But if ye will not hearken unto Me" – they stress the word "Me," saying that the verse refers to him "that knows his Master" but makes it his deliberate intention to rebel against Him, and citing Nimrod and the people of Sodom as examples.[8] By knowledge of God the Rabbis hence mean a consciousness of relationship to God. Wicked men possess that consciousness, too; in their wickedness they willfully, deliberately, rebel against Him.

The Rabbis speak of the man who denies God as one "who denies the root."[9] He that commits blasphemy "has

[6] שעובדי ע"ז אין מכירין אותו וכופרין בו והללו מכירין אותו וכופרין בו — Tosefta Shabbat XIII (XIV). 5, ed. Zuck.-Lieb., p. 129, and the parallels referred to. Add Tanḥuma, ed. Buber, IV, p. 48a which reads שעובדי ע"ז אינן מכירין את הקב"ה וכופרין בו. On the rendering here of Is. 57:8, see Rashi's gloss on Shabbat 116a, s. v. ואחר הדלת.

[7] See, for example, Rosh Ha-Shanah II.1.

[8] Sifra, בחוקותי, II, ed. Weiss, p. 111b.

[9] כופר בעיקר — e. g., Sanhedrin 38b. It is only in medieval Jewish philosophy that *'iḳḳar* (root) has the meaning of "dogma" or "fundamental principle." On the use of the word by the philosophers, see Albo, Sefer Ha-'Iḳḳarim, ed. Husik (Philadelphia: Jewish Publication Society of America, 1929), I, p. 55 f.

denied the root."[10] But repentance avails even for him. R. Eleazar declares that, though a man may have blasphemed in the marketplace, publicly, "the Holy One blessed be He says to him: Do *Teshubah* (repent) in private (lit., between Me and you), and I shall receive you."[11] Preceding this statement is one by R. Judah b. Simon: "'Return, O Israel, unto the Lord thy God' (Hos. 14:2) – even if you have denied the root."[12] Now repentance involves religious experience. If the Rabbis call upon him who denies God to repent, they must assume such denial to be a willful aberration. A Jew who denies God is to the Rabbis a person who rejects God despite his own experience of God.

Acceptance of God's Kingship, of *Malkut Shamayim*, is a sheer religious experience.[13] Similarly, when the Rabbis use the word מודה in reference to the acknowledgment of God, it is experience of God that the Rabbis have in mind. This is certainly the impression left by a rabbinic comment on Ps. 50:8 ff. "I will not reprove thee for thy sacrifices . . . If I were hungry I would not tell thee . . . I know all the fowls of the mountains . . . For every beast of the forest is Mine . . . Do I eat the flesh of bulls, or drink the blood of goats?" (ibid., vv. 8–13).[14] But the Psalm continues with: "Offer unto God the sacrifice of thanksgiving; and pay thy vows unto the Most High" (ibid., v. 14). Quoting these magnificent verses with their vivid disparagement of animal sacrifices, the Rabbis add to them a comment as to the attitude really required by God. By means of a play on תודה, "thanksgiving," the Rabbis so interpret this last

[10] See Sanhedrin 45b–46a, 49b.

[11] Pesiḳta de R. Kahana, ed. Buber, p. 163b.

[12] Ibid.

[13] See above, p. 212 f.; and comp. ibid., p. 198 and note 17 there.

[14] This is the order of the verses as quoted by the Rabbis. The rabbinic source is given in the next note.

verse that it is a fitting conclusion to the verses that precede. It is still God who is speaking, according to the Rabbis, and He says: "(I desire) that thou acknowledge Me — שתהא מודה בי — 'and pay thy vows unto the Most High.' "[15] The phrase, "that thou acknowledge Me," indicates that acknowledgment here is not the acceptance of a doctrine. Implied, instead, are an awareness of God — "acknowledge *Me*" — a recognition of relationship to God, fealty to God. Moreover, the phrase is a rabbinic conclusion to verses telling of God's otherness, and the consciousness of God's otherness is an aspect of the experience of God.[16] The entire passage is thus a reflection of rabbinic experience of God.

The next to the last benediction of the '*Amidah*[17] begins with the word מודים. The word here, according to Ginzberg, is most likely an affirmation of belief, not a term denoting gratitude.[18] There is, indeed, the soundest warrant, it seems to us, for regarding it in this conjunction as a term of acknowledgment. The Mishnah states that he who repeats the word מודים (in the benediction), saying it twice, is to be silenced.[19] Repetition of the word, the Babylonian Talmud explains, makes it seem as though there are "two Powers"[20];

[15] Tosefta Menaḥot VII.9, ed. Zuck.-Lieb., p. 522. See S. Lieberman, תוספת ראשונים (Jerusalem: Bamberger and Wahrmann, 1938), II, p. 253. The correct reading is obviously שאמרתי לך and this is the reading in Yalḳuṭ Shime'oni, Pekude, par. 418. From the Yalḳuṭ, too, it is evident that the phrase כבנים שמתפרנסין מאביהן in the Tosefta is a euphemism.

Ps. 50:14 is taken even by some modern commentators to refer to "an attitude of the heart" — see the commentary on Psalms by Chajes (Hebrew). Rashi on the verse takes תודה in the sense of "confession." See also Ibn Ezra on the verse.

[16] A parallel or version of the passage served us as an illustration of the way the Rabbis emphasize God's otherness when discussing the Temple sacrifices — see above, p. 315. See also ibid., p. 307.

[17] Prayer Book, ed. Baer, p. 99; ed. Singer, p. 51. It is one of the six benedictions required in all the '*Amidot*.

[18] Louis Ginzberg, Commentary etc., I, p. 211. See also the commentaries in 'Oẓar Ha-Tefillot, I, p. 179b f.

[19] Berakot V.3; Megillah IV.9.

[20] Berakot 33b.

and it is also undoubtedly this consideration that prompts R. Samuel b. R. Isaac to quote, in the comment of the Palestinian Talmud on the statement of the Mishnah, the verse "For the mouth of them that speak lies shall be stopped" (Ps. 63:12).[21] Now were מודים to mean "(We) thank," which is the way Moore translates the word, his remark that the statement in the Mishnah exhibits "some excess of scruple"[22] would be justified. This is not the way, however, that the word in the benediction should be rendered. In both Talmuds the word מודים in the benediction is linked with *Shema*ʻ – "he that says *Shema*ʻ, *Shema*ʻ is like him who says מודים מודים."[23] But *Shema*ʻ begins the declaration of *Malkut Shamayim,* and it is obvious, therefore, that for the Rabbis the term מודים, in this liturgical setting, has a similar connotation. In other words, if saying *Shema*ʻ twice would seem like acceptance of the sovereignty of "two Powers," saying מודים twice would seem like acknowledgment of "two Powers." Our benediction, then, ought to be rendered as follows: "We acknowledge unto Thee (מודים אנחנו לך) that Thou art the Lord our God and the God of our fathers for ever and ever. Thou art the Rock of our lives, the Shield of our salvation. Generation after generation we will give thanks unto Thee (נודה לך), and declare Thy praise, for our lives which are committed unto Thy hand," etc.[24] In the מודים דרבנן, the wording indicates con-

[21] Yer. Berakot V.3, 9c; Yer. Megillah IV.10, 75c. According to this statement, the prohibition extends only to public worship. The last two letters of דאת in Megillah 75c ought obviously to be deleted.

[22] G. F. Moore, op. cit., Vol. I, p. 365.

[23] This is the statement in Berakot 33b; see also Yer. Megillah, loc. cit.

[24] Ginzberg, loc. cit., briefly remarks that in this benediction, מודים is employed in the rabbinic usage and נודה in the biblical usage. For the phrases in question, see I Chron. 29:13 and Ps. 79:13. As to the Rabbis using a whole biblical phrase, and giving it a turn of their own, see above, p. 295 and the notes — the examples of *ʻOlam.* On the other hand, the Rabbis also employ our phrase in its biblical usage — in the last *Berakah* after the reading of the *Hafṭarah* (Baer, op. cit., p. 228), and in the parallel that is in the second *Berakah* of the grace after meals (ibid., p. 556). On the general prevalence of biblical phrases in the rabbinic

clusively that this rendering is correct. "We acknowledge unto Thee that Thou art the Lord our God and the God of our fathers, the God of all flesh, our Creator," etc.[25]

Everything about this acknowledgment of God reflects its character as a religious experience. It is linked with the declaration of *Malkut Shamayim*. It is expressed in terms of a relationship to God, a felt, mystical relationship—"We acknowledge unto *Thee, Thou* art the Lord our God." There is no such expression of relationship, to be sure, when the word occurs in the phrase כורעים ומשתחוים ומודים of our present liturgy; in these particular instances, however, the word is a later addition.[26]

Acknowledgment of God and acceptance of *Malkut Shamayim* are sometimes associated in the liturgy. According to the Mekilta, the people of Israel accepted the sovereignty of God at the Red Sea when they said, "The Lord will reign for ever and ever" (Exod. 15:18).[27] That idea has been incorporated into the liturgy. In the morning liturgy, toward the close of the long *Berakah* after the *Shema'*, the idea is given there as follows: "All of them together acknowledged—הודו—(Thee) and proclaimed (Thy) Kingship, and said, 'The Lord will reign for ever and ever.' "[28] We have here a verse and what is patently a liturgical introduction to the verse; indeed, in the evening liturgy, too, where the verse is again employed toward the end of the *Berakah* after the *Shema'*, the verse originally had the same

prayers, and especially in the *'Amidah*, see above, p. 207 and the notes there.

[25] Prayer Book, ed. Baer, p. 99; ed. Singer, p. 51.

[26] In our texts, it is found in the *'Alenu* prayer. But Seder R. Amram, ed. Frumkin, II, 151b, reads: ואנו כורעים ומשתחוים למלך וכו'; and Siddur R. Saadia Gaon, ed. Davidson and others, p. 221, reads: ואנו משתחוים למלך וכו'. In our texts, too, the word is found in the *'Abodah* Service of the Day of Atonement. Baer, op. cit., p. 7, points out, however, that it is "a superfluous word," since it is not to be found in the rabbinic sources of this service, or in the manuscripts of the *maḥzorim*. SEE NOTES, P. 371.

[27] See above, p. 19.

[28] Prayer Book, ed. Baer, p. 86; ed. Singer, p. 44.

introduction.[29] If the word הודו means "they gave thanks," the verse so introduced should have been one that also speaks of gratitude to God. But the word means here "they acknowledged (Thee)." It calls for no verse on its own account, since its connotation is similar to that of "they proclaimed (Thy) Kingship." The acknowledgment of God is an experience similar to that of accepting *Malkut Shamayim*.

Acknowledgment of God involves experience of God; denial of God is willful rejection of God despite that experience. Is there an implication of dogma in this use of מודה and כופר?

A rabbinic dogma is a belief which the Rabbis have singled out as one to which all must subscribe. A dogma is a matter of belief, not a matter of daily, personal experience. Acknowledgment of God, on the other hand, involves daily, personal experience; hence it is not a dogma, notwithstanding the terminology.[30] To this double use of terminology there is a parallel in the double use of the word "belief" itself. When the Rabbis speak of belief in God, as we may remember, they refer to faith or trust in God, and thus to normal experience of God.[31] The word "belief" also applies, however, to something that a person accepts as true but that has not occurred in his own experience, and this use of the word "belief," too, is found in rabbinic literature.[32]

[29] See Seder R. Amram, I, 191b, and Siddur R. Saadia Gaon, p. 27.

[30] For the same reason the statement, "There is justice and there is a Judge" (Bereshit R., XXVI.6, ed. Theodor, p. 252), is not a true dogma, in spite of its form. It is given in answer to those that say "There is no justice and there is no Judge" (ibid.), and it is an answer on the part of those who experience God's justice in daily life.

[31] See above, p. 42 f.

[32] See, for example, ibid., p. 136 — the rebuke by R. Joḥanan.

On the basis of the two meanings possessed by the word "belief," we can account for the difference between the passage in Mekilta, II, p. 143 f. and the version found in Mekilta de R. Simon, p. 82 f. In the former, belief refers to trust in

In the concept of *Mattan Torah* (the giving of Torah) we have both a value-concept and a belief. We have shown elsewhere that the term is a generalization, a concept — although it ordinarily refers to the giving of Torah on Sinai, it may stand for other occasions as well.[33] Being a value-concept, *Mattan Torah* allows for differences of opinion on the part of individuals. As against the opinion, for example, that the Glory descended on Sinai, R. Jose holds that "neither Moses nor Elijah went up to heaven, nor did the Glory come down below (i. e., to earth)."[34] In this and in other instances, the concept exhibits that indeterminacy that is characteristic of all value-concepts. Nevertheless, *Mattan Torah* differs from the usual value-concept. The usual value-concept is concretized, made determinate, in actual, everyday experience; *Mattan Torah* points only to occasions of the distant past. But if the concept is not actually concretized in everyday life, it has nonetheless an effect, a great effect, on everyday life. It functions as a belief, and as a belief that gives significance to Halakah and Haggadah.

The terms מודה and כופר are applied to this belief, and hence it is a dogma. Among those whom the Mishnah

God: "The Israelites would look at him and believe in Him who commanded Moses to do so." Compare the parallel in Rosh Ha-Shanah III.8 — "and would subject their heart to their Father in heaven." The Mekilta de R. Simon, however, takes "belief" in the ordinary sense, and hence the text there speaks not of trust in God but of Israel's belief in God's command: "When (the people of) Israel do the will of God and believe in what God commanded Moses, God does for them *Nissim* and *Geburot*." The passage holds to this understanding of "belief" throughout the rest of the interpretations there.

In another passage it is *trust* in God which is associated with *Nissim*. Just as God performed *Nissim* in Egypt, says the Sifra on Lev. 26:13, so will He in the future also perform those mentioned in the verses preceding. The expression used in this connection — "If you do not believe in Me" — refers to trust in God. See Sifra, ed. Weiss, p. 111b, and also Rashi on Lev. 26:13. SEE NOTES, P. 372.

[33] See Aspects of the Rabbinic Concept of Israel, Hebrew Union College Annual, Vol. XIX, pp. 61 ff. See also above, p. 58, note 14.

[34] See above, p. 74.

enumerates as having no portion in the world to come is he that says that the Torah was not (given) from heaven.[35] Those who "deny" in this manner are denying *Mattan Torah*; and it is these persons, apparently, that the version in the Tosefta characterizes as "those who deny the Torah."[36] Another passage states in so many words that "denial" of Torah is the denial of *Mattan Torah,* the giving of Torah. "I shall deny and say, 'Surely, Torah was not given from heaven.' "[37]

The terms indicative of dogmatic belief are applied not only to the Ten Commandments given at Sinai. "Everyone that acknowledges '*Abodah Zarah,*" the Rabbis deduce from biblical verses, "denies (כופר) the Ten Commandments, and what was commanded Moses, and what was commanded the prophets, and what was commanded (the) patriarchs; and everyone that denies '*Abodah Zarah* acknowledges (מודה) the entire Torah."[38] There were some Jews, as Lieberman has pointed out, who became idolaters "under duress or for lucrative reasons."[39] May not the denial of the Ten Commandments, and what was commanded the patriarchs, and so on, also represent actual attitudes of individuals or groups here and there? Another passage is somewhat clearer. According to Ben 'Azzai, the people of Israel were not exiled (to Babylon) until they had denied God, and the Ten Commandments, and circumcision, and the five Books of the Torah.[40] It may well be that Ben 'Azzai takes to task here individuals or groups in his own day. In any case, these passages reveal that the dogma included more than just the belief that

[35] Sanhedrin X.1.

[36] Tosefta Sanhedrin XIII.5, ed. Zuck.-Lieb., p. 434 — ושכפרו בתורה.

[37] Tanḥuma, ed. Buber, IV, p. 48b, and the notes there.

[38] Sifre on Numbers 15:22, ed. Horovitz, p. 116, and the notes and parallels there; (comp. Sifre on Deut. 11:28, ed. Friedmann, p. 86b, and parallels). Adam is reckoned here as among the patriarchs — see also above, p. 38, note 8.

[39] Lieberman, Hellenism in Jewish Palestine, p. 121.

[40] 'Ekah R., I.1, ed. Buber p. 21a, and the parallels.

the Ten Commandments were given by God. It was a matter of dogma that all the Books of the Pentateuch were given by God.[41]

The Books of the Prophets and the *Ketubim* (Hagiographa) are associated with this dogma. Israel said to Asaph, according to the Rabbis, "Is there then another Torah that you say, 'Give ear, O My people, to My Torah' (Ps. 78:1)? We have long ago received it from Mt. Sinai."[42] Asaph speaks in God's name, according to the rabbinic interpretation, and so his Psalm, his teaching, is God's teaching. "The sinners in Israel," the passage has him say, "contend that the Prophets and the *Ketubim* are not Torah, and they do not believe in them"; as to the Prophets, they are refuted by Daniel 9:10 – "Neither have we hearkened to the voice of the Lord our God, to walk in His Torot which He set before us by His servants the prophets"; and hence (the verses show) that the Prophets and the *Ketubim* are indeed Torah.[43] Of course, the entire argument is not Asaph's but that of the Rabbis themselves, and by "the sinners in Israel" they probably refer, as Schechter suggests, to the Samaritans.[44] As against those who "do not believe" in the Prophets and *Ketubim*, the Rabbis insist that the term "Torah" is to be applied not only to the Torah received at Sinai but to the Prophets and

[41] See also Mekilta, ed. Horovitz-Rabin, p. 211 and note 12 there. On the other hand, this dogma was not always strictly interpreted — see above, p. 75, as to the opinion of 'Abaye that the comminations in Deuteronomy were uttered "by Moses himself," and how this opinion contradicts, even in its wording, a specific formulation of the dogma.

[42] Tanḥuma Re'eh I.1; Tanḥuma, ed. Buber, V, 10a; comp. Midrash Tehillim on 78:1, ed. Buber, p. 172b, and see M. Arzt, פרקים ממדרש תהלים כת״י offprint from ספר היובל לכבוד אלכסנדר מארכס, p. 10.

[43] Ibid. Another verse from the *Ketubim* used as proof is Prov. 4:2; this verse also speaks of "My Torah" — the Rabbis again taking the possessive to refer to God.

[44] S. Schechter, Aspects etc., p. 122. He apparently implies that *Torati* (Ps. 78:1) is taken by the Rabbis as *Torotai*, plural.

Ketubim as well.[45] The Rabbis thus associate belief in the latter with the dogma that Torah was given at Sinai.

Mattan Torah is a dogma, but it is not merely a dogma. It must not be regarded merely as an event in the past, but must be felt as a present reality. " '(All the statutes and the ordinances) which I set before you *this day*' (Deut. 11:32) — let them be as beloved of you as though you received them from Mount Sinai this day, be as conversant with them as though you heard them this day."[46] This is not an exhortation only. It reflects the rabbinic attitude that the Torah and its commandments are, as it were, given to the individual, here and now.

This attitude is again illustrated in an inference that the Rabbis draw. Denial of God, we saw, is rejection of God, willful rejection in spite of experiencing Him. How can we tell that there has been, without actual blasphemy, such denial of God? We can tell by a man's overt actions, say the Rabbis. R. Reuben was asked, "Who is the most hateful man in the world?" The Rabbi replied, "He who denies his Creator"; and in explanation said that no man denies any of the Ten Commandments "until he has denied the root" (God), and that no man goes and commits a transgression unless he has first denied Him who has commanded concerning it.[47] This passage follows immediately after a comment on Lev. 5:21: " 'If any one sin, and commit a trespass against the Lord, and deal falsely with his neighbor in a matter of deposit' — no man deals falsely with his neighbor until he denies the root."[48]

[45] See the treatment in ibid., p. 123 f. For the manner in which this attitude of the Rabbis is reflected in the concept of *Ruaḥ Ha-Ḳodesh*, see above, p. 251.

[46] Sifre on Deut. 11:32; ed. Friedmann, p. 87a, and the reference there.

[47] Tosefta Shebu'ot III.6, ed. Zuck.-Lieb., p. 449 f.

[48] Ibid. See Lieberman, תוספת ראשונים, II, p. 177. (The entire passage is also quoted in ערוגת הבשם, ed. Urbach [Jerusalem: Meḳiẓe Nirdamim, 1939], I, p. 232. This was called to my attention by Lieberman).

Based on this interpretation is another given in Numbers R. IX.1, end,

Not only was the Torah given on Sinai, the Rabbis are saying here, but it is given to the individual here and now. Observance of the *Mizwot* of the Torah is an acknowledgment of God, bringing a heightened awareness of relationship to Him. This implies a steady consciousness on the part of the individual that the *Mizwot* were indeed laid on him by God. Even those who transgress a *Mizwah*, say the Rabbis, possess this consciousness. That is why the Rabbis can declare that he who violates a *Mizwah* has denied God, rejected Him, rebelled against Him.[49] *Mattan Torah* thus takes place anew, is concretized anew, in a sense, with every individual. The dogma remains, but it only reinforces the experience of the individual.

"Be as conversant with them as though you heard them this day." The Rabbis cannot say, of course, that he who does not study Torah denies God, since there is no actual manifestation of rebellion. But they do say of him who neglects the study of Torah that it is "as though he denies the Holy One blessed be He, for He gave Torah to Israel only that they may be engaged in it day and night, as it says, 'But thou shalt meditate therein day and night' (Josh. 1:8)"; and they add, citing proof texts, that "he who is engaged in the Torah and observes it, it is as though he received it from Mt. Sinai."[50] A passage in the Sifra teaches that a man who does not study will end by denying God. He that does not study also does not do; he will go

wherein the one "who deals falsely" is the adulteress dealing falsely with her husband. She denies (כופרת) both God and her husband — by being unfaithful to her husband, she denies Him "who laid upon her the commandment, 'Thou shalt not commit adultery' (Exod. 20:13)."

[49] As is true of the examples given in the previous paragraph, the *Mizwot* cited in this connection as a rule have to do with ethical or moral conduct. Thus also: No man utters slander until he denies the root — Yer. Pe'ah 16a. Again: Those who lend on interest deny the root — Tos. Baba Meẓi'a VI.17; Yer. ibid., V, end, 10d.

[50] Tanḥuma, Re'eh I.1; Tanḥuma, ed. Buber, V, p. 10a.

on to despise others, and then to hate the *Ḥakamim* (learned), and then to prevent others from doing, and then to deny the *Miẓwot* that were delivered at Sinai; finally, the man with all these characteristics will end by denying the root.[51] Here what the Rabbis evidently refer to is denial of God that is not merely implied but declared. They are describing the process of the growth of rebellion.

There is a further, and a far more radical, modification of the dogma. The Rabbis teach that the unwritten Torah is implicit in the written Torah, but this also means that they regarded as divine the laws and interpretations they derived from the written Torah. Moreover, they attribute divine sanction to purely rabbinic laws, laws not derived from the written Torah. In other words, the concept of Torah was, in practice, an indeterminate concept, and hence quite like other value-concepts; it was made determinate when it was concretized in new laws and in new interpretations.

The Rabbis taught that the oral Torah is implicit in the written Torah. " 'All this commandment which I command you' (Deut. 11:22) — learn Midrash, Halakot and Haggadot."[52] One must study the oral Torah if he is to know "all this commandment." "When the Holy One blessed be He came to give the Torah," say the Rabbis, "He taught it to Moses in the regular order — the Bible, and the Mishnah, and the Haggadah and the Talmud, as it says, 'And God spoke *all* these words' (Exod. 20:1), even what a faithful pupil will ask his master."[53] Moses, the passage continues, asked God to give Israel the oral Torah in writing, whereupon God told him that the time would come when the nations of the world would take over the written Torah and that

[51] Sifra on Lev. 26:14–15, ed. Weiss, 111b–c.

[52] Sifre on Deut. 11:22, ed. Friedmann, p. 84b.

[53] Tanḥuma, ed. Buber, II, p. 58b, and the parallels there.

then the oral Torah would serve as the demarcation between Israel and the nations.[54] In other versions, the point is more clear: the nations of the world, possessing the written Torah in translation, will claim, "We are Israel," and the true Israel will then be marked as such because of possessing also the unwritten Torah, Torah that the others could not take over.[55] Elsewhere, however, the Rabbis give a totally different explanation. God deliberately left many matters only implicit in Scripture, they say, in order that Israel, by deriving them, might "increase their reward."[56]

To say that the unwritten Torah is imbedded in Scripture is to say that the laws and interpretations derived by the *Ḥakamim* are divine. " 'But if ye will not hearken unto Me' (Lev. 26:14) – if ye will not hearken unto the Midrash of the *Ḥakamim*."[57] True, the Torah was given in such a way, according to the Rabbis, that the implicit laws could be brought forth by means of the hermeneutic rules; even so, conscious of their own contribution, they likened their work to that of the man who has been given wheat from which to make fine flour, and flax from which to make a garment.[58] Nor is it always the case that a law derived by a hermeneutic rule is felt to be really implicit in Scripture, as we saw above.[59] Again, the Rabbis themselves assert that the scriptural support for many laws is frail. "The halakot concerning the Sabbath, the offerings at the Festivals, and the diversion of sacred things to secular use (*me'ilot*) are like mountains hanging by a hair, for they (consist of) little Bible and many halakot (שהן מקרא מועט והלכות מרובות)."[60]

[54] Ibid.

[55] See Lieberman, Hellenism in Jewish Palestine, p. 207, and the notes there.

[56] See OT, p. 36.

[57] Sifra on Lev. 26:14, ed. Weiss, 111b.

[58] See OT, p. 34 f.

[59] Above, p. 126.

[60] Ḥagigah I.8; Tos. Ḥagigah I.9, ed. Zuck.-Lieb., p. 233; Tos. 'Erubin XI (VIII).23, ed. Zuck.-Lieb., p. 154.

The Talmud declares that these laws are essential parts of the Torah, as much so as are the laws with abundant scriptural support.[61] All this indicates how cognizant the Rabbis were of their creative rôle in the emergence of the oral Torah.

A rabbinic legend tells us much the same thing. When Moses ascended to heaven, the legend says, he found God occupied with ornamenting the letters (of the Torah) with crownlike tips. Having asked for an explanation, Moses was told that there would be a man, called 'Aḳiba the son of Joseph, who would, by interpretation, base mounds of halakot on each tip (of the letters). Moses then requested to be shown this man, and was told to go back eighteen ranks; he did so, and found that although he could hear the discussion well enough he was not able to understand what was being said.[62] The oral Torah is divine and is implied in the written Torah, the Rabbis are saying here, but they are also saying that it is being developed in their own times and by their own great leaders.

The Rabbis felt, then, that they contributed in no small degree to the development of the halakic aspect of the oral Torah. In regard to the Haggadah, they had an even stronger consciousness of their creative rôle. The Rabbis designate the haggadic method of interpretation as *derash*, distinguishing it thereby from the literal rendering, the *peshaṭ*.[63] True, the haggadic method still involves an association, a connection however faint with the Bible. The dichotomy itself, however, testifies to an awareness that this connection may be only tenuous. By the same token,

[61] Ḥagigah 11b, on the mishnaic statement הן הן גופי תורה. The Mishnah itself makes this statement only in regard to the laws having abundant scriptural support. See J. N. Epstein, מבוא לנוסח המשנה (ירושלים, תש"ח), II, p. 520.

[62] Menaḥot 29b. "Things that were not revealed to Moses were revealed to R. 'Aḳiba" — Pesiḳta de R. Kahana, ed. Buber, p. 39b. See Ginzberg, Legends, Vol. III, p. 114 f. and Vol. VI, p. 48, note 250.

[63] See above, pp. 100, 132.

it also testifies to the Rabbis' awareness of their own rôle in the creation of Haggadah.

We have spoken thus far of laws and interpretations regarded as being, in some sense, implicit in the written Torah. But the Rabbis felt empowered to enact legislation on their own authority. Designated as *taḳḳanot* (ordinances) and *gezerot* (prohibitory decrees), these enactments, solely rabbinic in origin, and avowedly such, constitute a considerable body of legislation.[64] Nor is this rabbinical legislation always only supplementary to the laws of the written Torah; sometimes the Rabbis find it necessary to set aside deliberately, or to suspend, biblical laws.[65] The legislative authority of the Rabbis is usually based on Deut. 17:11 – "According to the Torah which they shall teach thee, and according to the judgment which they shall tell thee, thou shalt do; thou shalt not turn aside from the sentence which they shall declare unto thee, to the right hand, nor to the left."[66] A tannaitic comment on "Thou shalt not turn aside from the sentence which they shall declare unto thee," after stating that this phrase refers to the tradition handed down from one man to another, adds: "Weighty (חמורים) are the words of the *Ḥakamim*, for he who transgresses their words is like him who transgresses the words of the Torah – indeed, the words of the *Ḥakamim* are more weighty than the words of the Torah, for among the latter there are light and weighty (precepts), whereas the words of the *Ḥakamim* are all weighty."[67] The rabbinic enactments are Torah, and in a certain respect are "more weighty" than the laws of the written Torah.

[64] See I. H. Weiss, דור דור ודורשיו, 4th ed. (Wilna: Romm, 1904), II, Chap. VII, where they are classified under ten headings.

[65] See ibid., p. 50 f.

[66] כל מלי דרבנן אסמכינהו על לאו דלא תסור — Berakot 19b. See also Weiss, op. cit., p. 49 f.

[67] Midrash Tannaim, ed. Hoffmann, p. 103, and the references there. But see Ginzberg, Commentary, I, pp. 150–2.

Among the purely rabbinic enactments are laws concerning the Sabbath light, the lights of Ḥanukkah, the *'erub*, the ritual washing of the hands, and a number of other rites.[68] All these matters were established by the Rabbis themselves and were recognized as such. Nevertheless, the Rabbis rule that the *Birkat Ha-Miẓwot* is to be said at these rites also, a ruling based on the general authority given them, according to one opinion, in Deut. 17:11, and according to another, in Deut. 32:7.[69] But does not the *Birkat Ha-Miẓwot* on the Ḥanukkah lights, for example, read as follows: "Blessed art Thou, O Lord our God, King of the world, who has sanctified us by His *Miẓwot*, and commanded us to kindle the light of Ḥanukkah?"[70] In the Rabbis' eyes, the rites ordained by them, too, are *Miẓwot* of God, and not only those rites that are ordained in the written Torah.

We have been concerned, in this discussion, with the rabbinic concept of Torah rather than with the historical development of rabbinic law. With few exceptions, the rabbinic value-concepts are dynamic, that is also to say, indeterminate, and the concept of Torah is no exception. It is always concretized in new laws and in new interpreta tions. The concept of *Mattan Torah*, on the other hand points only to occasions of the distant past; it stands for the belief that God gave the Torah on those occasions, a belief that must be subscribed to by everybody. But if the laws and teachings of the Rabbis themselves are also Torah, and these too are regarded as authorized by God, the giving of Torah is really not limited to the occasions represented by the term *Mattan Torah.* Upon such laws and teachings the dogma of *Mattan Torah* had comparatively little bearing. The dynamic, indeterminate concept of Torah

[68] See Maimonides, Mishneh Torah, Hilkot Berakot XI.3.

[69] See Shabbat 23a — specifically here in regard to the lights of Ḥanukkah. (See also Maimonides, loc. cit., and the כסף משנה, ibid.)

[70] Ibid. On the wording of the *Birkat Ha-Miẓwot,* see above, p. 267.

tends to modify, in no slight manner, the quasi-determinate concept of *Mattan Torah.*[71]

The Rabbis apply the terms מודה and כופר to the belief that God brought Israel out of Egypt, and hence this belief, also, is a dogma. " 'For I am the Lord that brought you up out of the land of Egypt' (Lev. 11:45) – on this account have I brought you up out of the land of Egypt, (that is), on condition that you accept upon yourselves the yoke of *Mizwot*; for everyone that acknowledges the yoke of *Mizwot* acknowledges (מודה) the exodus from Egypt, and everyone that denies the yoke of *Mizwot* denies (כופר) the exodus from Egypt."[72] Acknowledgment and denial of the exodus from Egypt are associated with acknowledgment and denial of the yoke of *Mizwot*, divine commandments, because of the conjunction of the biblical verses: immediately preceding Lev. 11:45 are verses dealing with the commandments regarding "swarming things."[73] Similarly connecting con-

[71] In an extended sense, the concept of Torah includes instruction in proper conduct in general. "When certain Jewish Boswells apologised for observing the private life of their masters too closely, they said, 'It is a Torah, which we are desirous of learning' (Berakot 62a). In this sense it is used by another Rabbi, who maintained that even the everyday talk of the people in the Holy Land is a Torah (that is, it conveys an object lesson) (Lev. R. XXXIV.7)" — Schechter, Aspects of Rabbinic Theology, p. 125 f.

Another concept used in an extended sense is that of *Ruaḥ Ha-Ḳodesh*, the Holy Spirit. Seder Eliahu teaches that the Holy Spirit rests on the learned (see OT, p. 37 f.); and above, (p. 251, note 126), we quoted Hillel's famous dictum that the Holy Spirit rests on the people as a whole. There is an obvious connection between such an extension of the concept of the Holy Spirit and the concept of Torah as a dynamic concept that is always concretized anew.

At the other extreme of a concept with an extended meaning would be one with an entirely contracted meaning. Were a concept so contracted as to be left with only one concretization, it would no longer be a value-concept at all but a dogma, pure and simple. See above, p. 318, note 57, where we discussed this matter in connection with the concept of vicarious atonement.

[72] Sifra on Lev. 11:45, ed. Weiss, p. 57b.

[73] The version in Yalḳuṭ Shime'oni, Shemini, par. 546, reads: "On this condition have I brought you up out of the land of Egypt, (namely), that you accept upon yourselves the yoke of My *Mizwot*. Weighty are 'swarming things'; for

secutive verses, and using the same phrasing, the Rabbis associate acknowledgment and denial of the exodus from Egypt also with the commandments concerning measures[74]; with the commandment concerning interest or usury[75]; and with the commandment concerning *ẓiẓit*.[76] To strengthen regard for the *Miẓwot*, the Rabbis thus taught that accepting or observing them is tantamount to acknowledging the exodus from Egypt. The folk in general evidently, not only the Rabbis, attached great importance to the belief that God brought Israel out of Egypt.[77]

The exodus from Egypt is mentioned in the long *Berakah* after the *Shema'*, both in the morning and in the evening liturgy as presently constituted.[78] This long *Berakah*, in each instance, restates and emphasizes the ideas found in the three sections of the *Shema'*.[79] In Babylon, however, during the early 'Amoraic period, the third section of the *Shema'* was not recited at the evening service,[80] and the exodus

everyone that acknowledges the *Miẓwot* concerning swarming things acknowledges the exodus from Egypt, and everyone that denies the *Miẓwot* concerning swarming things denies the exodus from Egypt."

[74] Sifra on Lev. 19:36, ed. Weiss, p. 91b; Yalḳuṭ Shime'oni, Ḳedoshim, par. 617, end.

[75] Sifra on Lev. 25:38, ed. Weiss, p. 109c. The Sifra here reads: "as if he denies the exodus from Egypt," but Yalḳuṭ Shime'oni, Behar, par. 666, has the same formula as in all the other passages, without "as if." Called to my attention by Dr. Bernard Heller.

[76] Sifre Zuṭṭa on Numbers 15:21, ed. Horovitz, p. 290. See Yalḳuṭ Shime'oni on the same verse, Shelaḥ, par. 750.

The connection between the exodus from Egypt and these various verses is given a different interpretation in Baba Meẓi'a 61b.

[77] Yehudah Ha-Levi (Kuzari, I, 11, 25) makes of this belief the cornerstone of his religious philosophy.

[78] Prayer Book, ed. Baer, pp. 85, 166; ed. Singer, pp. 43, 99.

[79] See Ginzberg, Commentary, I, p. 211.

[80] See ibid., pp. 207–209; comp. 206 f. Ginzberg argues that, in early 'Amoraic times, the third section of the *Shema'* was not recited in the evening at all in Babylon, whereas in Palestine they recited only Num. 15:37 and then Lev. 18:2. He adds that it is difficult to tell what was the practice in Palestine in tannaitic times.

was then recalled in the long *Berakah* after the *Shema'* in the following words: "We acknowledge unto Thee (מודים אנחנו לך),[81] O Lord, our God, that Thou hast brought us out of the land of Egypt and hast redeemed us from the house of bondage. And Thou didst perform for us *Nissim* and *Geburot* at the sea, and we sang unto Thee, ('Who is like unto Thee' etc.)."[82] This leads directly to the latter part of the *Berakah* as we have it today.[83] Thus, this composition, its dogmatic terminology included, was at one time part of the regular evening liturgy. It is the only instance we know of where a dogma is given as such in rabbinic liturgy.[84]

As in the case of *Mattan Torah,* the belief that God brought Israel out of Egypt, while a dogma, is not merely a dogma. The organismic complex allows for different interpretations of the exodus from Egypt, we saw above,[85] as it does for all events. What is more, the individuals in every generation endeavored to render the exodus from Egypt, imaginatively, a matter of personal experience. This imaginative reliving of the exodus is stimulated particularly by the Passover Seder conducted in the home by every householder, and by the symbols of the Seder.[86] It is the theme of the Passover Haggadah, the service of early rabbinic origin recited at the Seder.[87] "In every generation,"

[81] See ibid., p. 211.

[82] Berakot 14b, and Rashi a. l.; Yer. ibid., I.9, 3d. See Ginzberg, op. cit., p. 212. On *Nissim,* see above, pp. 152 ff., and on *Geburot,* ibid., p. 160.

[83] As Rashi indicates — see the previous reference.

[84] When מודים אנחנו לך is an acknowledgment of God, it has reference to the *experience* of God, not to dogma, as we pointed out earlier in this section; otherwise it is an expression of gratitude to God — see above, p. 345, note 24.

[85] Above, p. 73.

[86] In the organismic complex, symbols, as well as events, can be given *various* interpretations. Thus, among the symbols of the Passover Seder, for example, the four cups of wine are given a number of different meanings (Yer. Pesaḥim X.1, 37c, top); and several different meanings are given for the *ḥaroset* (Pesaḥim 116a and Tosafot, ibid., s. v. צריך). *Pasaḥ* itself is given two different interpretations — Mekilta, I, p. 57, and above, p. 319. SEE NOTES, P. 372.

[87] See the reference above, p. 237 note 70.

says the Passover Haggadah, "a man is duty bound to look upon himself as though he personally had gone forth out of Egypt; as it is said, 'And thou shalt tell thy son, saying: It is because of that which the Lord did for *me* when *I* came forth out of Egypt' (Exod. 13:8). Not only our fathers did the Holy One blessed be He redeem, but us also did He redeem with them; as it is said, 'And He brought us out from thence, that He might bring us in, to give us the land which He swore unto our fathers' (Deut. 6:23)."[88]

Finally, there is the belief in the resurrection or revivification of the dead, *Teḥiyyat Ha-Metim*. When the Mishnah lists those having no portion in the world to come, the first in that list is "he that says: There is no revivification of the dead."[89] Belief in the resurrection is a dogma; the Rabbis apply to this belief, also, the terms "deny" and "acknowledge." A baraita sees in the statement from the Mishnah just quoted an instance of "measure for measure": He has denied (כפר) the resurrection of the dead, therefore he will have no portion in the resurrection of the dead, for the Holy One blessed be He deals with man measure for measure.[90]

[88] We have here two versions that have been combined. The text through the quotation of Exod. 13:8 is precisely as it is given in Pesaḥim X.5; it represents the version current in tannaitic times. From ibid., X.4, it is evident that at that time the Haggadah began with the interpretation of Deut. 26:5—ודורש מארמי אובד אבי. Later, in Babylon of early 'Amoraic times, they added the long "introduction" with which our Haggadah as constituted at present begins — see Pesaḥim 116a, the statement of Samuel. In this new section, however, Exod. 13:8 is employed in the answer to "the wicked son." Raba, therefore, says that the verse in support of "In every generation," etc. should be Deut. 6:23 (see ibid., 116b). Versions in accordance with Raba's dictum, and hence not using Exod. 13:8 in the selection we quoted here, are that of Maimonides in his Code and the one in the Shibbole Ha-Leḳeṭ, ed. Buber, p. 99a.

Incidentally, the phrase "denied the root" in the section on "the wicked son" is probably an interpolation. It is not found in the manuscripts of the Mekilta, where this passage occurs — see Mekilta I, p. 167; nor in the parallel there, I, p. 149; nor in the version as given in Yer. Pesaḥim X.4, 37d.

[89] Sanhedrin X.1. The words מן התורה were not in the Mishnah originally. See L. Finkelstein, Mabo le-Massektot Abot ve-Abot d'Rabbi Natan (New York, 1950), p. 229, end of note 5.

[90] Sanhedrin 90a.

Again, included in the list given by the Tosefta of those having no portion in the world to come are persons "who have denied (ושכפרו) the resurrection of the dead."[91] The term "acknowledge" as applied to this belief is used in connection with the Samaritans. According to a statement at the end of Masseket Kutim, they are to be accepted as Jews if they have denied Mt. Gerizim (as the Temple site), and if they have acknowledged (והודו) Jerusalem and the resurrection of the dead.[92] We ought to add that one of the major issues between the Pharisees and the Sadducees was the dogma of the resurrection, a belief that the Sadducees negated.[93]

Acceptance of the dogma does not mean that there was no room for difference in opinion. Some hold that only those who died in the land of Israel will be resurrected[94]; others, also basing themselves on a biblical verse, declare that those who died outside the land will be resurrected as well.[95] Still another opinion has it that the resurrection will take place first in the land of Israel.[96] There are also further views, mainly variations on the opinions given here.[97]

Before the resurrection of the dead takes place, there will be the days of the Messiah. Regarding the duration of this period, a number of different views are given in a passage of the Talmud, all of them based on biblical verses — forty years, four hundred years, three hundred sixty-five years corresponding to the days of the solar year, seven thousand years.[98] The passage continues with a statement in the name

[91] Tosefta ibid., XIII.5.

[92] Masseket Kutim, Chap. II. See Geiger, op. cit., p. 85, note 1.

[93] See Finkelstein, The Pharisees, I, pp. 145 ff. and the references in II, p. 673, note 15. Comp., however, Geiger, op. cit., p. 84 f.

[94] Ketubbot 111a.

[95] Ibid.

[96] Bereshit R. LXXIV.1, ed. Theodor-Albeck, p. 857, and the references and notes there.

[97] See Tanḥuma, ed. Buber, I, 107b–108a, and the references there.

[98] Sanhedrin 99a. Also given there is Samuel's view — the period is to be as long as the time that has elapsed from the creation of the world to his own day.

of R. Joḥanan: "All of the prophets prophesied only concerning the days of the Messiah, *Yemot Ha-Mashiaḥ*, but (as to) the world to come — '(Whereof from of old men have not heard, nor perceived by the ear) neither hath the eye seen, O God, beside Thee, what He worketh for him that waiteth for Him' (Is. 64:4)."[99] This opinion, remarks the Talmud, is opposed to that of Samuel. "Samuel said, 'There will be no difference between this world and the days of the Messiah except only (delivery from) subjection to the empires.' "[100] R. Joḥanan's opinion, as the Talmud itself indicates, represents a conception of the days of the Messiah totally different from that held by Samuel.

A divergence even more striking is to be found in the views about the world to come. Some authorities believe that, upon death, the souls of the righteous are in the world to come; in other words, the world to come begins, for the righteous, immediately after they have ceased to exist in this world. This view is reflected in a statement like the following, a statement made with obvious regard for the scheme or order of things. "There is none to be compared unto Thee, O Lord our God, in *this world*, neither is there any beside Thee, O our King, for the life of the *world to come* (*Ha-'Olam Ha-Ba'*) ; there is none but Thee, O our Redeemer, for the *days of the Messiah*; neither is there any like unto Thee, O our Saviour, for the *resurrection of the dead*."[101] Another and more prevalent view, however, places the world to come at the end of all things, after the resurrection of the dead. This view is likewise reflected in rabbinic statements that emphasize the entire scheme of things; but now the series is given in the following order: this world, the days

[99] Ibid. (See Rashi on Is. 64:4, his interpretation of the verse in accordance with R. Joḥanan's statement here).

[100] Ibid.; and the parallels.

[101] From the Sabbath liturgy — Prayer Book, ed. Singer, p. 129; ed. Baer, p. 210 f., and the note on *Ha-'Olam Ha-Ba'*, ibid., p. 211. The passage is cited in Finkelstein, Mabo etc., p. 220.

of the Messiah, the resurrection of the dead, the world to come.[102] Our treatment here is based on Finkelstein's suggestive discussion of this problem, and he substantiates the thesis that there are these two distinct views regarding the world to come with other evidence as well.[103] He also points out that, in order to avoid the appearance of having decided in favor of either opposing view, the Rabbis are often deliberately ambiguous in their use of the term "the world to come."[104]

These "hereafter concepts," as we may call them, constitute a special group of concepts in themselves. All of them are, unlike the value-concepts in general, obviously not experiential concepts but beliefs. It is even a question whether, strictly speaking, they may be said to be value-concepts at all. To be sure, they combine organismically with the value-concepts; at the same time, they are connected with each other in a consecutive order, follow one upon the other *seriatim*, the order depending only on the interpretation of '*Olam Ha-Ba*'. The hereafter concepts are beliefs that are tied together in a series. Value-concepts are never connected in any *seriatim* order.

All of the hereafter concepts have a dogmatic character. We have seen that the resurrection of the dead is a rabbinic dogma. But if the belief in resurrection is itself only one in a series, we may well assume that the series as a whole has a certain dogmatic quality. Rabbinic statements support this assumption. A baraita quoted above says: "He has denied the resurrection of the dead, therefore he will have no portion in the resurrection of the dead."[105] Now the statement in the Mishnah to which our baraita refers speaks of those having *no portion in the world to come*[106]; our baraita,

[102] See Finkelstein, ibid.
[103] Ibid., pp. 212 ff.
[104] Ibid., p. 220 f. SEE NOTES, P. 372.
[105] See above, p. 361.
[106] Ibid.

therefore, equates the resurrection of the dead with the world to come. If these two beliefs can be equated, and the one, namely, the resurrection of the dead, is a dogma, then so is the belief in the world to come. Similarly, at least a tinge of dogmatism colors the belief in the days of the Messiah. The Talmud records a statement by R. Hillel (not Hillel the Elder) to the effect that Israel already "enjoyed" (lit. consumed) the Messiah in the days of Hezekiah, and that, as a result, "Israel has no Messiah" – a statement which causes R. Joseph to exclaim, "May his Master (God) forgive R. Hillel!"[107] We are thus justified in saying that the hereafter concepts as a whole have a dogmatic quality.

Yet here, too, we do not have pure dogma. Ordinarily, dogma is synonymous with uniformity in belief. In the case of the hereafter concepts, on the contrary, the chief impression is that of the variety of opinions and beliefs – and this, even though we could have added many more such instances.[108] Furthermore, dogma is hardly dogma if it is not clear cut and definite, yet the Rabbis are often ambiguous when they speak of the world to come. While the belief in the hereafter is a rabbinic dogma, it is a dogma in a modified, or a qualified, sense.

Rabbinic dogmas are beliefs which the Rabbis have singled out as those to which all must subscribe. They have to do either with events which a person must accept as having happened in the past, but which have not occurred in his own actual experience, or else with events that are

[107] Sanhedrin 99a. R. Joseph counters with the prophecy in Zechariah 9:9, made centuries after Hezekiah.

[108] See, for example, Tosefta Sanhedrin XIII.1–3, ed. Zuck.-Lieb., p. 434 — the various opinions as to the small children of the wicked, the righteous among the Gentiles, and the mediocre group of Israelites in the hereafter; also the discussion and references in Bereshit R., ed. Theodor-Albeck, p. 857, note 4 — the opinion regarding the resurrection of the dead also at the beginning of the days of the Messiah.

posited as taking place in the future. These events are: the bringing forth of Israel out of Egypt by God, the giving of Torah by God, and the resurrection of the dead in the future. The proper attitude to these events is that of "acknowledgment"; anything even associated with "denial" of them is a stigma. It is because the Rabbis apply the terms "acknowledge" and "deny" to these beliefs in such fashion that we take those beliefs to be rabbinic dogmas.

But the rabbinic dogmas are not pure dogmas. By means of the Passover Seder and its symbols, the exodus from Egypt is rendered, in the imagination, a matter of personal experience; that is to say, on that occasion the attempt is made to draw the exodus from Egypt out of the sphere of belief and into the sphere of experience. The giving of Torah, too, is projected into the sphere of personal experience. Each individual, according to the Rabbis, possesses the consciousness that the *Miẓwot* were laid by God on him personally; he who willfully violates a *Miẓwah* deliberately denies God, rejects Him, rebels against Him. Furthermore, the giving of Torah is not limited to any event in the past. The concept of Torah, like the other value-concepts, is a dynamic concept; it is concretized anew in enactments and teachings by the Rabbis themselves, new enactments and teachings that are recognized as such, but that are also felt to be authorized by God. As to the dogma of the resurrection, that too is modified, but in another way. The resurrection of the dead, in rabbinic belief, is to be an event in a whole series of events, and belief in the resurrection amounts to belief in that series of events as a whole. Instead of uniformity in belief, however, there is a striking variety of beliefs concerning these events of the future, and there is even definite conflict of opinion. Unlike creedal dogmas then, the rabbinic dogmas leave room, to some degree, for the play of personality, either in the realm of experience or in the realm of opinion.

The rabbinic dogmas are not marshaled into a creed; neither are they otherwise presented as the basic principles of Judaism. Of the dogmatic character of the belief in the exodus, we are made aware merely in the course of the regular midrashic interpretation of certain sections of Leviticus. The dogma of the resurrection and that of the giving of Torah are, it is true, set off more prominently, for those who deny them head the list given of "those who have no portion in the world to come."[109] But there are others in that list, and among them those who engaged in certain practices apparently characteristic of sectaries.[110] What we have here is an anathema against such sectaries, evidenced by the fact that not only beliefs but practices are mentioned, and not a statement of the basic doctrines of Judaism.[111] Indeed, it is quite likely that the very crystallization of the rabbinic dogmas was primarily due to the sectarian conflicts of those times.[112]

The absence of a statement of basic principles on the part of the Rabbis was among the most serious difficulties with which medieval formulators of creeds had to cope. Albo says this in so many words. "In fine the knowledge of the essential principles of divine law is very difficult. And a more serious difficulty still is that we find no clear pronouncement upon this matter in the discussions of the Rabbis."[113]

The rabbinic dogmas are vastly different from the dogmas of medieval Jewish theology. The rabbinic dogmas do not constitute a creed, and they even permit, in some degree, the play of personality.

[109] Sanhedrin X.1.

[110] Particularly the practice of using Exod. 15:26 as an incantation over illness, and that of pronouncing the Name as it is spelled — ibid. The latter practice was that of the Samaritans; see Yer. Sanhedrin X.1, 28b, and S. Lieberman, Tarbiz XX (1949), p. 117 and n. 108 there.

[111] We called attention above to the anti-sectarian character of some of the statements on the dogmas — see above, pp. 349, 350, 362. Also, p. 364, n. 104.

[112] See the preceding note.

[113] Albo, op. cit., I, p. 63.

Notes

P. 40, n. 12

For an analysis of the rabbinic concept of *Ḥasid,* see now L. Jacobs, "The Concept of *Ḥasid* in Biblical and Rabbinical Literature," The Journal of Jewish Studies, VIII (1957), pp. 143–154. See also L. Gulkowitsch, Die Bildung des Begriffes *Ḥasid* (Tartu, 1935).

P. 56, n. 8

(The plural, *Yisre'elim,* is also found—see 'Erubin VI.1; 'Abodah Zarah IV.11.)

P. 83, n. 8

Contrast this statement with what the novelist Joyce Cary says: "Each of us . . . must decide what he wants . . . even a primitive savage, with his extremely limited range of thought and action makes such a choice. He can excel as farmer or hunter, drummer or dancer, he can be genial or surly, cooperative or rebellious, he can be respected among men or ignored or perhaps feared"—First Trilogy (New York: Harper, 1957). Preface, p. ix.

P. 93, n. 13

Striking examples: Raba qualifies a certain law with regard to *Zimmun* on the basis of an analogy with a law regarding *Ṭum'ah* (Berakot 50a-b); a law in regard to meal-offerings is taken as a principle, and the principle is applied to *ḥaliẓah* and other matters (Yebamot 104b, and the references).

P. 94, n. 15

Albeck demonstrates that the redaction by Rabbi Judah the Prince was not intended as a code and that it did not function as such; see his Mabo La-Mishnah (Tel-Aviv: Dvir, 1959), pp. 105 ff.

P. 95, n. 24

On the various aspects of divergence in law, see now G. Alon, Toledot Ha-Yehudim Be-'Ereẓ Yisra'el Bi-Teḳufat Ha-Mishnah Weha-Talmud, I (Tel-Aviv, 1952), pp. 193 ff.

P. 103, n. 22

See also I. Heinemann, Die wissenschaftliche Allegoristic des jüdischen Mittelalters, Hebrew Union College Annual, XXIII (1950–1951), pp. 611–643, who shows that the medieval Jewish philosophers engaging in allegorical interpretation of the Bible found scientific or philosophic ideas there as "the deeper meaning." He also shows that the texts so interpreted were limited to a rather small number, and that laws were never so interpreted, and this in accordance with the approach to allegorical interpretation outlined by the philosophers themselves.

P. 123, n. 6

See also Mechilta de-R. Simon b. Jochai, ed. Hoffmann, p. 8. Also Yer. Ḳiddushin II.1, 62a, and קרבן העדה ad loc.—one person acts for the whole family.

P. 129, n. 33

See also Tosefot Yom Ṭob on Sukkah III.3, s.v. כשרה, and on ibid., III.4, s.v. שלשתן. But there are exceptions—see, e.g., Tosafot, Giṭṭin 20b, s.v. ספר.

P. 148, n. 16

See also Boaz Cohen, Proceedings of the American Academy for Jewish Research, XX (1951), p. 152, n. 89.

P. 175, n. 32

The rule applies to the *Birkat Ha-Miẓwot* but not necessarily to other *Berakot*—see the Kesef Mishneh toward the end of the comment on Maimonides, Mishneh Torah, Hilkot Tefillah VII.3.

P. 175, n. 37

Comp., however, the characterization by Saadia—Siddur R. Saadia Gaon, ed. Davidson and others (Jerusalem: Meḳiẓe Nirdamim, 1941), pp. 82, 94

P. 180, n. 58, (i)

The latter has to do with Books of Scripture "defiling" *terumah*. On the entire matter of these halakot see now Albeck's long note in his Commentary on Seder Ṭoharot (Tel-Aviv: Dvir, 1958), pp. 608 f.

P. 180, n. 58, (ii)

On the maintenance of a number of laws of *Ṭum'ah* after the fall of the Temple see G. Alon, op. cit., I 162 f.

P. 203, n. 9

Occasions for this *Berakah* include damage to one's property—see Yer. Berakot VI.3, 10c.

P. 207, n. 18

"Know thou that the language of the *Tefillah* is based on the language of the Bible"—Sefer Abudraham, ed. Ch. L. Ehrenreich (Klausenberg, 1927), p. 42.

P. 221, n. 82

This passage is often quoted in Kabbalistic literature. On the difference between the manner in which it is used there and the rabbinic meaning, see now I. Tishby, Mishnat Ha-Zohar II (Jerusalem: Bialik Institute, 1961), p. 8, and especially the last paragraph there.

P. 260, n. 148

See now his Jewish Gnosticism, Merkabah Mysticism, and Talmudic Tradition (New York: Jewish Theological Seminary of America, 1960) wherein he indicates that Jewish esoteric mysticism goes back to as early a period as the second century.

P. 268, n. 11

In the Bible such a shift in person is to be found only "in poetic (or prophetic) language"—see Gesenius-Kautzsch. Hebrew Grammar, trans. A. E. Cowley (2nd English ed., Oxford, 1910), p. 462 *p*. Here, however, the shift is in plain prose.

P. 327, n. 13

On סוד as used by Naḥmanides, see G. Scholem, Reshit Ha-Kabbalah (Jerusalem–Tel Aviv: Schocken, 1948), pp. 150 f.

P. 346, n. 26

Dr. Saul Lieberman, on the basis of very early sources, says in the following communication that מודים in the *'Alenu* prayer ought not be deleted:

ואשר ל"מודים" של תפלת עלינו אין להוציא אותה משם שכן אנו מוצאים בספר עתיק, והוא בקטע למכילתא דברים (שפרסם שכטר בסה"י לכבוד ר' ישראל לוי עמ' 192 שו' 10): לכריעה ולהודיה ולהשתחויה ולתפילה מכל (=בכל) מקום. ובמנהיג ה' תפילה סי' ס"א (ד' ברלין י"ח ע"א): שאנו מודים לך פירוש משתחוים לך. ובאבודרהם (סדר תפלות של חול ד"ה מודים ד"ו שכ"ו ל"ט ע"א): והירחי פי' מודים משתחוים כדמתרגמינן (ש"ב ט"ז־ד') ואשתחוה אל המלך ומודינא למלכא ואמרינן בבראשית רבה (ויחי ריש שיטה חדשה, הוצ' תיאודר־אלבק ע' 1199) כי לא שאול תודך ומי הוא מודה מי שהוא חי ו מ ש ת ח ו ה .

P. 348, n. 32
The verb *ma'amin* may at times be used in the sense of "belief," but the noun *'Emunah* always means "trust." *'Emunah* in the sense of "a belief" is not rabbinic.

P. 360, n. 86
For other interpretations of *ḥaroset,* one of which even involved calling it by a different name, see S. Lieberman, Hayerushalmi Kiphshuto (Jerusalem: Darom Publishing Company, 1934), p. 520. See also the examples in D. Goldschmidt, The Passover Haggadah (Hebrew), (Jerusalem and Tel Aviv: Schocken, 1947), pp. 17 f., and the sources there.

P. 364, n. 104
Berakot IX.5 records that the *Minin,* sectarians, insisted there was only this world, and that to counteract them a phrase was added in the *Berakot* as these were recited in the Temple to indicate the belief in two worlds, this world and the world to come. Lieberman's illuminating discussion of this mishnah demonstrates that the two different views of the world to come resulted in two different versions of the addition or insertion in the *Berakot,* both of them well attested. See his Tosefta Ki-Fshuṭah, I (New York, 1955), pp. 122 f.

Albeck, in his commentary on Seder Nezikin (Jerusalem–Tel Aviv, 1953), p. 454, says that the world to come, according to the Rabbis, will take place after the resurrection of the dead, and that the Rabbis refer to "the world of the souls" by other terms. He adds that it was Maimonides who designated "the world of the souls" by the term "world to come."

Appendix

BY SIMON GREENBERG

Questions based on The Rabbinic Mind

CHAPTER I

1. What is the basic problem the book undertakes to discuss?
2. How can we identify rabbinic values?
3. What is meant by the statement, "Rabbinic value terms are undefined concepts?"
4. How do value-concepts function both in stabilizing society and in giving expression to the self?
5. Differentiate between "values, value-judgments and value-concepts."
6. Why have "value-concepts" gone unnoticed?
7. What is the relationship between "value-concepts" and "significance?"
8. What are the implications of the statement that "value-concepts are dynamic?"
9. How is the idea of "value-concept" related to our understanding of the place of the individual and society in religion?
10. Distinguish between the author's "descriptive terms" and the rabbinic "value-concept."
11. What is the fundamental relationship between Halakah and Haggadah?
12. What does the author have to say about the problem of rabbinic anthropomorphism?
13. What does he say about the relationship of subconscious and conscious to human personality?

CHAPTER II

1. What virtue did Schechter find in the lack of logical system in rabbinic thought?

2. What problem did he leave unsolved?
3. How does the author solve this problem?
4. What is the relationship of the subconcepts to the general concepts?
5. What are "conceptual phases?"
6. How are the concepts interrelated? Can you give an illustration?
7. Why does he speak of four of the concepts as "tracer" or fundamental concepts rather than "dominant" concepts?
8. What is the relationship between the meaning of a rabbinic concept and the process of its integration with other value-concepts?
9. What is the relationship between the "integration" and the "individuation" of the concepts?
10. What distinction does the author draw between a physical and a mental organism? Do you consider this a valid distinction?
11. What form of coherence other than organismic does he find among the rabbinic value-concepts?
12. What is the relationship between the value-concepts and normal everyday experience?
13. What was the fundamental source of difficulty for those who heretofore attempted to systematize rabbinic thought?
14. What pitfalls does the author find in our attempt to understand modern religion by studying primitive religion?

CHAPTER III

1. What is the test for establishing the presence of a genuine rabbinic concept?
2. Of what are the value-concepts abstractions?
3. What do the terms *Goy*, *Nokri* and *'Ummot Ha-'Olam*, and *'Emunah*, *Biṭṭaḥon*, connote in rabbinic thought?
4. What does he say about the "static aspect" of the rabbinic organismic complex?
5. What is the relationship between a concept other than a value-concept and its definition?
6. How are rabbinic value-concepts defined?

7. What is the difference in origin between a value-concept and other concepts?
8. Explain: "The conceptual term does not act as a label."
9. What is the nature of rabbinic "auxiliary" ideas? Name some such ideas mentioned by the author.
10. What does he say about the term "chosen people?"

CHAPTER IV

1. What is the difference between organizing and integrating data?
2. What makes possible the consecutive but different and even contradictory interpretations of the same biblical verse?
3. Wherein does the unity of the haggadic composition inhere?
4. What is the basic difference in function between the cognitive and value-concepts?
5. How is the concept of organic thinking helpful in relating the self to the "social mind?"
6. Explain: "The concretization of the value-concepts in law—Halakah—is not legalism."
7. What makes it possible for "a group character to go hand in hand with full development of differentia in the individual?"
8. Wherein does the author see the basic difference between primitive and civilized society?
9. What was the role of the Rabbi and the Haggadah in making value-concepts vivid and their use frequent?

CHAPTER V

1. What basically different assumptions underlie the figurative interpretation of a Bible text and the rabbinic or haggadic interpretation of it?
2. Explain: "Between halakic definitions there is always an explicit or implicit nexus; between rabbinic value-concepts there is no implicit nexus."
3. Explain: "In a literal sense, there is no real demarcation between the valuational situation and the individual who experiences it."
4. Explain: "A haggadic statement (as contrasted with a sermon

of the Rabbis) derived its unitary character from the value-concepts it embodies rather than from its form and rhythm."

5. What two types of expression are included in the "category of significance?"
6. What one important feature do Haggadah and poetry have in common?
7. What is the basic distinction between the halakic and the haggadic approach to the Bible text?
8. What aspect of the value-concepts "makes it possible for them to cultivate and express the differentia of each human personality?"
9. Explain: In haggadic interpretation the text is "a non-determining stimulus."
10. What do you understand by the author's concept of "Indeterminacy of Belief?"
11. What concepts appear to be "compounds of cognitive and valuational concepts," and what problems do such "compound concepts" present?
12. What is the relationship between the value-concept *Nes* and the concept *sidre Bereshit*?
13. How does the author distinguish between a conceptual phase and a subconcept?
14. Wherein is the concept *Nes* unique in the "rabbinic value-complex" and how is this uniqueness reflected?
15. How did the Rabbis make the "category of significance steady as well as extensive?"
16. What is the relationship between *Ḳedushah* and daily conduct?
17. What is the difference between objects which are "holy in themselves," and objects whose holiness derives from their association with a religious rite?
18. Explain: "Reflected in those halakot is reverence for *Ḳedushah* rather than any notion of efficacy."
19. How is *Ḳedushah* concretized in "days" as in "objects?"
20. How is Halakah related to the "category of significance?"
21. What is the difference between the role of the concept "angel" and that of *shed* in rabbinic thought?

CHAPTER VI

1. What does the author designate as normal mysticism?
2. How does he relate de Laguna's words "a privacy which is inexpressible to ourselves and incommunicable to others" to his discussion of the Hebrew terms for God?
3. How do we *experience* God and how is that related to the mystic experience?
4. To what five contexts is the use of the terms *'El*, *'Eloah*, and *'Elohim* limited in rabbinic literature?
5. How does the Halakah "facilitate the expression of the value-concepts?"
6. Explain: "Through the agency of the Halakah . . . the spiritual leader brought the common man up to his own level."
7. How does the "mystical experience of God" rise to expression?
8. How do the Rabbis express their reaction to the presence of evil in the world?
9. What conclusion does the author draw from the fact that ideas like God's omniscience, omnipotence and omnipresence are not represented by conceptual terms in rabbinic thought?
10. What is meant by treating an auxiliary idea "as a subject in itself?"
11. In what special context do the rabbis use *Shekinah* as an appellative for God?
12. In what respect is *Gilluy Shekinah not* typical of the value-concepts?
13. Where is the term *Gilluy Shekinah* actually mentioned by the Rabbis? What conclusion does the author draw from the fact that it is so rarely mentioned?
14. How does he explain the difference between the Sadducees and the Pharisees regarding the offering of incense in the Holy of Holies on the Day of Atonement?
15. How is *Gilluy Shekinah* associated with prophecy?
16. What reconciliation does the author suggest between the statements that God "withdrew His *Shekinah*" and that "*Shekinah* is everywhere?"

17. What does he have to say about the relation of *Shekinah* to the idea of "immanence of God?"
18. Explain: "The awareness or experience of God is thus a phenomenon associated with the integration of the self."
19. Are *Bat Ḳol* and *Gilluy Shekinah* in any way to be related?
20. What is the special characteristic of the relationship of the Rabbis to God?
21. How does the author interpret the shift from second to third person in *Berakot*?
22. What are the three main features of normal mysticism?

CHAPTER VII

1. Do the Rabbis take a stand on anthropomorphism? Explain your answer.
2. What, according to the author, uniquely characterizes Judaism? Is it an *idea* of God?
3. How can we prove that rabbinic thought is a development of biblical thought?
4. In their relationship to the Bible what types of rabbinic concepts can be identified? Illustrate.
5. What are "emphatic rabbinic trends?"
6. How do the Rabbis express their sense of the otherness of God?
7. What difference does the author find between the rabbinic attitude towards the otherness of God and their attitude towards His justice and love?
8. What idea does he find expressed in the rabbinic discussions of anthropomorphism?
9. How does he explain the attitude of Onkelos to anthropomorphism?
10. To what do the Rabbis refer when they speak of the acknowledgment or denial of God?
11. What are the two meanings of "Belief?"
12. What is the difference between viewing *Mattan Torah* as a dogma or as a value-concept?
13. What are the three rabbinic dogmas according to the author?
14. What is the peculiar characteristic of rabbinic dogmas?

Index

Index

Aaron, all Israel eligible for priesthood only until God chose, 61; experienced several *Dibberot*, 237n.

'Abaye, 75n., 92, 105n., 152, 153, 157, 158, 162n., 165, 247n.

R. 'Abba bar Judan, 257.

Abba Saul, 169.

R. 'Abba b. Zabda, 56n.

R. 'Abbahu, 157n., 233.

'Aberah, obverse of *Miẓwah*, 27; in reference to the "faint-hearted," 100; "crowds off the feet of the *Shekinah*," 228. *See also* Sin; Transgression.

'Abigedor Kohen Ẓedeḳ, 158n.

'Abodah, applied both to prayer and study of Torah, 213.

'Abodah Zarah (idolatry), in worship of human beings, 54; generic terms for God as applying to, 195 f., 199; cannot hear prayer, 195; "cancelling" of, 197; forms of accepting or acknowledging, 197; concept of, as negating heathen gods, 206; entire Torah acknowledged when there is denial of, 349. *See also* Idolatry.

'Abot (patriarchs), concept of, limited in generalizing power, 38; Rabbis sometimes speak of seven, 38n. *See also* Patriarchs.

Above, an appellative for God, 204.

Abraham, as patriarch, 38n.; Israel redeemed from Egypt because of, 73; crossing of the Red Sea because of, 73; made converts, 99; appeals to God's mercy in behalf of Sodom, 99; God visits him on his sickbed, 141; contrast between inhabitants of land of Israel and, 199; *Shekinah* began to descend to earth because of, 226.

R. Abraham b. David of Posquières, 235n., 283n.

Abraham Ibn Ezra, 249n., 293, 294n., 297, 344n.

R. Absalom the elder, 74.

Abstract thought, value-concepts represent a form of, 37.

Abṭalyon, 74.

R. Abun, 187.

Academies, the, *see bet ha-midrash.*

Achan, 135.

Adam, referred to as a patriarch, 38n., 349n; death as due to sin of, 53; death of, attributed to sins of descendants, 53; death of, caused by serpent's slander, 60n.; God acts as best man at wedding of Eve and, 141; given promise of everlasting life, 219.

R. 'Adda bar 'Ahabah, 163.

Adulteress, denies both God and her husband, 352n.

Aesthetic forms, function of, 68.

Aesthetic significance, 111–12; compared with valuational significance, 112–14. *See also* Art.

Affirmation, in haggadic statements, 135–36.

Agadot Ha-Tannaim (Heb. trans.) (W. Bacher), 87, 119n., 120n.

Agard, W. R., 112n.

Agency, principle of, 123.
R. 'Aḥa bar Jacob, 185.
Ahaz, not named among those having no portion in the world to come, 137.
'Akatriel, a name for God, 234, 261n.
'*Aḳedat Yiẓḥaḳ* (Isaac Arama), 328.
R. 'Aḳiba, 71, 90, 100, 104, 123, 127, 131n., 212, 218n., 235, 238, 240n., 241n., 355, 355n.
'*Akkum*, a term imposed by censorship, 41n.
Albeck, Ch., 62, 73n., 369n., 370n., 372n.
Allegorical interpretation, 370n.; Maimonides' rationale of, 102–4. *See also* Figurative interpretation.
'*Alenu* prayer, 197, 266.
Alon, G., 369n., 370n.
Altar, Jerusalem as locale of, 61; sanctifying power of, 179.
Amalek, enemy of Israel, 19; God fought battle of, 20.
'*Am Ha-'Areẓ, see* Ignorant.
'*Amidah*, Daily, warrant for Eighteen Benedictions in, 127; biblical phrases in, 207n.; relationship to God in, 266; *Teshubah* in, 301; of Rosh Ha-Shanah, 131n.; the meaning of *modim* in, 344–46.
R. 'Ammi, 76, 256.
'Amoraim, the, 90; *Nissim* in times of, 157.
Angels, student's vision of, 136; as a cognitive concept, 184, 186–88; concept of, used exclusively in concretizations of value-concepts, 186–87; associated with *Ḳedushah*, 184, 187–88; indeterminacy of belief with respect to, 187; have no efficacy of their own, 188; question of their presence in Holy of Holies, 234n.; do not see the Glory (God), 235.
Anthropology, and the study of developed religion, 32–33.
Anthropology (R. R. Marett), 146n.
Anthropomorphism, Haggadah teems with, 141–42; term not in rabbinic universe of discourse, 225; neutralizing of, 230; the question of, 273 ff.; Rabbis not concerned with problem of, 274 f.; unqualified in many statements, 276–77; Rabbis take no stand on, 280, 304–5; and modern scientific thought, 286n.; idea of God's otherness does not involve a stand on, 320–21; and Targum Onkelos, 325 ff. *See also* Corporeality of God.
Antoninus, among the righteous Gentiles, 28; parable of, 274–75.
Appellatives for God, the, *Shekinah* is one of, 225; express consciousness of relationship to God, 271; the relation of *Memra'*, *Yeḳara'*, and *Shekinta'* to the, 332–33. *See also* God, epithets or appellatives for.
Aristotle, 341.
Aristotleianism, pagan element in, 285.
Art, unity achieved in, 111–12.
Articles of Faith, of Maimonides, 106.
'*Arugat Ha-Bosem* (ed. E. E. Urbach), 351n.
Arzt, M., 350n.
Asaf, S., 174n.
Asaph, insists that Prophets and *Ketubim* are Torah, 350.
R. 'Ashi, 116, 155, 158.
'*asmakta*, 124.
Aspects of Rabbinic Theology, Some (Solomon Schechter), 9, 14, 79n., 142, 169, 170, 184n., 205n., 221, 257n., 275, 279, 312n., 322, 350, 358n.
Association of ideas, as connecting haggadic statements, 61.
Atonement, subconcept of God's loving-kindness, 15. *See also* Vicarious atonement.
Atonement, Day of, *see* Day of Atonement.
Authority, and haggadic statements, 72; derived from *Gilluy Shekinah*,

252; biblical basis for rabbinic, 356–57; Rabbis felt empowered to legislate on their own, 356–57.

Auxiliary idea(s), 52 f.; is static, 53–54; how it differs from value-concept, 54; freedom of the will is an, 53, 54–55; God's omnipotence is an, 55, 220; God's eternity is an, 55; God's omnipotence and omnipresence are, 220; and "independent attributes," 55n.; not given conceptual terms in rabbinic literature, 220; idea of otherness of God is not an, 307.

Awareness, value-concepts and realm of, 13.

Babylonian myths, vestiges in Haggadah of, 140n.

Bacher, W., 87, 100nn., 119n., 120n., 124n., 251n., 312n.

Baer, S., 36nn., 131n., 168n., 183n., 187n., 197n., 207n., 210n., 212n., 266n., 267n., 269n., 300n., 346n., 363n.

baḥor, does not necessarily imply selection, 56.

R. Banaah, 73.

Balaam, designated as wicked, 27.

Balaam's ass, and the *Nes* of, 154.

Bamberger, B. J., 292nn., 293n.

Bat Ḳol, several kinds of, 261–62; not associated with experience of God, 262; often rejected by Halakah, 262; "is not to be taken into account," 262n.; sometimes identified with Holy Spirit, 262n.; sometimes used as a cognitive concept, 263.

"Battle," as symbol of discussion of Torah, 118.

Belief, in the existence of God, 42; of a determinate nature, 135–36; not in the sense of "trust," 347 (*see also 'Emunah*); as trust in God, 347n.; *Mattan Torah* both a value-concept and a, 348. *See also* Indeterminacy of belief.

Beliefs, rabbinic dogmas have to do with certain, 365–66.

Ben 'Azzai, 349.

Benediction(s), on the Torah, 56; on the lection from the Prophets, 56–57; on a new home, 64; in grace after meals, 127; when seeing a place where *Nissim* were done for Israel, 163. *See also Berakah*; *Berakot*.

Ben Sira, Book of, charity in, 88n.; quoted by Rabbis, 199.

Berakah, on bread, 167–68; as worship, 168; "praise" rather than "blessing," 168n.; in grace after meals, 168n., 345n.; on the light of the day, 168; on the twilight, 169; the formula at a rite, 170; *Birkat Ha-Miẓwot* as a distinctive, 175, 370n., said also at purely rabbinic rites, 357; relationship to God implied in a, 202; evil tidings also occasion for a, 203, 219n., 371n.; formula for beginning of, 208; "Thou" conjoined to "He" in a, 267, views of medieval authorities on, 268–69; on *'Olam* in the formula of the, 295; as a structural stereotype, 308, 311; after the reading of the *Hafṭarah*, 345n.; after the *Shema'*, ideas in the sections of *Shema'* emphasized in, 359. *See also* Benediction; *Berakot*.

Berakot (Benedictions), in daily, Sabbath and Festival prayers, 209; "a hundred every day," 209n.; eighteen, of the *Tefillah*, 42–43, 209, warrant for, 127, room for private petitions in, 211.

Bereshit, as a conceptual term, 35–36; as a value-concept, 149–52; as an overlapping concept, 150–51; has a connotation of universalism, 150–51; the waters of, 35. *See also sidre Bereshit*.

Bereshit R., and its relation to the Pesiḳta, 67n.

Bergmann, J., 79n.

Bergson, H., 88.

*Bet Din Ha-Gadol (*The Great Court), ordinances and verdicts of, 94–95.

bet ha-keneset (synagogue), holiness of, 179.

bet ha-midrash, the study of Torah in, 79; creative function of, 85.

Bet Hillel, 262n.; "Halakah is according to," 262n.

Bet Shammai, 262n.

"Beyond," as a term for the otherness of God, 307n.

Bible, the, meaning of *Goy* in, 40; conceptual terms in, 55; interpretations of biblical texts are usually concretizations of rabbinic concepts, 98–99; as stimulus for Haggadah, 114–16; relation of rabbinic value-concepts to ideas of, 117, 228 f.; a living bond unites rabbinic thought with, 298 f.; as a division of Torah, 116–17; haggadic interpretations may contradict statements in, 133–35; events of Esther regarded as end of all *Nissim* in, 155; word *Nes* has different meaning in, 161–62; generic terms for God in, 200; prayers contain phrases from, 207; how rabbinic emphasis on God's love affects interpretation of, 219; acquaintance of the folk with, 216–17; rôle of the individual in, 298n.; dependence of the rabbinic Halakah on, 299–300; and normal mysticism, 300–1; God's love in, 302; idea of otherness of God in, 305; Rabbis recognized many laws have frail support in, 354; Rabbis sometimes suspend laws of, 356; basis for rabbinic authority in, 356–57. *See also* Pentateuch; Prophets, Books of; Hagiographa.

Bible as Read and Preached in the Old Synagogue, The (Jacob Mann), 63, 65n.

Bildung des Begriffes Ḥasid, Die (L. Gulkowitsch), 369n.

binyan 'ab, 91n.

Birkat Ha-Miẓwot, see Berakah.

Biṭṭaḥon, as distinguished from *'Emunah*, 42–43.

Biure Onkelos (S. B. Schefftel), 333n.

Blasphemy, is denial of God, 342–43.

Blau, L., 262.

Blessings, by God, 64.

Blind, the, excluded from appearance at the Temple, 240.

Bread, forbidden to eat on Passover leavened, 18; *Berakah* on, 167–68; as symbol for Torah, 118.

"Bridegroom," God spoken of as, 270.

Brother, God is to Israel a, 74; as term for God, 270.

Buber, Solomon, 208n., 313n., 349n.

Buddha (H. Oldenberg), 202n.

Buddhist mysticism, 202n.

Cary, Joyce, 369n.

Cassirer, E., 145, 146.

Cassuto, M. D. (U.), 140n., 300n.

Category of significance, the, and Haggadah, 107 ff., 192–93; and Halakah, 121 ff., 183, 193; and the element of indeterminacy, 131 f.; a rabbinic rite is an epitome of, 176; summary of, 189 f. *See also* Significance.

Chajes, Z. H., 164n.

Chajes, Z. P., 344n.

"Chariot," *see Ma'aseh Merkabah.*

Charity, as subconcept, 15; enables man to receive presence of *Shekinah*, 30; the concept of, as concretized in the Halakah, 79, 109; connoting love, 110; early use of term, 88n. *See also Ẓedaḳah.*

Chastisements, subconcept of God's justice, 15. *See also Yissurin.*

Child, *Nes* done for man with suckling, 152.

Chosen people, the, *see* Election of Israel.
Circumcision, the rite of, exodus from Egypt reward for, 73; crossing of Red Sea because of, 73; led to martyrdom, 80–81.
Classification, of the laws in the Mishnah, 90; generic term for God not really a, 198–200.
Coghill, E. G., 24.
Cognitive concept, the, 50 f.; not dependent on a definition, 50–51; has reference to perceptual experience, 50–51; how it differs from the value-concept, 51–52, 68–69; a disintegrating mental agent, 68–69; is readily translatable, 77; the definite, objective character of, 107–8 (*see also* Defined concept, the); does not indicate significance, 110; "angel" as a, 184; "demon" as a, 184–86.
Cognitive concepts, generally consistent dichotomy of value and, 143 f., 151–52.
Cognitive term(s), ritualistic objects that are designated by, 171; the question of *sefarim* as a, 172.
Cohen, Boaz, 370n.
Coherence of rabbinic thought, *see* Organismic coherence of value-concepts.
Coherence, supplementary forms of, 26, 40n. *See also* Organismic coherence.
Collected Papers of C. S. S. Pierce (ed. Hartshorne and Weiss), 30n., 286n.
Collective nouns, may be conceptual terms, 56.
Commentary on the Bible (Ibn Ezra), 249n.; 294nn., 297, 344n.
Commentary on the Bible (S. D. Luzzatto), 75n.
Commentary on the Bible (Rashi), 312n., 344n., 348n., 363n.
Commentary on Ḳohelet (Hebrew) (H. L. Ginsberg), 294n.
Commentary on the Pentateuch (Naḥmanides), 223n., 251n., 268, 294n., 326, 327.
Commentary on Psalms (Hebrew) (Z. P. Chajes), 344n.
Commentary on the Mishnah (Maimonides), 106, 155, 341.
Commentary on the Mishnah (Ch. Albeck), 370n., 372n.
Commentary to Moreh Nebukim (Abarbanel), 327.
Commentary on the Palestinian Talmud, A (L. Ginzberg), 28n., 35, 43, 73n., 94, 127n., 128, 129n., 184, 209n., 226n., 253, 344, 345n., 356n., 359, 359n., 360nn.
Comminations, those in Deuteronomy uttered by Moses himself, 75.
Commonplace, the, significance of, 169.
Communicability, of normal mysticism, 201 f.
Communication, Haggadah is a supplementary form of, 84.
"Communion with God," not a rabbinic concept, 57.
Composition, forms of, in Haggadah, 62 f.
Concentration, before and after prayer, 208. *See also Kawwanah.*
Concepts, *see* Cognitive concept; Defined concept; Value-concept.
Conceptual phases, not crystallized in conceptual terms, 17; concept of *Nes* has two, 161.
Conceptual term(s), valuational, is only suggestive or connotative, 23, 38–39; is always a noun-form, 35 f.; is an abstract term, 37; are part of the common vocabulary, 37; differ in their generalizing powers, 38; is a stable term, 44; value-concept must have a, 52–53; "election of Israel"

not given a, 55; "Israel" as a, 55–56; a collective noun may be a, 56; use of a non-rabbinic, 57–58; auxiliary ideas not given, 220; those found in rabbinic literature but not in Bible, 288–90; biblical words with new and wider connotations in rabbinic usage, 290 f.; words having one meaning in Bible and another in rabbinic usage, 295–97; of secondary importance in philosophy and science, 46; the generic terms for God as, 194 f.

Conceptualization, of perceived things, 50; in the valuational life, 51.

Concretization, as a major characteristic of the value-concepts, 79–81; of the concept of charity, 109; when concepts cease to be indeterminate, 131; "anthropomorphisms" and the necessity for vividness in haggadic, 141; angelology makes for vividness in, 187; definition of, 191; concept of *Gilluy Shekinah* allows for contradictions in, 230–31.

Conduct, *Ḳedushah* as bearing upon, 169–70, 176.

Connotation, each conceptual term has its own, 38 f.; function of conceptual term is, 38–39, 46; same terms in Bible and rabbinic thought differ in, 290 f.

Contradictions, in haggadic statements, 74–76. *See also* Haggadah; Multiple interpretation.

Convert(s), Jethro and Rahab were, 28; and the "making" of a soul, 114; laws regarding marriage of *kohen* with, 292n. *See also Ger*; Proselytes.

Corporate justice, as a conceptual phase, 17; and Adam's sin, 53; exodus from Egypt interpreted as, 73.

Corporate personality, of the group, 82; and corporate responsibility, 218.

Corporeality of God, held as a principle by some medieval authorities, 282–83; and motion, 325, 327. *See also* Anthropomorphism.

Corrections of the Soferim, the, Lieberman's theory on, 336n.

Creed, *'Emunah* has no connotation of, 42; rabbinic dogmas are not a, 367.

Cruse of oil lasting for eight days, *Nes* of, 160n.

dabar 'aher, and haggadic interpretation, 71–72; its use in Halakah, 72n.

Daniel, prayers attributed to, 128n.; *Nes* ordained from Creation for, 154; the question as to his being among the prophets, 251n.

Darke Ha-Agadah (I. Heinemann), 40n., 105n., 114n., 117n., 278n., 297nn., 298n.

Darke Ha-Mishnah (Z. Frankel), 91n., 92n., 242n.

David, referred to as among the patriarchs, 38n.; all Israel eligible for kingship only until God chose, 61.

Davidson, Israel, 210n.

Day, *Nissim* that occur every, 159; occasions for experiencing normal mysticism every, 203; *Berakah* on the light of the, 168; as manifestation of God's love, 168.

Day of Atonement, atoning power of, 182; the controversy regarding offering of the incense on, 245 f.

Days of the Messiah, the, before the resurrection, 362; differences of opinion in regard to, 362–63; differences between world to come and, 363.

Death, opinion that it is result of sin, 76.

Deeds of loving-kindness, as subconcept, 15; concept of, refers also to deeds beyond what is required by law, 80.

Defined concept(s), the, definite character of, 108; present where there is a dichotomy of value and cognitive concepts, 152.

Definition, value-concepts not given, 45 f.; performs function of abstraction and classification, 46; the attempts to give value-concepts, 83; in Halakah, 109; for the idea of regularity in nature there is no, 149.

de Laguna, G. A., 50, 51, 51n., 68, 201.

Deluge, the, God mourns over, 141.

Democracy, attempts at defining it, 83n.; rôle of intellectuals in, 89n.; weakness of value-concepts of, 138.

Demons, as a cognitive concept, 184–86; as a popular belief, 185–86; view that they ceased from the world when Tabernacle was built, 186.

Denotation, a characteristic of cognitive concepts, 51.

derash, and *peshaṭ*, 99–101, 115–16, 117n.; in Halakah no dichotomy of *peshaṭ* and, 123–26; and the element of indeterminacy, 132.

Derek Ereẓ, subconcept of Torah, 15, 16; as classifying term, 36–37; prohibits building with wood of fruit-bearing trees, 36; behavior of the stranger as, 36.

Deuteronomy, Book of, comminations in, 75.

Development, rabbinic thought as a, *see* Organismic development.

Dibberot, relation to land of Israel, 61; Aaron experienced several, 237n.

Dibbur, the, an appellative for God, 204; as God's utterance to the prophets, 236; to all Israel at Sinai, 236n.; as associated with *Gilluy Shekinah*, 250; as an overlapping concept, 251.

Dichotomy, concept of *Gilluy Shekinah* an exception to, 233.

Dictionary (Jastrow), 171n., 295n., 302n.

Differences of opinion, in Halakah, 93 f.; in regard to resurrection of the dead, 362–63; in regard to period of days of Messiah, 362–63; regarding the world to come, 363–64. *See also* Contradictions; Variety of opinion.

Diḳduḳe Soferim (R. N. Rabbinovicz), 36n., 124n., 147n.

Distributive justice, as a conceptual phase, 17.

"Divine Light," a medieval idea, 282; *Shekinah* and Providence as, 325.

Dogma, how a value-concept may contract into a, 319n., 358n.; the term *'iḳḳar* as meaning, 342n. *See also* Rabbinic dogma.

Dor Dor We-Doreshaw (I. H. Weiss), 134n., 356nn.

R. Dosa, 235.

Duran, Simeon, 155n.

Durkheim, E., 48n., 49n.

Eagle, God's love and analogy of, 71–72.

Edeles, Samuel, 196n., 309n.

Efficacy of Torah, as a conceptual phase, 17; as related to the righteous and the learned, 29.

Egypt, *Dibberot* in, 61; why the ten plagues were visited on, 140; *Shekinah* withdrew to highest firmament because of sins of, 226.

'El, as a generic term for God, 194, 195–96.

R. Eleazar, 19, 58n., 231n., 343.

R. Eleazar b. Azriah, 73, 74.

Election of Israel, is an auxiliary idea, 55–57; no conceptual term for, 55; in the liturgy, 56–57.

Elementary Forms of the Religious Life, The (E. Durkheim), 48n.
R. Eliezer, 71, 92n., 94, 125, 127, 164, 166, 239n.
Elijah, opinion that he did not go up to heaven, 74, 232; appears to individuals in rabbinic times, 259.
'Eloah, as a generic term for God, 194 f.; used as a proper noun, 199.
'Elohim, as referring to God, 196, 198; used as proper noun, 200; when used as an oath or vow, 206, 207; associated with *Middat Ha-Din* (God's justice), 217; relation between biblical and rabbinic usage, 300n.
'Elohot, a plural term, 198–99; not to be confused with *'Elohut*, 199n.
Emanation, an epithet for God does not represent an, 205.
Emperor-worship, negated by *Malkut Shamayim*, 131n.
Emphatic trend(s), biblical plea for justice turned into plea for mercy, 99; rabbinic thought characterized by, 297–98; otherness of God as an, 321–24.
'Emunah, as distinguished from *Biṭṭaḥon*, 42–43, 372n.; has not the connotation of creed, 42. *See also Biṭṭaḥon*; Faith.
Ha-'Emunot Weha-De'ot (Saadia), 325n.
Encyclopaedia Britannica, 48n.
Enelow, H. G., 120, 212n.
Ephodi, 153n.
Epstein, A., 199.
Epstein, J. N., 355n.
'erub, a rabbinic enactment, 357.
Essay on Man, An (E. Cassirer), 145, 146.
Esther, events of, regarded by some as end of all biblical *Nissim*, 155.
Eternity of God, *see* God's eternity.
Ethical outlook, breadth of, 28.
Euphemism, examples of, 312n., 313n., 344n.
Eusebius, 157n.
Event, multiple interpretation of an, 73–74.
Evil, reaction of the Rabbis to presence of, 218; *Berakah* over a tiding of, 203, 219n.
Evil Yeẓer, Israel's reward for withstanding, 187–88; may incite belief that God eats and drinks, 315.
"Existence of God," as a phrase used in medieval Jewish philosophy, 341.
Exodus from Egypt, *Malkut Shamayim* accepted by Israel at, 21; given various interpretations, 73–74; as a rabbinic dogma, 358–61; "acknowledgment" of the yoke of *Miẓwot* associated with "acknowledgment" of, 358–59; mentioned in *Berakah* after the *Shema'*, 359–60; a personal experience, imaginatively, at Passover Seder, 360–61.
Experience, *see* Religious experience.
Experience of God, as expressed in concepts, 202; in prayer, 209 f.; and the acceptance of *Malkut Shamayim* (God's Kingship), 212–13; the study of Torah and, 213–14; associated with integration of the self, 257–58; *Bat Ḳol* not associated with, 262; was not sporadic, 265–66; relation between biblical and rabbinic, 300 f.; acknowledgment of God involves, 343–47. *See also* Normal mysticism; Relationship to God.
Experiential concepts, 30 f. *See also* Value-concepts.

"Faint-hearted," the law concerning the, 100.
Faith, he that prays loudly is among those of little, 209. *See also 'Emunah.*

Fast-days, symbol on, 128.

Father, as term for God in prayer, 210.

"Father in heaven," 183; an appellative for God, 204, 270; "would subject their heart to their," 348n.

Fear of God, whilst studying, 29. *See also Yir'at Shamayim.*

"Feet of the *Shekinah*," see *Shekinah.*

Festival of Tabernacles, nexus in connection with law concerning, 93.

Festivals, the, *Berakah* on, 64; as occasions for instruction, 86.

Figurative interpretation, Haggadah is not, 102 f.; Maimonides' rationale of, 102–4; no indeterminacy of belief in, 139. *See also* Allegorical interpretation.

Finkelstein, Louis, 237n., 246n., 253n., 361n., 362n., 363n., 364.

Fire, as a symbol for Torah, 230n.

First Commandment, as expressing *Malkut Shamayim,* 21.

First Trilogy (J. Cary), 369n.

Folk, the, interaction of Rabbis with, 84 f., 319n.; Rabbis instructed and trained, 86–87; Haggadah and, 113; and indeterminacy of belief, 133; possessed quasi-scientific concepts of regularity in nature, 147 f.; and normal mysticism, 204, 211; and Halakah, 211; their acquaintance with the Bible, 216–17; opinion that Holy Spirit rests on, 251n.

Folk-tales, some haggadot based on, 140.

Food, *Berakot* on, 168.

Forgiveness, prayer for, 210; God taught Moses prayer for, 309.

Form(s), function of, 68; as achieving unity in work of art, 112.

Four cups of wine, given various interpretations, 360n.

Frankel, Z., 91n., 92n., 242n.

Freedom of speech, not an evaluating concept, 4.

Freedom of the will, an auxiliary idea, 53, 54–55.

Friedlaender, Israel, 103n.

Friedmann, M., 274n.

"Friend," as term for God, 270.

Frisch, E., 79n.

From Adam to Noah (Heb.), (M. D. [U.] Cassuto), 300n.

From Noah to Abraham (Heb.), (M. D. [U.] Cassuto), 140n.

"From the Torah," compared with *'asmakta,* 125–26.

Fruit-bearing trees, prohibition against building with wood of, 36.

Frumkin, L., 210n., 269n.

Fundamental concepts, 15; possess subconcepts, 15; possess also conceptual phases, 17; as tracer concepts, 22–23; interweave with other concepts, 24; concept of *Gilluy Shekinah* interweaves with, 228–29. *See also Middat Ha-Din*; *Middat Raḥamim*; Torah; Israel.

R. Gamaliel, 87n., 180n., 254, 255.

R. Gebiha of Argiza, 116.

Geburah, an appellative for God, 225.

Geburot geshamim, 160.

Geiger, Abraham, 235n., 240n., 243n., 244, 321n., 362nn.

Gemilut Ḥasidim, see deeds of loving-kindness.

Genizah Studies I (L. Ginzberg), 60n., 65n., 67n., 200n.

Gentile(s), Holy Spirit can rest on, 52, 135–36; recompensed for good deeds, 135–36; generic terms for God used in discussion with, 206–7; reference to rabbinic comments on, 28; righteous among the, 41.

Ger, as a value-concept, 184; differences between biblical and rabbinic connotations of, 290–93; universalistic connotation of concept of, 291–93. *See also* Convert; Proselytes; *Gerim.*

Gere Ha-'Arez, semi-proselytes, 39n.

Gere 'Ummot Ha-'Olam, semi-proselytes, 39n.

Gerim (proselytes), subconcepts of, 39n.; as a subconcept of Israel, 56; Abram and Sarai made, 99.

Geschichte der Attributenlehre (D. Kaufmann), 282n.

Gesenius, W., 162n.

gezerot, see Halakah.

Gilluy Shekinah, not limited to occasion at Sinai, 57–58; in the enlarged Jerusalem, 118n.; the manifestation of God to human senses, 228 f.; not necessarily associated with a particular *Nes,* 230; and the giving of the manna, 230–31; experience of, 233; does not take place "in this world," 234–35; *Dibbur* as a form of, 236; term itself occurs only once, 237; assumption that pilgrims in Temple could experience, 241, 244; Mishnah rejects assumption that pilgrims could experience, 242–44; as a subject of controversy between Sadducees and Pharisees, 245–49; associated with prophecy in two ways, 250–52; as associated with *Dibbur,* 250; the authority derived from, 252; its relation to normal mysticism, 254–55; *Merkabah* mysticism not the same as, 260–61. *See also* God; *Shekinah.*

Gilluy Shekinah, the concept of, interweaves with the four fundamental concepts, 228–29; often associated with concept of Israel, 229; often imbedded in statements, 229–30; allows for contradictory concretizations, 230–31; involves sensory experience, 231–32; an admixture of the valuational and the cognitive, 233; largely not applied to rabbinic times; 234 f.; restriction of, 238–39; instances in Halakah of, 239 f.; its restriction in the Halakah, 245; restricted early in rabbinic period, 248; as an overlapping concept, 251.

Ginsberg, H. L., 294n.

Ginzberg, Louis, 28n., 35, 38n., 43, 44n., 60n., 65n., 66, 66nn., 67n., 73n., 85, 86, 90n., 94, 95, 122, 127n., 128, 129n., 140, 184, 199n., 209n., 226n., 231n., 253, 253n., 270n., 344, 345n., 355n., 356n., 359, 359n., 360nn.

Glory, the, *see Ha-Kabod.*

God, blesses man, 64; blessings by, 64; power of, contrasted with man's, 64; slandered by serpent, 60n.; studies Torah daily, 66; judges the world daily, 66; sustains the world daily, 66; laughter by, 66; is a Brother to Israel, 74; hears whispered prayer, 195; epithets or appellatives for, 204–6; appellatives for, as a factor in normal mysticism, 205; addressed as "Thou," 202, 210; fills His world, 221; shares Israel's sorrow and joys, 224; will reveal Himself in world to come, 229; revealed Himself at Red Sea as a hero whilst at Sinai as an old man full of mercy, 229; fights Israel's battles for them, 230; cannot be seen by men in their lifetime, 235; nearness of, in contexts both of normal mysticism and *Gilluy Shekinah,* 254; is the locus of the world, 256; sanctifies His Name in Israel, 275; taught Moses prayer for forgiveness, 309; *Imitatio hominis* on the part of, 277, 278, 322, 324; *Shekinah* as a name for, 326; *Minim* "know God and deny Him," 341–42; "denial of the root" is denial of, 342–43; acknowledgment of God involves experience of God, 343–47; *Malkut Shamayim* linked with acknowledgment of, 346–47; acknowledgment of God is experience and not dogma, 347; a transgression implies denial of, 351; neglect of study of Torah is tantamount to denial of, 352–53; neglect of study of Torah finally results in denial of, 352–53; immoral conduct implies denial of, 352n. *See also* Experience of God; Normal mysticism; Relationship to God; *Shekinah*; *Gilluy Shekinah*; *Middat Ha-Din*; *Middat Raḥamim*; Otherness of God; Appellatives for God.

God, "belief in existence of," 42; idea of, not inferred, 48, 49; *'Eloah*, *'El* and *'Elohim* as conceptual terms for, 194 f., are not really generic, 198–200, used as proper nouns, 199–200, are limited to five contexts, 206–7, express consciousness of relationship to God, 270–71, point to otherness of God, 307; concept of, is *sui generis*, 200–1; "implications" to be found in Jewish tradition of an abstract conception of, 284; source of Judaism not a *concept* of, 286–87.

God's eternity, is an auxiliary idea, 55.

God's forgiveness, an aspect of His love, 219.

God's justice, universality of, 52; the many aspects of, 218; tempered by His mercy, 219. *See also Middat Ha-Din.*

God's justice, the concept of, subconcepts of, 15; the conceptual phases of, 17; integrated with concept of *Malkut Shamayim*, 19 f.; imbedded in statement, 52; as concretized in legends and episodes, 141, 142; interweaves with concept of *Gilluy Shekinah*, 228–29; *Middah Tobah* and *Middat Pur'anut* are subconcepts of, 219n.; *Nes* is a subconcept of God's love and, 162n.

God's Kingship, *see* Kingship of God; *Malkut Shamayim.*

God's love, manifestations of, 52; manifested to Israel, 20; and as depicted in Song of Songs, 105; and analogy of eagle, 71–72; Abraham's emphasis on, 99; as manifested in giving sustenance, 168; as manifested in light of day, 168; as associated with repentance, 215; metaphorical expressions of, 270. *See also Middat Raḥamim.*

God's love, the concept of, subconcepts of, 15; interweaves with concept of *Malkut Shamayim*, 20; *Nes* is a subconcept of God's justice and, 162n.; as a dominant theme, 219–20, 302–3; interweaves with concept of *Gilluy Shekinah*, 229; as concretized in legends and episodes, 141–42. *See also Middat Raḥamim.*

God's mercy, tempers His justice, 219.

God's omnipotence, an auxiliary idea, 55.

God's omniscience, an auxiliary idea, 53–54; a static idea, 54; implicates idea of God's otherness, 319–20.

Golah we-Nekar (E. Kaufmann), 290n., 291n., 292n., 293n.

Goldman, Solomon, 85, 286n.

Goldschmidt, D., 372n.

Good deeds, subconcept of Torah, 15, 16.

Gottesdienstlichen Vorträge der Juden (L. Zunz) 86, 234n., 260.

Goy(im), the concept of, distinctive connotation of, 40–41; rabbinical usage not the same as biblical, 40; connotes a status in rabbinic usage, 295; who do not forget God, 41.

Grace after meals, benedictions in, 127, 168.

Grammar, Rabbis' approach to, 101.

Grass, growth of, a manifestation of God's love, 52.

Great Court, The, *see Bet Din HaGadol.*

Greek in Jewish Palestine (Saul Lieberman), 39n., 87, 158n.

Greenberg, Simon, 169n.

Group, the, and the interaction with the self, 81–83; corporate personality of, 82.

Gulack, A., 73n.

Gulkowitsch, L., 369n.

Guttmann, A., 158n., 165n., 167n.

Guttmann, M., 102n., 124, 127, 129n., 206.

Hadrian, designated as wicked, 27.

Hafṭarah, the, and the rabbinic sermons, 63; *Berakah* after reading, 345n.

Haggadah, its relation to Halakah, 11; occasionally influences Halakah, 128; and halakic methodology, 120; each haggadic statement a unit by itself, 59 f.; independent character of interpretations in, 65–67, 71, 72 f.; association of ideas as connecting device in, 61; examples of exegetical, 61–62; forms of composition in, 62 f., 68; as public instruction, 62–63; variety of opinion in, 71 f.; and multiple interpretation, 120–21; examples of multiple interpretation in, 72–73; contradictory statements in, 74–76; reflects relation between "social mind" and individual mind, 76 f.; is a supplementary form of communication, 84; attitude of Rabbis toward, 87; interpretations of Bible texts are usually concretizations of rabbinic concepts in, 98–99; is not figurative interpretation, 102 f.; as representing the folk, 113; its kinship with poetry, 113; as interpretation of Bible, 114–15; biblical texts as stimulus in, 114–16; its conceptual kinship with the Bible, 117; Maimonides on, 118–19; has features characterized by indeterminacy, 132; and indeterminacy of belief, 133 f.; affirmations in, 135–36; "erasure" of interpretations in, 137–38; vestiges of Babylonian myths in, 140n.; and the category of significance, 192–93; made value-concepts vivid, 258–59; as a reflection of actual experience, 324. *See also* Haggadic interpretation.

Haggadic interpretation, *dabar 'aḥer* in, 71–72; no demand for consistency in, 72–73; different for scholars and for masses, 87–88; why each statement is a complete entity in, 110–11; *peshaṭ* and *derash* in, 115–16; "sequence of thought" required between text and, 118–19; thirty-two rules for, 119–20; early origin of rules for, 120n.; how it differs from halakic interpretation, 122 f.; and the element of indeterminacy, 132; may contradict biblical statements, 133–35.

Haggadic stereotypes, *see* Structural stereotypes.

Hagiographa, and the proem form, 62.

Ḥakam, concept of, and concept of *Talmid Ḥakam*, 43. *See also* Learned, the.

Ḥakamim, the, respect for, 137; representing majority opinion, 239; he that does not study Torah will hate, 353; divine character of laws and interpretations derived by, 354–56; conscious of their creative rôle, 355–56; the authority of, 356.

Halakah, relation of Haggadah to, 11; Haggadah and methodology of, 120 (*See also* Halakic interpretation); occasionally influenced by haggadot, 128; Yelammedenu sermon begins with, 64; reflects qualities of the value-concepts, 72n., 93–95, 130;

logic in, 75–76; as concretizing the value-concepts, 79–81, 109; is not "legalism," 80; nexus in, 89 f., 369n.; divergence of opinion in, 93 f.; divergence in practice, 94–95; majority rule in, 94–95; definitions in, 109; rules of interpretation in, 122–23; inferences from the Bible in, 123; and the liturgy, 130; *Nissim* not to be taken account of in discussions of, 163–65; how it makes for recurrent or fixed concretizations of value-concepts, 167 ff.; ritualistic objects are governed by, 170–71; on *Ḳedushah*, 178 f.; gives character to the holy days, 181; and the category of significance, 183, 193; as it affected prayer, 208–9, 210 f.; and the folk, 211; and normal mysticism, 212; instances of *Gilluy Shekinah* in, 239 f.; restriction of concept of *Gilluy Shekinah* in, 245; often rejects *Bat Ḳol*, 262; "is according to Bet Hillel," 262n.; its dependence on the Bible, 299–300; eliminated magic from ritual, 300; and the dictum that "Torah speaks according to the language of man," 321n.; *taḳḳanot* (ordinances) and *gezerot* (prohibitory decrees) avowedly rabbinic in origin, 356–57. *See also halakah le-Moshe mi-Sinai.*

halakah le-Moshe mi-Sinai, and kindred halakot, 92n.; and *'asmakta*, 124n.

Halakic interpretation, how it differs from haggadic interpretation, 122–26; occasionally analogous to haggadic interpretation, 126–27; multiple interpretation in, 129; non-Massoretic readings also utilized in, 240; many laws are like "mountains hanging by a hair" with regard to scriptural support in, 354. *See also* Halakah.

Halakic Midrashim, and their relation to Mishnah, 121–22.

Hallel, at Passover Seder, 158.

R. Ḥama bar Ḥanina, 72, 73n., 105.

R. Ḥananel, 93n., 171n., 251n.

Hananiah, Mishael and Azariah, *Nes* wrought for them, 160; *Nes* ordained from creation for, 154.

R. Ḥananiah ben Antigonos, 200.

R. Ḥananyah ben Ḥalnisi, 74.

Handwörterbuch (W. Gesenius), 162n., 194n., 294n.

R. Ḥanina ben Dosa, wife of, "accustomed to *Nissim*," 157.

Ḥanukkah, *Nes* of, 155; acknowledgment of *Nissim* on, 159–60; on the question of the holiness of the lights of, 172n.; lights of, a rabbinic enactment, 357.

ḥaroset, given various interpretations, 360n., 372n.

Ḥasid, superior to *Ẓaddiḳ*, 39; concept of, as possessing its own connotation, 39–40; related to *Ẓaddiḳ*, 40n. *See also* Pious, the.

Ḥasidim, customs in regard to prayer practiced by early, 208.

Hayerushalmi Kiphshuto (S. Lieberman), 372n.

Heaven, opinion that Moses and Elijah did not go up to, 74; stood still at behest of Moses, 156.

Heaven, an appellative for God, 204.

Hebrew Reborn (Shalom Spiegel), 286n.

Heinemann, I., 40n., 105n., 115n., 117n., 153n., 166, 166n., 278n., 281n., 297nn., 298n., 370n.

Hekalot, in *Merkabah* mysticism, 260.

Hellenism in Jewish Palestine (Saul Lieberman), 73n., 101n., 120n., 123n., 261, 319n., 336n., 349n., 354n.

Hellenistic philosophers, and allegorical interpretation, 102.

Heller, Bernard, 359n.
Henotheism, and monotheism, 48.
"Hereafter concepts," are beliefs rather than value-concepts, 364; dogmatic character of, 364–65; variety of opinion with respect to, 365n.
Hermeneutic rules, and the halakic nexus, 91; of Hillel and R. Ishmael, 123; kinship with methods of rhetors, 123n.
Heschel, A. J., 252n.
Hezekiah, regard for honor of, 137; opinion that Israel had enjoyed Messiah in days of, 365.
Hezekiah bar Ḥiyya, 313.
Hidden meaning, in allegorical interpretation, 103.
Hierarchical order, value-concepts have no, 25–26.
Hierarchy of holiness, in holy days, 181.
High-priest, the, and the offering of incense on Day of Atonement, 245 f.
Hillel, 85, 95, 123, 251n. *See also* Bet Hillel.
R. Hillel, 365.
R. Hillel b. Eliakim, 241n.
Ḥillul Ha-Shem, concept of, interweaves with other concepts, 45n.; as compared with antecedent in the Bible, 288–89; and daily actions, 289.
Historical Geography of the Holy Land (G. A. Smith), 48.
Historical Survey of Jewish Philanthropy, An (E. Frisch), 79n.
History of Medieval Jewish Philosophy (I. Husik), 282n.
R. Ḥiyya, 118n.
Hoffmann, D., 42n., 240n.
Holiness, gives significance to rites, 7; a rite evokes consciousness of, 173–74; hierarchy of, 178 f. *See also Ḳedushah.*
Holy, ritual objects characterized as, 177.
Holy days, the, Halakah objectifies, 181.
Holy of Holies, the, question of *Gilluy Shekinah* in, 245 f.
Holy One blessed be He, the, an appellative for God, 204.
Holy Scriptures, "make the hands unclean," 180n.
Holy Spirit, the, can rest on Gentiles and slaves, 52, 135–36; ceased when the last prophets died, 250–51; as resting on the folk, 251n.; as conceived in medieval Jewish philosophy, 282. *See also Ruaḥ Ha-Ḳodesh.*
Honi the circle-drawer, 156.
Honoring of parents, commandment of, given at Marah, 58n.
hosha'na', as a synonym for myrtle, 171n.
Hospitality, caused *Shekinah* to rest on prophet of Baal, 250.
How Natives Think (L. Lévy-Bruhl), 33, 144, 146.
Huichol, the, conceptual "identities" among, 144.
Human equality, a concept not produced by logic, 6.
R. Huna, 256.
R. Huna bar Nathan, 116.
Husik, I., 282n.

Ibn Samuel, J. (J. Kaufman), 103nn.
Idea of the Holy, The (R. Otto), 176n., 307n.
Ideals of the Jewish Prayer Book (Simon Greenberg), 169n.
Idioms, value-concepts less translatable than, 78.
Idolaters, "do not know God and deny Him," 341.
Idolatry, will be uprooted, 19; adultery, murder, and, defiling character

of, 170; obverse of *Malkut Shamayim*, 27. *See also 'Abodah Zarah.*

Idols, in Egypt, 61; become "gods" as soon as they are made, 195; *Molek* as a generic term for, 200. *See also 'Abodah Zarah.*

Ignorant, the, as subconcept, 15, 28–29; obverse of the learned, 27.

Imitation of God, and *Ḳedushah*, 169–70; refers to imitation of aspects of God's loving-kindness, 219.

Immanence of God, not expressed in term *Shekinah*, 255–56; and the idea of God as locus of the world, 256–57.

Immersion, of the proselyte, 292.

Incantation(s), against demons, 185, 186; Exod. 15:26 as an, 367n.

Incense, the controversy between Pharisees and Sadducees regarding offering of, 245 f.

Incest, laws of, given at Marah, 58n.

"Independent attributes," are auxiliary ideas, 55n.

Indeterminacy, range of value-concepts characterized by, 38; and the category of significance, 131 f.; as exhibited by concept of *Mattan Torah*, 348; of the concept of Torah, 353–58.

Indeterminacy of belief, 131 ff.; can harden into determinate belief, 135–38; with respect to angelology, 187; and the idea of God's otherness, 323–24. *See also* Belief.

Individual, the, and society, 1 f., 8; over-stressed in some theories of religion, 7–8; in primitive societies, 82–83, 298n., 369n.; concern of Bible with, 298n. *See also* Personality; Self, the.

Ineffability, *see* Communicability.

Instruction, occasions for, 86.

Integration, rôle of the fundamental concepts in process of, 18; illustrated by passages on *Malkut Shamayim*, 18 f.; process of, 22 f.; data integrated by each value-concept, 59–60; of the self, 81; of the value-concepts, experience of God associated with, 214–15. *See also* Organismic coherence.

Interest, "acknowledgment" of exodus from Egypt associated with "acknowledgment" of commandments concerning, 359.

Interpretation, accompanies every modern presentation of rabbinic thought, 8 f.; simple or literal, 99–101; Haggadah is not figurative, 102 f.; how rabbinic interpretation differs from philosophic, 103–5; comparison of methods in halakic and haggadic, 122 f.; how emphasis on God's love affects rabbinic, 219; non-Massoretic readings also utilized for, 240. *See also* Hermeneutic rules; Multiple interpretation.

Interpretation of the Bible in the Mishnah, The (Samuel Rosenblatt), 101n.

Introduction to the Talmud (M. Mielziner), 91n.

Introduction to the Talmud and Midrash (H. L. Strack), 42n., 67nn., 90n., 91n., 122n., 147n., 157n.

Intuition, in Bergson's view, 88.

Isaac, as patriarch, 38n. *See also* Sacrifice of Isaac.

R. Isaac, 91, 117n., 134, 168, 257, 294.

Isaac Abarbanel, 327.

Isaac Arama, on Targum Onkelos, 328–29.

R. Ishmael, 73, 91, 123, 127, 234.

R. Ishmael b. R. Jose b. Ḥalafta, 233.

Israel, subconcepts of, 15, 55–56; as a conceptual term, 55–56; concept of, wider connotations of rabbinic, 293; as referring to individual members of the people, 55, 55n.; preceded creation although realized later, 16n.; and the rule of the nations, 19; failed at Red Sea, 19; God's loving-kindness to, 20; God's rule over, 20; accepted *Malkut Shamayim* at exodus from Egypt and at Sinai, 21; excellence of, 21; the wicked of, 27; extolled by the Rabbis, 42; all qualified for priesthood until Aaron was chosen, 61; all eligible for kingship until David was chosen, 61; patriarchs and prophets offered their lives in behalf of, 61–62; trusted in God at Red Sea, 74; God is a Brother to, 74; its love for God depicted in Song of Songs, 105; the *familia* of God, 169; *Miẓwot* as a source of holiness to, 170; received two *Ḳedushot*, 187; rewarded when withstanding *Evil Yeẓer*, 187–88; are called children of *Maḳom*, 205; *Shekinah* accompanies, 223, 255–56; *Shekinah* left because of sinning of, 224, 256; *Shekinah* dwelt below for the sake of, 224; God shares sorrows and joys of, 224; gathered "under the wings of the *Shekinah*," 227; God will reveal Himself in world to come to, 229; God fights their battles for them, 230; and *ziw Ha-Shekinah*, 231; *Dibbur* at Sinai to all, 236n.; God sanctifies His Name in, 275; God makes known His love for, 275; marked off from the nations by possessing oral Torah, 353–54; nations of the world will claim that they are, 354; opinion that in days of Hezekiah Messiah had been enjoyed by, 365; a sinner does not lose his status as a member of, 56n. *See also* Election of Israel, the; Land of Israel.

Jacob, as patriarch, 38n.; opinion that he did not die, 134.
Jacobs, L., 369n.
R. Jeremiah ben Eleazar, 154, 156, 162n.
Jerusalem, as chosen, 61; crossing of Red Sea because of, 73; its boundaries will reach Damascus, 117n.
Jethro, righteous before conversion, 28.
Jew and the Universe, The (Solomon Goldman), 85, 286n.
Jewish Gnosticism, Merkabah Mysticism, and Talmudic Tradition (G. G. Scholem), 371n.
Job, referred to as a patriarch, 38n.
R. Joḥanan, 117n., 134, 136, 139, 160n., 186, 250, 302, 309, 316, 363.
R. Joḥanan ben Dahabai, 242, 244.
R. Joḥanan Ha-Sandelar, 85.
R. Joḥanan b. Zakkai, 87n.
Jonah, *Nes* ordained from Creation for, 154.
R. Jonah Girondi, 208n.
R. Jonathan, 154.
Jonathan the *shed*, 186n.
R. Jose, 74, 94, 117n., 232, 253n.
R. Jose the Galilean, 100, 104, 127, 310n.
R. Jose ben Ḥalafta, 233, 257.
R. Jose ben Ḳisma, 250.
R. Joseph, 152, 153, 211n., 365.
Joseph Albo, 283n., 294n., 342n., 367.
R. Joseph Ibn Plat, 150n.
Joseph the *shed*, 186n.
Joshua, responsible for the defeat at Ai, 135.
R. Joshua b. Ḥananiah, 41, 58n., 85, 164, 231n., 262n.
R. Joshua b. Ḳorḥa, 196.
R. Joshua b. Levi, 128, 209n., 241n.
Joy, Israel accepted *Malkut Shamayim* with, 21; given the righteous, 29.
Jubilee, use of *'olam* for, 294.

R. Judah, 117n., 230, 242, 243, 244.
R. Judah bar Ezekiel, 157.
Rabbi Judah the Prince, 21, 74, 75, 91, 182, 212n., 239n., 242, 274.
R. Judah b. Tema, 242n., 244n.
Judaism in the First Centuries of the Christian Era (G. F. Moore), 28n., 42, 67n., 79n., 101n., 279, 292, 332, 345, 367n.
R. Judan, 313.
R. Judan b. R. Simon, 313, 316, 320, 343.

Ha-Kabod (the Glory), as name for God, 74; as referring to *Gilluy Shekinah*, 74n., 253n.
Kabyakol, as a mitigating expression, 279, 311n.
Kadushin, Phineas, 309n.
R. Kahana, 115n.
Kaufmann, D., 282n.
Kaufmann, Ezekiel, 283, 284, 285, 286, 287, 290n., 291n., 292nn., 293n., 298n., 300, 321n., 330n.
Kaufman, J., *see* Ibn Samuel, J.
Kawwanah, the recital of the *Shema'* and, 212–13; study of Torah requires, 213. *See also* Concentration.
Ḳedushah, as affecting daily conduct, 169–70, 176; an experiential concept, 222; as imitation of God, 169–70, 277; ritualistic objects classified as, 171; not a power to be "utilized," 178; does not have any efficacy, 178 f.; halakot on, 178 f.; hierarchy contains idea of reverence for, 180–81; *Ṭum'ah* as obverse of, 180n.; holy days are fixed concretizations of, 181; angels associated with, 184, 187–88; associated with figure of "under the wings of the *Shekinah*," 227; child born to proselytes is born in, 227. *See also* Holiness.
Ḳedushah of the *'Amidah*, 44, 187n.
Ḳedushat Ha-Shem, and the concept of *Ḳiddush Ha-Shem*, 44; former generations laid down lives for, 158.
Ḳedushat Ha-Yom, of the Day of Atonement, 182.
Ḳedushot, as a term for holy objects, 172; Israel received two, 187.
Ḳeri'at Shema', not prayer but study of Torah, 131n. *See also Shema'*.
Kesef Mishneh, 182n., 212n., 357n., 370n.
Ḳiddush, for the Sabbath, 56.
Ḳiddush Ha-Shem, obverse of *Ḥillul Ha-Shem*, 27; and concept of *Ḳedushat Ha-Shem*, 44; in story of woman and her seven sons, 140; and angels, 187; awareness of God involved in, 214; as compared with its antecedent in the Bible, 288–89; and daily actions, 289.
King of the kings of kings, the, an appellative for God, 204.
Kingship of God, the, extends everywhere, 18; and the Tetragrammaton, 212n. *See also Malkut Shamayim*.
Ḳiẓẓur Ha-Talmud (C. Tchernowitz), 207n.
Klatzkin, J., 153n.
Kohen, laws regarding marriage of convert with, 292n.
Kohler, W., 25.
Kol Bo, 158n.
Korah, and *Nes* of his destruction, 154.
Krauss, S., 172n.
Krochmal, N., 63, 87, 87n., 92n., 93n.
Ḳuppah, community chest, 79.
Kuti, is not a *Goy*, 41n. *See also* Samaritans.
Kuzari (Yehudah Ha-Levi), 223n., 281, 359n.

"Labor," holy days differentiated by what is classified as, 181.

Land of Israel, the, relation of *Dibberot* to, 61; relation to God of him who dwells in, 195; opinion that *Gilluy Shekinah* accompanies study of Torah in, 233; *Shekinah* may reveal itself outside of, 250; every-day talk in Holy Land is Torah, 358n.; and the resurrection of the dead, 362.
Language, as an organic whole, 69; "portmanteau" words in primitive, 146n.
Lauterbach, J. Z., 234n., 249n.
"Law of participation," the, governs conceptual identities in primitive societies, 144.
la'w she-bikelalot, 72n.
Learned, the, as subconcept, 15, 28–29; as obverse of the ignorant, 27; related to the righteous, 29. *See also Ḥakam; Talmid Ḥakam.*
Le'atid Labo, general acceptance of *Malkut Shamayim* postponed to, 19.
Lectern, as a *tashmish*, 178.
"Legalism," Halakah is not, 80.
Legends, in Haggadah, 139–40; as used in concretization of concepts, 318–19.
Legends of the Jews, The (L. Ginzberg), 38n., 270n., 355n.
leḳeṭ, for the poor, 79; defined by laws, 109.
Levi, tribe of, why they diminished in numbers, 229.
R. Levi, 87, 99.
R. Levi bar Ḥayta, 105n.
Leviathan, God's sport with, 66, 140.
Levy, Jacob, 150n.
Lévy-Bruhl, L., 33, 144, 145.
lex talionis, rabbinic interpretation of, 91.
Lieberman, Saul, 39n., 60n., 63n., 73n., 87, 101n., 120n., 123n., 131n., 139n., 157n., 158n., 174n., 186n., 261, 311n., 319n., 336n., 344n., 349, 351n., 354n., 367n., 371n., 372nn.
Light, a manifestation of God's love, 52.
Liturgy, the, election of Israel in, 56–57; interweaving of the value-concepts in, 130; acceptance of *Malkut Shamayim* and acknowledgment of God linked in, 346–47; a rabbinic dogma was at one time in, 359–60. *See also* Prayer; *Berakah.*
Locutions, *Gilluy Shekinah* and, 231–32; absent in normal mysticism, 252.
Logic, value-concepts not the product of, 6; ways of applying value-concepts are result of, 6; rabbinic thought not coördinated into a system governed by, 31 f.; in Halakah, 123.
"Logic of revealed religion," negated, 106.
Love, as connoted by charity, 110.
lulab, as ritualistic object, 170.
Lumholtz, C., 144.
Luria, David, 155n.
Luzzatto, S. D., 75n., 286n., 329, 330, 331nn., 333n., 334n., 334.

ma'aleh 'ashan, "smoke raiser" put into incense, 247.
Ma'aseh Bereshit, refers to section in Genesis, 36n.; in Maimonides' view, 102; and *Ma'aseh Merkabah*, mystic lore taught privately, 260.
Ma'aseh Merkabah, refers to section in Ezekiel, 36n.; and *Ma'aseh Bereshit*, mystic lore taught privately, 260. *See also Yorede Merkabah.*
Mabo La-Mishnah (Albeck, Ch.), 369n.
Mabo le-Massektot Abot ve-Abot d'-Rabbi Natan (L. Finkelstein), 361n., 363n., 364.
Mabo Le-Nusaḥ Ha-Mishnah (J. N. Epstein), 355n.

Mafteaḥ Ha-Talmud (M. Guttmann), 124n., 127n., 129n., 206.
Magen 'Abot (Simeon Duran), 155n.
Magic, excluded by value-complex, 158n.; former practices reinterpreted by Rabbis, 158n.; in paganism, 300.
Maharam of Lublin, 197n.
Maḥzor Vitry (ed. Hurwitz), 208n., 269.
Maimonides, 155, 171n., 175n., 177n., 182n., 220n., 292n., 321n., 341, 357nn., 370n.; and allegorical interpretation, 102–4; and revelation of the Torah, 106; on Haggadah as poetic expression, 118–19; on the Thirteen *Middot*, 126; on miracles, 153–55; on *Shekinah*, 223; on anthropomorphism and Targum Onkelos, 325–26.
Major Trends in Jewish Mysticism (G. Scholem), 234n., 260, 261, 307n.
Maḳom, a term for God, 20n., 29n., 204; why God is called, 256.
Malbim, 127n., 246n., 248n., 249n.
Malkut Shamayim, as an imbedded concept, 3–4; process of integration as illustrated by passages on, 18 f.; as expressed in the *Shema'*, 130, 212; expressed in a declaration, 79–80; a mystical experience, 212–13; by individual daily, 197; by Israel at Sinai, 21; by Israel at exodus from Egypt, 21; acceptance of, 18n.; as expressed in First Commandment, 21; and God's rule over Israel, 20; obverse of idol-worship, 27; its negation of emperor-worship, 131n.; will ultimately be recognized by whole world, 19, 197; affirmed in a parable, 257. *See also* Kingship of God.
Malkuyyot, on Rosh Ha-Shanah, 131n.
Malter, H., 325n.
Man, concept of, 16n.; has connotation of universalism, 150; as an overlapping concept, 150.
"Man," as referring to God by "prophetic license," 314–15.
Mankind, will ultimately accept God's kingship, 197.
Manna, the, created on eve of first Sabbath, 154; giving of, and *Gilluy Shekinah*, 230–31.
Mann, Jacob, 63, 64n., 65.
Marah, commandments given at, 58n.
Mar bar Rabina, 157.
Marduk's struggle with Tiamat, haggadic echo of, 140.
mar'eh Dibbur, 236–37; experienced by Moses, 236.
Marett, R. R., 146n.
Marmorstein, A., 204n., 217n., 277.
Martyrdom, as an expression of the self, 80–81; of R. 'Aḳiba, 131n.; brings home to others awareness of God, 214.
Master of the world, as appellative for God, 205.
Mattan Torah, not limited to Sinai, 57–58; is both a value-concept and a belief, 348; allows for differences of opinion, 348; as a rabbinic dogma, 348 f.; Books of the Prophets and *Ketubim* associated with, 350–51; takes place anew, as it were, with every individual, 351–52; as modified by the dynamic concept of Torah, 353 f., 357–58.
maẓẓah, mandatory character of *Miẓwah* of, 175.
Mead, G. H., 82.
"Measure for measure," subconcept of God's justice, 15, 16; as applied to the learned, 29; and the ten plagues, 140; in regard to denial of resurrection of the dead, 361.

Measures, "acknowledgment" of exodus from Egypt associated with "acknowledgment" of commandments concerning, 359.

Medieval exegetes, use of *peshaṭ* and *derash* by, 100.

Medieval Jewish philosophy, and allegorical interpretation, 102; conceptualizes God's omniscience, 220; on *Shekinah*, 223; and anthropomorphism, 225; and the concept of *Ruaḥ Ha-Ḳodesh*, 251n.; and "negative attributes", 282; and Targum Onkelos, 327–28; belief in existence of God in, 42; "existence of God" as a phrase used in, 341; the term *'iḳḳar* as meaning "dogma" in, 342n. *See also* Philosophy.

megillah, reading of, introduced by the prophets, 252n.

Meḥḳere Ha-Yahadut (S. D. Luzzatto), 286n.

R. Me'ir, 61n., 90, 209n., 219n., 224, 239n. *me'ilot*, laws regarding diversion of sacred things to secular use, 354.

Memra', as an appellative for God, 205; *Yeḳara'*, and *Shekinta'*, and, are not "buffer-words", 332; are reverential terms that cultivate awareness of God's otherness, 333.

Mental habit, a value-concept represents a common, 37.

Mental organism, value-complex is a, 25.

Merit of the children, subconcept of God's justice, 15; an aspect of corporate justice, 17; and Ahaz, 137.

Merit of the fathers, subconcept of God's justice, 15; an aspect of corporate justice, 17; Israel redeemed from Egypt because of, 73; instances of, 73, 74; concretized in legend of the sacrifice of Isaac, 318–19.

Messiah, opinion that in the days of Hezekiah Israel had enjoyed, 365. *See also* Days of the Messiah.

mezuzah, as holy, 171, 177; the two different meanings of word, 172n.

middaḥ, as referring to rules of nature, 148; in the sense of a "quality", 216, 216n.

Middah Tobah, a subconcept of God's justice, 219n.

Middat Ha-Din, 15; and the "fainthearted," 100; world created in accordance with both *Middat Raḥamim* and, 215; sometimes personified, 216; associated with *'Elohim*, 217; normal mysticism rendered communicable by concepts of *Middat Raḥamim* and, 217; as compared with its antecedent in the Bible, 288 f. *See also* God's justice.

Middat Pur'anut, a subconcept of God's justice, 219n.

Middat Raḥamim, 15; imbedded in statement, 52; Abraham's appeal to, 99; world created in accordance with both *Middat Ha-Din* and, 215; associated with Tetragrammaton, 217; thirteen *Middot* of God associated with, 216n.; normal mysticism rendered communicable by concepts of *Middat Ha-Din* and, 217; as compared with its antecedent in the Bible, 288 f. *See also* God's love; God's mercy.

Midrash 'Ekah, and its relation to Wayyiḳra R., 67n.

Midrash Ḳohelet, a later Midrash, 67n.

Midrashic method, *and peshaṭ*, 115–16; requires sequence of thought between text and interpretation, 118–19. *See also* Haggadic interpretation; Halakic interpretation.

Mielziner, M., 91n.

Mi-Ḳadmoniyyot Ha-Yehudim (A. Epstein), 199n.

Ha-Mikra We-Targumaw (Heb. trans.) (Abraham Geiger), 235n., 240n., 243n., 244n., 362nn.

Mind, Self, and Society (G. H. Mead), 83.

Minim, "know God and deny Him," 341–42. *See also* Sectaries.

Miracle, philosophic idea of a, 153; Maimonides on, 153–55. *See also Nes.*

Mishnah, the, classification of laws in, 90; divergent opinions in, 93–94; relation to Halakic Midrashim of, 121–22.

Mishnat Ha-Zohar (I. Tishby), 371n.

Mishneh Torah (Maimonides), 171n., 175n., 177n., 182n., 209n., 262n., 283n., 341, 357nn., 361n., 370n.

Mizwah, obverse of *'Aberah*, 27; why consciousness of holiness does not accompany performance of each and every, 174; God's protection of Israel in Egypt because of a, 319.

Mizwot, subconcept of Torah, 15, 16; concept of, interweaves with concept of *Hillul Ha-Shem*, 45n.; involved in recital of the *Shema'*, 130; practical implication of *Malkut Shamayim* is observance of, 20; Israel redeemed from Egypt because of, 73; martyrdom for, 80–81; as a source of holiness to Israel, 170; a rite is a representative part of, 173; why many do not require a *Berakah*, 174; yoke of, "acknowledgment" of exodus from Egypt associated in the "acknowledgment" of, 358–59.

modeh and *kofer*, as terms indicating rabbinic dogma, 341 ff. *See also* Rabbinic dogma.

Modern concepts, examples of those not rooted in rabbinic tradition, 57.

modim, prohibited to repeat, 344–45; linked with *Shema'*, 345; in *'Alenu* prayer, 346, 371n.; in *'Abodah* of Day of Atonement, 346n.

Molek, as a generic term for idols, 200.

Monotheism, and henotheism, 48; and Greek philosophy, 285.

Moore, G. F., 28n., 42, 67n., 79n., 101n., 279, 292, 322.

Moreh Nebuke Ha-Zeman (N. Krochmal), 63, 87, 87n., 92n., 93n.

Moreh Nebukim (Maimonides), 102, 103, 119, 153, 220n., 223n., 321n., 325, 326, 341.

Moses, prepared Israel to accept *Malkut Shamayim*, 21; designated as seventh patriarch, 38n.; faith in, 42; as "chosen," 56, 57; crossing of Red Sea because of prayer of, 74; opinion that he did not go up to heaven, 74, 232; comminations in Deuteronomy attributed to, 75; God does the last honors to, 141; heavens stood still at behest of, 156; and *ziw Ha-Shekinah*, 231; did not see God, 235–36; alone experienced *mar'eh Dibbur*, 236; why God revealed Himself in a bush to, 254; God taught prayer for forgiveness to, 309; astonished at command to build a sanctuary, 316; was taught not only written but oral Torah, 353; heard but did not understand interpretations of R. 'Akiba, 355.

Motion, as implying corporeality, 325, 327.

mufla' she-bebet din, 73n.

Müller, J., 172n.

Multiple interpretation, biblical verses given, 71–73; in Halakah, 72n., 129; examples in Haggadah of, 72–73, 120–21; as a rabbinic principle, 104–6; and the element of indeterminacy, 132. *See also* Haggadic interpretation; Halakic interpretation.

Myrtle, also called *hosh'ana'*, 171n.

Mystic, in Bergson's view, 88.
Mystic power, and the "law of participation", 144–45.
Mystical Element in Religion, The (Friedrich von Hügel), 176n.
Mystical experience, not incommunicable, 201 f. (*see also* Normal mysticism); not a separate kind of experience, 176; and recital of *Shema'*, 213; in Buddhism, 202n. *See also Yorede Merkabah.*

Nadab and Abihu, feasted on effulgence of *Shekinah*, 231n.
R. Naḥman, 117n.; daughters of, 158n.
Naḥmanides, 251n., 268, 293; on the Thirteen *Middot*, 126; his theory on legends, 139; on *Shekinah*, 223; on anthropomorphism and Targum Onkelos, 326–27.
Nahum of Gimso, 157.
Naḳdimon ben Gorion, 156.
Name, the, as an appellative for God, 204; prohibition of pronouncing, 367n.
R. Nathan, 73, 80, 168n.
Nations of the world, the, and their rule over Israel, 19; the wicked men among, 27; the righteous men of, 27–28; challenge God, 66; God makes His love for Israel known to, 275; oral Torah serves as demarcation between Israel and, 353–54; will claim that they are Israel, 354. *See also 'Ummot Ha-'Olam.*
"Natural order," concepts of, 143 f., 147 f.
Nature, repetition of the number "twelve" in, 148.
Nebuchadnezzer, proclaimed himself god, 53.
"Negative attributes," as a doctrine of medieval Jewish philosophy, 282.
Neoplatonism, and medieval Jewish thought, 282; pagan element in, 285.
Nes, the concept of, 152 ff.; subconcept of God's love and God's justice, 162n.; concept of, as a change in *sidre Bereshit*, 152 f.; frequently found in rabbinic literature, 156–58; aspect in which question of *sidre Bereshit* does not enter, 159–61; has two conceptual phases, 161; phase involving change in *sidre Bereshit* restricted, 162 f., no consistency in restriction of abstract phase, 165–66; presence of a rationalistic tendency in regard to, 155–56, a tendency to limit *Nissim* to biblical period, 155–56; of the "day of Rameses," 71; at Mt. Sinai, 71; done for man with suckling child, 152; corroboration by a passage in Eusebius of a, 157n.; performed only through worthy agent, 158n.; wrought in a sick person's recovery, 160; regarding cruse of oil lasting for eight days, 160n.; question of major and minor, 161n.; biblical and rabbinic usages of word are different, 161–62; biblical antecedents of, 296; as a sign, 164; man's sustenance as daily, 168. *See also Nissim.*
Nexus, in Halakah, 90 f., 369n.
Nimrod, rebelled against God, 342.
Nishmat prayer, second part of, 210.
Nissim, performed by the Rabbis, 156–57; Tannaim "accustomed to," 157; were within expected order of things, 157; in later generations of 'Amoraim, 157; only the work of God, 158; in daily life, 159; benediction on, 163–64; trust in God associated with, 348n. *See also Nes.*
Noah, referred to as a patriarch, 38n.
Nokri, concept of, distinctive connotation of, 41.
Normal mysticism, 194 ff.; everyday occasions for experiencing, 203; and

the ordinary man, 204, 211; unusual temperament not required for, 252–53; visions and locutions absent in, 252; a steady aspect of normal valuational life, 214–15; experiential character of, 221–22; appellatives for God as a factor in, 205; and prayer, 207 f.; and study of Torah, 213–14; acceptance of *Malkut Shamayim* is, 212–13; term *Shekinah* used in contexts of, 227–28; and its relation to *Gilluy Shekinah*, 254–55; and the felt relationship to God, 265 f.; as an emphatic trend, 300–303; its divergence from other forms of mysticism, 307n.; rendered communicable by concepts of God's love and God's justice, 217; the private element and the expressible elements in, 307–8. *See also* Experience of God.

"Nothing," as a term for the otherness of God, 307n.

Noun-form, conceptual term is always a, 35 f. *See also* Proper nouns.

Oath, *'Elohim* used as vow or, 206, 207; High Priest obliged to take an, 248.

R. Obadiah of Bertinoro, 125n., 151n.

Obverses, a supplementary form of conceptual relationship, 26–27, 40n.; parallelism of, 28–29; *Ḳedushah* and *Ṭum'ah* as, 180n.; *Goy* and *Ger* as, 295–96.

Oheb Ger (S. D. Luzzatto), 239, 331nn., 333n., 334n., 335.

'Olam, has connotation of universalism, 150; as an overlapping concept, 150–51; how the rabbinic usage of the word differs from the biblical, 293–95; as referring to mankind, 294. *See also* World, the.

'Olam Ha-Ba', concept of, as a subconcept of *'Olam*, 151. *See also* World to come, the.

Oldenberg, H., 202n.

Old Rabbinic Doctrine of God, The (A. Marmorstein), 204n., 217n., 277.

Omer-offering, law of, 125.

"Operational terms," do not convey significance of an act, 190.

Oral Torah, *see* Torah.

Organismal Conception, The (Ritter and Bailey), 24.

Organismic coherence, value-concepts possess an, 5, 14 ff., 22; as a process of integration and a process of individuation, 24.

Organismic development, 288 ff.

Origins, theory of, 47–48, 49n.

Otherness of God, the, 303 ff.; in the Bible, 305; as an idea cultivated by the Rabbis, 305 f.; as expressed through structural stereotypes, 308–11; as expressed by the term "to soothe the ear," 312; in the attributing of comparisons to "prophetic license," 313–15; God does not partake of the sacrifices, 315–16; He has no need of light in the Temple, 316; Moses astonished at command to build a sanctuary, 316; taught in the several interpretations of Exod. 12:13, 317–18; implicated in idea of God's omniscience, 319–20; does not involve a stand on anthropomorphism, 320–21; as an emphatic trend, 321–24; idea has no real power of generalization, 322–23; and the element of indeterminacy, 323–24; taught by Targum Onkelos, 331 f.; an awareness cultivated by *Memra'*, *Yeḳara'*, and *Shekinta'*, 333; as taught by deviations because of reverence, 333–35.

Otto, Rudolf, 176n., 307n.

Overlapping concepts, 29, 29n.; man, *'Olam* and *Bereshit* are, 150–51;

Gilluy Shekinah, *Dibbur*, and *Ruaḥ Ha-Ḳodesh* are, 251; *Ẓedaḳah* and *Gemilut Ḥasadim* are, 297; vicarious atonement and merit of the fathers as, 318n.

'Oẓar Ha-Munaḥim etc. (J. Klatzkin), 153n.

'Oẓar Ha-Shirah Weha-Piyyuṭ (I. Davidson), 210n.

'Oẓar Ha-Tefillot, 344n.

Paganism, the common ground in all, 284–85; as an element in Greek philosophy, 285; magic in rituals of, 300.

Pantheism, pagan element in, 285.

R. Papa, 157, 158, 162n.

Parable, of a man shielding his son with his body, 72; of Antoninus and his sons, 274–75.

Parallels, in midrashic texts, 66–67.

Paschal lamb, the, law of, 123; circumcised *Ger* could eat of, 290.

Passover, eating of leavened bread forbidden on, 18; eating of *maẓẓah* on, 175; martyred for the observance of, 81.

Passover Haggadah, 237; imaginative re-living of exodus through recital of, 360–61; combined versions in present, 361n.; phrase "denied the root" an interpolation in, 361n.

Passover Haggadah, The (D. Goldschmidt), 372n.

Passover Seder, symbols of, are given various interpretations, 360n.; renders imaginatively the exodus as a personal experience, 360–61.

Past and Present (Israel Friedlaender), 103n.

Patriarchs, the, as subconcept, 15; offered their lives in behalf of Israel, 61; associated with prayers, 128. *See also 'Abot.*

Patriarchs of the world, refer to seven individuals, 38n.

pe'ah, left for the poor, 79; defined by laws, 109.

Pentateuch, and the proem form, 62; and the triennial cycle, 63; a matter of dogma that it was given by God, 349.

Perception, is largely conceptualized, 50.

Personality, statements as expression of, 5; realm of awareness and, 13; and range of value-concepts, 82–83; projected by means of the value-concepts, 111; and the indeterminacy of the value-concepts, 131; and valuational events, 190.

peshaṭ, and *derash*, 99–101, 115–16, 117n.; principle that a biblical verse never loses its, 104; as stimulus for haggadic ideas, 115–16; as a nondetermining stimulus, 132; in Halakah no dichotomy of *derash* and, 123–26.

Pesiḳta, the, and its relation to Bereshit R., 67n.

Pharaoh, designated as wicked, 27.

Pharisees, the, controversy regarding *Gilluy Shekinah* between the Sadducees and, 245–49; belief in resurrection an issue between Sadducees and, 362.

Pharisees, The (L. Finkelstein), 246n., 362n.

Philosophy, static character of statements of, 6; rabbinic interpretation differs from interpretation of Scripture in works of, 12; contrasted with rabbinic thought, 31–32; rabbinic thought is not, 107, 280 f., 286, 336–37, 341; concepts defined in, 45; as a system of concepts, 106; idea of miracle in, 153; criticism by Yehudah Ha-Levi of, 281; pagan

element in, 285. *See also* Medieval Jewish philosophy.
R. Phinehas ben Ya'ir, 156.
Pierce, C. S. S., 30n., 286n.
Pilgrims, *see* Temple.
Pillars of Caesarea, shed tears at death of R. 'Abbahu, 157n.
Pious, the, as subconcept, 15, 56. *See also Ḥasid.*
Pious women, redeemed Israel from Egypt, 73.
Place of Value in a World of Facts, The (W. Kohler), 25.
Platonism, pagan element in, 285.
Poetry, rôle of stimulus in, 113.
Poor, the, halakic provisions for, 79.
"Portmanteau" words, primitive languages run to, 146n.
Prayer(s), subconcept of God's love, 15; concept of *Bereshit* as used in, 35; crossing of Red Sea because of Moses', 74; patriarchs associated with, 128; attributed to Daniel, 128n.; God teaches Israel, 141–42; acknowledgment of *Nissim* in, 159; study of Torah as a parallel to, 213; *'Abodah Zarah* cannot hear, 195; God hears whispered, 195; phrases adapted from the Bible in, 207; and normal mysticism, 207 f.; nearness of God in, 208–9; Halakah established aids to, 208–9, 210 f.; injunction against loud, 209; experience of God in, 209 f.; for forgiveness, 210; of praise, 210 (*see also Nishmat* prayer); stimuli for, 211; private petitions, 211; direction when standing in, 226; Rabbis opposed to those of *Merkabah* mystics, 261; shift from "Thou" to "He" in, 268; God taught Moses prayer for forgiveness, 309. *See also 'Alenu* prayer; *'Amidah*; *Berakah*; Liturgy.
Prayer Book (ed. S. Baer), 36n., 56, 131n., 168, 169, 170, 183n., 207n., 209nn., 212n., 266, 267, 269n., 300n., 344, 345n., 346nn., 359, 363n.
Prayer Book, ed. P. Birnbaum, 268.
Prayer Book (ed. Singer), 144, 159, 169, 183, 187n., 197, 200, 210, 266, 267, 268, 293n., 363.
"Pre-connections," as classifications in primitive societies, 144–47.
Presence (or face) of *Shekinah, see Shekinah.*
Primitive religions, do not have variety of abstract concepts, 32–33.
Primitive society, and the individual, 82–83, 298n.; no dichotomy of value and cognitive concepts in, 144–47; admixture of the cognitive and the valuational in, 147.
Proem, a haggadic form, 62.
Proper nouns, are not conceptual terms, 56; conceptual terms for God used as, 199–200.
Prophecy, no longer possible in rabbinic times, 250–51; associated with *Gilluy Shekinah* in two ways, 250–52.
Prophets, the, did not infer idea of God, 48, 49; as "chosen," 56, 57; offered their lives in behalf of Israel, 61; maid servant at Red Sea saw more than all, 231; all had visions of God, 250; could neither introduce nor abrogate law, 252n.; universalistic idea of, 291; bond between rabbinic Halakah and, 300.
Prophet of Baal, *Shekinah* once rested on, 250.
Prophets, Books of the, benediction on lesson from, 56–57; and the rabbinic sermons, 63; *Ketubim* and, also associated with dogma of *Mattan Torah*, 350–51.
"Prophetic license," *see* Otherness of God.

Proselytes, brought "under the wings of the *Shekinah*," 227; children born to them are born in *Ḳedushah*, 227. *See also* Convert; *Ger*; *Gerim*.
Proselytism in the Talmudic Period (B. J. Bamberger), 292nn., 293n.
Providence, conceived by philosophers as a "Divine Light," 325.
Pseudo-Rashi on Ta'anit, 134n.
Psychological study of Rabbinic Judaism, 10 f.
Purim, acknowledgment of *Nissim* on, 159–60.

Rab, 92, 163, 180n., 208, 211n.
Raba, 92, 165, 178, 361n., 369n.
Rabba, 211n.
Rabbanan, representing majority opinion, 239.
Rabbinic interpretation, differs from philosophic interpretation of Scripture, 12; usually interprets Scripture in terms of rabbinic concepts, 98–99. *See also* Haggadic interpretation.
Rabbinic dogma, 340 ff.; "acknowledge" and "deny" as terms indicating, 341 ff.; definition of, 347; acknowledgment of God, an experience and not, 347; *Mattan Torah* as a, 348 f.; giving of Ten Commandments by God a matter of, 349; that Pentateuch was given by God is a matter of, 349; exodus from Egypt as a, 358–61; at one time there was an instance in the liturgy of a, 359–60; resurrection of the dead as a, 361 f., 372n.; has to do with beliefs regarding certain events, 365–66; not pure dogma, 366; does not constitute a creed, 367.
Rabbinic thought, *see* Philosophy.
Rabbis, the, interaction with the folk, 84 f.; not a professional class, 85; as representative of the folk, 85–86; instructed and trained the folk, 86–87; their attitude toward Haggadah, 87. *See also* *Ḥakam*; *Ḥakamim*.
Rabbinovicz, R. N., 36n., 124n.
Rahab, righteous before conversion, 28.
Rain, a manifestation of God's love, 52; in response to prayers of Rabbis, 156–57; *Nes* of, 160.
Rainbow, the, created on eve of first Sabbath, 154.
Rasha', as a value-concept, 4, 184. *See also* Wicked, the.
Rashi, 39, 45n., 90n., 105n., 135n., 138, 147n., 154n., 164n., 171n., 172n., 175n., 177n., 181n., 182n., 186n., 187n., 195nn., 209n., 211n., 243n., 244n., 249n., 295n., 312n., 315n., 342n., 344n., 348n., 360nn., 363n.
Ratiocination, religious concepts not result of, 48–49. *See also* Philosophy.
Rationalistic tendency, in regard to *Nes* (miracle), 155–56.
Red Sea, Israel's failure at, 19; variety of opinion in accounting for crossing of, 73–74; condition imposed upon, 154; God revealed Himself at, 229, 231.
Relationship to God, the, 202, 205; implied in a *Berakah*, 202; a consciousness not expressed by a concept, 264; a mystical consciousness, 269–72; the intimacy of "Thou," 266; "Thou" conjoined with "He," 267–70; expressed metaphorically in terms of human relationships, 270–71; expressed in generic terms and appellatives for God, 271.
Religion, difficulties with some modern theories of, 7–8.
Religious experience, everyday situations and actions make for, 167–68. *See also* Experience of God.
Repentance, the concept of, as concretized by the Halakah, 79; ten days of, 79; Day of Atonement and, 182;

as associated with God's love, 15, 215; avails even him who denied God, 343. *See also Teshubah.*

Reshit Ha-Kabbalah (G. G. Scholem), 371n.

Resurrection of the dead, the, as a rabbinic dogma, 361 f.; no portion in world to come for him who denies, 361–62; an issue between Pharisees and Sadducees, 362; differences of opinion in regard to, 362–63; days of the Messiah before, 362.

Reuben, opinion that he did not sin, 136.

R. Reuben, 351.

"Revelation," not equivalent to *Mattan Torah*, 57–58. *See also Gilluy Shekinah.*

Reverence for holy objects, 180–81; for holy things in speech, 181n.

Rhetors, kinship of hermeneutic rules with methods of, 123n.

Righteous, the, a subconcept of Israel, 15, 56; as obverse of the wicked, 27; related to the learned, 29; given joy, 29; among the Gentiles, 41; why they suffer in this world, 218n.; God suffers over the spilled blood of, 224; seven groups of, will greet the presence of *Shekinah*, 228; death of, as vicarious atonement, 318n. *See also Ẓaddiḳ.*

Rites, 169 f.; not primarily symbols of society, 7; the question of the holiness of objects used at, 170–72; representative of the *Miẓwot* as a whole, 173; evoke consciousness of holiness, 173–74; mandatory character of, 175; epitome of the category of significance, 176; Halakah eliminated magic from, 300; some are purely rabbinic enactments, 357.

Ritual uncleanness, *see Ṭum'ah.*

Ritualistic objects, *tashimishe Miẓwah* not holy in themselves, 170–72; those that are classified as holy, 171, 177 f.

Ritter and Bailey, 24.

Rod of Moses, created on eve of first Sabbath, 154.

Roḳeaḥ, 174n., 212n.

Rosenblatt, Samuel, 101n.

Rosh Ha-Shanah, *Malkuyyot* in *'Amidah* for, 131n.

Ruaḥ Ha-Ḳodesh, as an overlapping concept, 251; as divine inspiration in rabbinic times, 251n.; as used in an extended sense, 358n.; a degree below prophecy in medieval view, 251n. *See also* Holy Spirit, the.

Saadia Gaon, 209n., 281, 325n., 370n.

Saadia Gaon (H. Malter), 325n.

Sabbath, the, *Ḳiddush* for, 56; as occasion for instruction, 86; things created on eve of the first, 154; why God is said to have rested on, 276; Rabbis recognized there is frail scriptural support for halakot concerning, 354; the light of, a rabbinic enactment, 357; Commandment of, given at Marah, 58n.

Sachs, Chaim, 100n.

Sacrifices, the, interpreted symbolically, 300n.; God does not partake of, 315–16.

Sacrifice of Isaac, God passed over Israel in Egypt because of, 317–19; legend of actual sacrifice, 318; as concretization of *Kapparah* or *Zekut 'Abot*, 318.

Sadducees, *see* Pharisees.

Sake of Heaven, the, the study of Torah for, 29.

Samaritans, term *Goy* does not apply to, 41; may be referred to as "sinners in Israel," 350; accepted if they acknowledge Jerusalem and resur-

rection, 362; pronounced the Name as spelled, 367n.
Samson, and *Gilluy Shekinah*, 232.
Samuel ('Amora), 92, 163, 199, 208n., 361n., 362n., 363.
R. Samuel b. R. Isaac, 345.
R. Samuel b. Naḥman, 211n.
Sanctuary, Moses astonished at command to build a, 316.
Sarah, Abraham and, made converts, 99.
Satan, Leviathan as symbol for, 66, 140.
Schechter, Solomon, 9, 14, 79n., 101, 142, 156, 169, 170n., 184n., 205, 221, 257n., 275, 279, 306, 312n., 313n., 322, 350, 358n.
Schefftel, S. B., 333n.
Scholem, G. G., 234n., 260, 261, 307n., 371nn.
School of Hillel, 94. *See also* Bet Hillel.
School of R. Ishmael, 105.
School of Shammai, 94. *See also* Bet Shammai.
Science, "law of participation" prevents development of, 146; not affected adversely by value-concepts, 191–92.
Scientific, concepts of regularity in nature are only quasi-, 149.
Sectaries, "anathema" against, 367. *See also Minim.*
Seder R. Amram Gaon (ed. Frumkin), 210n., 269n., 346n., 347n.
Seder Eliahu, as a haggadic composition, 66.
sefarim, characterized as holy, 171, 177; as a cognitive term, 172.
Sefer Abudraham, 371n.
Sefer Ha-'Iḳḳarim (Joseph Albo), 283n., 294n., 342n., 367.
Sefer Ha-Miẓwot (Maimonides), 126.
Sefer Ha-Pardes (ed. H. L. Ehrenreich), 174n.
sefer-Torah, characterized as holy, 171, 177; *Ḳedushah* associated with objects connected with, 178–79; actions reflecting holiness of, 181.
Selected Works (H. G. Enelow), 212n.
Self, the, rôle of value-concepts in development of, 2–3; rôle of the value-concepts in integration of, 81; the distinctive character of the group and, 81–82; martyrdom as an expression of, 80–81. *See also* Individual, the; Personality.
"Sequence of thought," in poetry, 113–14; between biblical text and haggadic statement, 118–19; in halakic interpretation, 126–27.
Sermons, of the Rabbis, 62–65.
Serpent, slanders God, 60n.
Shammai, 95. *See also* Bet Shammai.
shed, a term for demon, 185n.
She'eltot, 87n.
Sheheḥeyanu, as a *Berakah* on the Festivals, 64.
Sheḳi'in (Saul Lieberman), 139n.
Shekinah, is a reverential name for God, 223–25, 326; name used in contexts of normal mysticism, 227–28; word is used in contexts of revelation of *Shekinah*, 228; name used in contexts of God's nearness, 225–28; the two contexts in which term is used, 253–55; term does not express immanence of God, 255–56; *Ha-Kabod* and, 74n., 253n.; charity enables man to receive the presence of, 30; he that studies in *bet ha-midrash* greets the presence of, 229; to be regarded as before one in prayer, 208; abides with those who study Torah, 214, 227; with ten persons in a synagogue, 227; is with Israel, 255–56; when worthy Israel is gathered "under the wings of the," 227; proselytes are brought "under the wings of the," 227; with

Israel in their affliction, 223; dwelt below for the sake of Israel, 224; Israel's sinning caused removal of, 224, 256; transgression "crowds off the feet of the," 228; ascended to higher firmaments when man sinned, 225–26; descends to earth because of succession of righteous men, 226; dwelt in Tabernacle and Temple, 226, 255; withdrew when Temple was destroyed, 226, 254; question as to its presence in Second Temple, 231, 253n., 255; "is in every place," 226, 254; is in the west, 226; primarily does not reveal itself outside land of Israel, 250; once rested on prophet of Baal, 250; medieval Jewish philosophy on, 223; conceived by philosophers as "Divine Light," 325. *See also Gilluy Shekinah.*

Shekinta', see Memra'.

Shem, referred to as a patriarch, 38n.

Shema', the, biblical warrant for recital of, 125; value-concepts involved in recital of, 130; acceptance of *Malkut Shamayim* daily in recital of, 197; *Berakot* of, 209; composition of, 212; *Kawwanah* in recital of, 212–13; linked with *modim*, 345; ideas contained in its three sections emphasized in *Berakah* after, 359. *See also Ḳeri'at Shema'.*

Shema'yah, 74.

R. Sheshet, 226, 233n.

Shibbole Ha-leḳeṭ (ed. Buber), 158n., 175n., 295n., 361n.

shikḥah, left for the poor, 79; defined by laws, 109.

shofar, law of, 128.

Siddur R. Saadia Gaon (ed. Davidson and others), 209n., 346n., 347n.

sidre Bereshit, concept of, as expressing idea of regularity in nature, 147 f.; a *Nes* as a change in, 152 f.; departure from, ordained from creation, 154; things created after, 154–55; aspect of *Nes* in which no question is raised regarding, 159–61.

sidre 'Olam, concept of, as expressing idea of regularity in nature, 147 f. *See also 'Olam.*

Sign, *Nes* as a, 164; as philosophic term for miracle, 153n.

Significance, only in a whole situation, 110; value-concept indicates, 110; a situation may have a many-toned, 110–11; aesthetic as compared with valuational, 112–14; of the commonplace, 169. *See also* Category of significance.

R. Simeon b. Laḳish, 186, 302.

Simeon the Righteous, 234.

Simeon of Teman, 73.

R. Simeon b. Yoḥai, 21, 73, 157, 235, 239n.

R. Simlai, 198.

Sin, a person remains an Israelite despite committing, 56n.; opinion that death and suffering are result of, 76; opinion in regard to certain biblical characters and their connection with, 136; causes withdrawal of *Shekinah* from Israel, 224, 256; *Shekinah* ascended to higher firmaments because of, 225–26. *See also 'Aberah.*

"Sinners in Israel," may refer at times to Samaritans, 350.

Sinai, *Malkut Shamayim* accepted by Israel at, 21; Torah received at, 21; God descended to, 74; opinion that God did not actually come down to, 74, 232; God revealed Himself as an old man full of mercy at, 229.

Slave, Holy Spirit can rest on, 52, 135–36.

Smith, George A., 48.

"Social mind," the, problems concerning, 76–77.

Society, the individual and, 1 f., 8; rôle of value-concepts in stabilization of, 2–3; overstressed in theories of religion, 7; in Bergson's view, 88.
Sodom, people of, rebelled against God, 342.
Song of Songs, as an allegory, 105, 278.
Sons of Eli, opinion that they did not sin, 136.
Sons of Jacob, the, designated as patriarchs, 38n.; crossing of the Red Sea because of merit of, 74.
Sons of Samuel, opinion that they did not sin, 136.
Speech: Its Function and Development (G. A. deLaguna), 50, 51.
Speech, reverence in, 181n.
Spender, Stephen, 113.
Spiegel, Shalom, 286n., 318, 318nn., 319n.
Strack, H. L., 42n., 67nn., 90n., 91n., 122n., 147n.
Structural stereotypes, idea of otherness of God as expressed through, 308–11; how the *Berakah* differs from the haggadic, 310–11.
Students, Scholars and Saints (L. Ginzberg), 85, 86.
Studies in Judaism, (S. Schechter), 79n., 101, 156n.
Study of Torah, subconcept of Torah, 15; and the concept of the learned, 28; the concept of, as concretized by the Halakah, 79; as enjoined in Bible, 125; as a means of experiencing God, 213–14; *Kawwanah* required in, 213; *Shekinah* is with persons engaged in, 227; presence of *Shekinah* greeted by those engaged in, 229; opinion that *Gilluy Shekinah* accompanies, 233; tantamount to denial of God is neglect of, 352–53; denial of God final result of neglect of, 352–53. *See also* Torah.
Subconcepts, fundamental concepts possess, 15; are concepts in their own right, 16; kinship of, 16; of two concepts, 27.
Suffering, opinion that it is result of sin, 76.
sukkah, as ritualistic object, 170.
Sustenance, *Nes* wrought in daily, 160; God's love as manifested in His giving, 168.
"Swarming things," "acknowledgment" of exodus from Egypt associated with "acknowledgment" of commandment concerning, 358.
Symbol(s), for Torah, 117–18, 230n.; on fast-days, 128; sacrifices interpreted as, 300n.; on Passover, are given various interpretations, 360n.
Synagogue, characterized as holy, 177; *Shekinah* with ten persons in a, 227. *See also bet ha-keneset.*

Ṭa'ame Ha-Miẓwot Be-Sifrut Yisra'el (I. Heinemann), 281n.
Tabernacle, the, demons ceased to be after it was built, 186; *Shekinah* dwelt in the Temple and, 226, 255.
takkanot, see Halakah.
Talmid Ḥakam, the, regard for, 86; the concept of, and concept of *Ḥakam*, 43. *See also* Learned, the.
Talmud, the, discussions of 'Abaye and Raba in, 92; discussions of Rab and Samuel in, 92; establishment of halakic nexus in, 92–93.
Talmudische Archäologie (S. Krauss), 172n.
tamḥuy, community plate, 79.
R. Ṭarfon, 341.
Targum Jonathan, term *Bereshit* in, 36; anthropomorphisms and, 223n.
Targum Onkelos, and the *peshaṭ*, 101; and anthropomorphism, 223n., 325 ff.; and medieval Jewish philosophy, 327–28; teaches idea of

God's otherness, 331 f.; deviations reflecting rabbinic ideas and laws in, 331n.; *'Elohim* interpreted as the Tetragrammaton in, 333n.; deviations because of reverence in, 333–35.

tashmishe Ḳedushah, as differentiated from *tashmishe Miẓwah*, 171–72; objects connected with *sefer-Torah*, 178–79.

tashmishe Miẓwah, as differentiated from *tashmishe Ḳedushah*, 171–72.

Tchernowitz, C., 122n., 124n., 207n., 299n.

Tefillah, see Prayer.

tefillin, characterized as holy, 171, 177.

Teḥiyyat Ha-Metim, see Resurrection of the dead.

Temple, the, God will punish those who destroyed, 19; *Shekinah* dwelt in the Tabernacle and, 226; *Shekinah* withdrew upon the destruction of, 226, 254; *ziw Ha-Shekinah* and dedication of First, 231; question as to presence of *Shekinah* in Second, 231, 253n., 255; *Gilluy Shekinah* to High-Priests of Second, 233-34; blind excluded from appearance in, 240; assumption that *Gilluy Shekinah* could be experienced by pilgrims in, 241, 244; the Mishnah rejects assumption that *Gilluy Shekinah* could be experienced by pilgrims in, 242–44; list of those exempt from appearance in, 242–43; God has no need of light in, 316. *See also* Sacrifices; Sanctuary.

Ten Commandments, the, begin with second statement, 21; a matter of dogma that they were given by God, 349; denial of God implied in transgression of any of, 351.

Ten plagues, the, and "measure for measure," 140.

Ten Sayings, world created with, 151.

Terminologie (Heb. trans.) (W. Bacher), 100nn., 124n., 251n., 312n.

teru'ot and *teḳi'ot*, on Rosh Ha-Shanah, 127.

Teshubah, as compared with its antecedent in the Bible, 288 f. *See also* Repentance.

Tetragrammaton, the, and God's Kingship, 212n.; Rabbis associate *Middat Raḥamim* (God's love or mercy) with, 217.

Theodor, J., 73n., 313, 320, 320n.

Thirteen *middot* of God, qualities associated with God's love, 216n.

Thirteen *Middot* of R. Ishmael, 123. *See also* Hermeneutic rules.

Thirty-two rules, for haggadic interpretation, 119–120.

"This world," *Gilluy Shekinah* does not take place in, 234–35; the concept of, as a subconcept of *'Olam*, 151. *See also* World, the.

"Thou," in addressing God in *Berakot*, 202, 210; as reflecting intimacy of relationship to God, 266.

Tiamat, haggadic echo of her struggle with Marduk, 140.

Tishby, I., 371n.

Tithes, halakic nexus in connection with law on, 93.

Tobit, Book of, term "charity" in, 88n.

Toledot Ha-'Emunah Ha-Yisre'elit (Ezekiel Kaufmann), 283, 284, 285, 286, 287, 291n., 292n., 298n., 300, 321n., 330n.

Toledot Ha-Halakah, (C. Tchernowitz), 122n., 124n., 299n.

Toledot Ha-Yehudim Be-'Ereẓ Yisra-'el Bi-Teḳufat Ha-Mishnah Weha-Talmud (G. Alon), 369n., 370n.

Torah, received at Sinai, 21; benediction on the, 56; God tested words of the, 56n.; studied daily by God, 66;

from heaven, dogma of, 75 (*see also Mattan Torah*); not rendered adequately by word "law", 77; public reading of, 79; reading of, led to martyrdom, 81; involved in recital of the *Shema'*, 130; "speaks according to the language of man," 321n.; he that denies *'Abodah Zarah* acknowledges the entire, 349; implicit in the written is the oral, 353–55; Israel marked off from the nations by possessing oral, 353–54; in extended sense includes proper conduct in general, 358n.; everyday talk in Holy Land is, 358n.; sub-concepts of, 15; conceptual phases of the concept of, 17; Torah, the concept of, interweaves with concept of *Malkut Shamayim*, 20–21, interweaves with concept of *Ḥillul Ha-Shem*, 45n., is an indeterminate concept, 353–58; quasi-determinate concept of *Mattan Torah* is modified by the dynamic concept of, 353 f., 357–58. *See also* Efficacy of Torah; *Mattan Torah*; Study of Torah.

Ha-Torah Weha-Miẓwah (Malbim), 127n., 246n., 248n.

Tosafot, 105n., 125n., 161n., 175n., 178n., 181n., 212n., 261, 360n., 370n.

Tosefeth Rishonim (Saul Lieberman), 344n., 351n.

Tosefot Yom Ṭob, 208n., 244n., 370n.

Tosefta Ki-Fshuṭah (Saul Lieberman), 372n.

"To soothe the ear," *see* Otherness of God.

Transgression, denial of God implied in commission of, 351. *See also 'Aberah*; Sin.

Translation, value-concepts largely not amenable to, 77–78.

Triennial cycle, in Palestine, 63.

Trisagion, *see Ḳedushah* of the *'Amidah*.

Trust in God, *'Emunah* and *Biṭṭaḥon* as, 42–43; Israel crossed Red Sea because of, 74; associated with *Nissim*, 348n.

Ṭum'ah, as "a power," 180n.

Ṭur, Oraḥ Ḥayyim, 209n.

"Twelve," as a number repeated in nature, 148.

"Two Powers," revelation of *Shekinah* negates idea of, 229; repetition of word *modim* is acknowledgment of, 344–45.

Two Sources of Morality and Religion, The (H. Bergson), 88.

Tylor, E. B., 47, 49n.

'Ummot Ha-'Olam, concept of, distinctive connotation of, 41.

Eine unbekannte jüdische Sekte, (L. Ginzberg), 38n.

Universalism, man, *'Olam* and *Bereshit* have a connotation of, 150–51, 295; of the prophets, 291; as embodied in rabbinic concept of *Ger*, 291–93; as an emphatic rabbinic trend, 297–98.

Unpredictability, combination of value-concepts characterized by, 23, 24.

Valuation, in primitive societies, 144–47.

Value-complex, is a mental organism, 25; supplementary forms of conceptual relationship in, 26 ff.; functions easily, 30.

Value-concept(s), the, are not defined, 2; not a wholly satisfactory term, 4–5; flexible character of, 2; factors in development of self and in stabilization of society, 2–3; and the integration of the self, 81; endow a group with a special character, 77–

78; often imbedded in a situation or statement, 3–4, 52, 54, 59–60, 111; made vivid by Haggadah, 258–59; are embodied in the Halakah, 79–81; Halakah as reflecting the qualities of, 72n., 93–95, 130; how Halakah makes for recurrent or fixed concretizations of, 167 ff.; both Halakah and Haggadah are concretizations of, 11; dynamic character of, 5; are not the result of inference, 47 f., 49n.; are not an inference from events, 298n.; are not the product of logic, 6; the realm of awareness and, 13; interweaving of, 22 f.; have no hierarchical order, 22, 25; are inseparable from experience, 30; as abstracting and classifying terms, 36–37; represent a form of abstract thought, 37; usually indeterminate range of, 38; how it differs from cognitive concept, 51–52, 68–69; how it differs from cognitive and defined concepts, 108; their relation to cognitive concepts, 109–110; their relation to the other types of concepts, 108–110; generally consistent dichotomy of cognitive and, 143 f., 151–52; must have a conceptual term, 52–53; served by auxiliary ideas, 54; relation of rabbinic to biblical, 55; are integrating mental agents, 59–60, 69; are largely not translatable, 77–78; transmission of, 78, 84 f.; are part of the common vocabulary, 78; drive toward concretization of, 79–89, 111; supply means of expression to personality, 81, 111, 190; expression of personality depends on the range of, 82–83; the attempts to define, 83; democracy and, 89n., 138; connotative character of, 46, 108; indicate significance, 110; are not external to a situation, 110; interweave in the liturgy, 130; as indeterminate, 131; potential determinacy of, 191; do not affect science adversely, 191–92; are not vestiges of primitive mentality, 146; are never classified by means of another value-concept, 177; angelology used exclusively with concretizations of, 186–87; as expressing experience of God, 202; experience of God and the normal functioning of, 214–15; the relation of biblical ideas to rabbinic, 288 f.; extended sense of some, 358n.; dogma results from complete contraction of, 358n.

Variety of opinion, in Haggadah, 71 f.; in accounting for crossing of Red Sea, 73–74; with respect to "hereafter concepts," 365n. *See also* Differences of opinion; Multiple interpretation.

Vicarious atonement (*Kapparah*), as subconcept, 15; as concretized in legend of sacrifice of Isaac, 318; death of the righteous as, 318n.

Visions, all prophets had, 250; absent in normal mysticism, 252; in *Merkabah* mysticism, 260.

von Hügel, F., 176n.

wadd'ai, as equivalent to *peshaṭ*, 100.

Walls of *bet-hamidrash*, and the *Nes* as a sign, 164.

"Water," as symbol for Torah, 118.

Wayyiḳra R., and its relation to Midrash 'Ekah, 67n.

Weiss, I. H., 134n., 275n., 356nn.

Well, the *Nes* of the, 154.

Weltanschauung, not the same as a value-pattern, 13.

Whitehouse, O. C., 48n.

Wholes, as fraught with significance, 110.

Wicked, the, individuals designated as among, 27; of Israel, 27; why given tranquility in this world, 218n.; God suffers over the spilled blood of, 224; penalty exacted from, 276; deliberately rebel against God, 342; the concept of, as a subconcept, 15, 27; as the obverse of the righteous, 27; as a subconcept of Israel, 56. *See also Rasha'.*

"Wings of the *Shekinah,*" *see Shekinah.*

Wolfson, H. A., 282.

Woman and her seven sons, *Ḳiddush Ha-Shem* of, 140

Women, present at sermons, 87.

World, the, created in accordance with both *Middat Raḥamim* and *Middat Ha-Din,* 215; God is the locus of, 256–57.

World to come, the, kings having no portion in, 137; those having no portion in, 348–49, 361; full accounting reserved for, 218; God will reveal Himself in, 229; difference between days of the Messiah and, 363; two distinct views regarding, 363–64, 372n.

Worship, a *Berakah* as, 168; study of Torah regarded as, 213.

Wörterbuch über die Talmudim und Midraschim (Jacob Levy), 150n., 199n.

R. Yannai, 129n., 163.

Yehudah Ha-Levi, 223, 281, 282, 286, 359n.

Yeḳara', as an expression of reverence, 328–29. *See also Memra'.*

Yelammedenu, the, sermons in, 63–65; the term *'Elohim* in, 199.

Yesode Ha-Mishpat Ha-Ibri (A. Gulack), 73n.

Yir'at Shamayim, and freedom of the will, 54–55. *See also* Fear of God.

Yissurin, sent to purify men, 218.

Yorede Merkabah, experience not the same as *Gilluy Shekinah,* 260–61.

Yoẓer prayer, angels in, 187n.

Ẓaddiḳ, the concept of, as possessing its own connotation, 39–40; as a value-concept, 4, 184. *See also* Righteous, the.

Ẓedaḳah, difference between biblical and rabbinic usage of word, 297; has connotation of love, 297. *See also* Charity.

Ha-Ẓedaḳah Be-Yisra'el (J. Bergmann), 79n.

Zimmun, 369n.

ziw Ha-Shekinah, 231.

ẓiẓit, as a ritualistic object, 171; "acknowledgment" of exodus from Egypt associated with "acknowledgment" of Commandment of, 359.

Zunz, L., 86, 234n., 260.

Printed in the United States of America

ABOUT THE AUTHOR

MAX KADUSHIN is Visiting Professor in Psychology of Religion at the Jewish Theological Seminary of America. Dr. Kadushin received his B.A. from New York University, and degrees of M.A. and Rabbi, D.H.L., and Litt. D. (honoris causa) from the Jewish Theological Seminary.

Other books published by Dr. Kadushin include *The Theology of Seder Eliahu, A Study in Organic Thinking* (1932); *Organic Thinking, A Study in Rabbinic Thought* (1938); and *Worship and Ethics, A Study in Rabbinic Judaism* (1964).